One House Per Day *no.001–365*

Andrew Bruno

ORO EDITIONS

Foreword
Keith Krumwiede

If you're reading this foreword you've likely already skimmed through the book. You've flipped through the houses—loving some, questioning others—and started to form opinions about this menagerie of domestic dreams. If you're like me, you don't read the foreword to a book until after you've checked out the main attraction. You may even skip it entirely, I often do. So these thoughts are less about describing what you'll see and more about offering some reflections upon what you've presumably already seen: 365 houses, drawn over the course of 365 days. Which, let's face it, is a bit crazy. One could be tempted to see this as the work of a madman (think Jack Nicholson in *The Shining* relentlessly typing out "all work and no play makes Jack a dull boy"). Except here our madman wakes each day and thinks: "oh shit, one more house is due today, what have I gotten myself into?" And it is a bit mad, but it's also more than a bit beautiful, and instructive. *One House Per Day* tells us a lot about who we are as architects, but it also tells us about who we are as humans, seeking and making nests to support our lives and the lives of those with whom we live.

The detached house, isolated in its own little Eden, has long been the privileged domain of the single family. It has also long been seen by architects as the ideal building type through which to exercise their formal ambitions. Its seemingly stable program (a collection of rooms designated for living, cooking, dining, sleeping, washing, etc.) allows the architect to imagine (or imagine they're imagining) new and exciting arrangements of architectural matter—walls, roofs, doors, windows. And while there may be some pretense toward programmatic invention, more often than not an architect working on a house is an architect working on their architecture. The imagined inhabitants, if any are imagined, are simply witnesses to the formal drama of the architect dreaming up architecture.

A house, however, is not simply a formal exercise. Every house organizes and frames the lives of its inhabitants, charting a loose choreography for their domestic life. Andy Bruno knows this, and in these houses—lovingly executed day in and day out—he explores other arrangements for how we live and how we might live, both alone and, more importantly, together. I don't imagine that he sees any of these houses as complete, as definitive solutions (although he surely has his favorites). Each one is simply another in a series of quickly expressed thoughts aimed at upending our expectations—as conventional hierarchies and typical room designations are subverted—of what a house might be and do. With each iteration Andy lovingly reflects upon the relationship between our domestic routines and the spaces in which they are performed. He offers us, with *One House Per Day*, a hymnal of houses, architectural liturgies in which the patterns of domestic life, often mundane and occasionally sublime, take on a kind of ritual significance.

The achievement of this book is less in any of these houses individually than in the collection as a whole. There are some inspired designs here (alongside what I'm sure even Andy would admit are a few duds), but in the end, what resonates is the idea that ideas are not a limited resource. The idea that if, day after day, we let go of our ego and forgo our drive for perfection, the ideas will flow one after the other. That beyond the next house, there's another house, and another, and another…And that in each of these possible houses there are possible lives, both wonderful and tragic.

(Re)thinking the House & its Family
Malcolm Rio

Four decades after writing in an unpublished 1846 manuscript with Karl Marx, "the first division of labour is that between man and woman for the propagation of children,"[1] Friedrich Engels expanded on this claim:

> *The first class antagonism which appears in history coincides with the development of the antagonism between man and woman in monogamian marriage, and the first class oppression with that of the female sex by the male. Monogamy was a great historical advance, but at the same time it inaugurated, along with slavery and private wealth, that epoch, lasting until today, in which every advance is likewise a relative regression, in which the wellbeing and development of the one group are attained by the misery and repression of the other.*[2]

In this passage from *The Origin of the Family, Private Property, and the State* (1884), Engels connected his and Marx's materialist view that social life is determined by the means of production of immediate life—i.e., food, tools, shelter—to the production of biological life itself—i.e., reproductive sex—in order to argue that the social organizations of human cultures are determined not only by their stage of development of labor but also by their kinds of kinship relations.[3] Thus, the modern bourgeois family was the result of a specific kind of historical development, not a "natural" (i.e., patriarchal) given.

Prior to the 1860s, a history of the family would have been almost unthinkable within the culture from which Marx and Engels were writing. The patriarchal form of the family was presumed to have been determined by both nature/biology and divine revelation: men are the natural providers and women the natural caretakers, as evidenced in the relationships of Adam, Eve, and their descendants. However, in 1861, Swiss anthropologist and Roman law professor Johann Jakob Bachofen published *Das Mutterrecht* (Maternal Law/Mother Right), which put forth the first developmentalist theory and history of the family. Bachofen claimed that early human societies lived in unrestricted sexual promiscuity with one another (hetaerism) and women and men were held in common with one another through communal marriages. Further, these early societies were gynarchal because matrilineality was the only indisputable form of descent and kinship bond. The emergence of male-dominant religious ideals, Bachofen argued, led to a transition away from sexual hetaerism toward sexual monogamy and a social (re)organization from matrilineality to patrilineality—from maternal law to paternal law. Thus, for Bachofen, the roots of patriarchy could be located in religion or ideology.[4]

Marx and Engels were dissatisfied with this theory because it lacked a materialist conception of history. However, it was not until 1877 that a materialist argument for the development of the family was made in American anthropologist Lewis Henry Morgan's *Ancient Society*. To align Morgan's argument with Marxist thinking, Engels worked with Marx's posthumous notes and described the origin of the family wherein

> *[i]n a profoundly significant move for some versions of feminism, [Engels's] reading of Morgan led him to suggest that the female act of reproduction—the production of children—should be understood as on a par with the provision of the means of existence, of which there were few higher human callings in Marx's and Engels's materialist template.*[5]

The oppression of women and this privileging of heterosexual monogamy were, therefore, to be understood as co-constitutive components of class exploitation. Consequently, the rise of the monogamous and patrilineal family form was arguably coeval with the rise of private property: the domus. The advent of the iron plowshare shifted horticultural labor from a collective practice organized and regulated by women to an individual practice done by men.[6] This shift, which coincided with the domestication of animals, restructured other social and labor relations including craft specialization and the accumulation of resources, effectively removing women as the dominant food producers of settlement societies.

To ensure the continuation of bountiful crops across generations, and thus the reproduction of immediate life, individual male farmers were tasked with teaching their sons the proper skills and techniques of plowshare horticulture, inaugurating the idea of "passing down" trade and craft along paternal lines. This, according to Engels, "abolished the tracing of descent by female lineage and the maternal right of inheritance, and instituted descent by male lineage and the paternal right of inheritance."[7] Engels further argued that because a genealogy along the paternal line was unknowable for societies with common or group marriage (hetaerism), women were forced into monogamy to ensure indisputable patrilineality: "to secure the faithfulness of the wife, and hence the reliability of paternal lineage, the women are delivered absolutely into the power of the men."[8]

Engels went on to write that "monogamy was the first form of the family not founded on natural, but on economic conditions, viz.: the victory of private property over primitive and natural collectivism."[9] Coetaneous with women's compulsion into monogamous kinship formations was their relegation to the private/domestic sphere; to ensure patrilineality and the patrilineal inheritance of property, women were isolated from their larger gens, both materially and socially, within the separate and exclusive dwellings of their husbands.[10] Private property and the exclusive domestic home are therefore co-constitutive not only of the paternal family unit but also of privatized monogamous sexual relations. The family unit and the private dwelling unit serve as sites of sexual intimacy to reproduce the property relationship—or, in a more vulgar read, the reproduction of private property equals reproductive sex. Correspondingly, the non-private space (i.e., the public) was to be neutered of any sexual relations, and non-reproductive sex pathologized.[11]

The Origin of the Family, of course, has numerous shortcomings. Marx and Engels based their historical development of the family off the limited, fragmentary, and in many ways naive evidence provided in the late nineteenth century from the relatively new sciences of anthropology, archeology, and philology, all of which were susceptible to Orientalist and specious reasoning. Engels himself recognized the paucity of historical information on the family and primeval societies, amending *The Origin of the Family* when subsequent anthropological and archaeological research challenged, contradicted, or even made untenable the theses of Morgan and Bachofen.

Contemporary appraisals of Engels and Marx's claims remain mixed. British historian Tristram Hunt argues that twenty-first century academic discourse widely dismisses Engels's text due to a lack of substantive evidence of historic gender equality in early societies, while researchers from Cambridge University have argued that the "nuclear family" has a more extensive lineage than previously thought, dominating the social organizations of most known human societies throughout world history.[12] Conversely, Dr. Kit Opie at the University of Bristol has argued that modern monogamy is a recent social development.[13] The very contradiction between these two stances demonstrates that claims regarding the historicity of the nuclear family rest on the cultural assumptions of these researchers as they impact method, interpretation, or what counts as evidence for or against the development of monogamous kinship formations. Furthermore, drawing universal evolutionary conclusions from the specific ethnographic and anthropological studies of human and non-human social organization, both past and present, is always methodologically precarious.

Despite *The Origin of the Family's* faults, Marx and Engels offer a materialist argument that at least opens a space for challenging the (nuclear) family and the domestic (home) as timeless, absolute kinship relations. They also provide a crucial link between gender and sex and property and ownership that is specifically manifested within the figure of the home. Rethinking the historical construction of the family, as a construct of written history and comparative law, may allow architects to rethink the typology of the home.

Notes

1 Karl Marx and Friedrich Engels, *The German Ideology* [1867], ed. C. J. Arthur (London: Lawrence & Wishart, 1970), 51.
2 Friedrich Engels, *The Origin of the Family, Private Property and the State* [1884] (Chippendale NSW: Resistance Books, 2004), 73.
3 Engels, "Preface to the First Edition 1884," in *The Origin of the Family* (2004), 25–26.
4 It is important to note that while Bachofen's work offers novel notions of family structure, his theories overall are profoundly conservative and reify male-female dichotomies and biases. Peter Davies, "Myth and Maternalism in the Work of Johann Jakob Bachofen," *German Studies Review* 28, no. 3 (October 2005): 501-18.
5 Tristram Hunt, "Introduction," In *The Origin of the Family, Private Property and the State* [1884] (Kindle Edition) by Friedrich Engels. (New York: Penguin, 2010), kindle location 189-92.
6 Pat Brewer, "Introduction" in *The Origin of the Family* (2004), 19, 21.
7 Friedrich Engels, *The Origin of the Family, Private Property, and the State* [1884] (Chicago: Charles H. Kerr & Company, 1908) 69.
8 Engels, *The Origin of the Family* (1908), 71.
9 Engels, *The Origin of the Family* (1908), 79.
10 The ability of labor and private property to separate from and exclude the larger gens/common is also reiterated by John Locke's theory on private property. See: John Locke, *Two Treatises of Government* [1689] (Cambridge: Cambridge University Press, 1988), 288-89.
11 See Michel Foucault, *The History of Sexuality* [1976] (New York: Vintage, 1990); George Chauncey, "Privacy Could Only Be Had in Public: Forging a Gay World in the Streets," in *Gay New York: Gender, Urban Culture, and the Making of the Gay Male World 1890-1940*, (New York: Basic Books, 1994), 179–205.
12 See the Cambridge Group for the History of Population and Social Structure. Hunt, "Introduction," kindle location 346-77.
13 Kit Opie, et. al., "Male Infanticide Leads to Social Monogamy in Primates," *Proceeding of the National Academy of Sciences of the United States* 110 (2013): 13,328–32.

Transcending the American Dream: House, Family & Domesticity

Alessandro Orsini & Nick Roseboro

Traditionally, we refer to the house as the structure to protect the intimacy of the family. It provides shelter and separates us from work (although it might support work). In other words, it is the space that protects the biological life of the occupants. The house comprises an envelope that allows for further subdivision into smaller spaces—what we call rooms. Such rooms present a defined hierarchy—what we call privacy, set forth by the homeowner, giving individuals the possibility to separate from the rest of the occupants, a value "highly praised by family ideology."[1] This value is deeply rooted in the individualism of the family as an entity and its members. The demarcation of rooms and their functions reiterates the nuclear family structure and allows for the separation of the family from the outside world and of each individual within the house. This quality of the house enables inhabitants to define what can be presented to the public and what stays private.

The conventional organization of the house revolves around a central room where the owner may host guests, while the remaining space is subdivided into smaller rooms shaped according to different domestic activities, usually more private. In this paradigm, architecture hides spaces such as the kitchen, laundry room, and bathroom, where women have traditionally performed domestic labor. This organization defines the relationship between the house and its rooms as one of power and gender, between the male head of the household and its constituents, including a woman in the case of the traditional family. Women have conventionally attended to the governance and sustenance of the household through tasks that guarantee the reproduction of the family,[2] such as preparing food and raising children, in contrast to the labor performed by the patriarch that occurs outside the domestic space. Thus, the spatiality of the single-family house is the direct outcome of the nuclear family structure centered around the patriarchal relationship within it, master and slave, husband and wife, father and children.

In analyzing the origin of the word family, from the Latin *familia*, we observe its original meaning: "the slaves of a particular household."[3] The word indicates that the family is a collective body of people—not necessarily linked by blood—but connected by a pact of ownership within the estate

See Red Women's Workshop: Feminist Posters 1974-1990. Creative Commons license CC BY-NC-SA 3.0

of the house. Therefore, the house not only represents the space of family accommodation but also symbolizes the social status and acquired power of the paterfamilias[4]—the owner or landlord—over his estate.[5] Over the centuries, the power structure of the house and the notion of property have become two of society's most critical ordering principles, manifesting capitalistic values "via speculative finance, mortgage debt, and property development."[6]

After World War II, the history of the single-family house in the United States became inextricably linked to the creation of suburbia. The house embodied the concept of mass ownership, primarily aimed toward white families, who were the beneficiaries of racially divisive government policies through which they obtained middle-class status and privileges such as education, pensions, and homes. The migrations to the suburbs established patterns of car dependency, a preference of privacy versus community, and the cult of domesticity based on the principles of "piety, purity, [and] submissiveness" of the woman to the patriarch;[7] their participation in church activities transformed the household into a territory for the "most significant religious experiences."[8]

New housing developments defined by standardization, typological repetition, and low-cost materials "did not involve careful site planning, provision of community space, or any design input from architects. These houses were bare boxes to be filled up with mass-produced commodities," such as the washer and dryer, vacuum cleaner, and other tools for domestic labor extraction.[9] Additionally, single-family zoning, which regulates the architectural form of most suburban and urban America, was used to prohibit the construction of anything other than a single house on a single lot, "segregating family from non-family,"[10] and deterring any forms of community association. Zoning practices allowed developers to design the segregation of African, Indigenous, and White Americans through a system of discriminatory selling contracts such as the infamous ones adopted in Levittown, Long Island.[11] Racist and capitalist tendencies shaped the spatial division of cities and their surrounds, as government-sponsored mortgages were offered only to white owners for "the cultivation of the dweller as a consumer."[12] In addition, as architectural theorists Pier Vittorio Aureli and Maria Shéhérazade Giudici explain: "Designed to be cleaned, refurbished, and beautified, the house or apartment incurs expenses, encouraging workers to earn more to improve it and further forcing women into un-paid labor to maintain it."[13]

Furthermore, sociologist Jon Bernardes states that the "wage labour and the ideology of motherhood and housework"[14] drove the cyclical nature of economic extraction using the house as a device at its center, furthering "the division of the public and the private, the division of the sexes and the division of labour."[15] The house symbolizes the desire and achievement of the American dream, a commodity that serves as an escape from the working environment and a shelter from the elements—and at the same time, a tool for segregation.

Today, we must rethink domestic space to give agency to the multiple and diverse forms of association, cooperation, and collectivity that would reject the racial and gender segregation of the single-family house and the capitalistic financial paradigm of work, profit, and living. The house, its network, and its form must be rearranged with aspects of collective living that address the dialectical elements of domesticity that oppose processes of individualization. A family, in its most transgressive definition, is not configured around people related by blood. Even so, in such a definition, it becomes a personal choice retaining aspects of comfort and safety understood in terms of the traditional family. Paradoxically, we can use those historical values to look toward the model of the collective, replacing the nuclear to redefine the meaning of family. New definitions of the family and related domesticity can enhance the possibilities of outcomes that transgress the political and social barriers within and outside the house. Such new definitions need not necessarily erase heteronormative families, but they may further define and promote sharing structures that will transcend the individualism of family ideology.[16]

Therefore, the form of the house would become "spatially flexible, changeable over time according to household size and composition,"[17] in support of household diversity beyond the binary notion of gender. Furthermore, in the words of autonomist feminist Marxist activist Silvia Federici, "we cannot build an alternative society and a strong self-reproducing movement unless we redefine our reproduction in a more cooperative way and put an end to the separation between the personal and the political, and between political activism and the reproduction of everyday life."[18] The house will have agency for the collective and oppose the individualism of the suburban house that demarcates social boundaries through ownership and gender roles. Via a more radical discourse, architects and designers have been slowly moving toward the "transgressive home," a space that operates with the people and the genius loci of the land, planned and designed in conversation with its inhabitants through agreements that will place the house in the new social sphere of the collective.

Notes

1 Jon Bernardes, "'Family Ideology': Identification and Exploration," *Sociological Review* 33, no. 2 (May 1985): 279–82.
2 For more on the definition of family in relation to reproduction, economy, and society, see Pier Vittorio Aureli and Maria Shéhérazade Giudici, "Familiar Horror: Toward a Critique of Domestic Space," Log, no. 38 (2016): 113.
3 See Roman History definition, Oxford English Dictionary, "'familia, n.'.," n.d., https://www.oed.com/view/Entry/67955?redirectedFrom=familia.
4 See Roman Law definition Oxford English Dictionary, "'paterfamilias, n.'," n.d., https://www.oed.com/view/. Entry/138753?redirectedFrom=paterfamilias.
5 For more about the domestic sphere, See Pier Vittorio Aureli and Maria Shéhérazade Giudici, "Familiar Horror: Toward a Critique of Domestic Space," *Log*, no. 38 (2016): 111–15.
6 Helen Hester and Nick Srnicek, "Shelter Against Communism," E-Flux (blog), accessed February 6, 2022, https://www.e-flux.com/architecture/workplace/430312/shelter-against-communism/.
7 Barbara Welter, "The Cult of True Womanhood: 1820-1860," *American Quarterly* 18, no. 2 (1966): 152, https://doi.org/10.2307/2711179.
8 Charles F. Irons, "The Cult of Domesticity, Southern Style," ed. Scott Stephan, *Reviews in American History* 38, no. 2 (2010): 253.
9 Dolores Hayden, *The Grand Domestic Revolution: A History of Feminist Designs for American Homes, Neighborhoods, and Cities* (Cambridge, Mass: MIT Press, 1981), 23.
10 Leslie Kanes Weisman, *Discrimination by Design: A Feminist Critique of the Man-Made Environment*, Illini Books ed. An Illini Book (Urbana, Ill.: Univ. of Illinois Press, 1994), 132.
11 Richard Rothstein, *The Color of Law: A Forgotten History of How Our Government Segregated America*, First edition (New York ; London: Liveright Publishing Corporation, a division of W. W. Norton & Company, 2017), 82–83.
12 Aureli and Giudici, "Familiar Horror: Toward a Critique of Domestic Space," 126–27.
13 Aureli and Giudici, 127.
14 Bernardes, "'Family Ideology': Identification and Exploration," 278.
15 Bernardes, 280.
16 Bernardes, 279–82.
17 Weisman, *Discrimination by Design*, 125.
18 Silvia Federici, *Re-Enchanting the World: Feminism and the Politics of the Commons*, Kairos (Oakland, CA: PM Press, 2019), 112.

One House Per Day

no.001–365

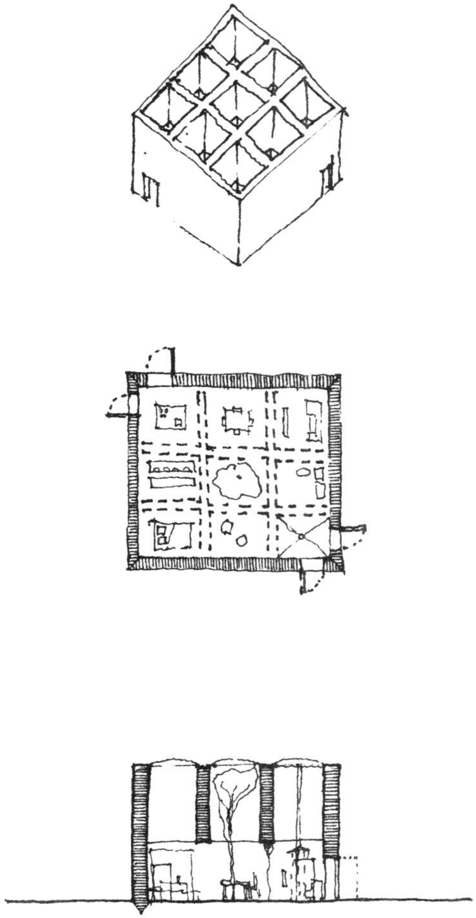

no.001

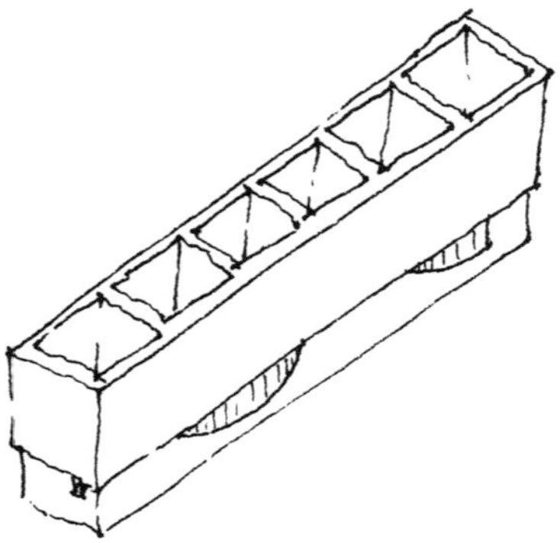

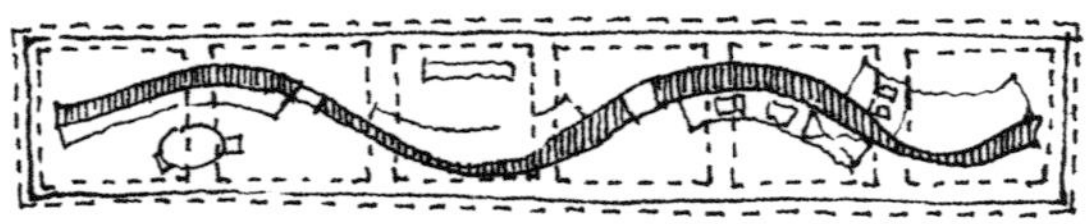

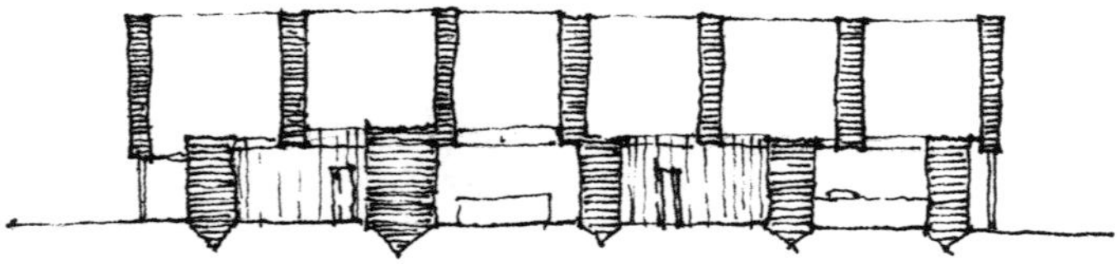

no.002

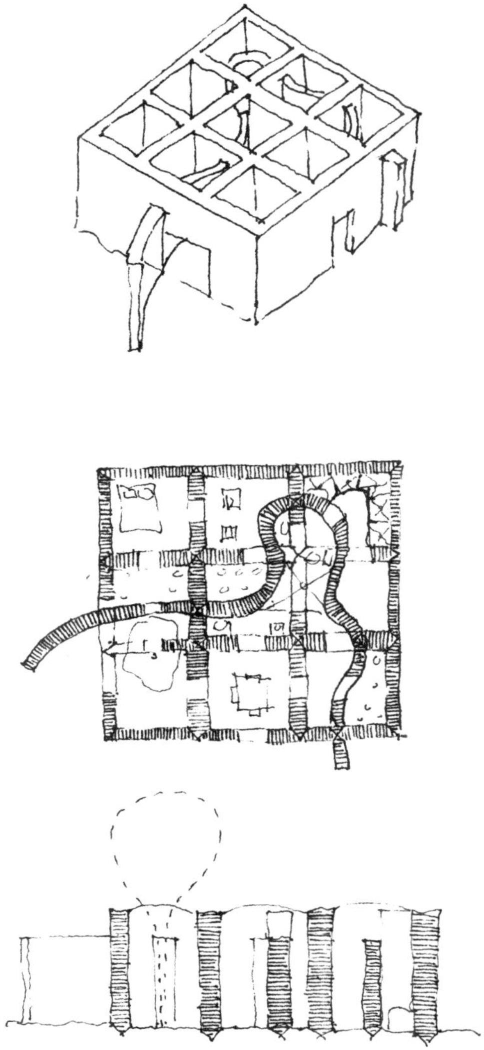

no.003

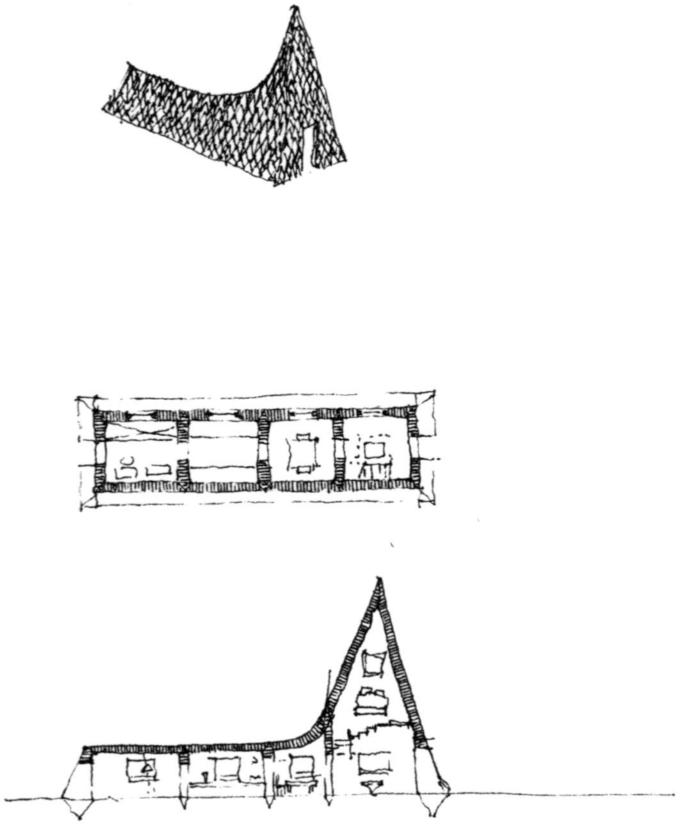

no.004

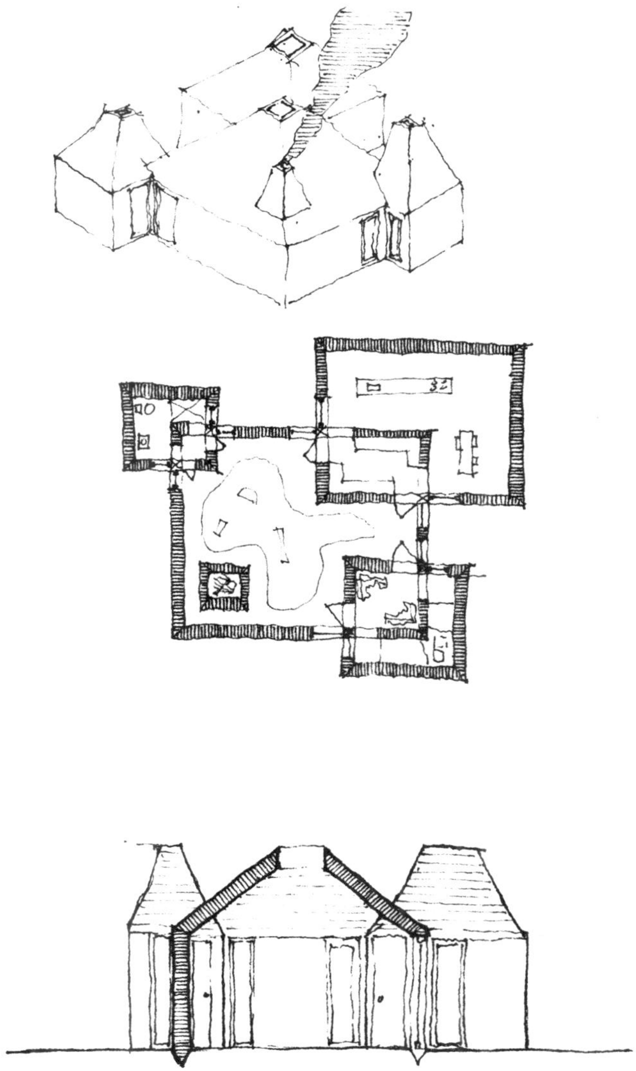

no.005

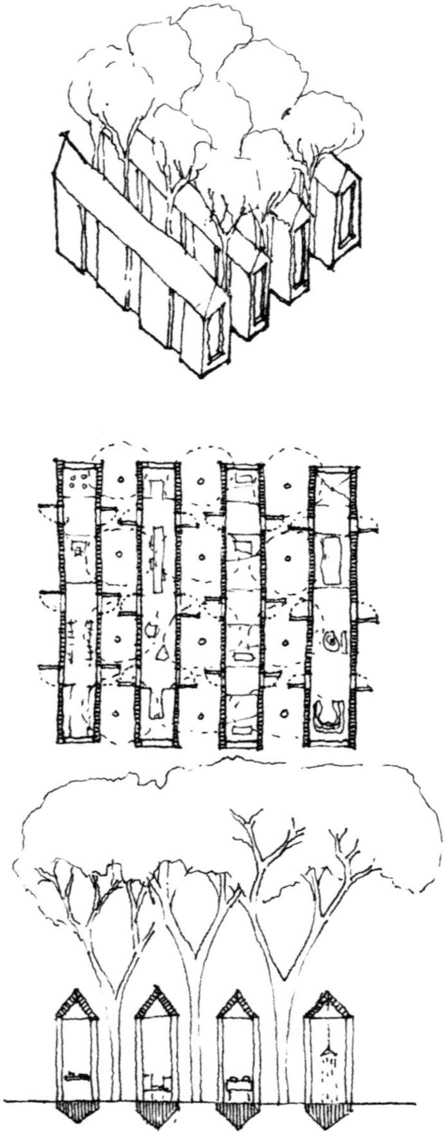

no.006

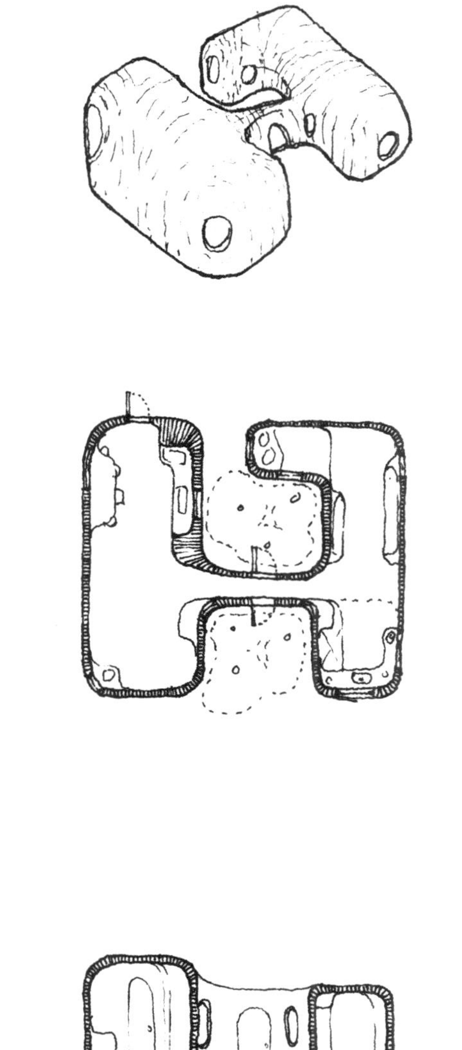

no.007

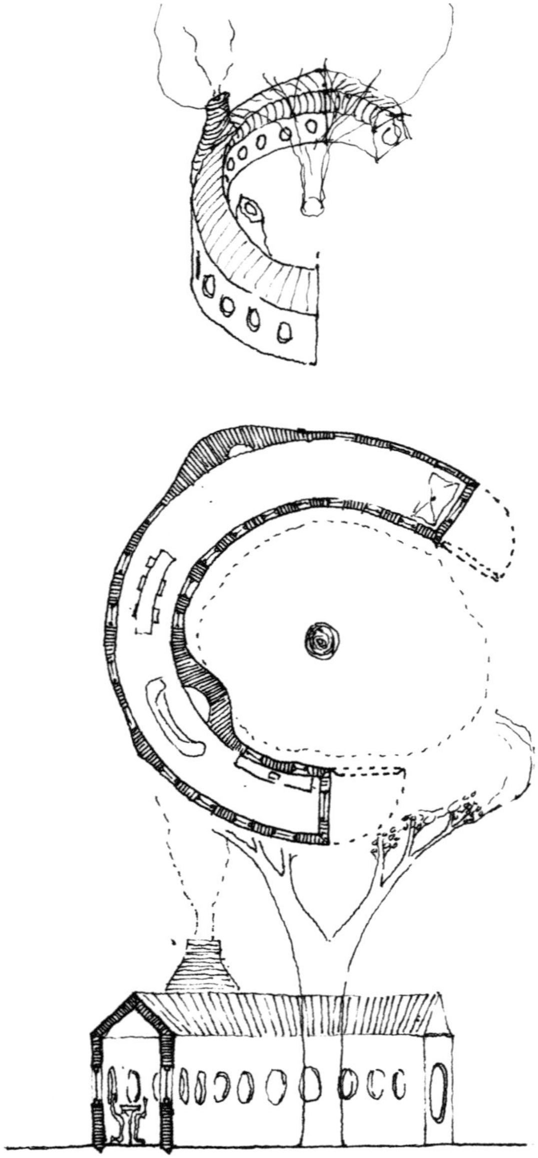

no.008

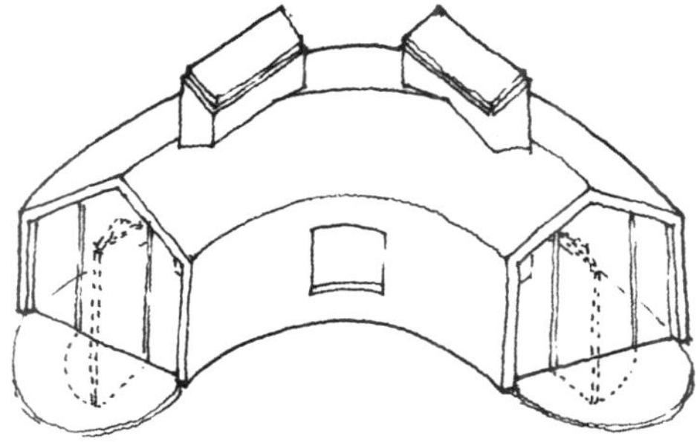

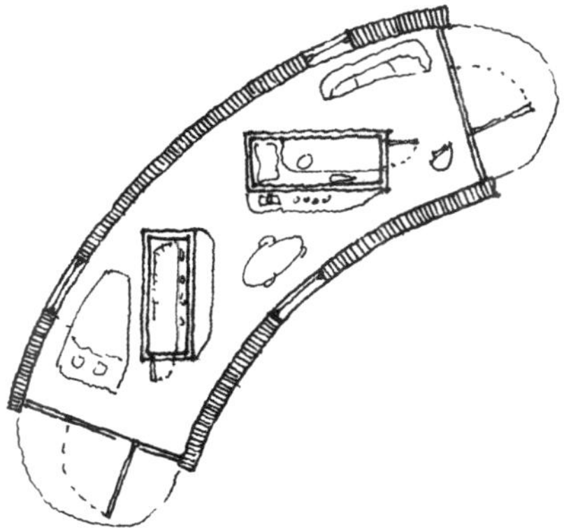

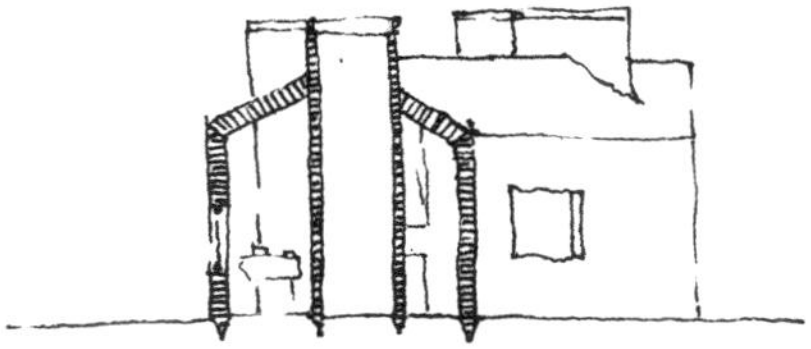

no.009

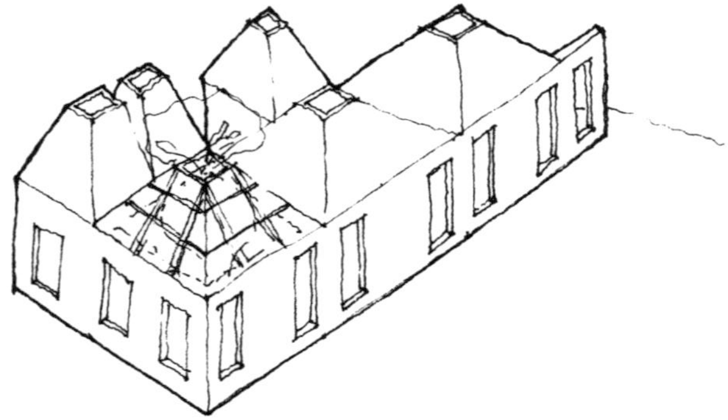

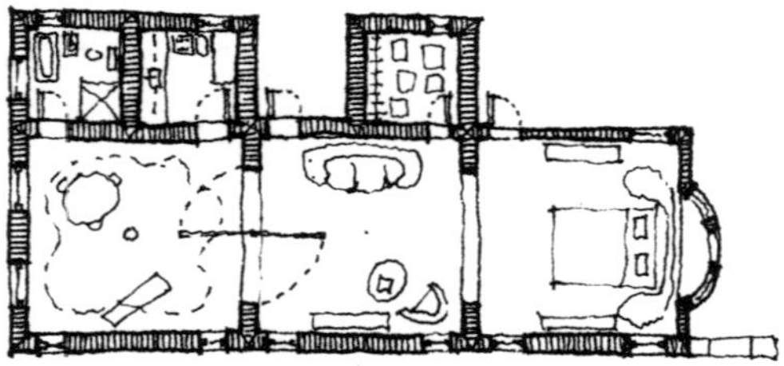

no.010

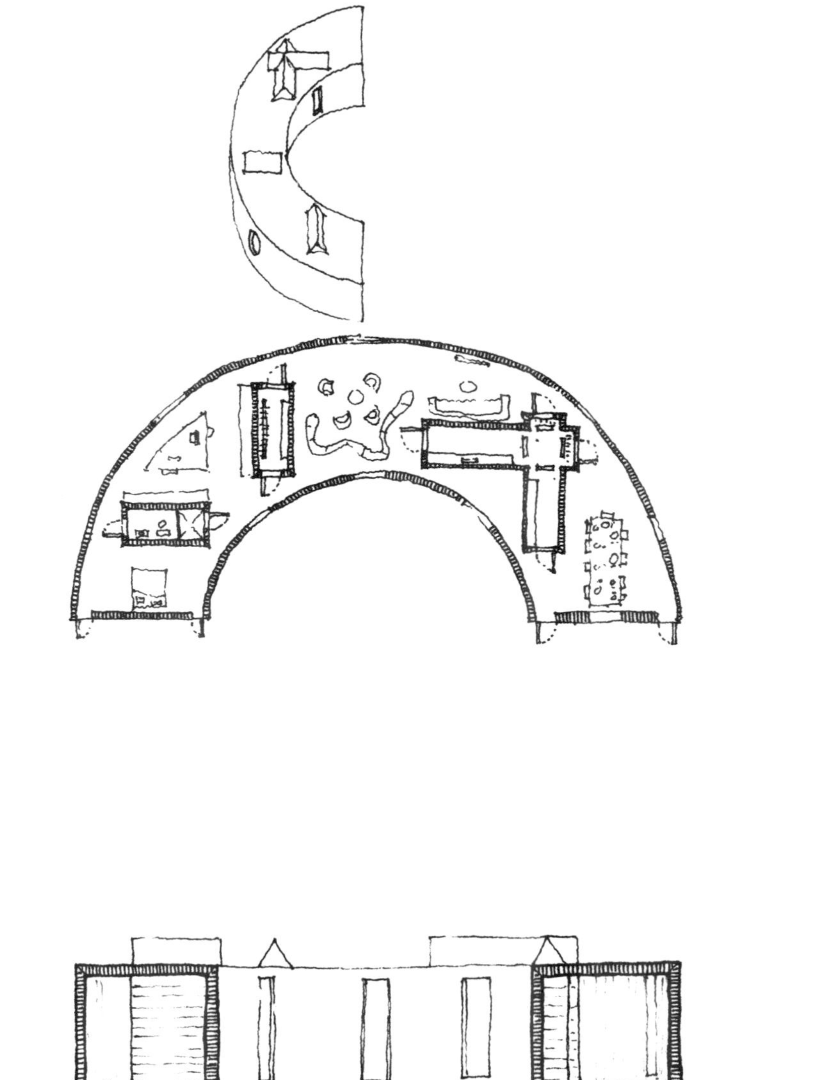

no.011

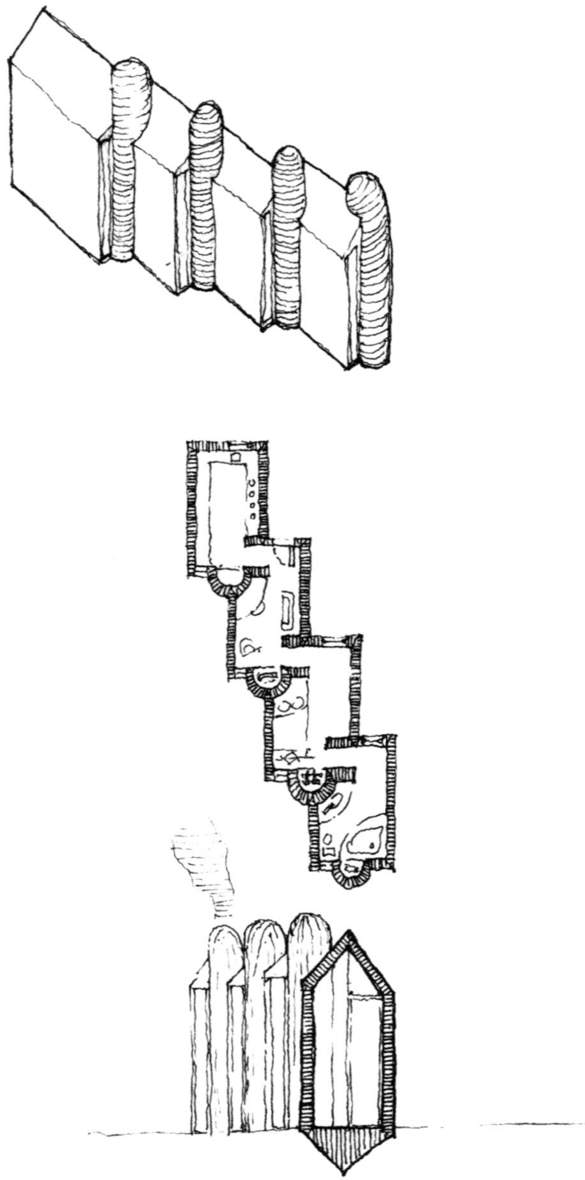

no.012

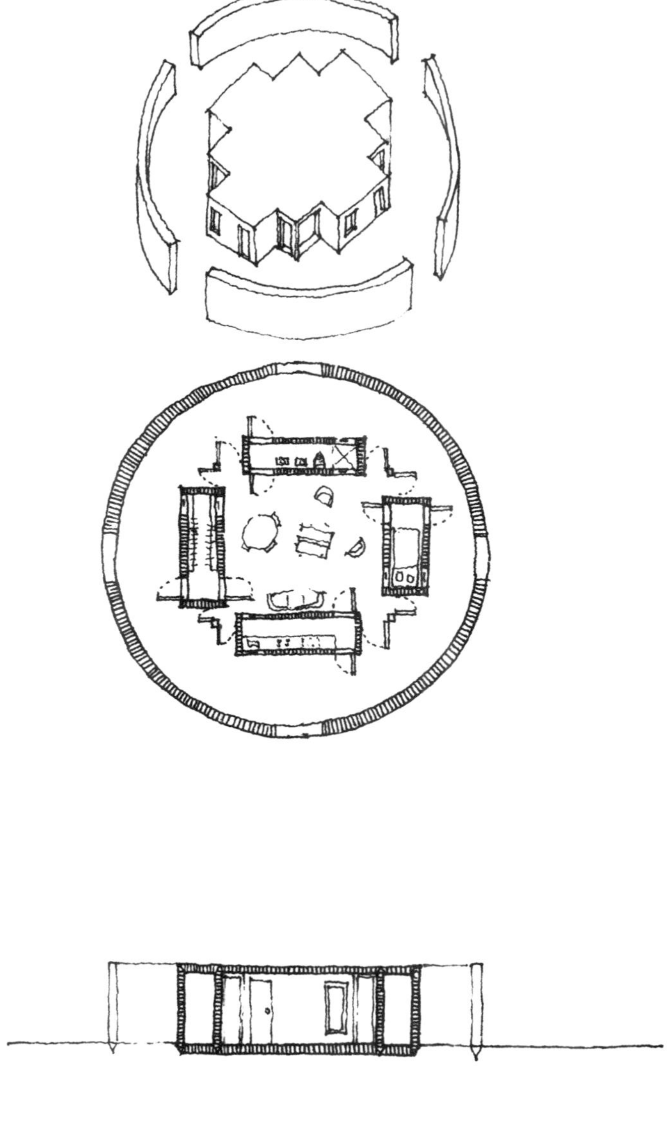

no.013

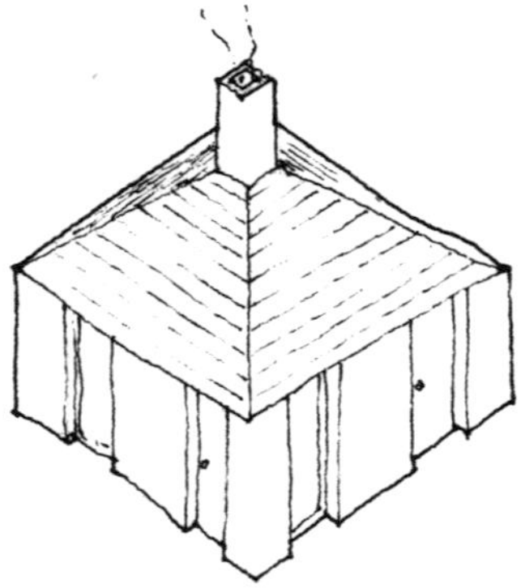

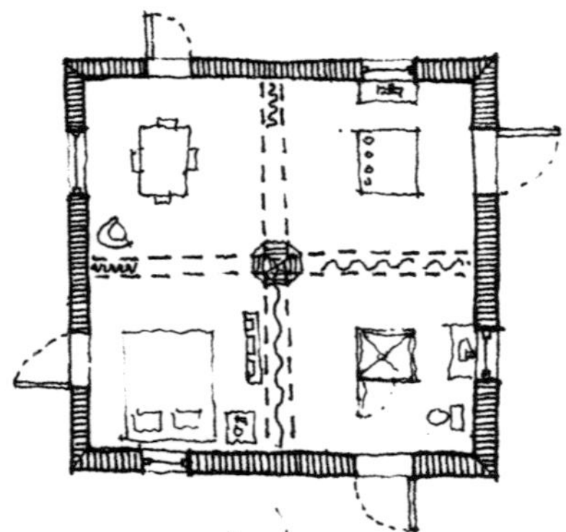

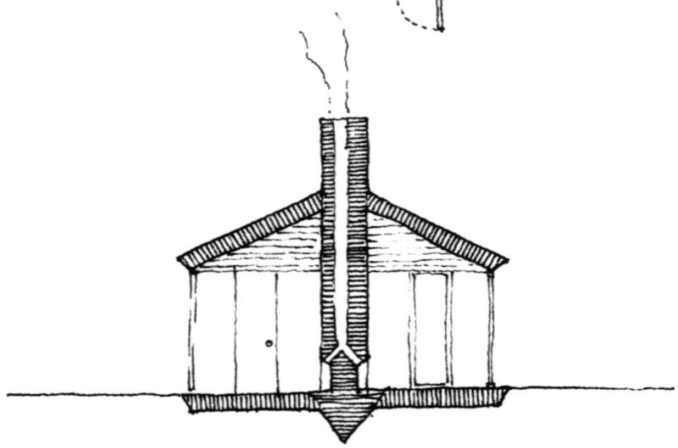

no.014

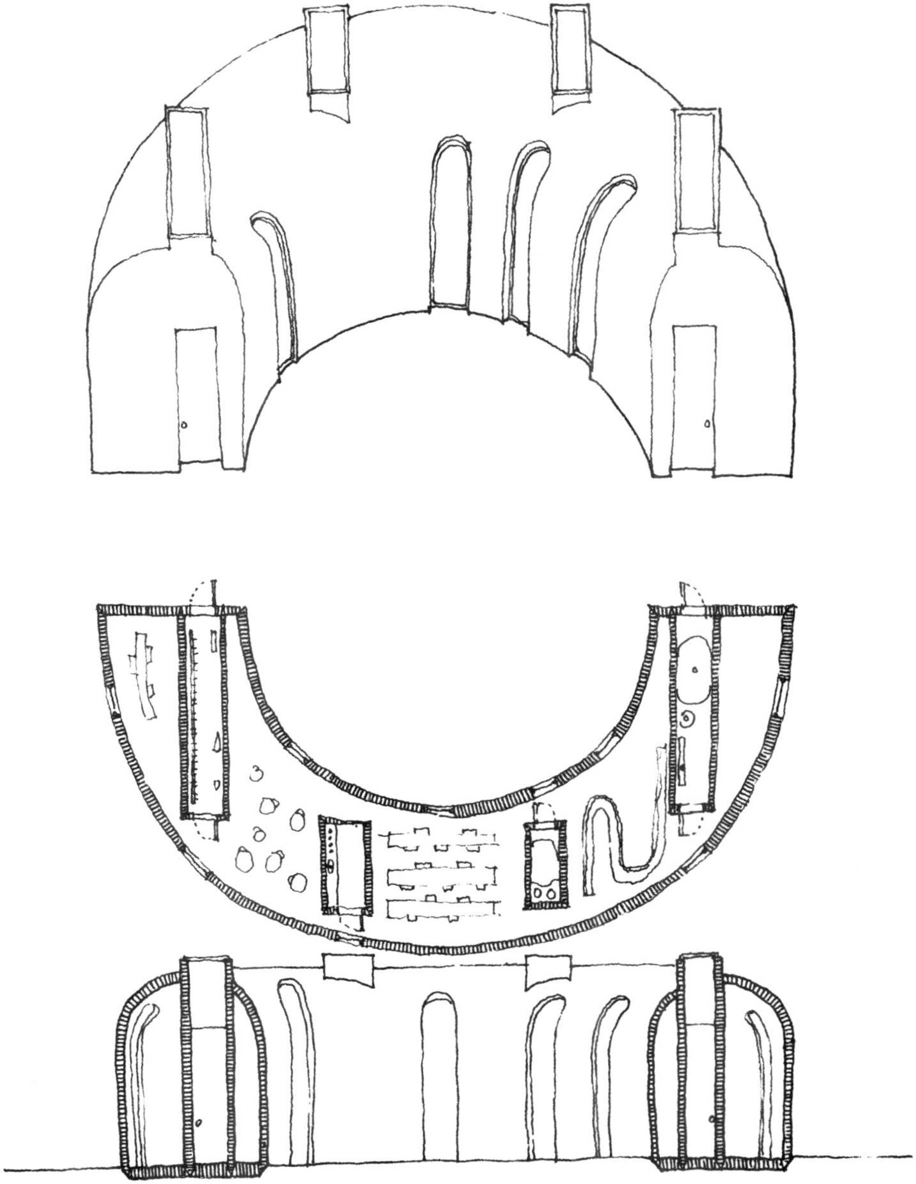

no.015

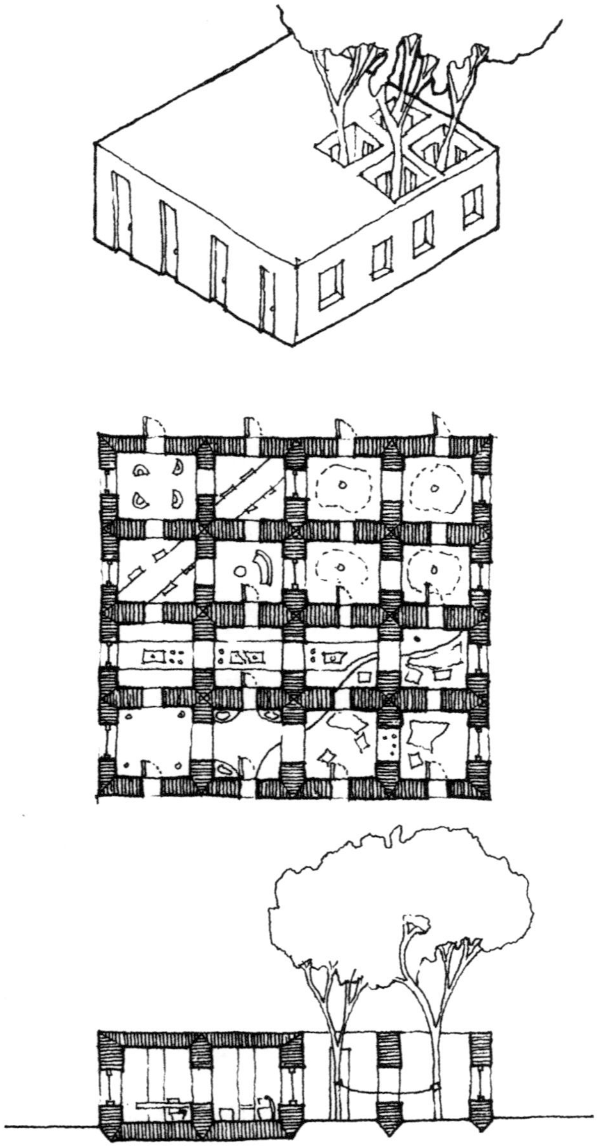

no.016

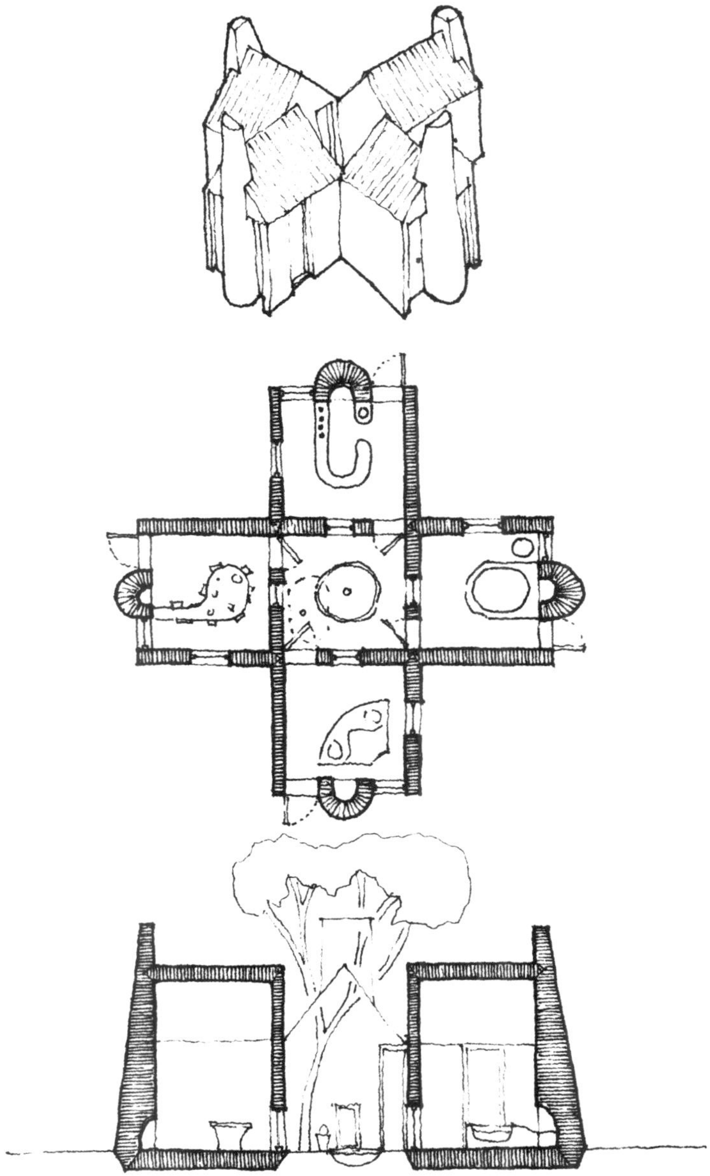

no.017

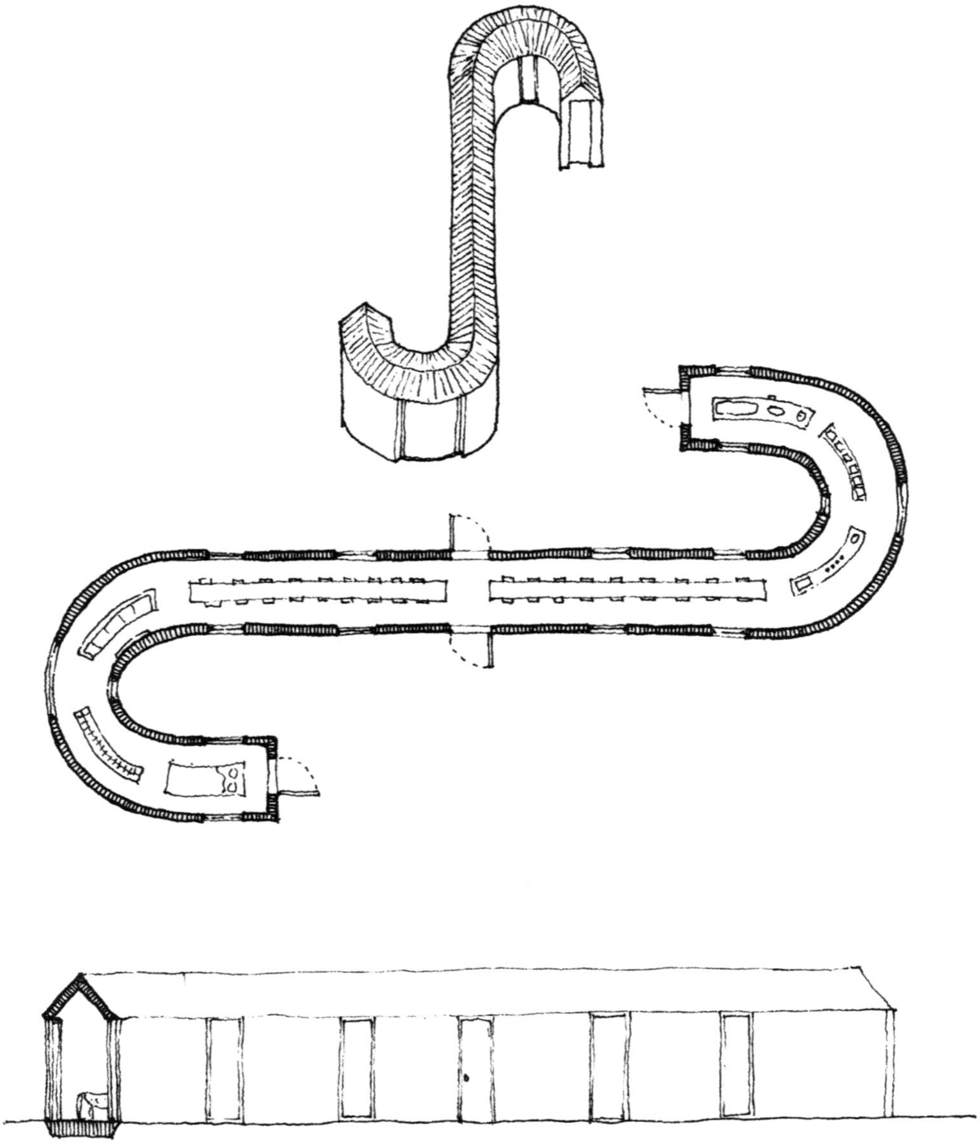

no.018

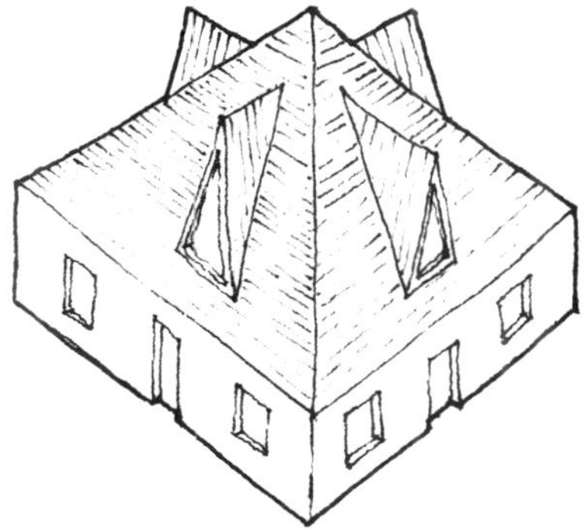

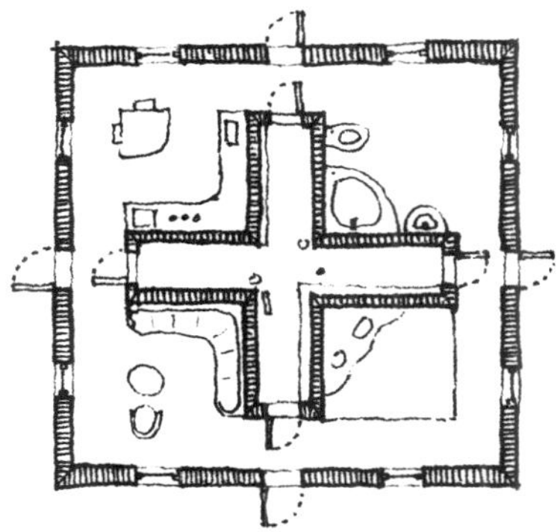

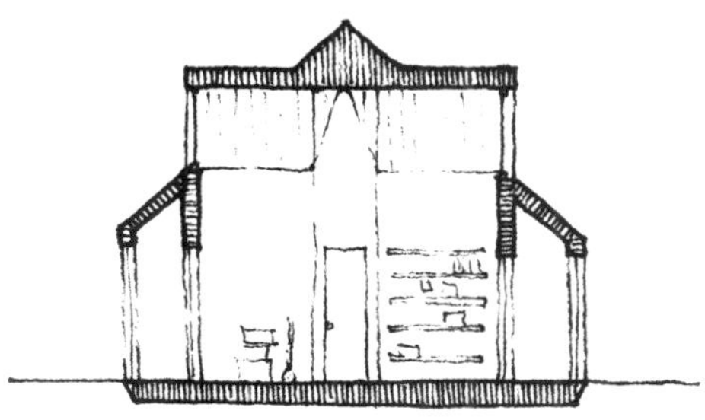

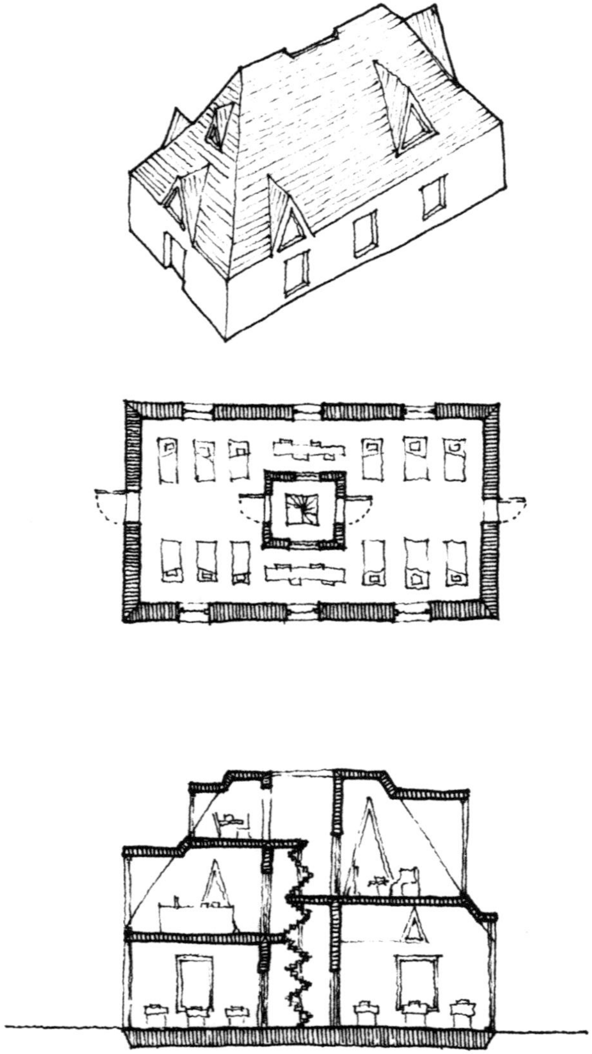

no.020

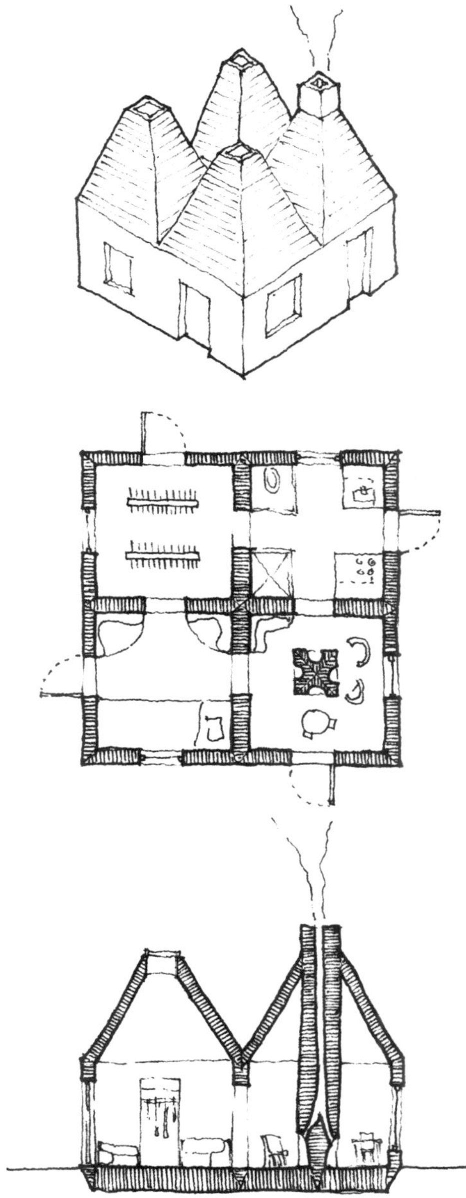

no.021

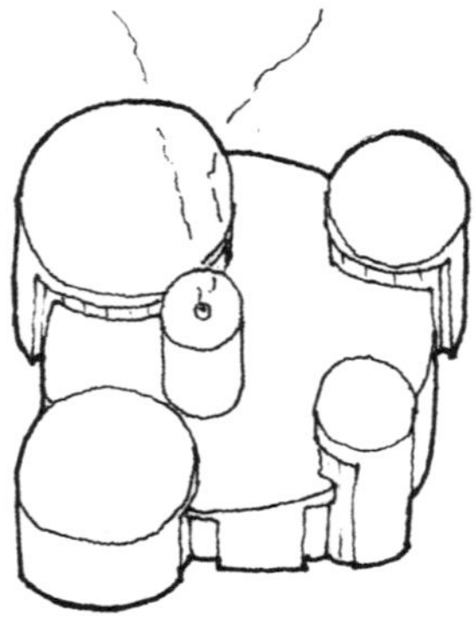

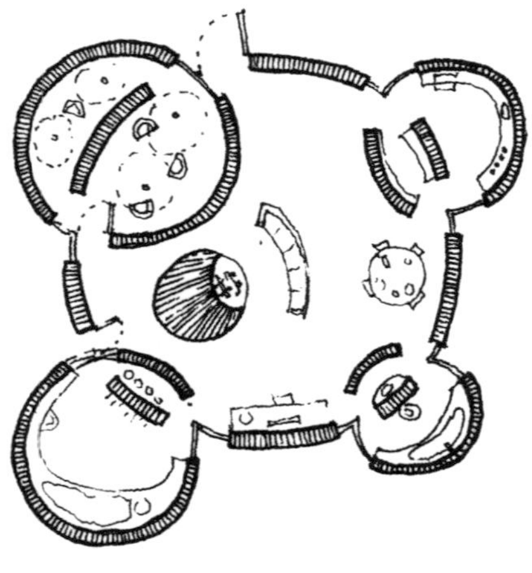

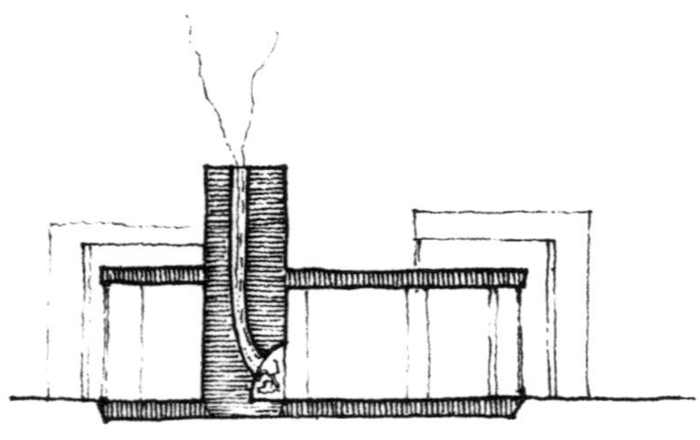

no.022

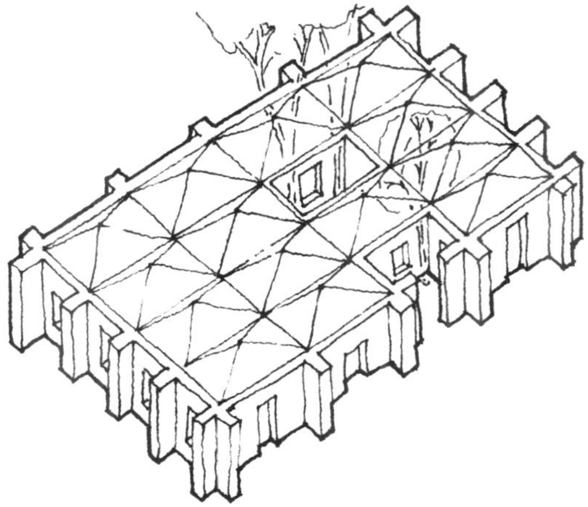

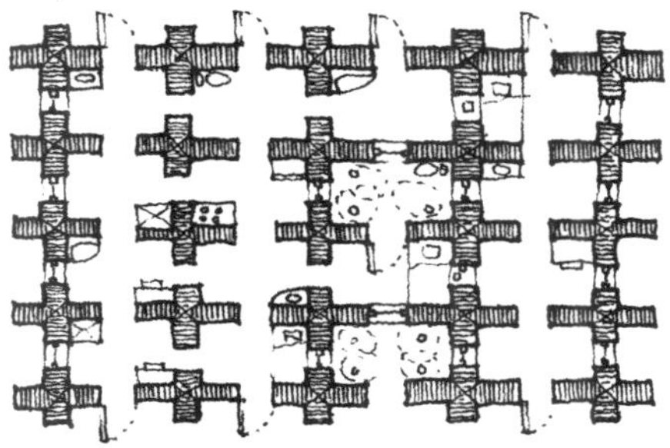

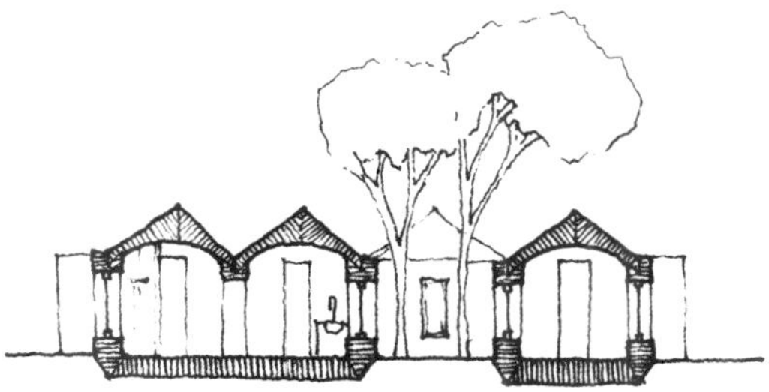

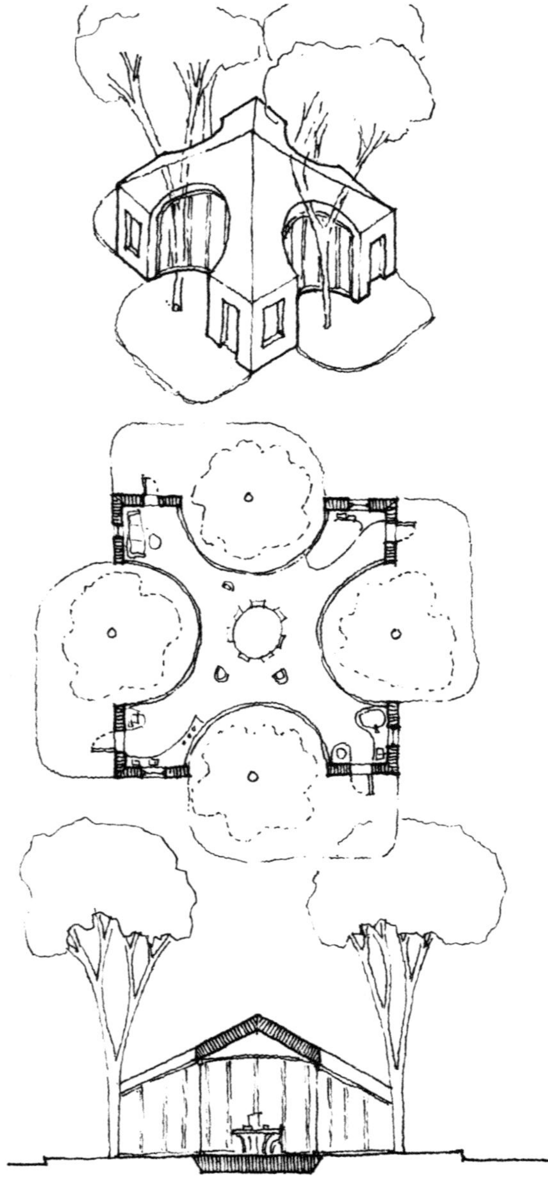

no.024

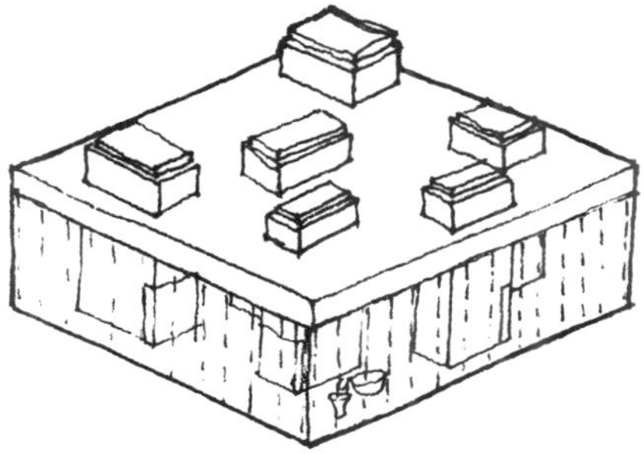

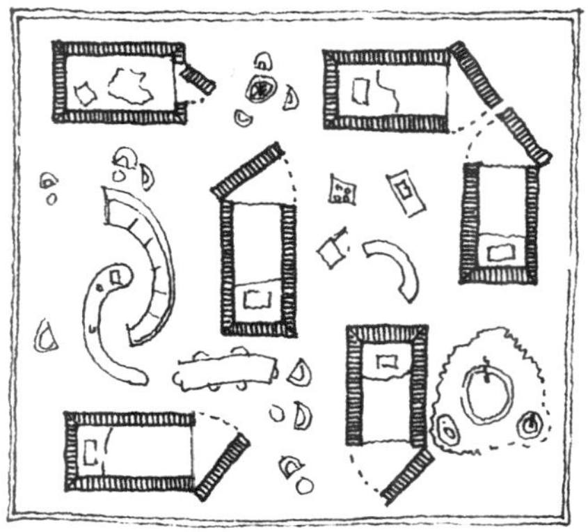

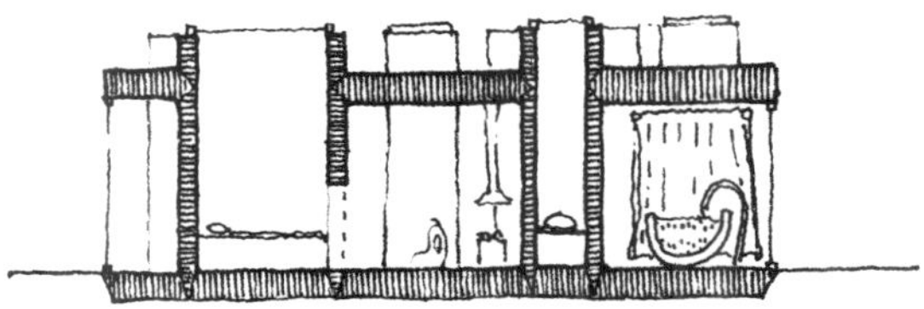

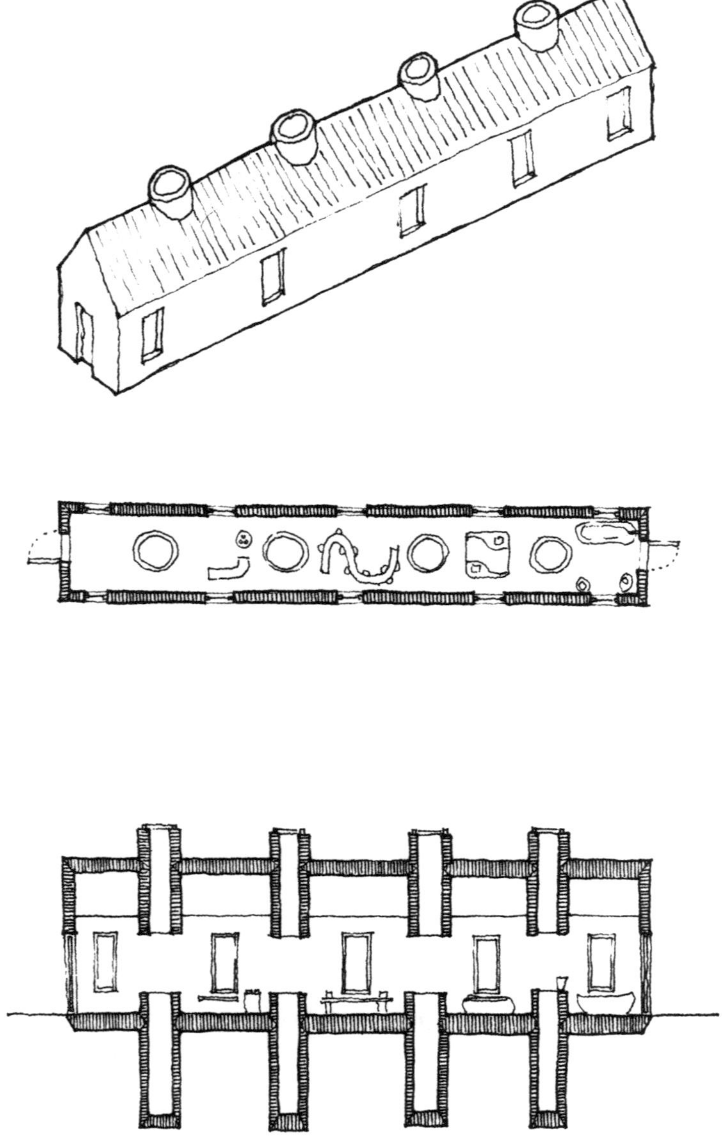

no.026

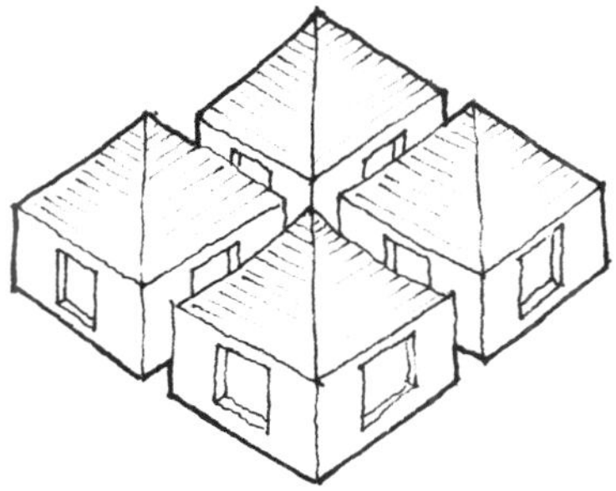

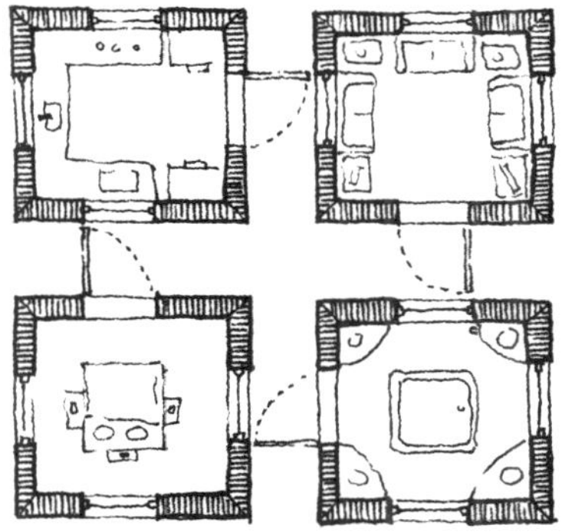

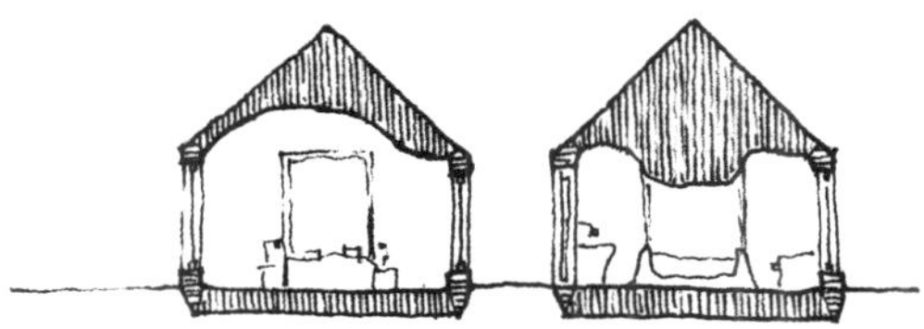

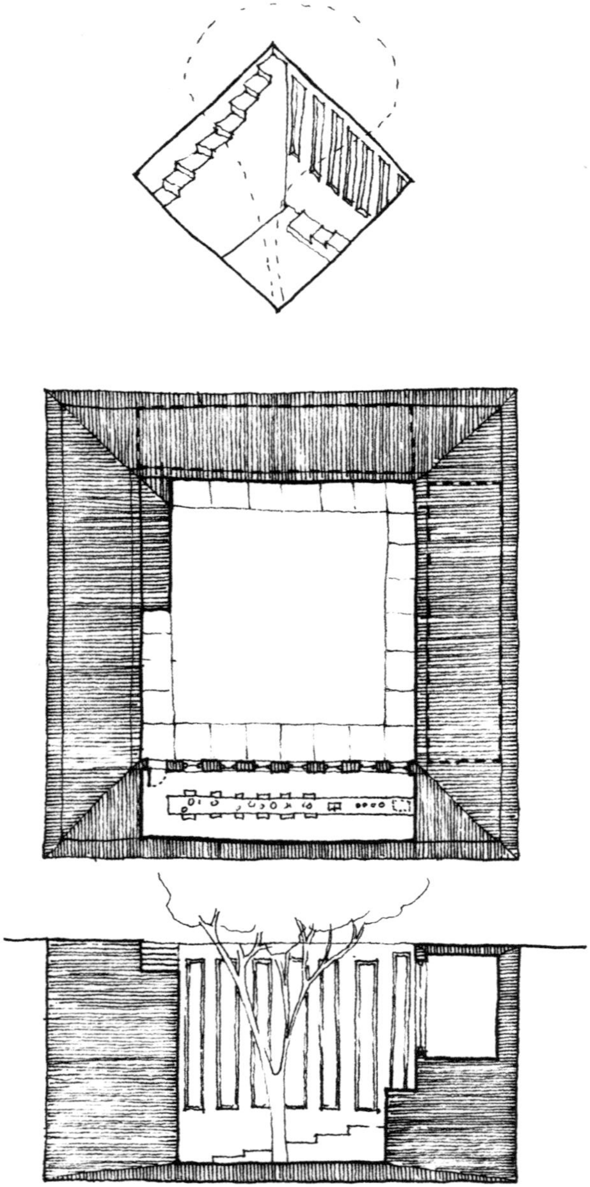

no.028

no.029

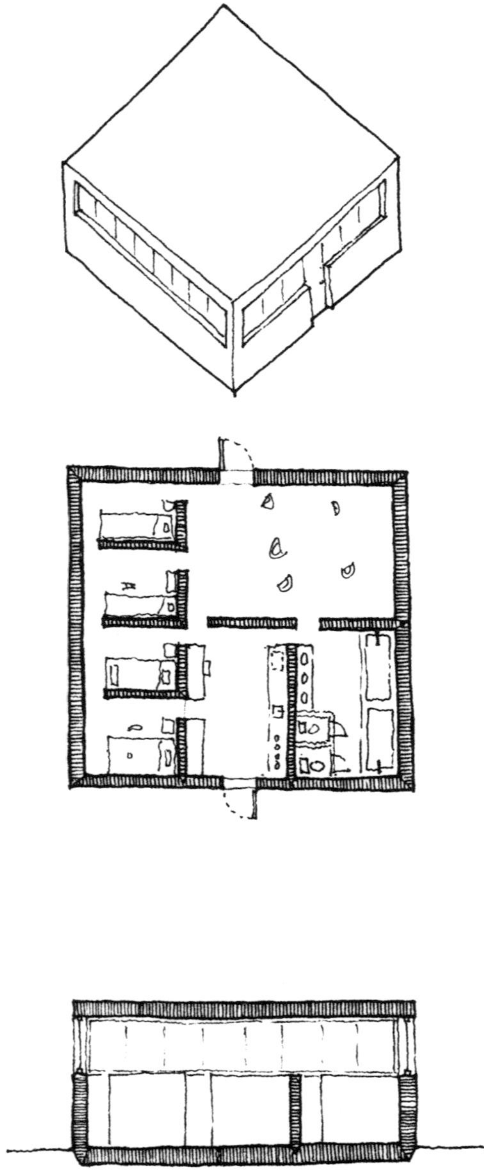

no.030

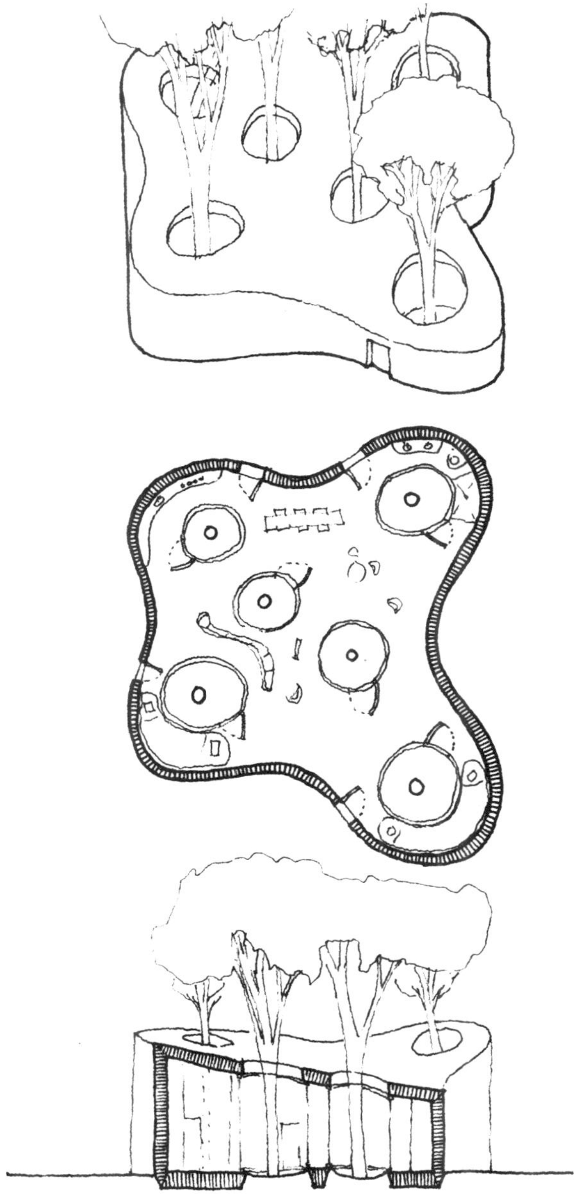

no.031

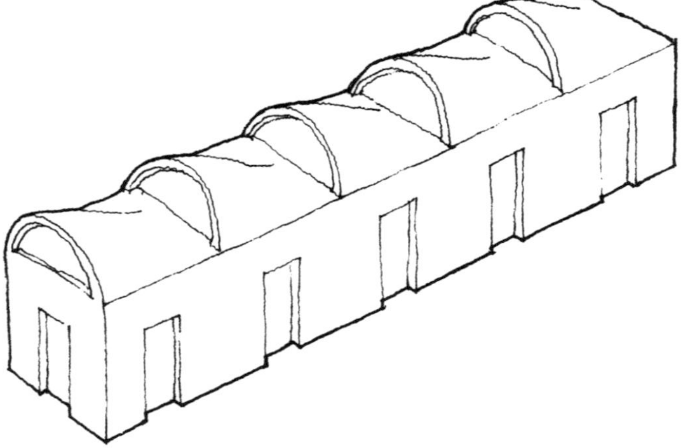

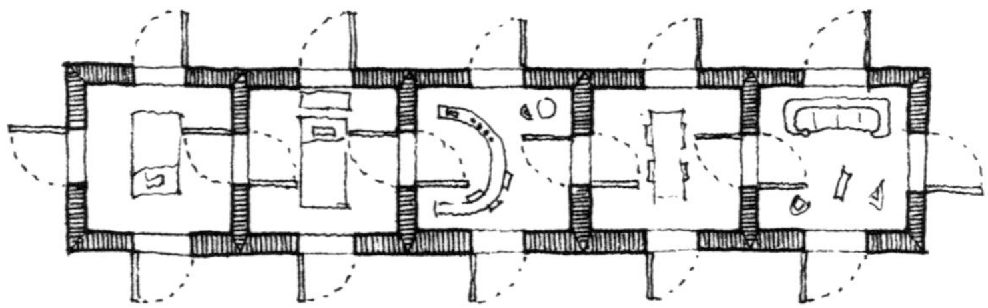

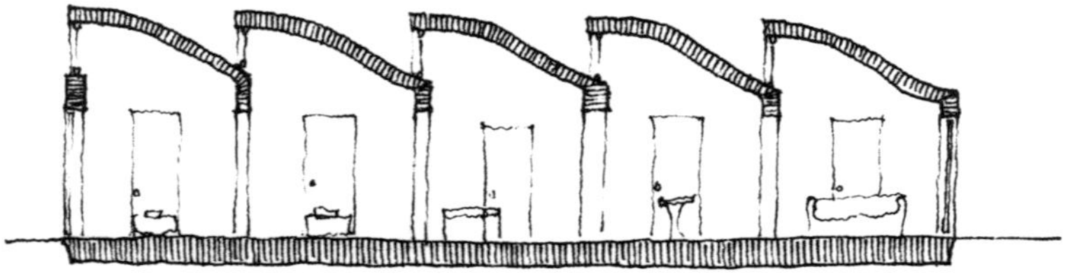

no.032

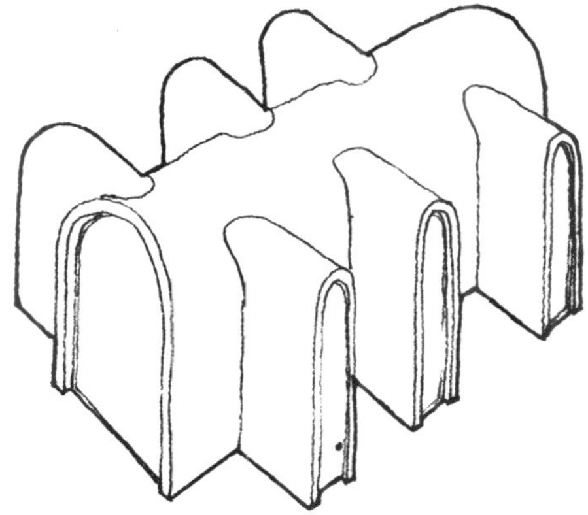

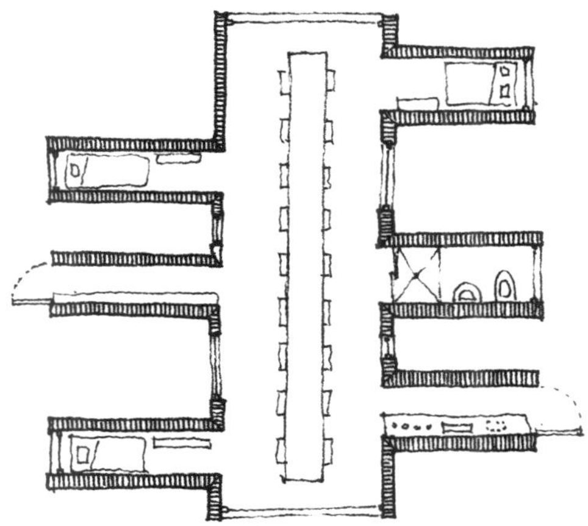

no.033

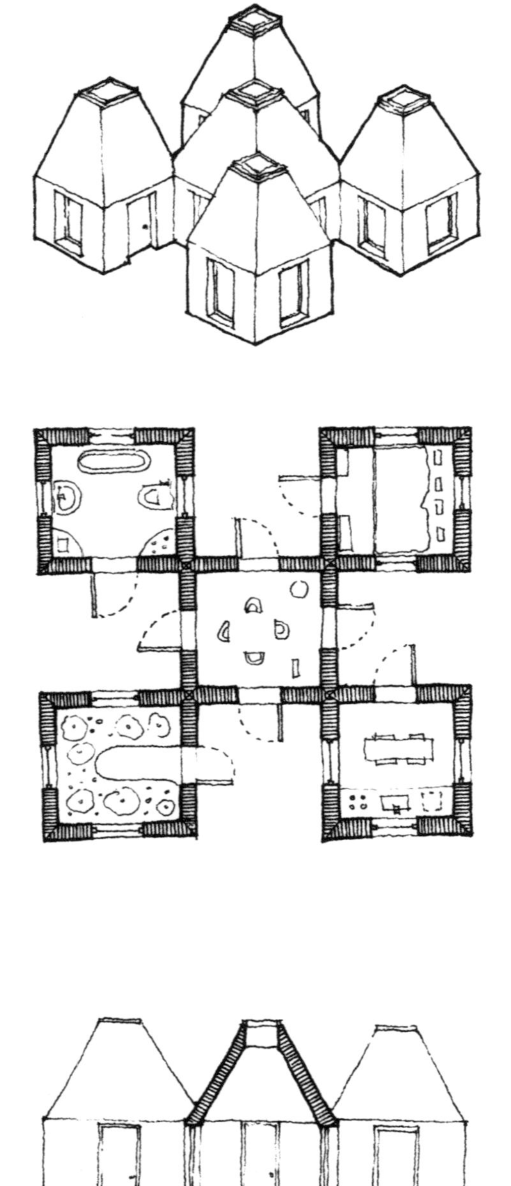

no.034

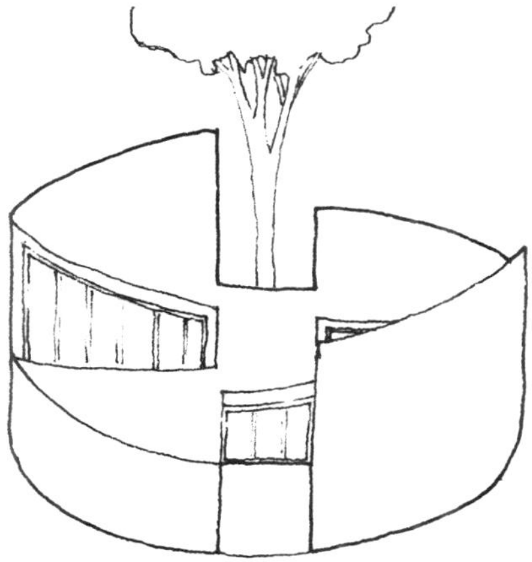

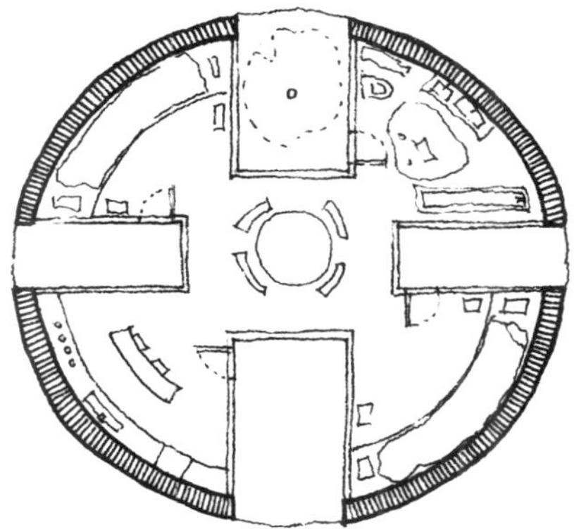

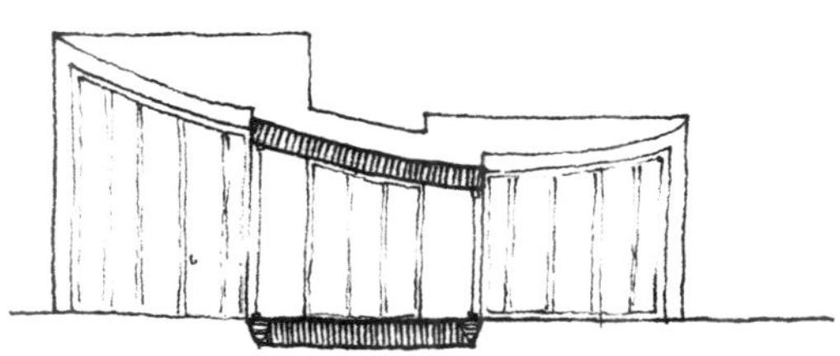

no.035

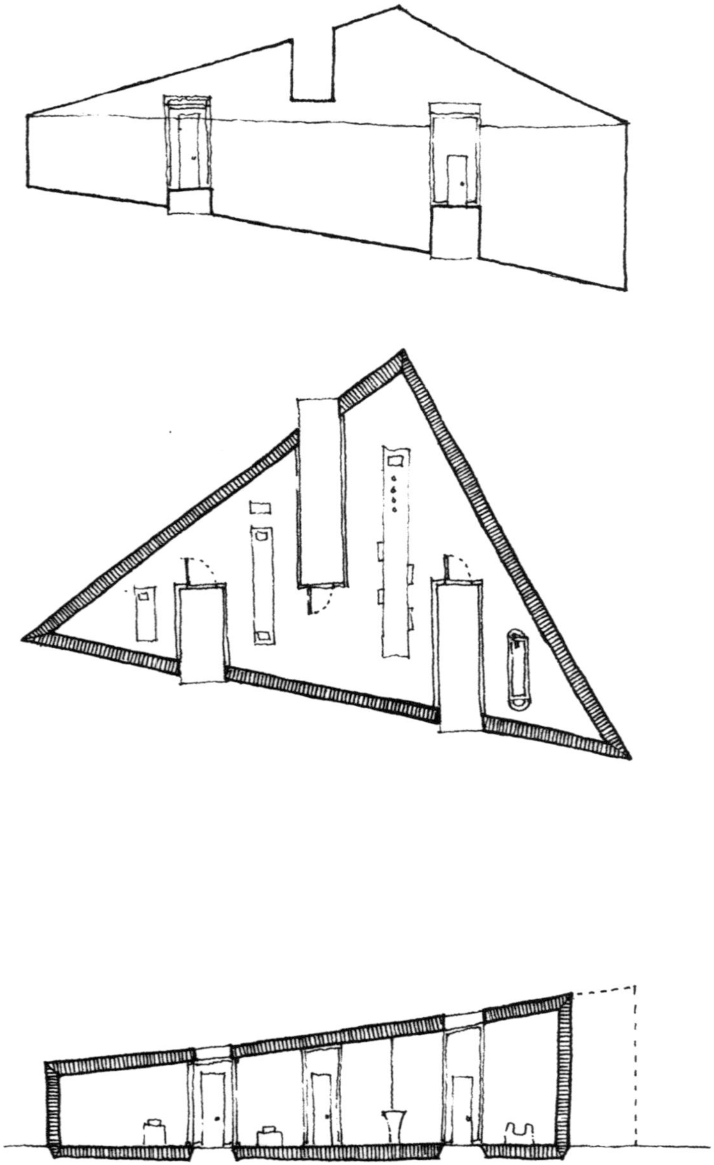

no.036

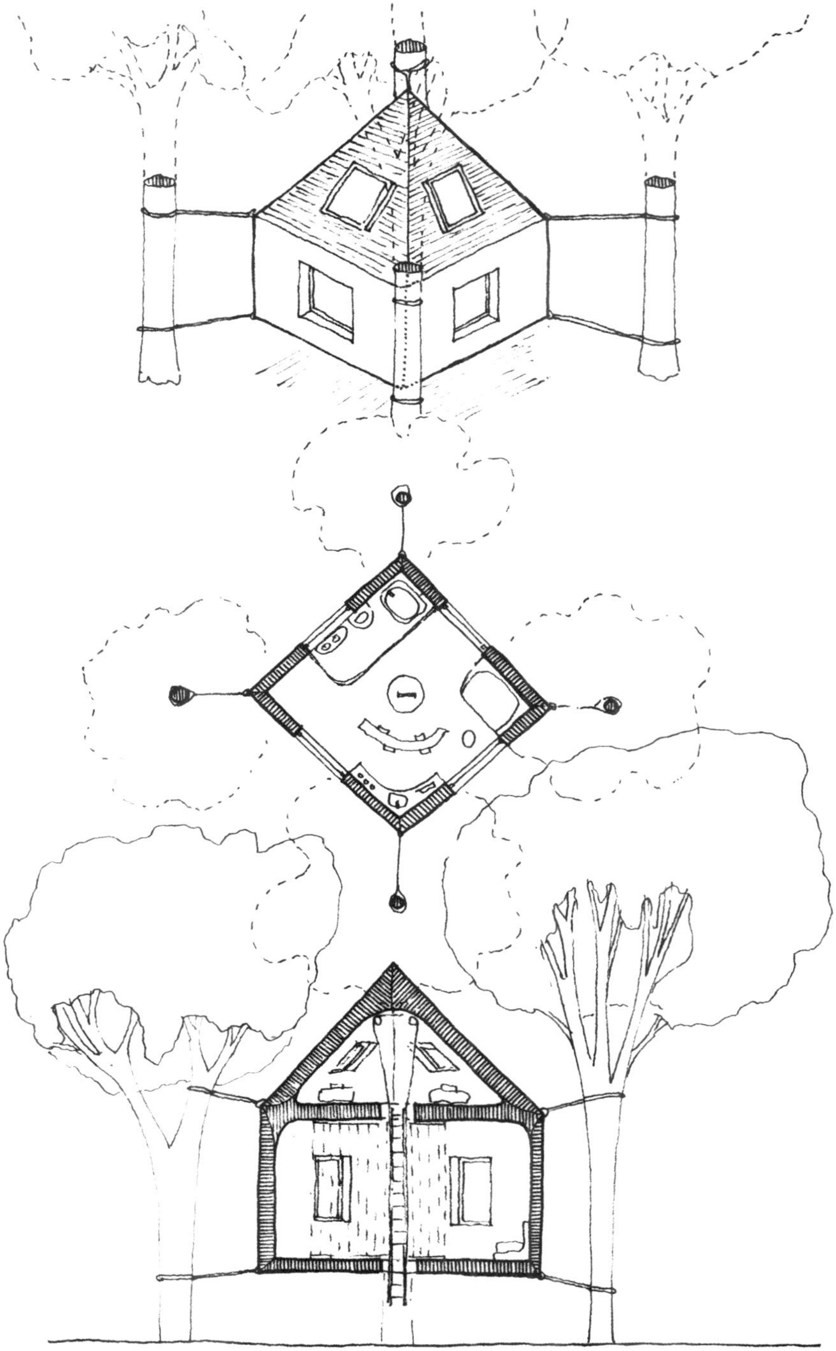

no.037

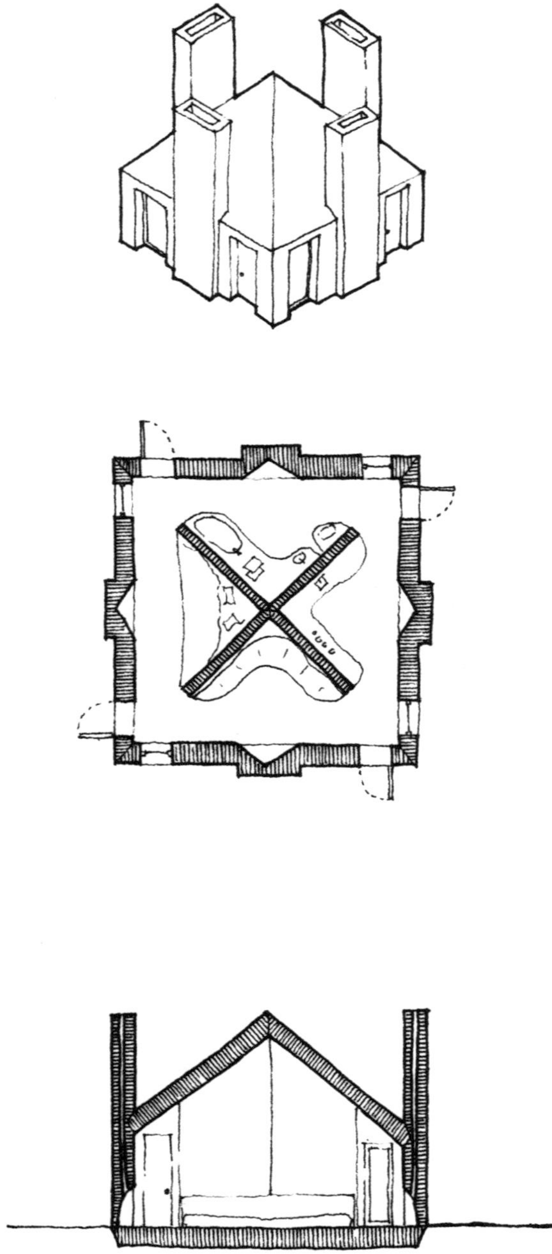

no.038

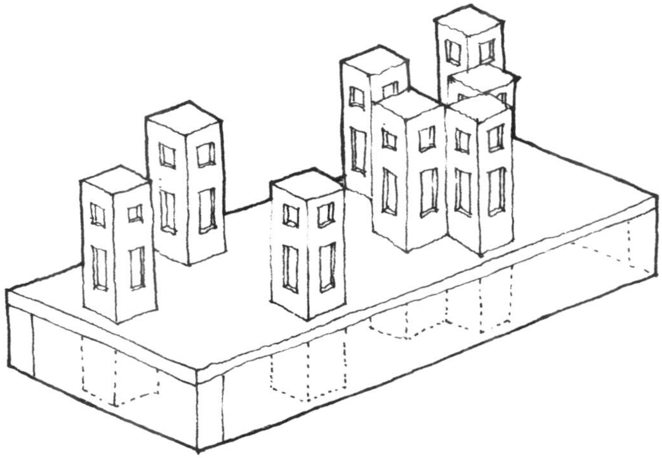

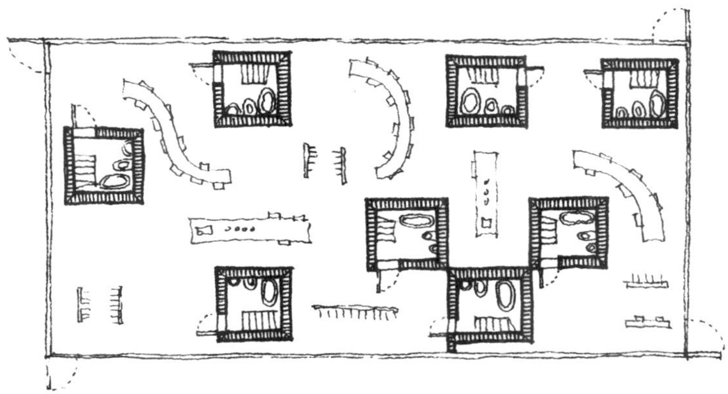

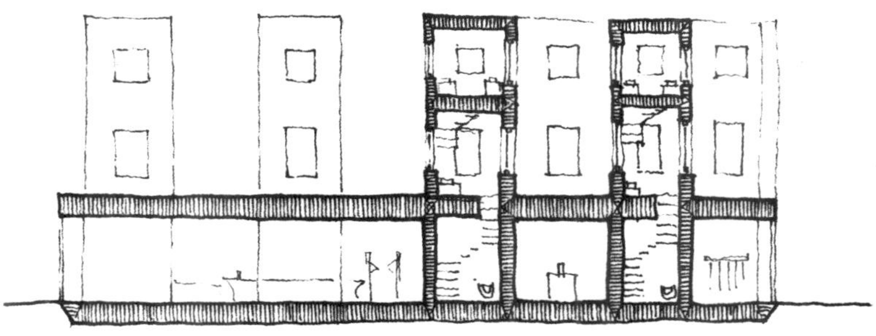

no.039

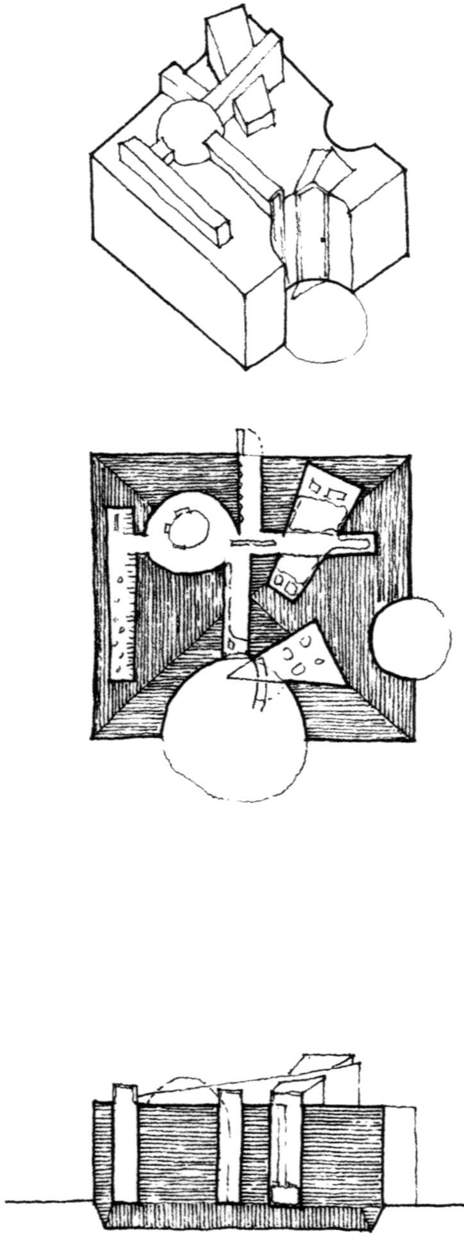

no.040

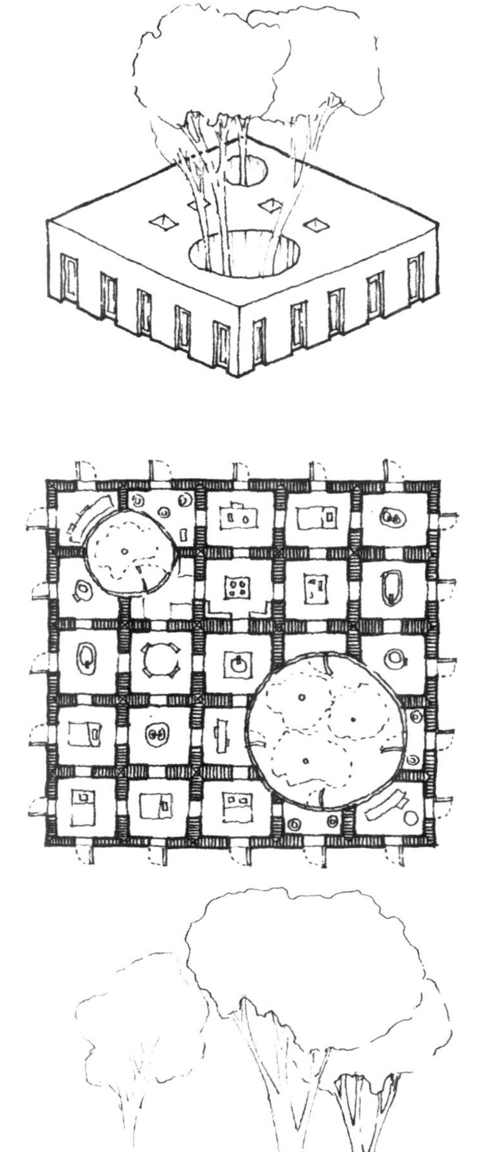

no.041

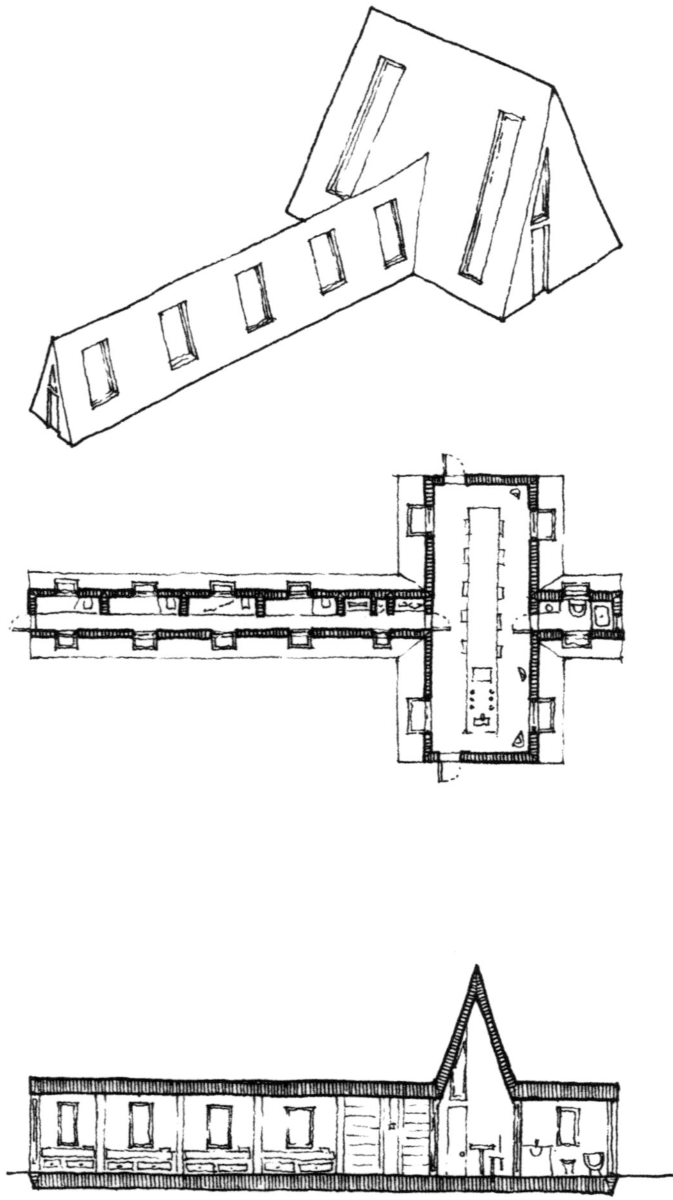

no.042

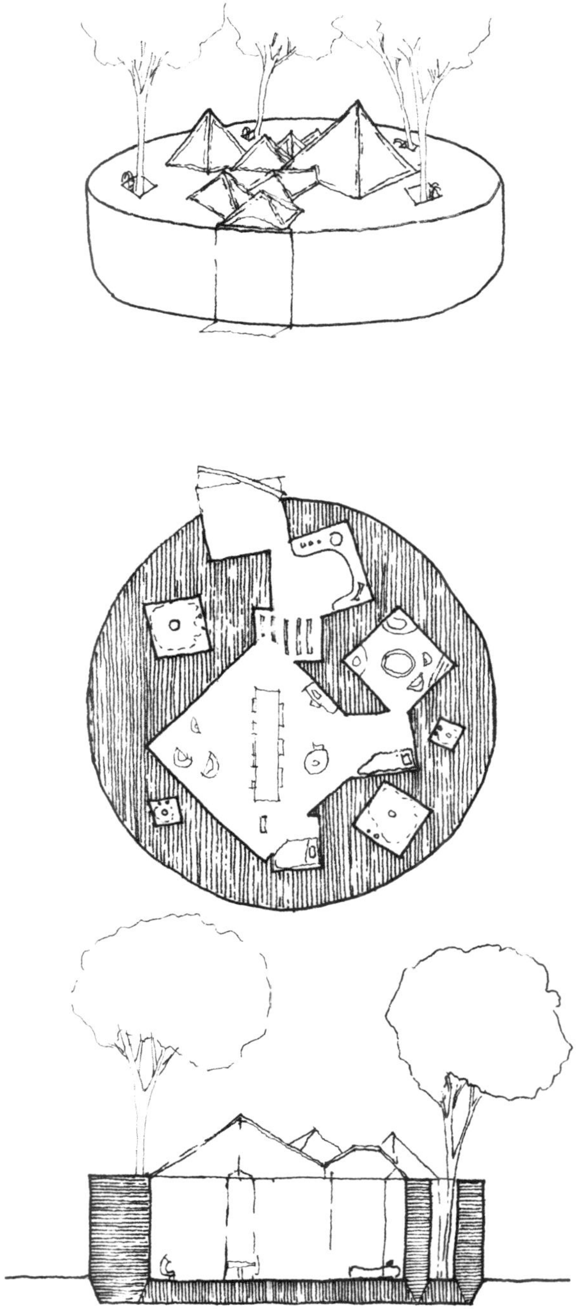

no.043

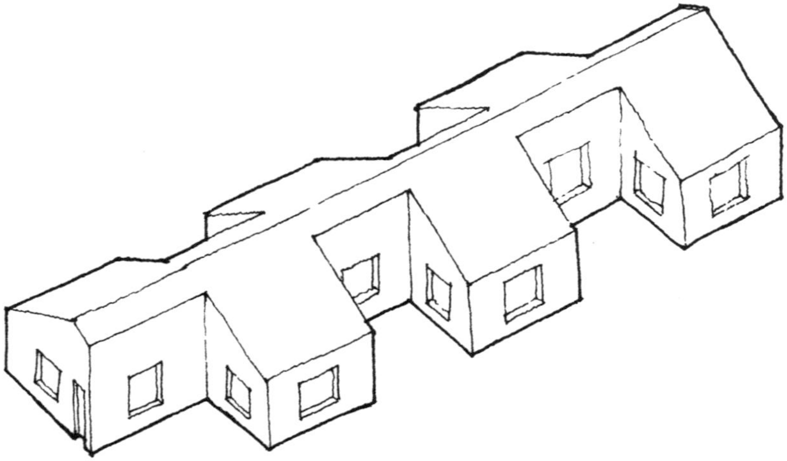

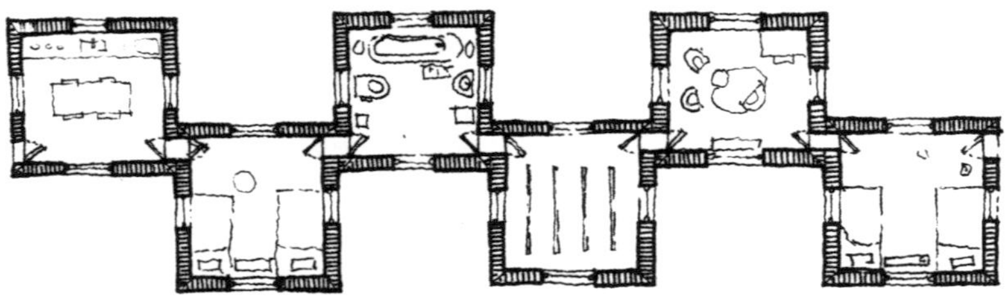

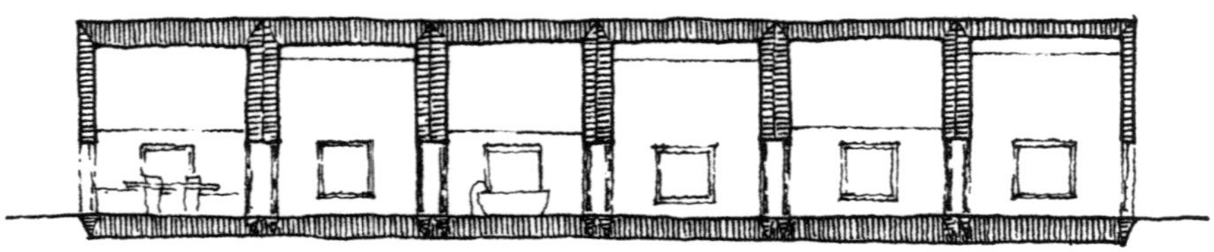

no.044

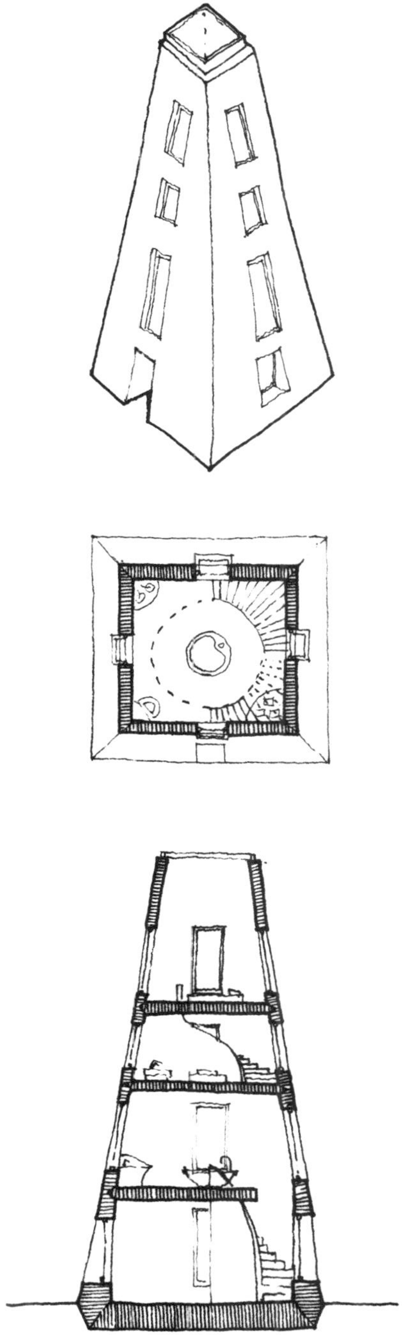

no.045

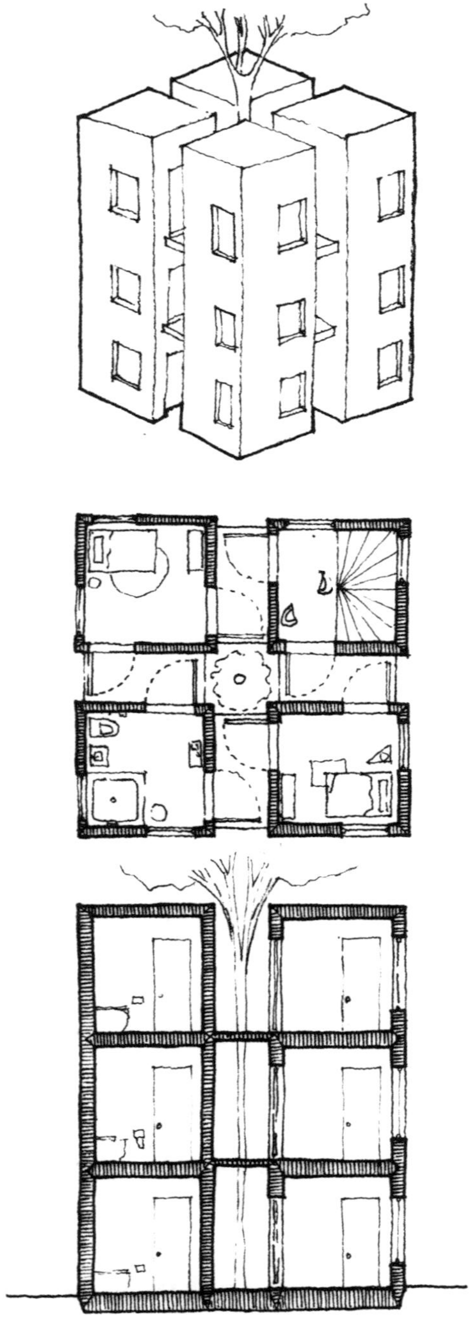

no.046

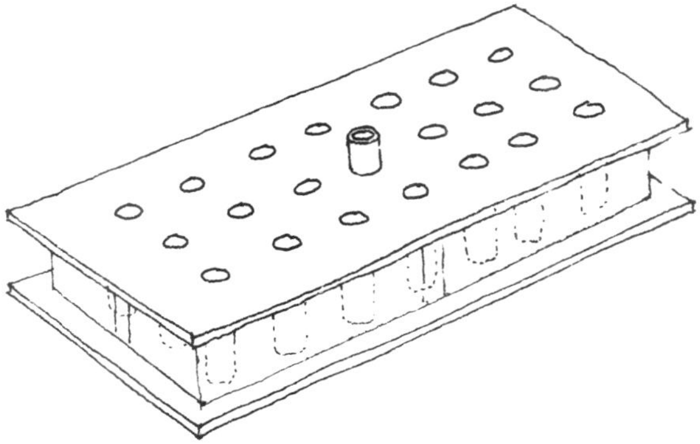

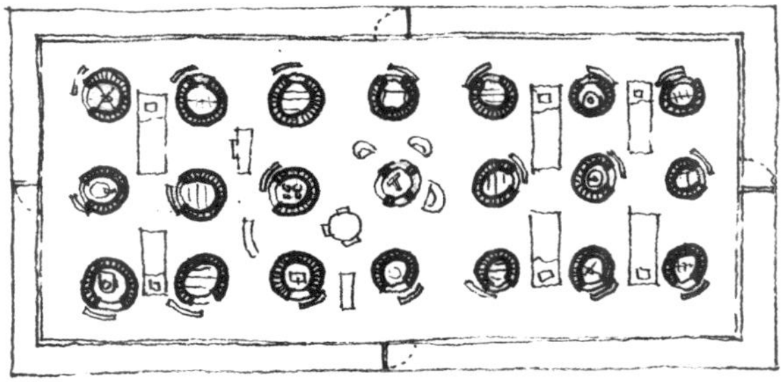

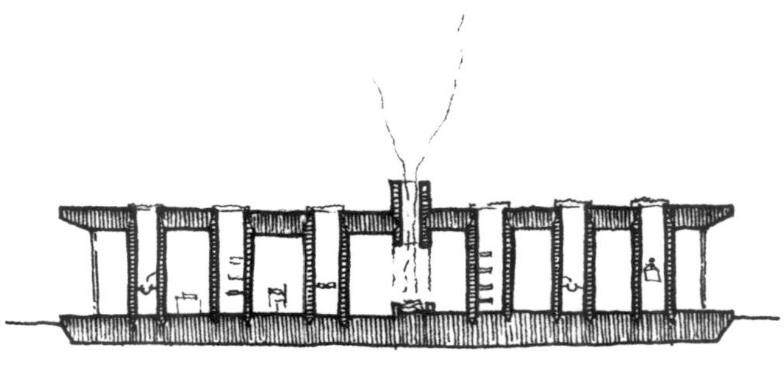

no.047

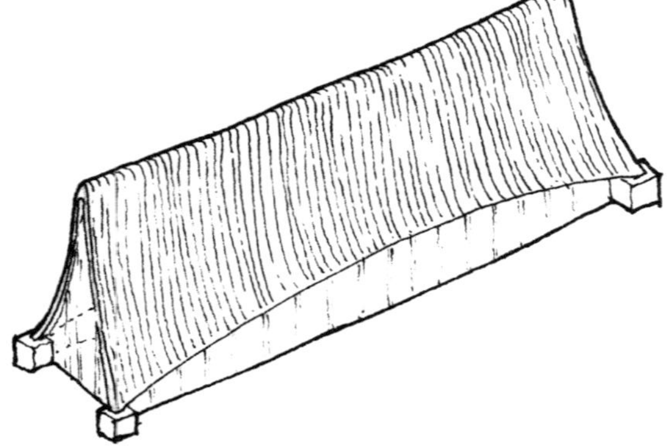

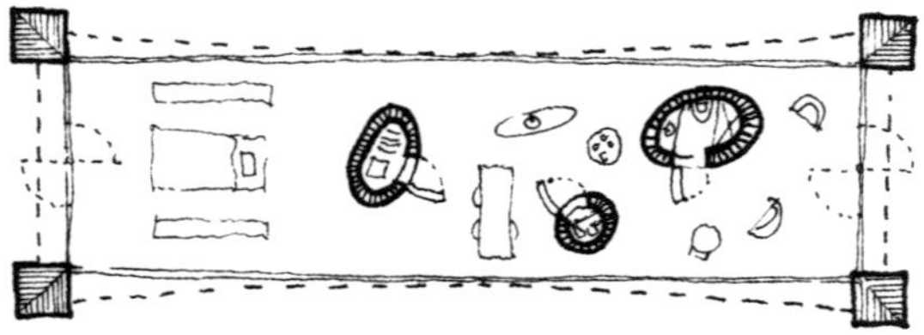

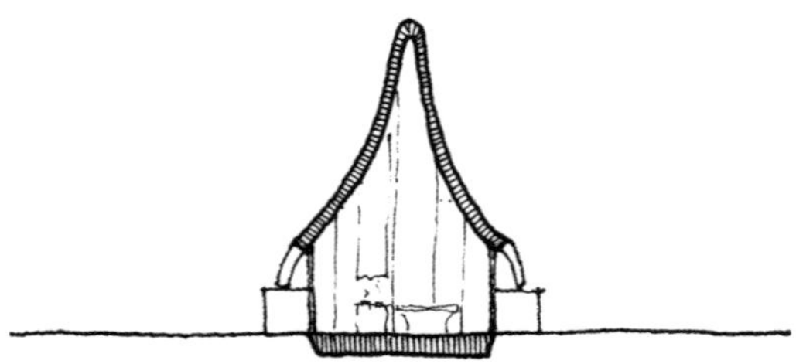

no.048

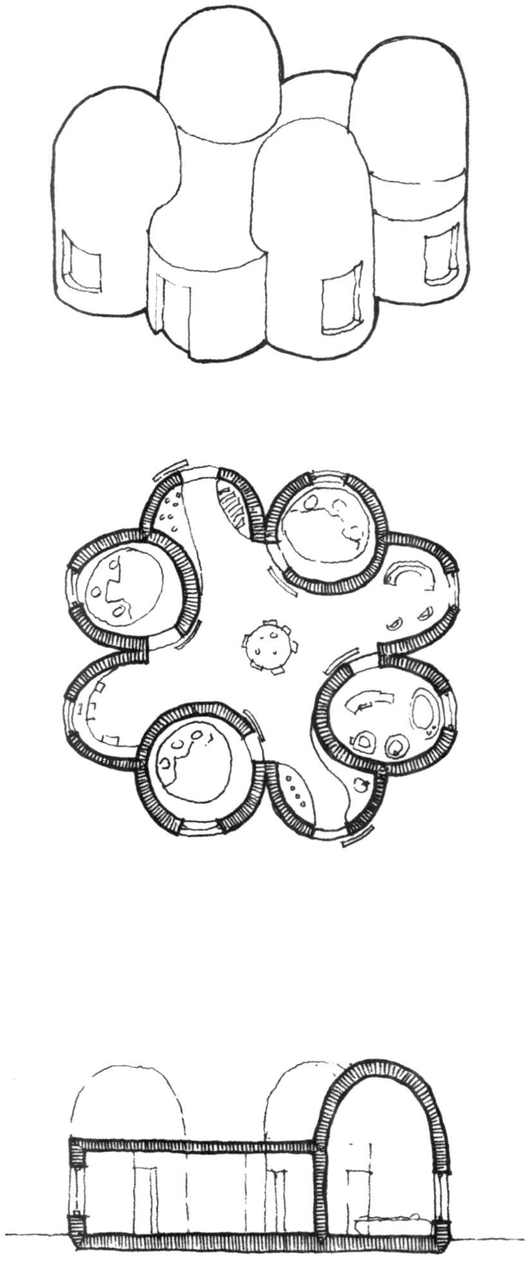

no.049

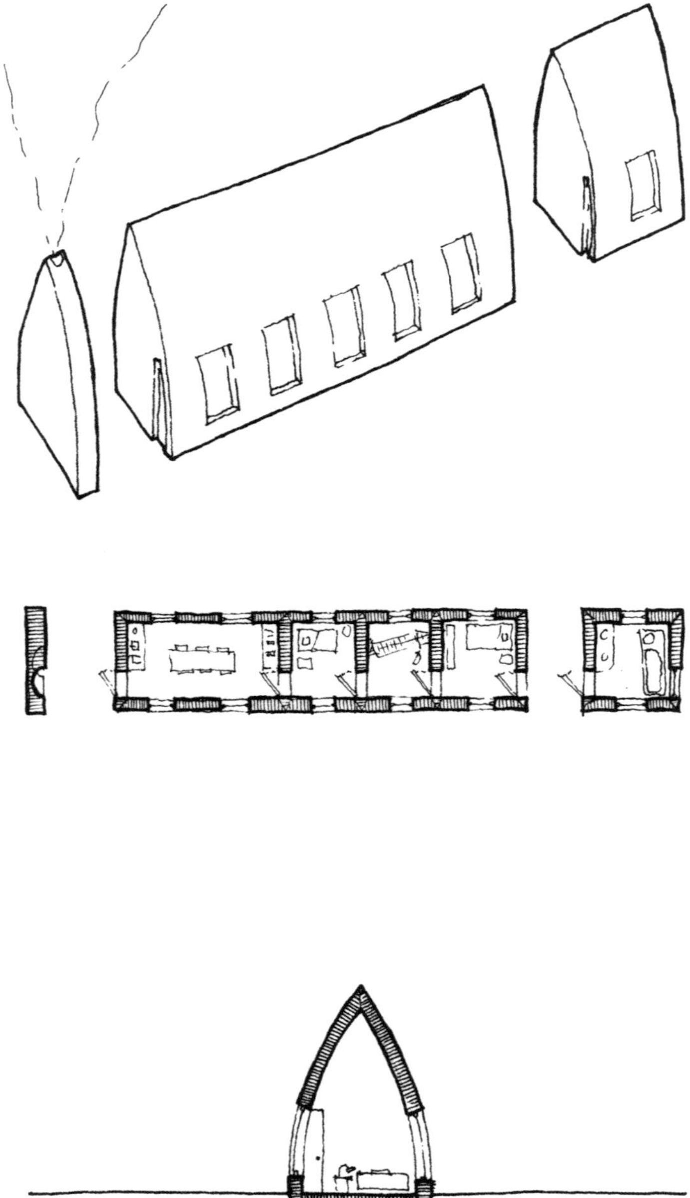

no.050

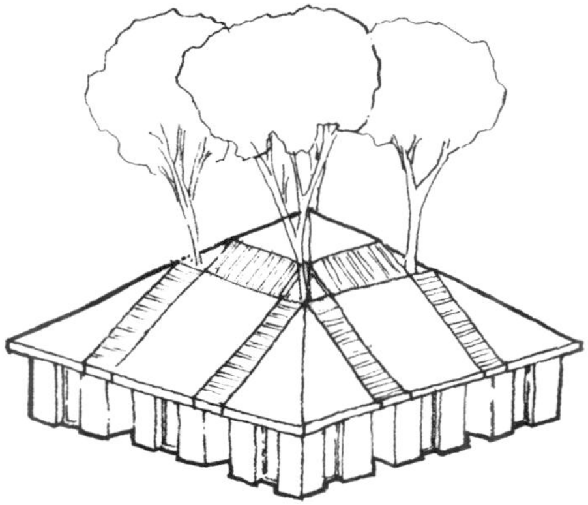

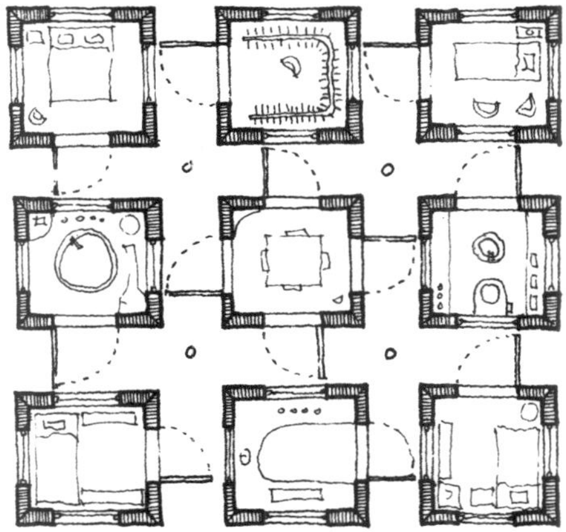

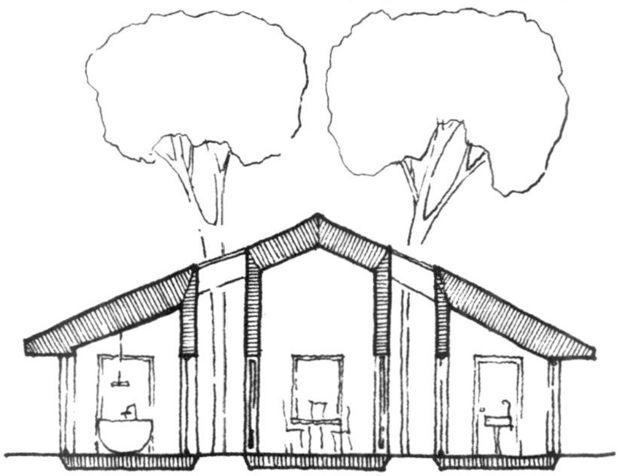

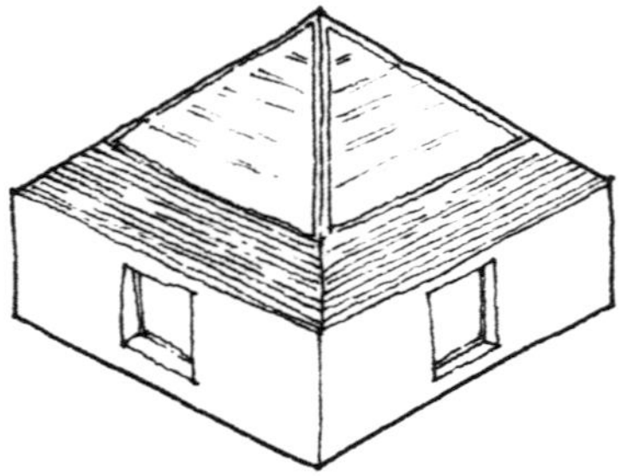

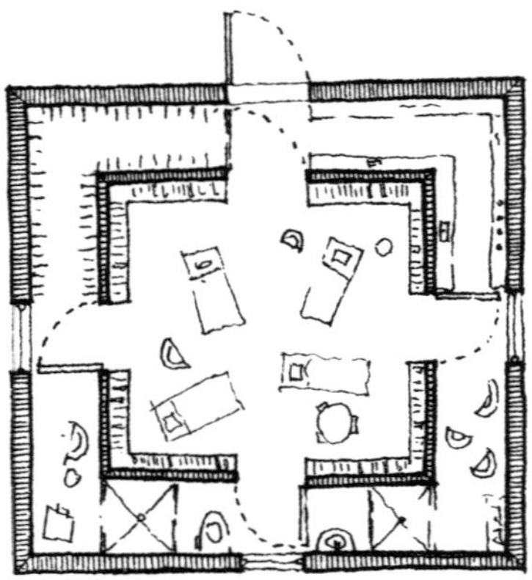

no.052

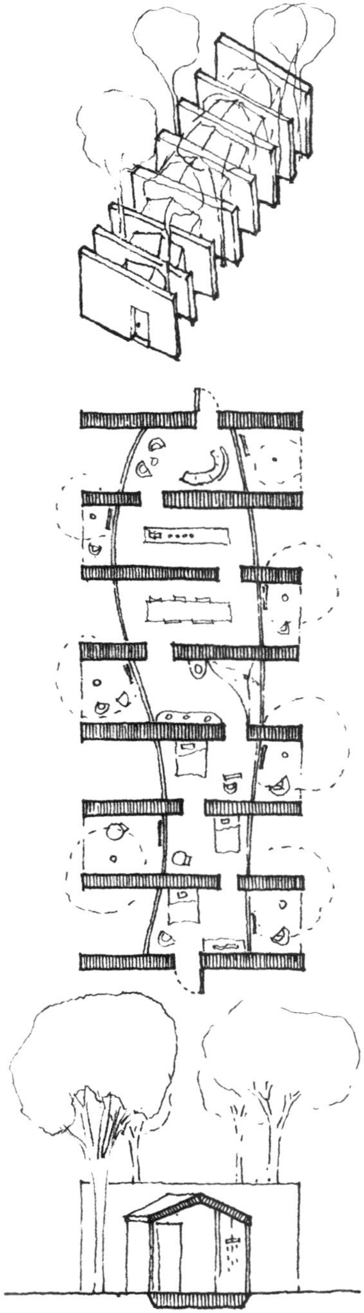

no.053

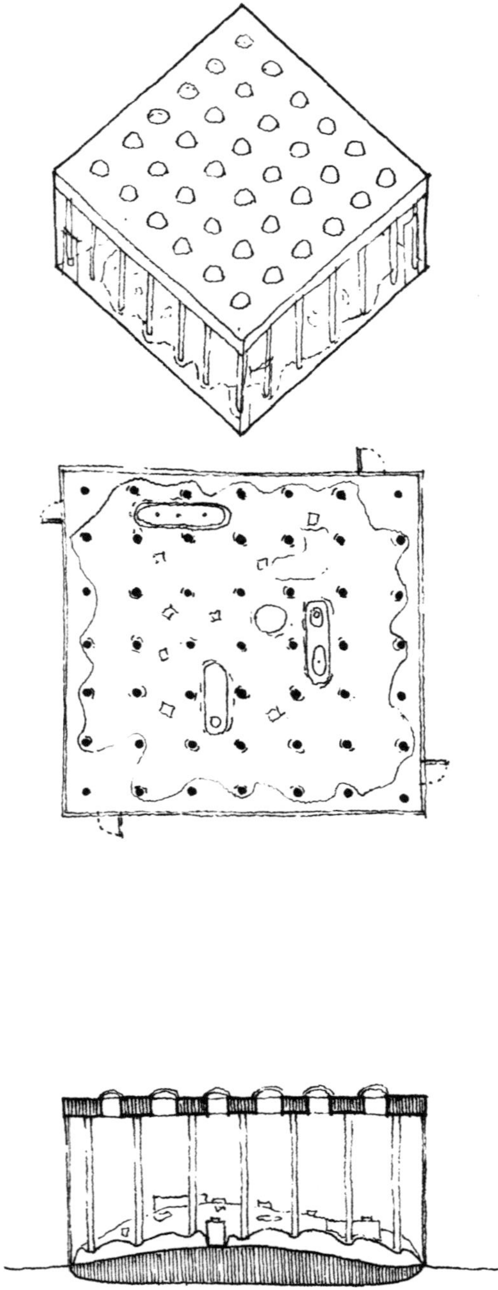

no.054

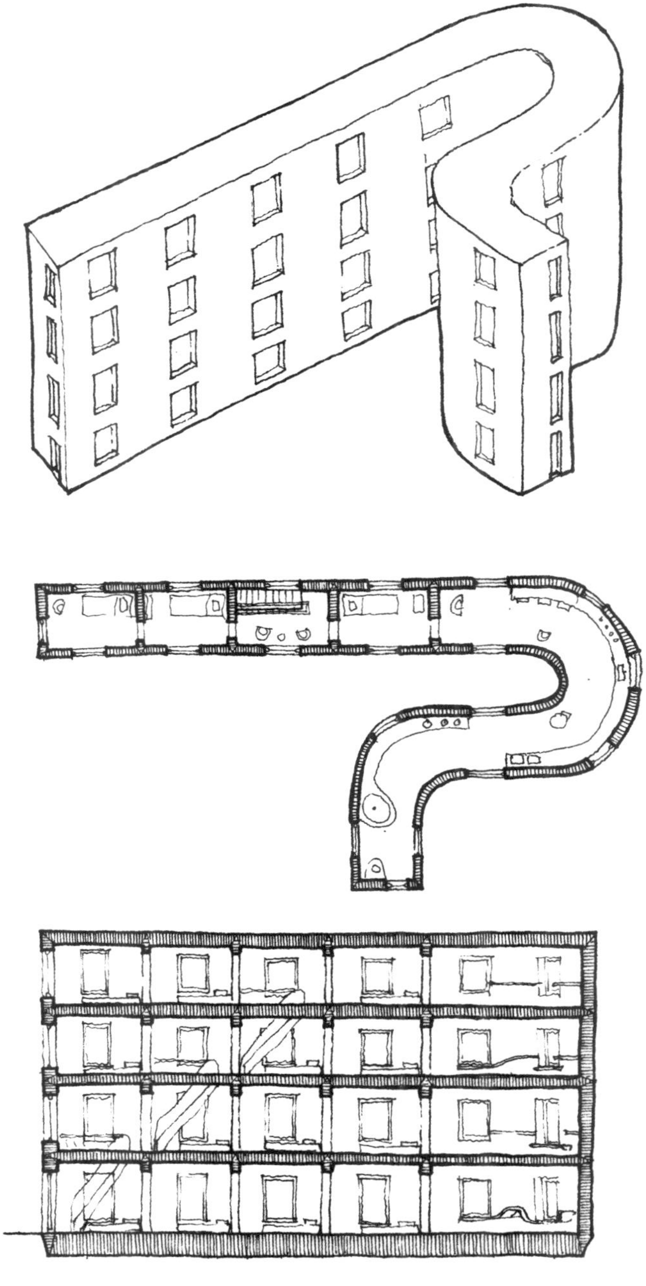

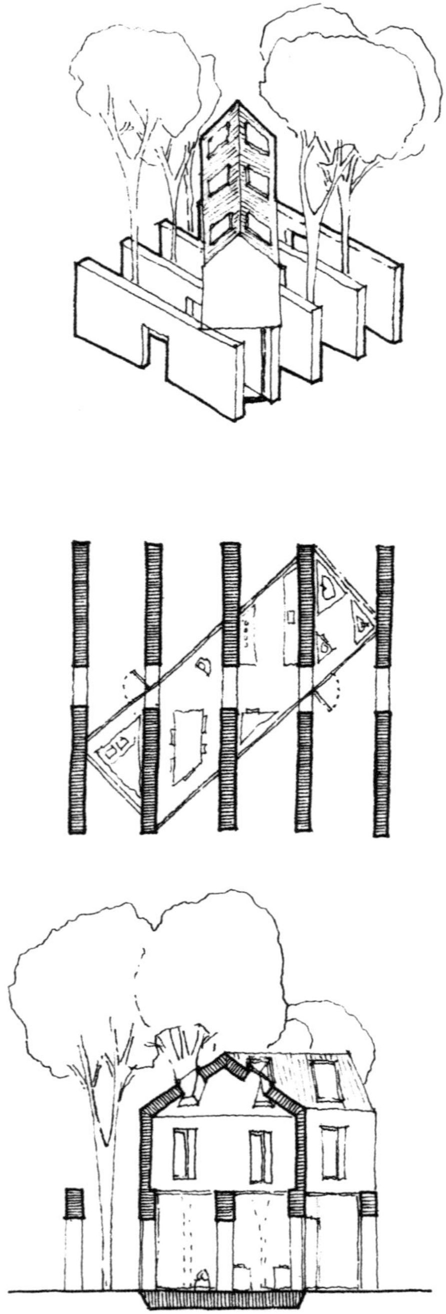

no.056

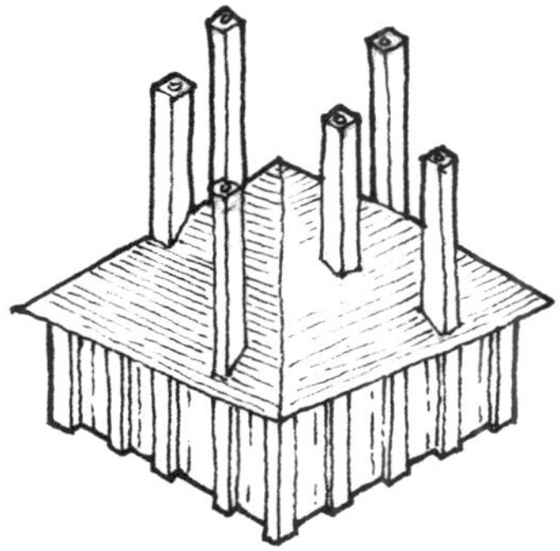

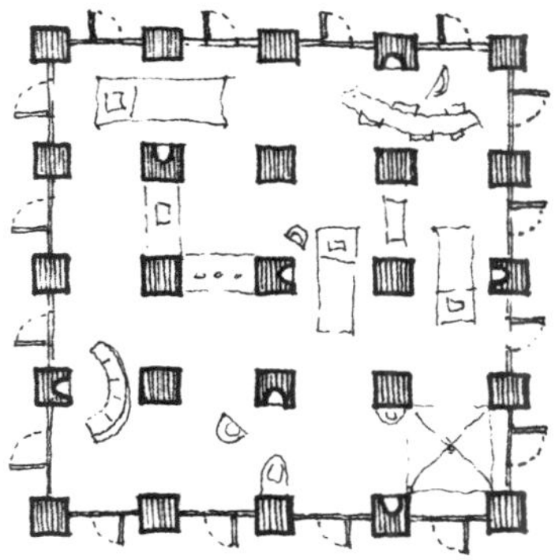

no.057

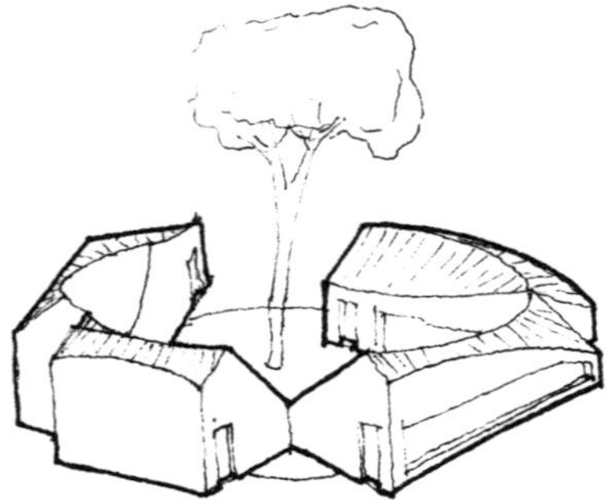

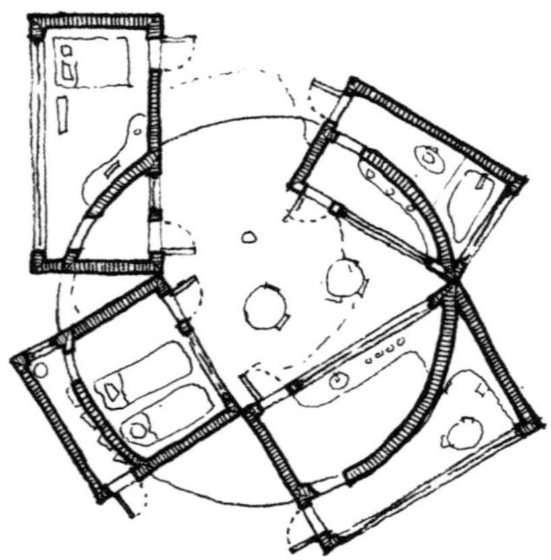

no.058

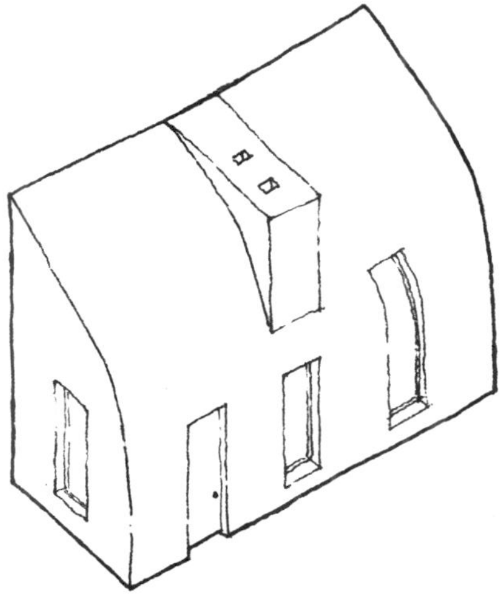

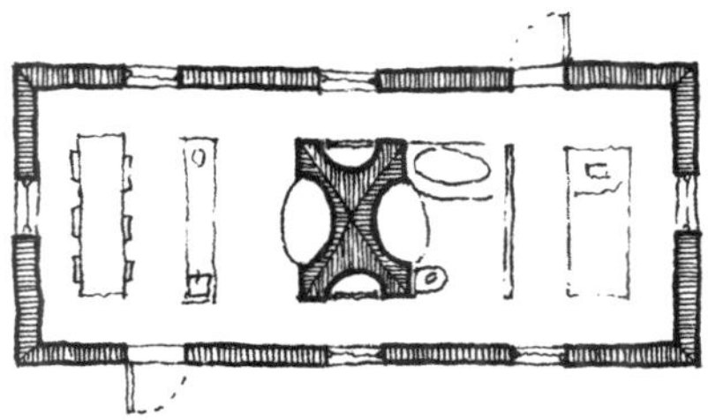

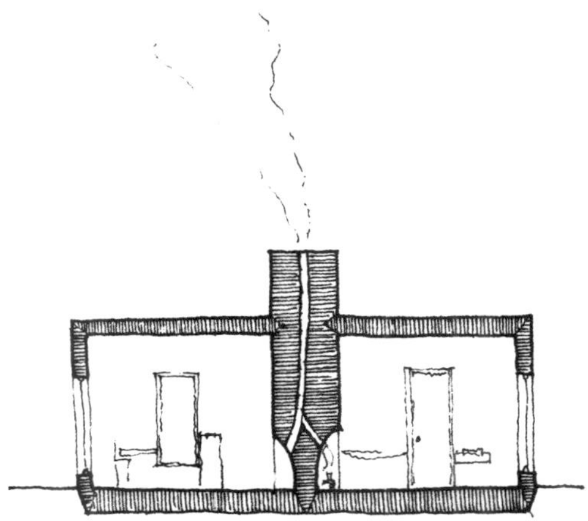

no.059

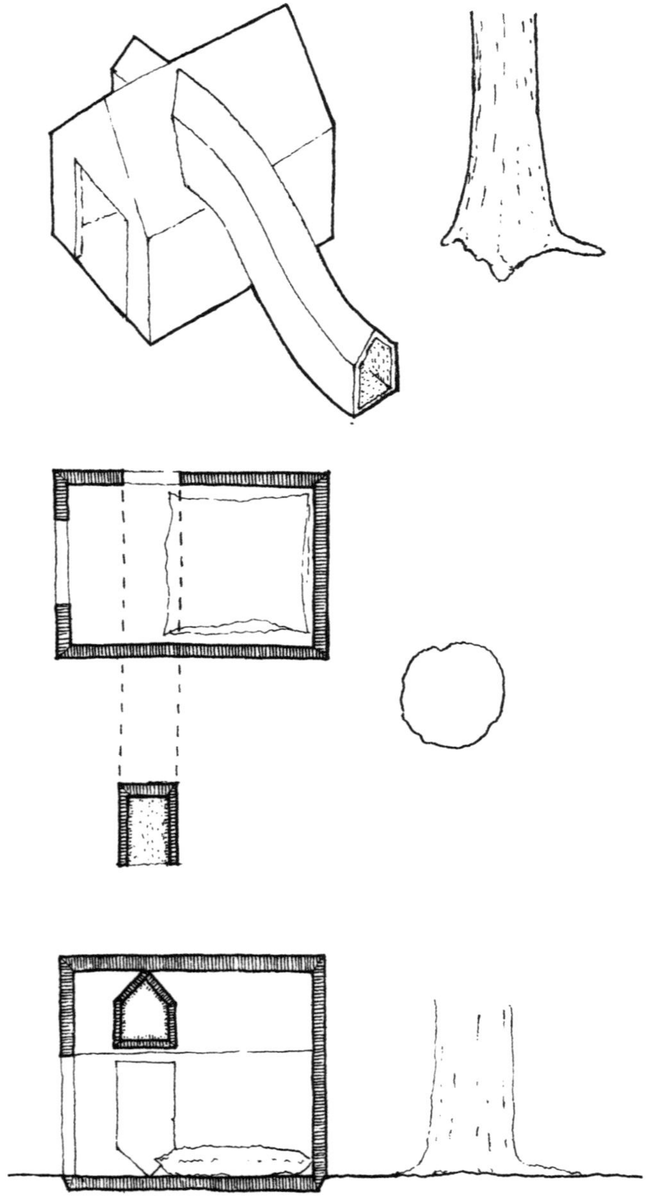

no.060

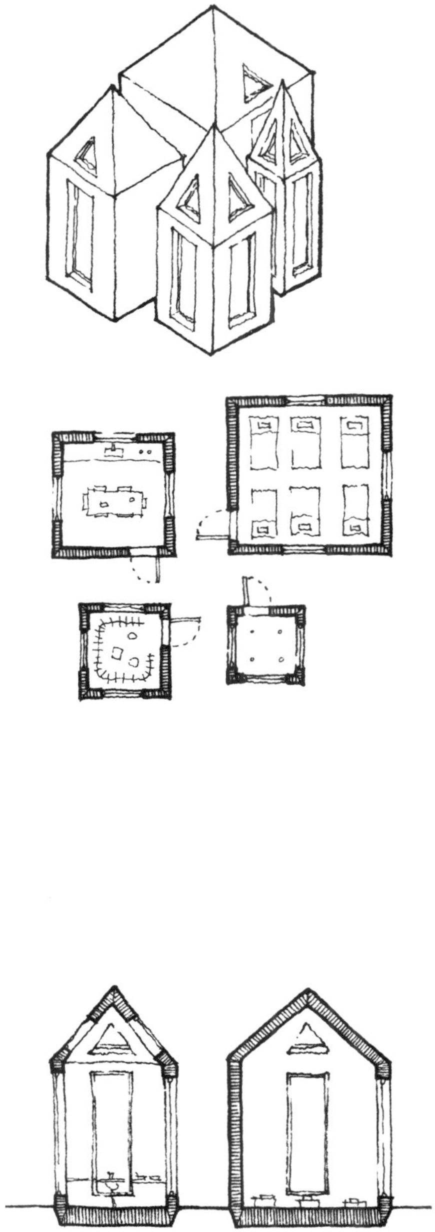

no.061

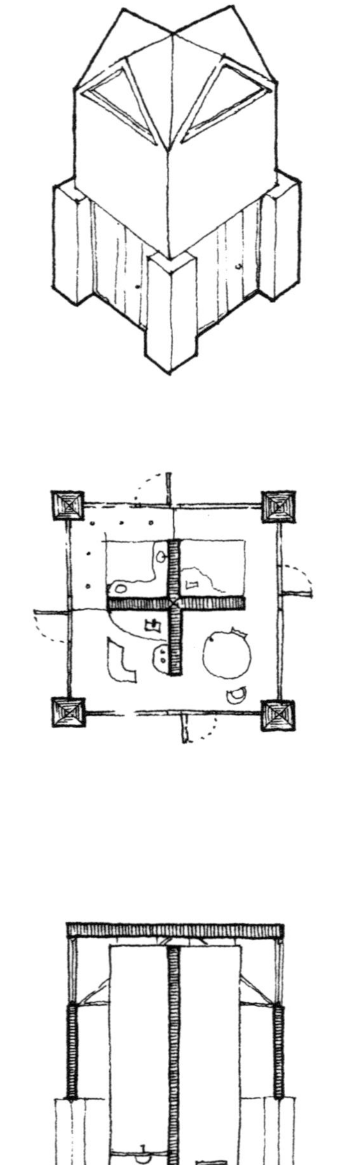

no.062

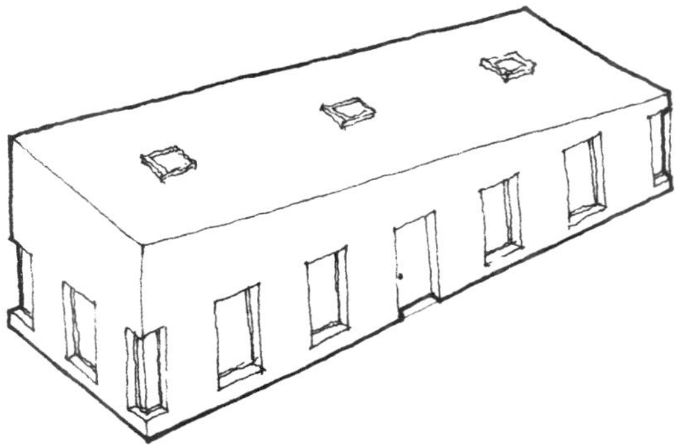

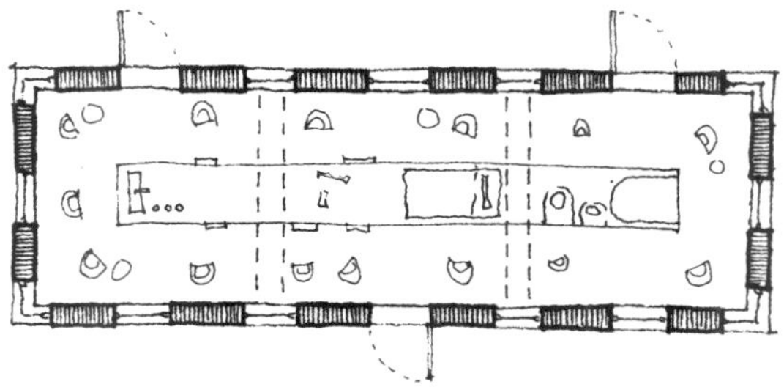

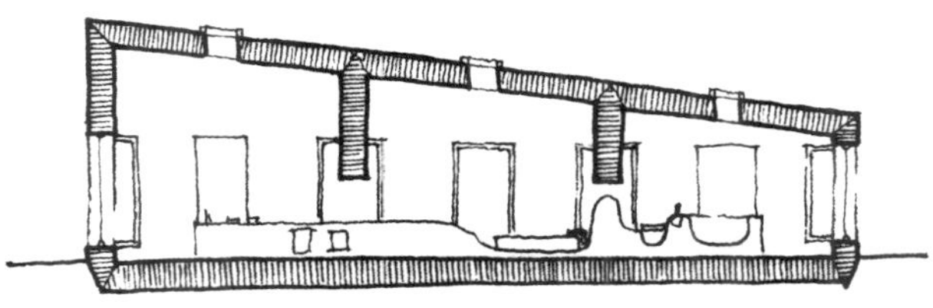

no.063

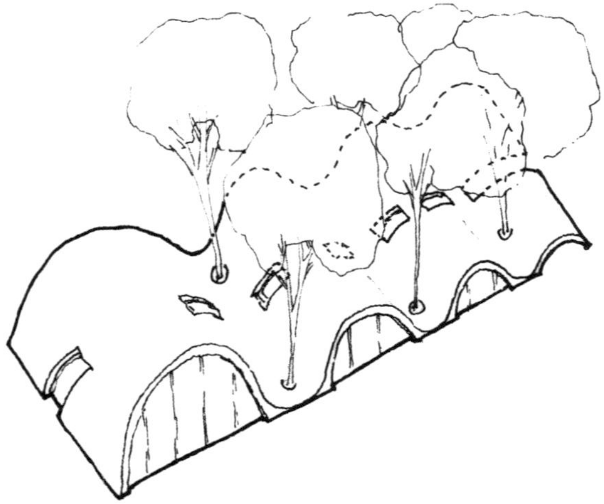

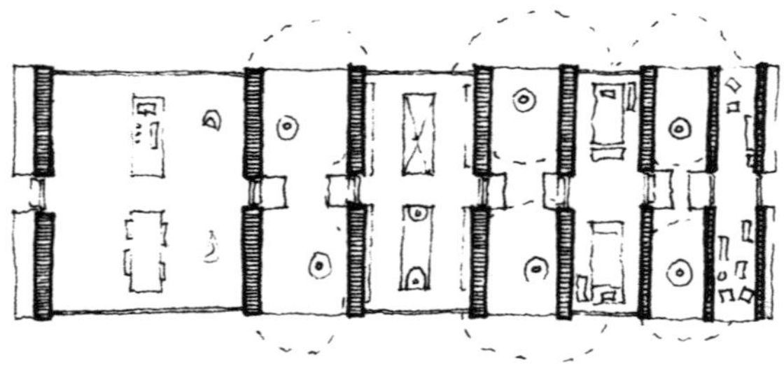

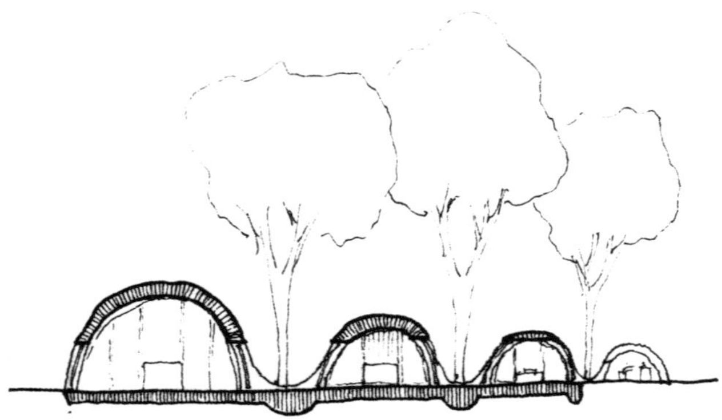

no.064

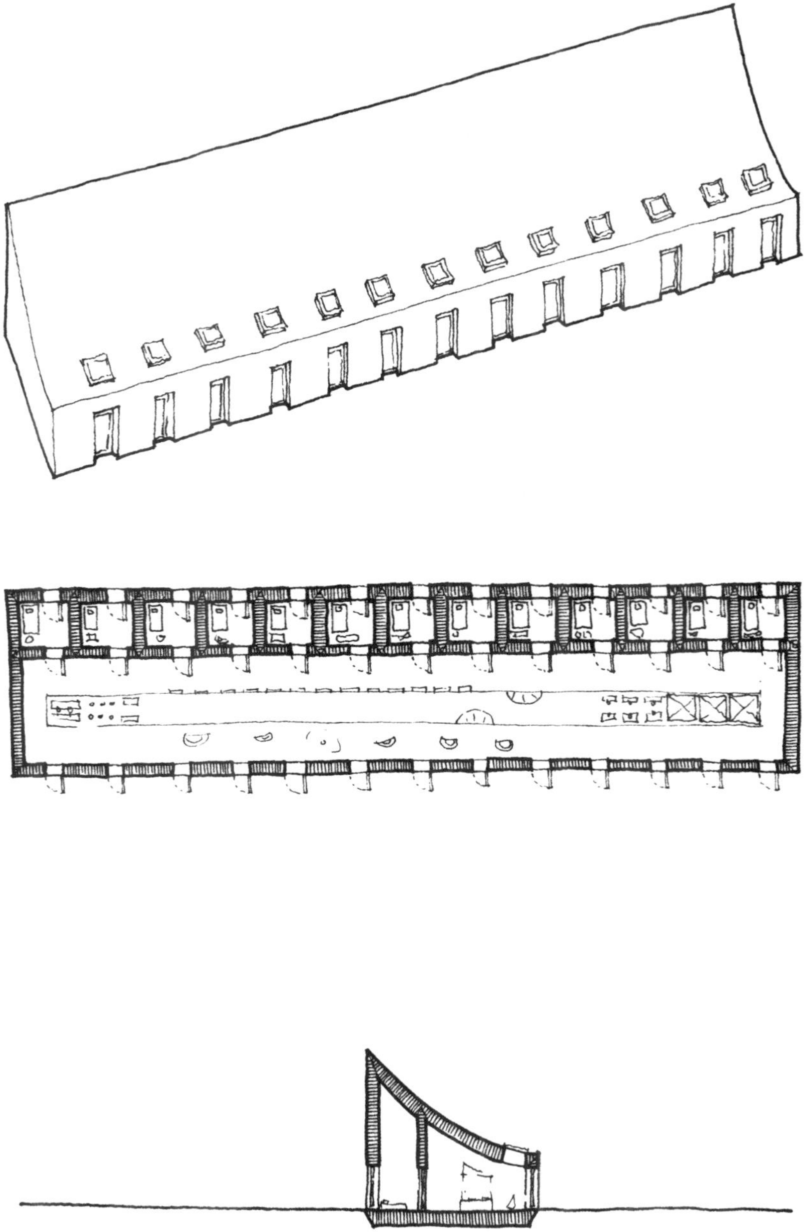

no.065

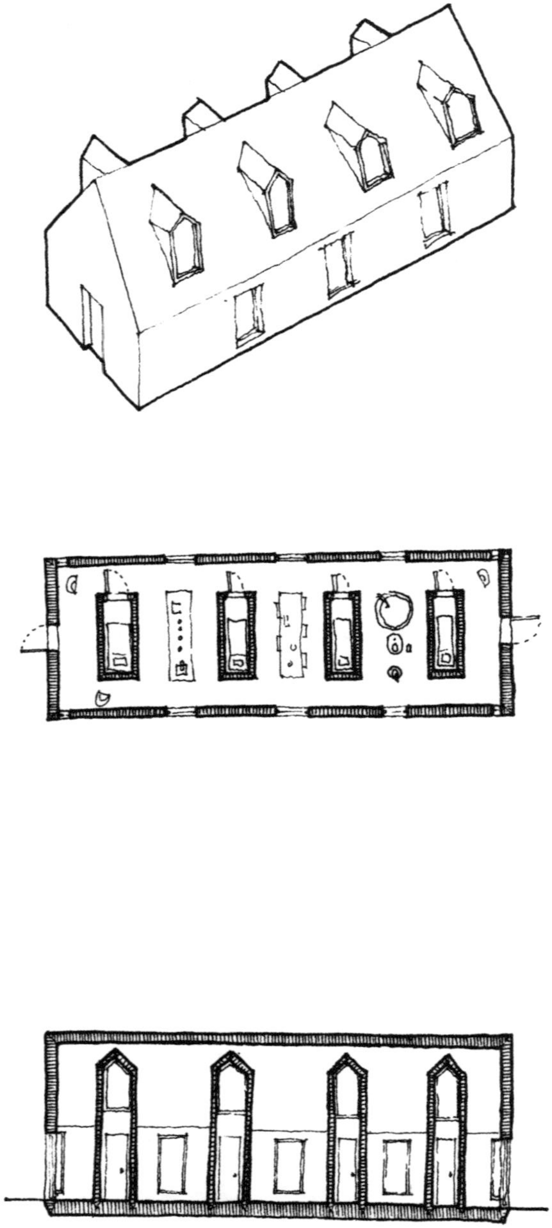

no.066

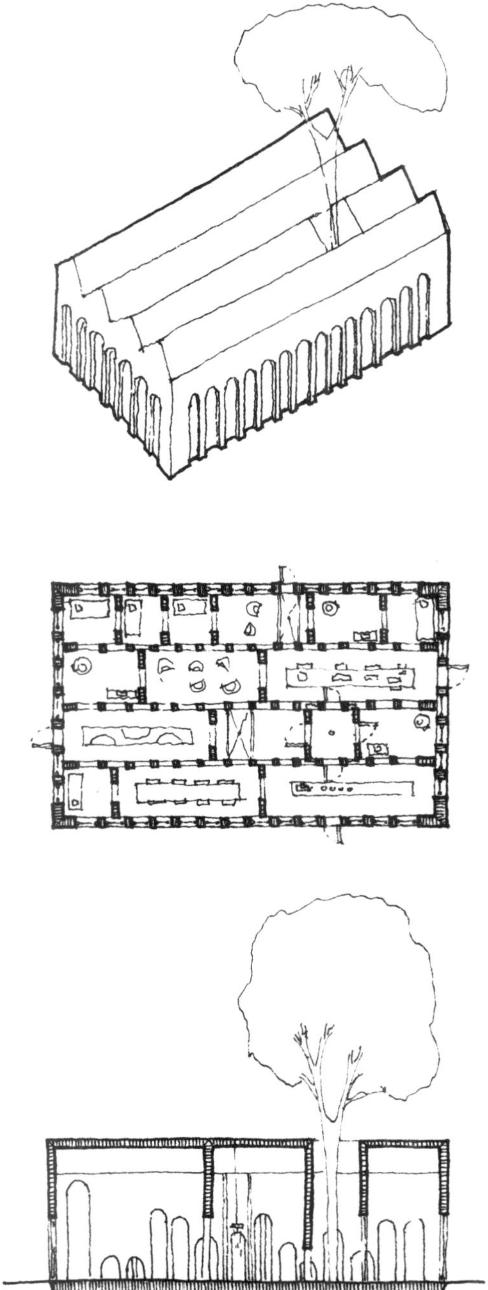

no.067

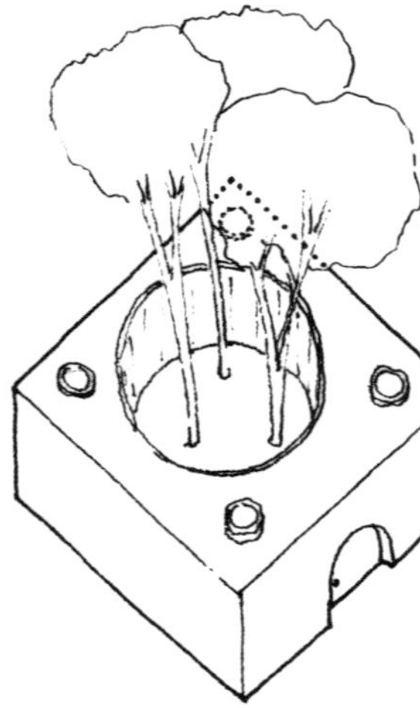

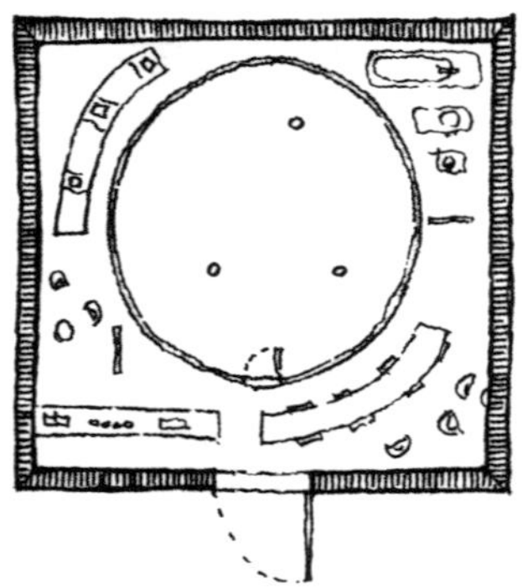

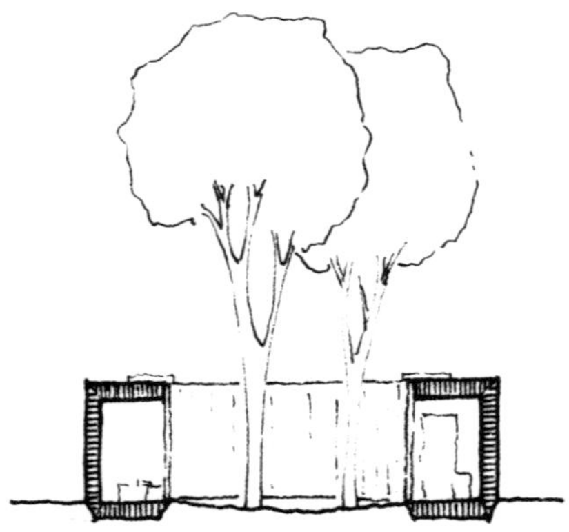

no.068

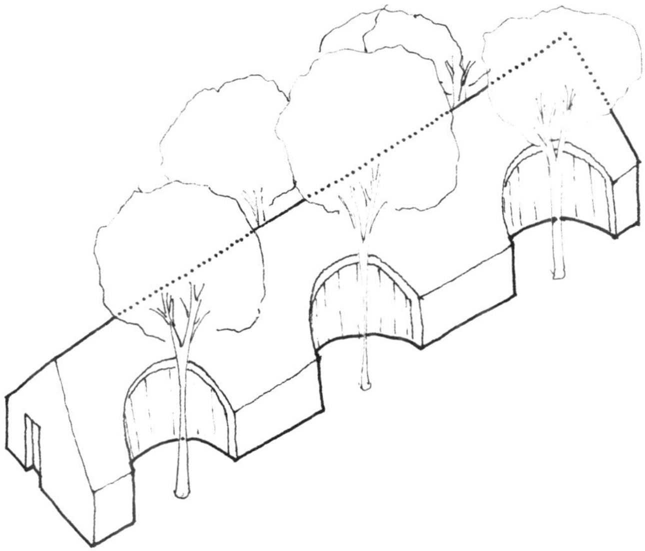

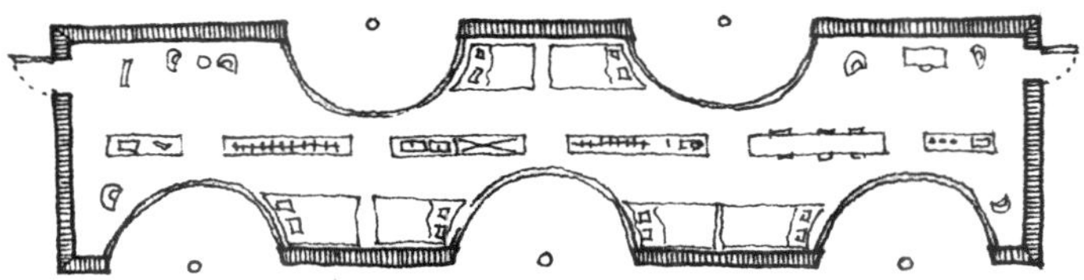

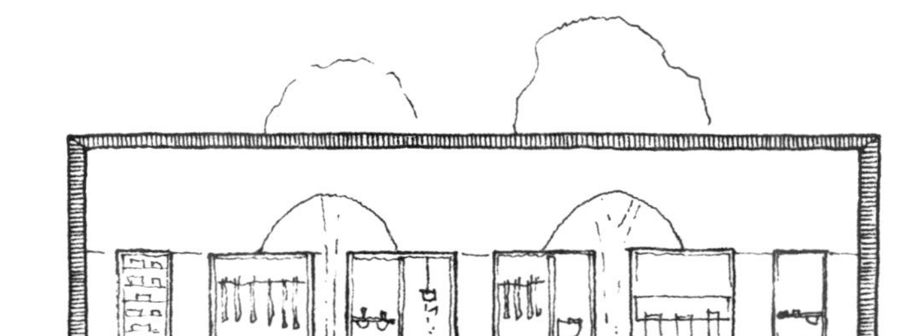

no.069

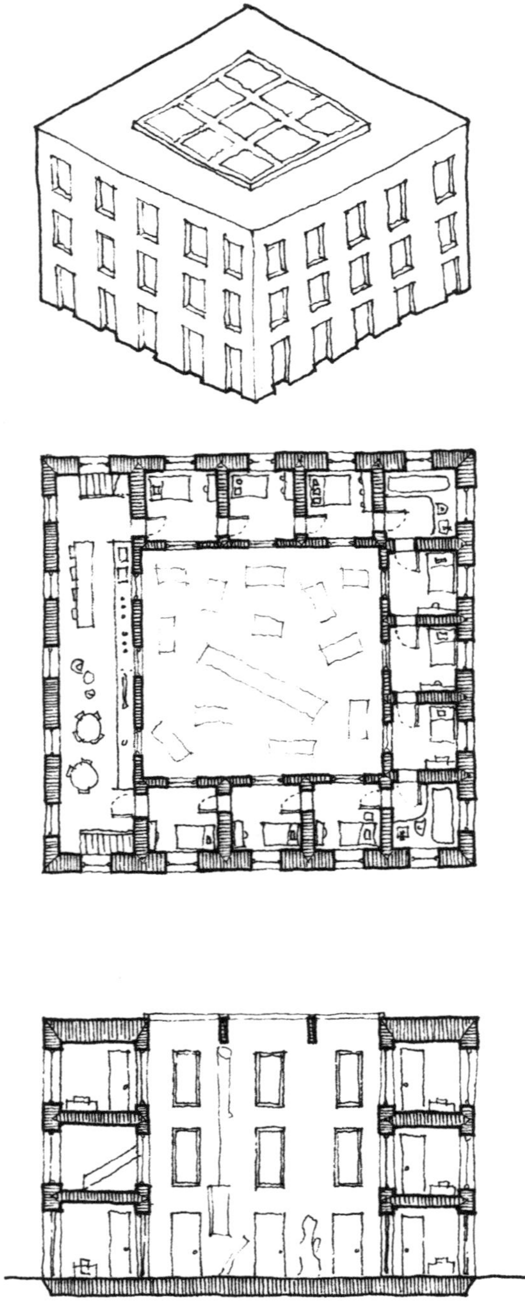

no.070

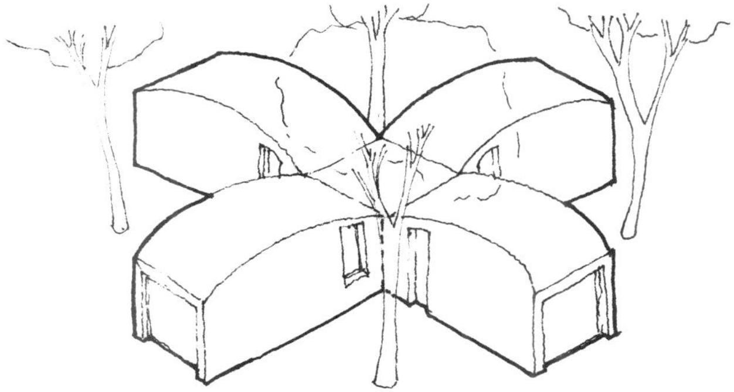

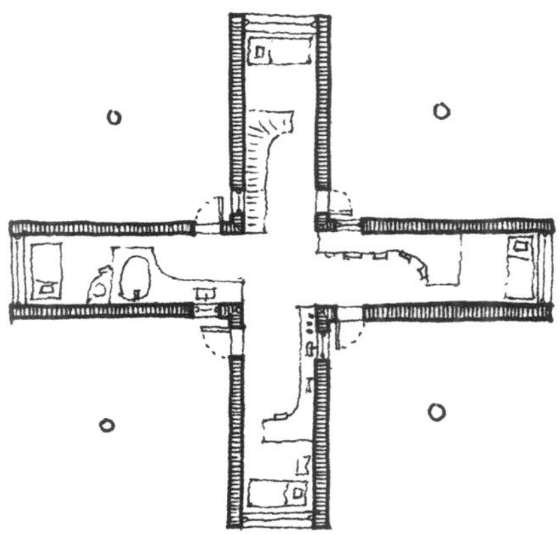

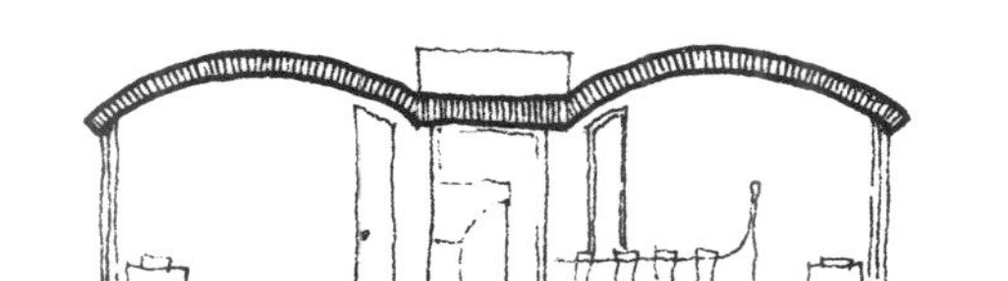

no.071

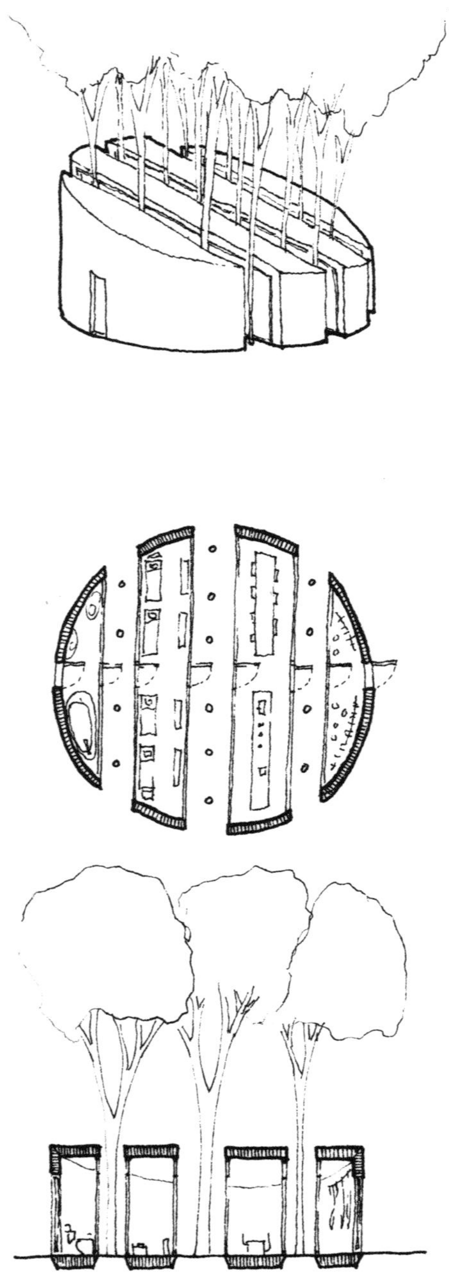

no.072

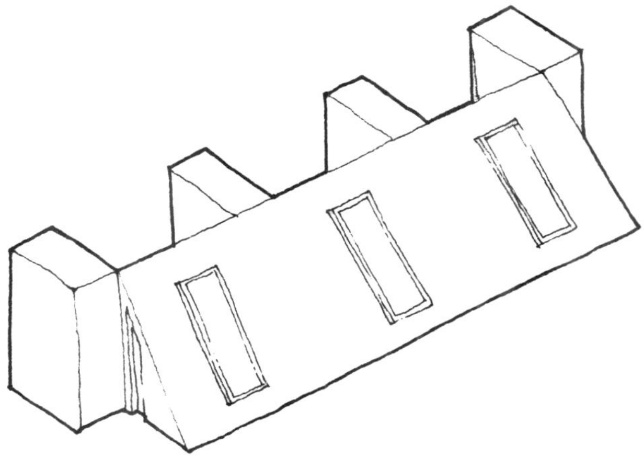

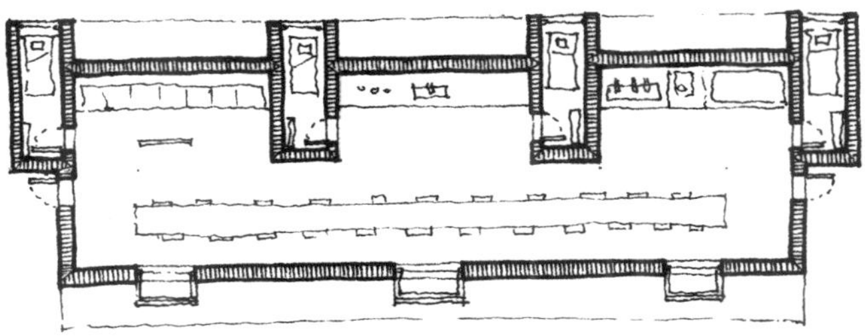

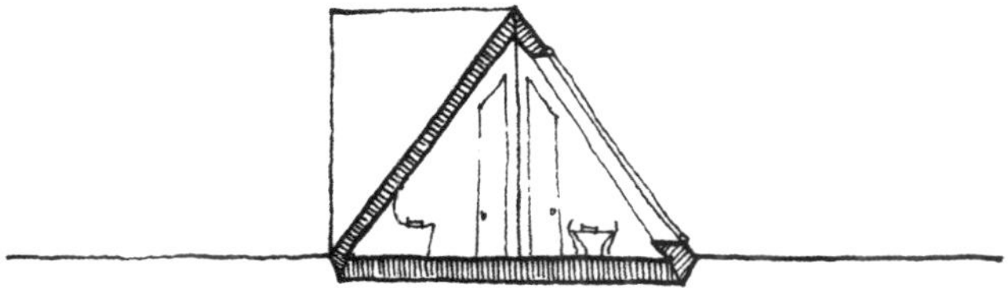

no.073

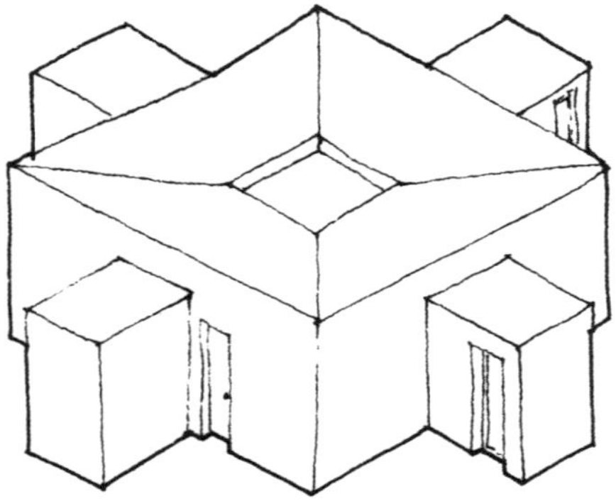

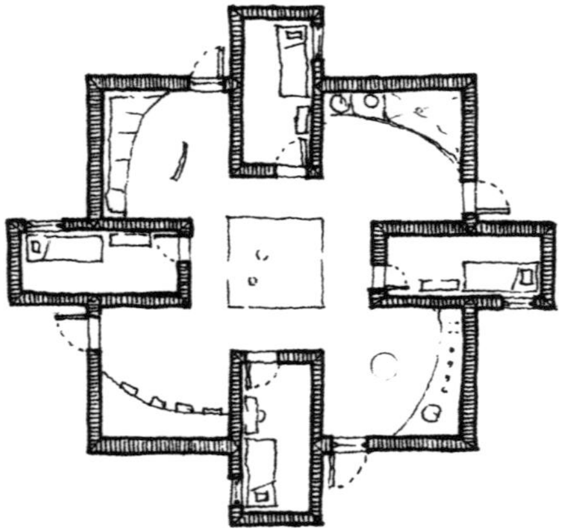

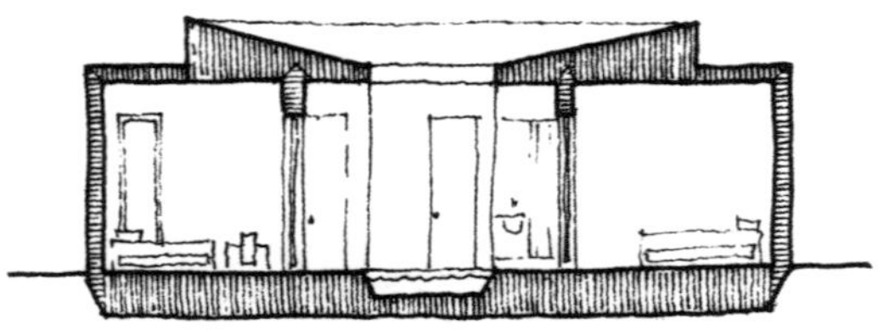

no.074

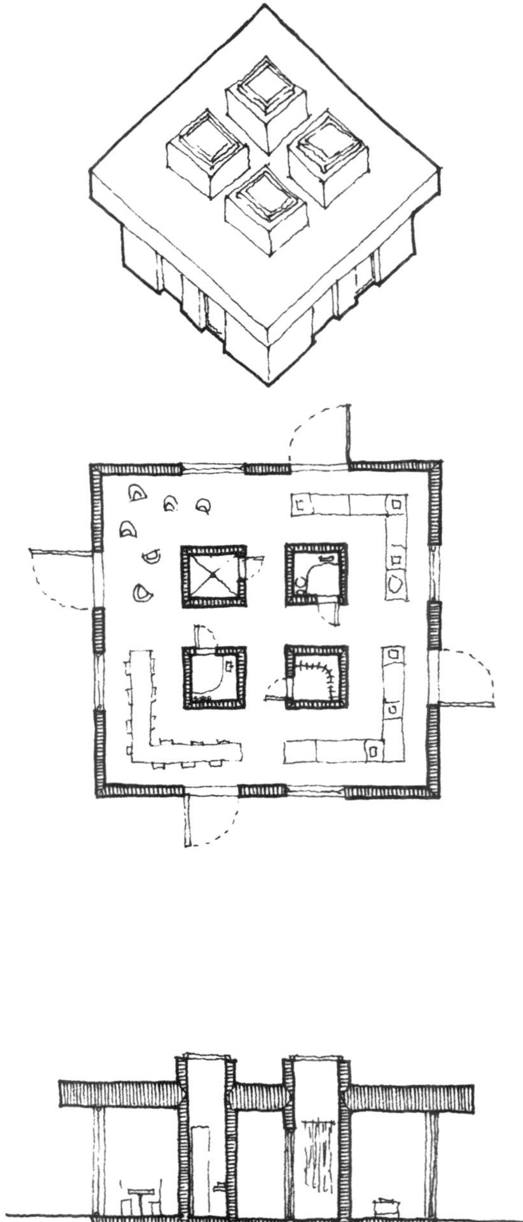

no.075

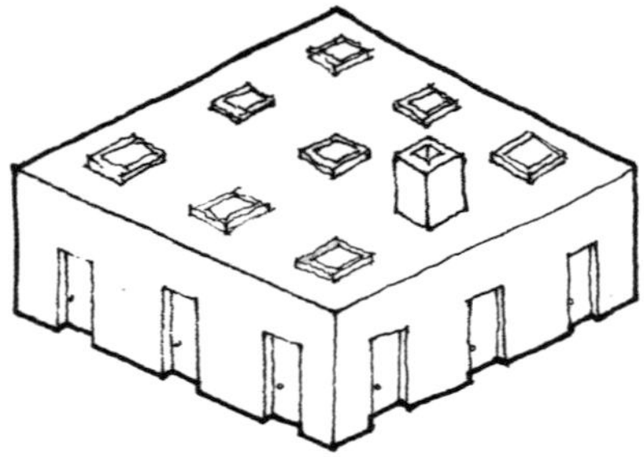

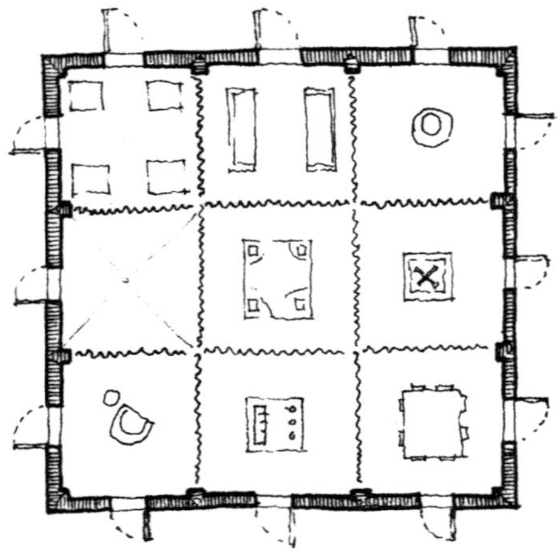

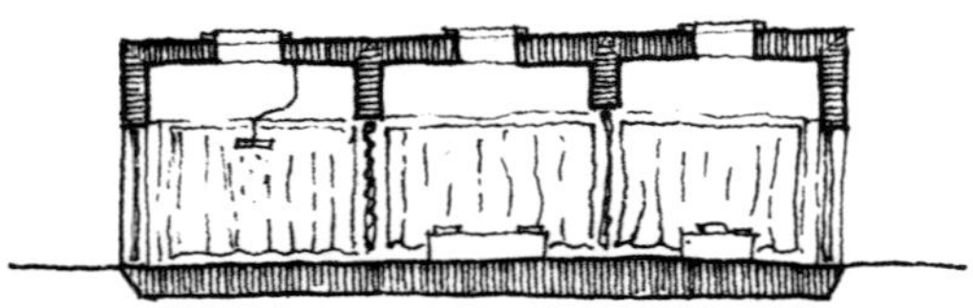

no.076

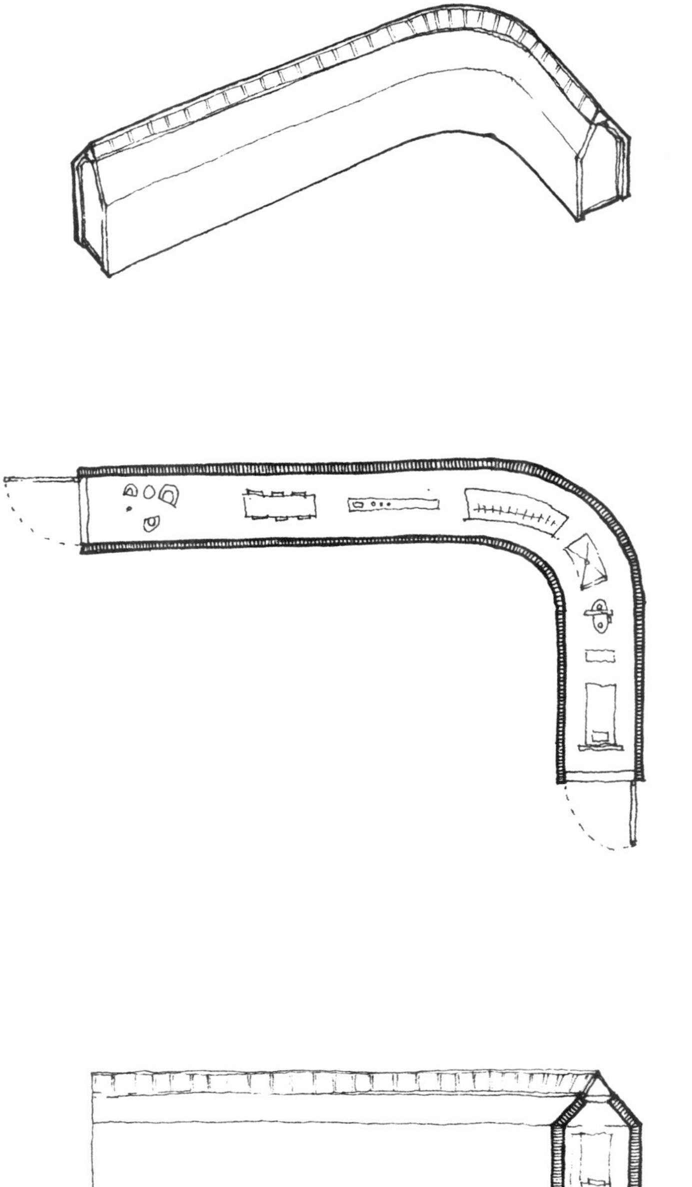

no.077

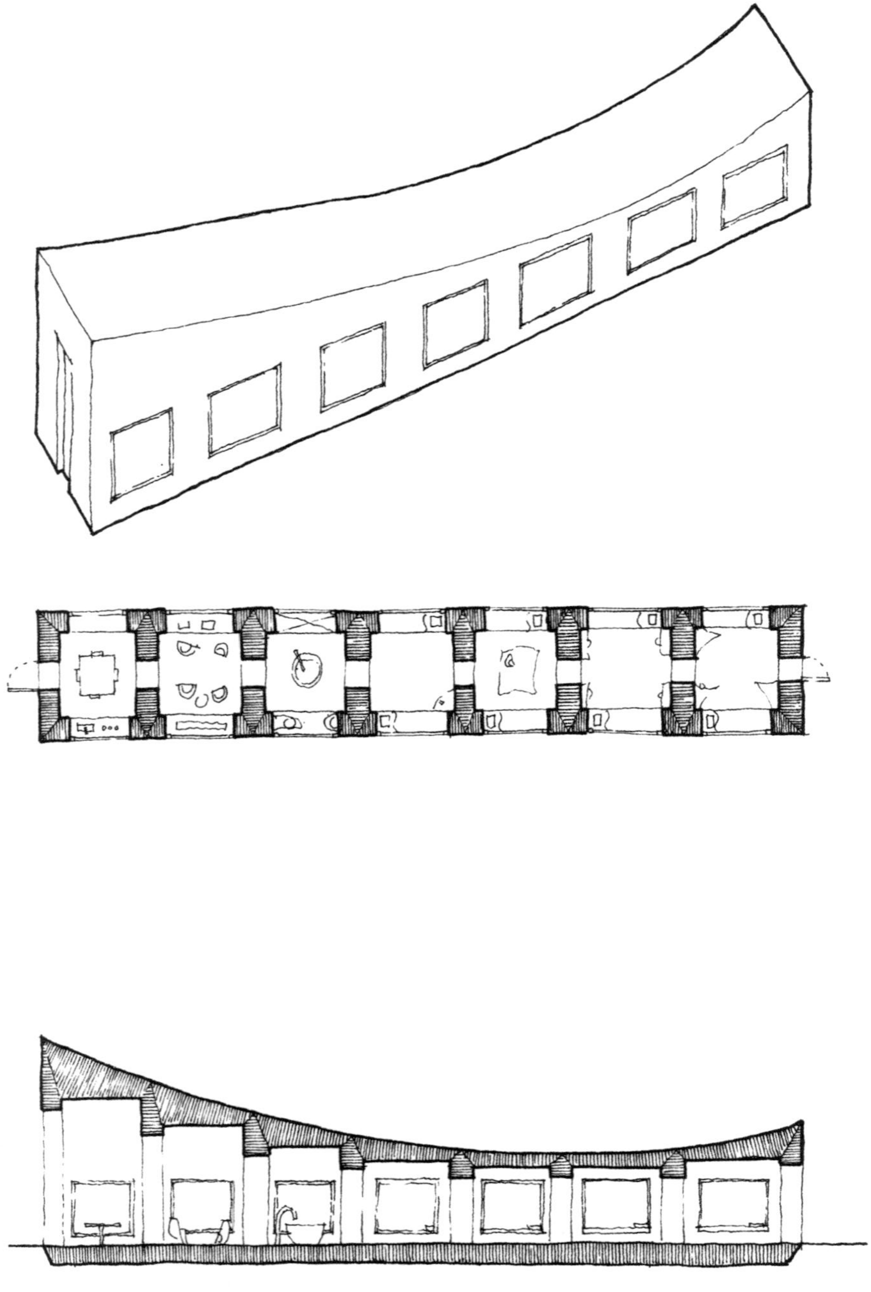

no.078

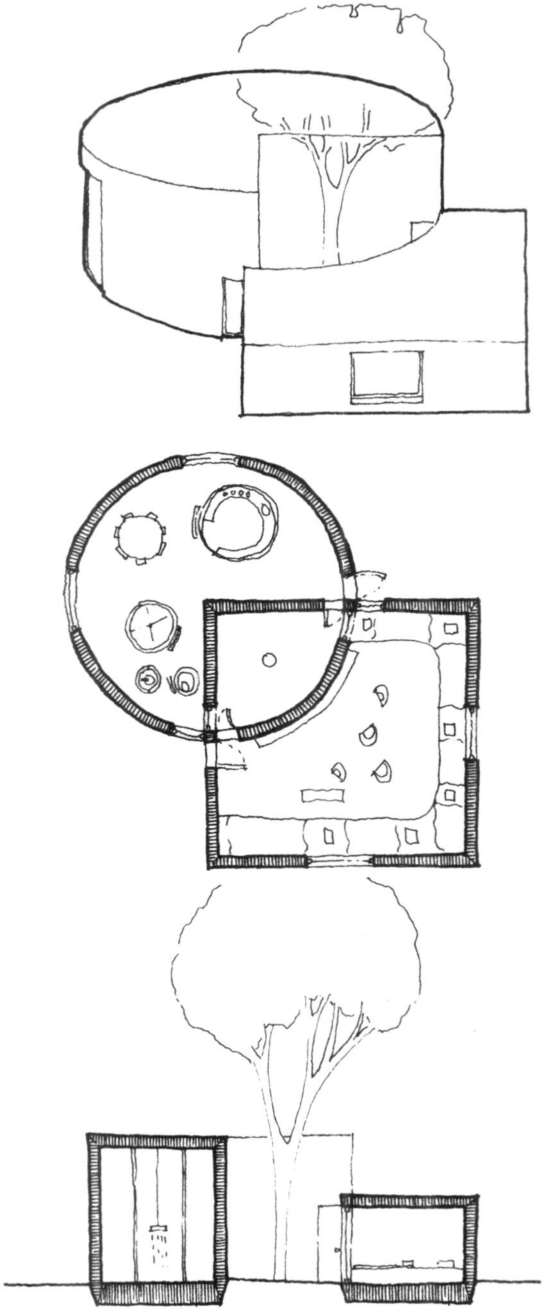

no.079

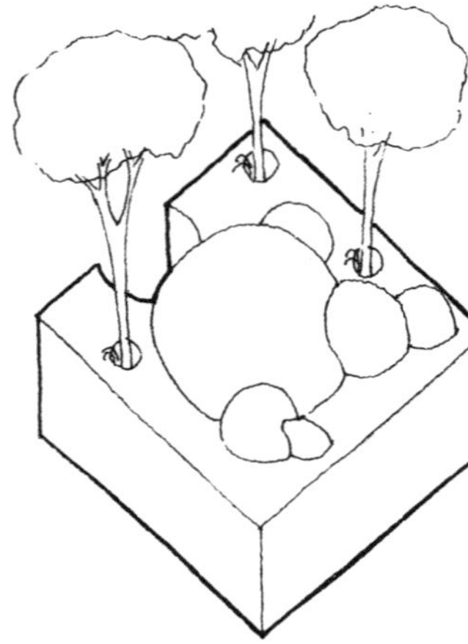

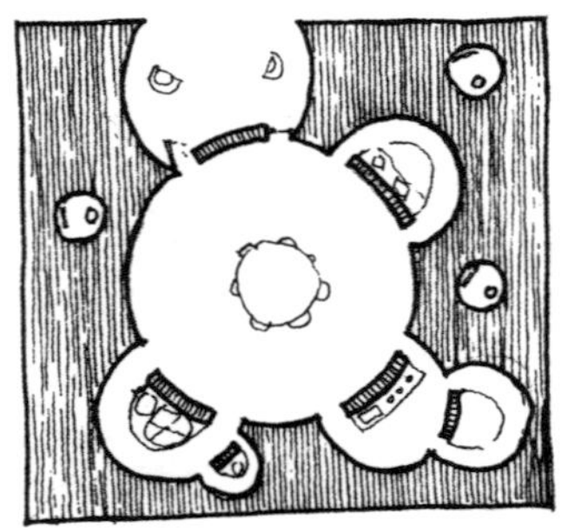

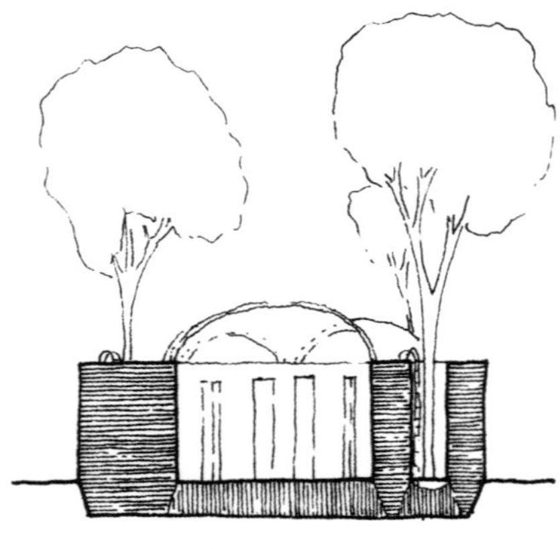

no.080

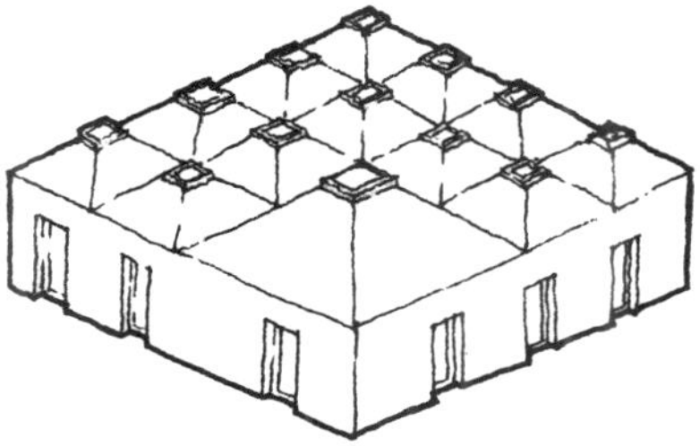

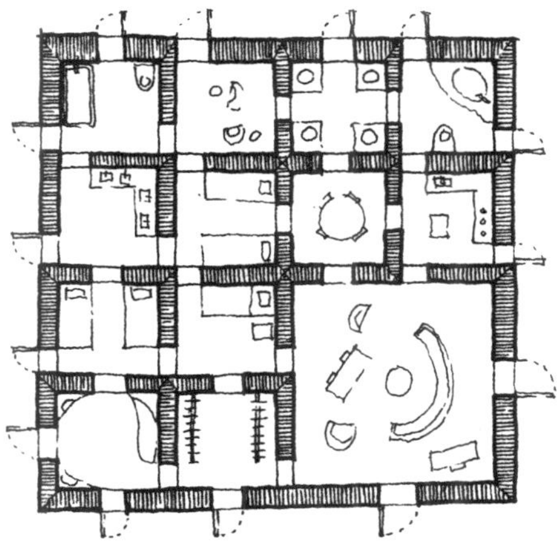

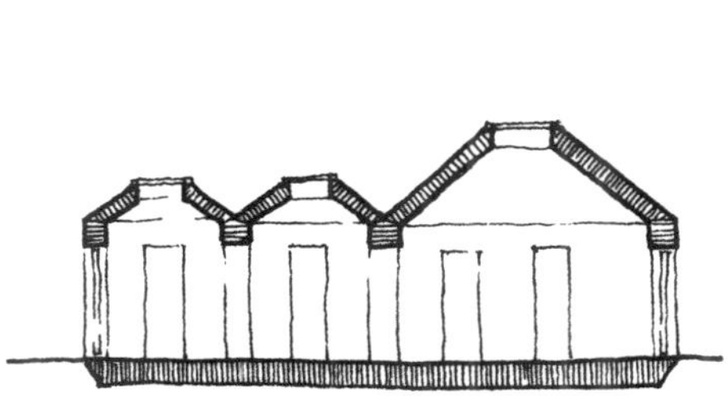

no.081

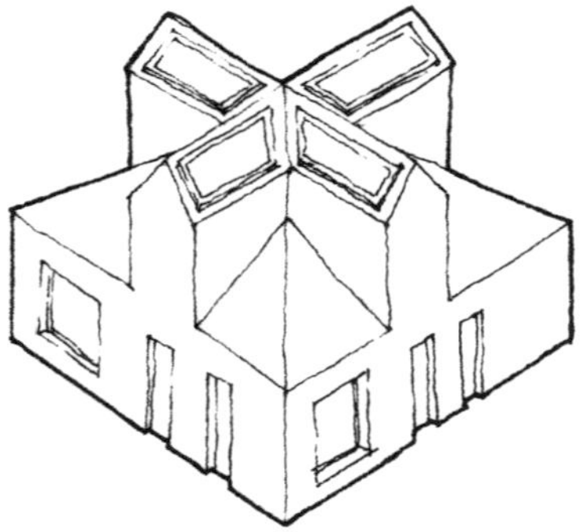

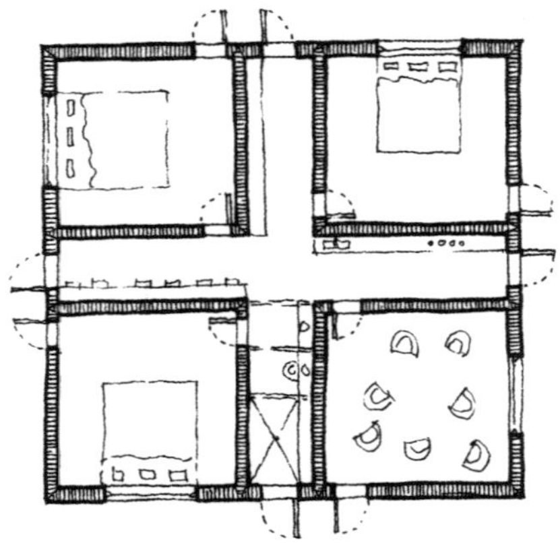

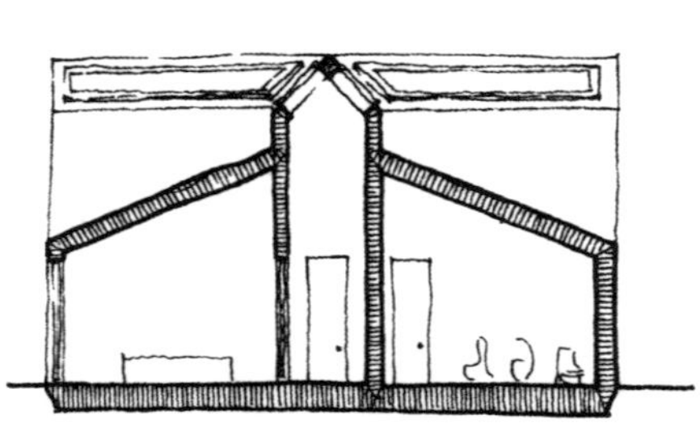

no.082

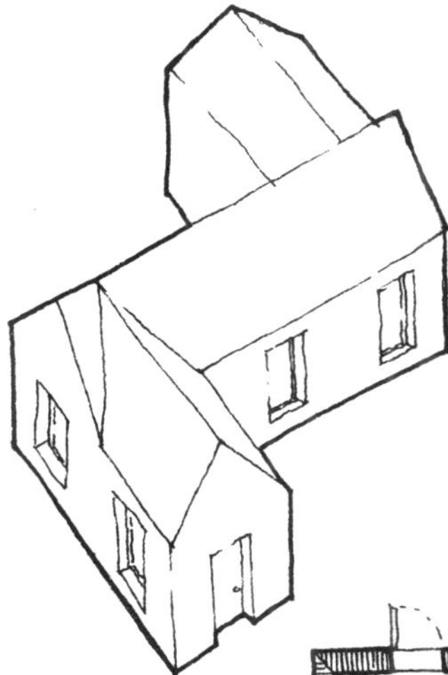
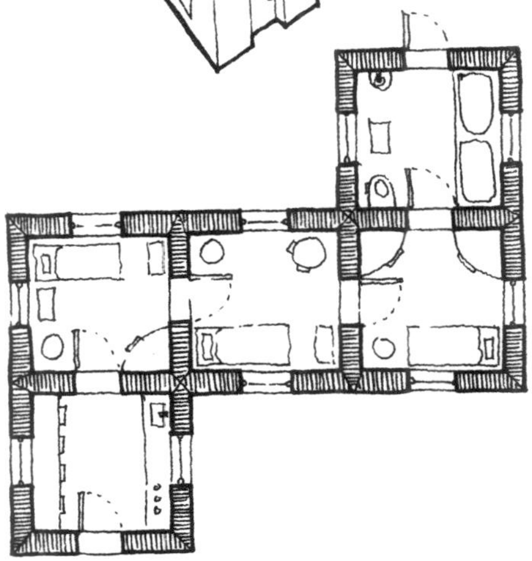

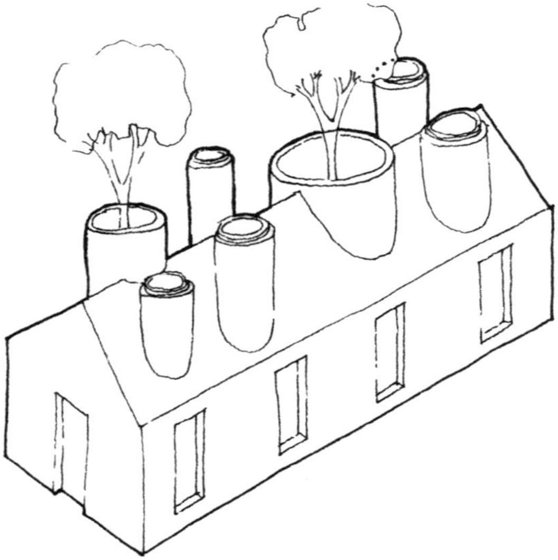

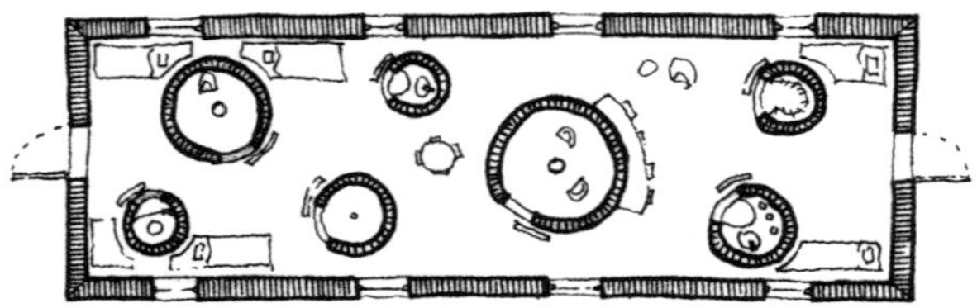

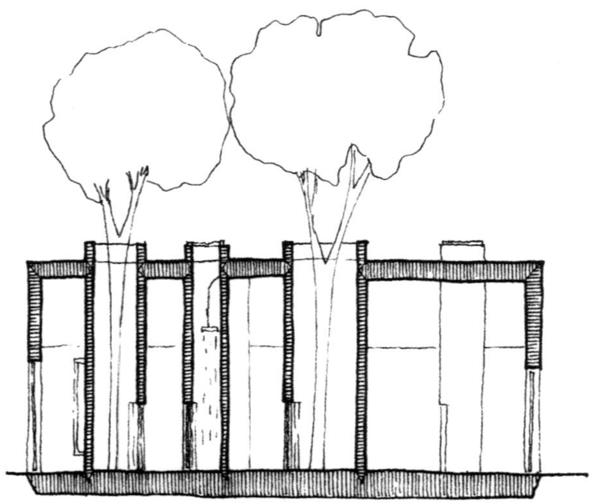

no.084

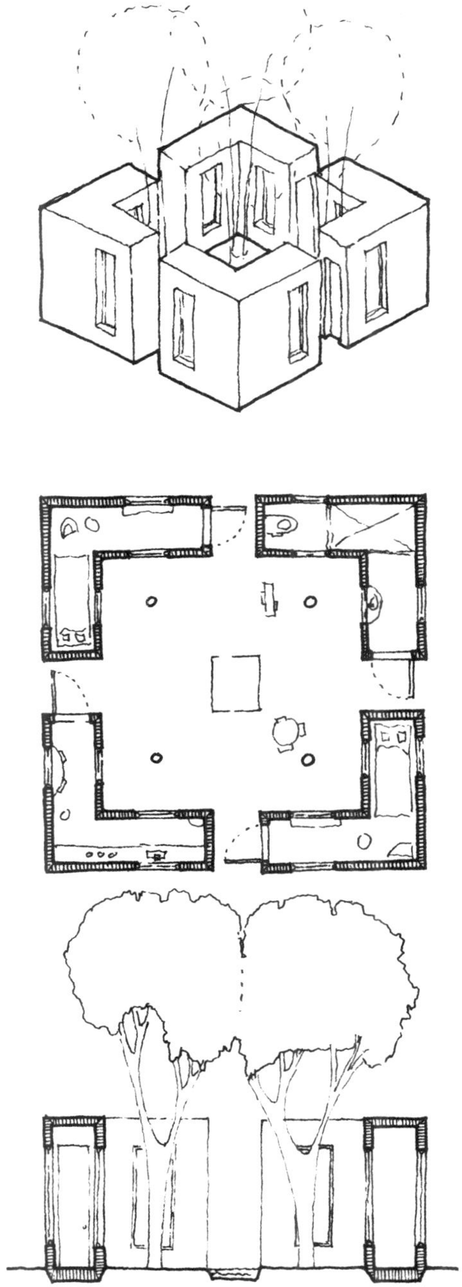

no.085

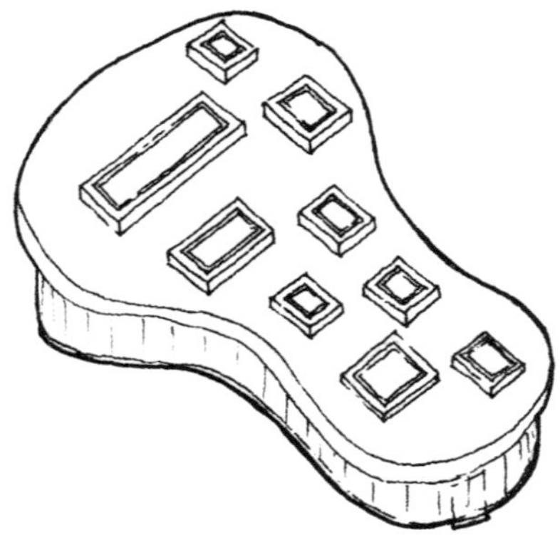

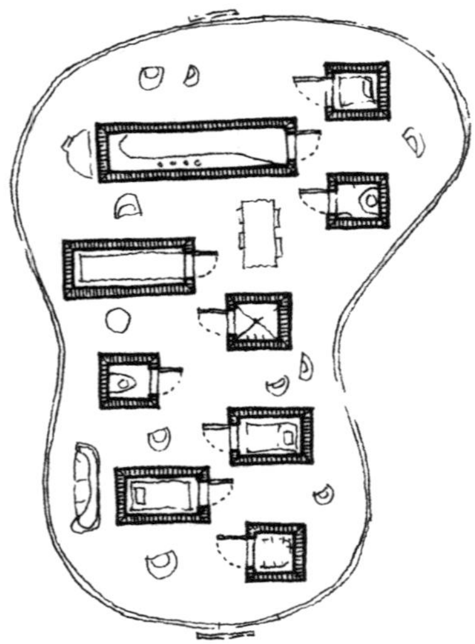

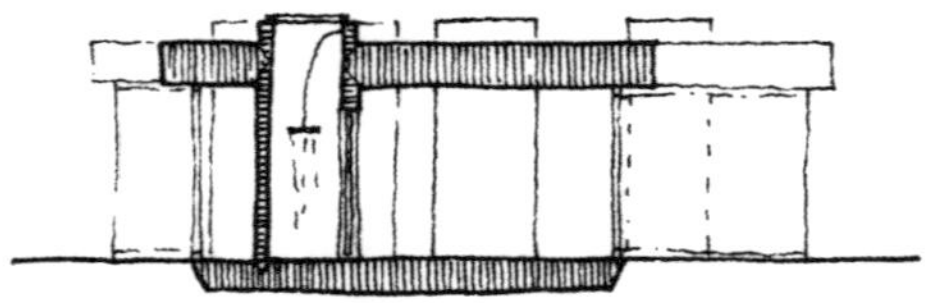

no.086

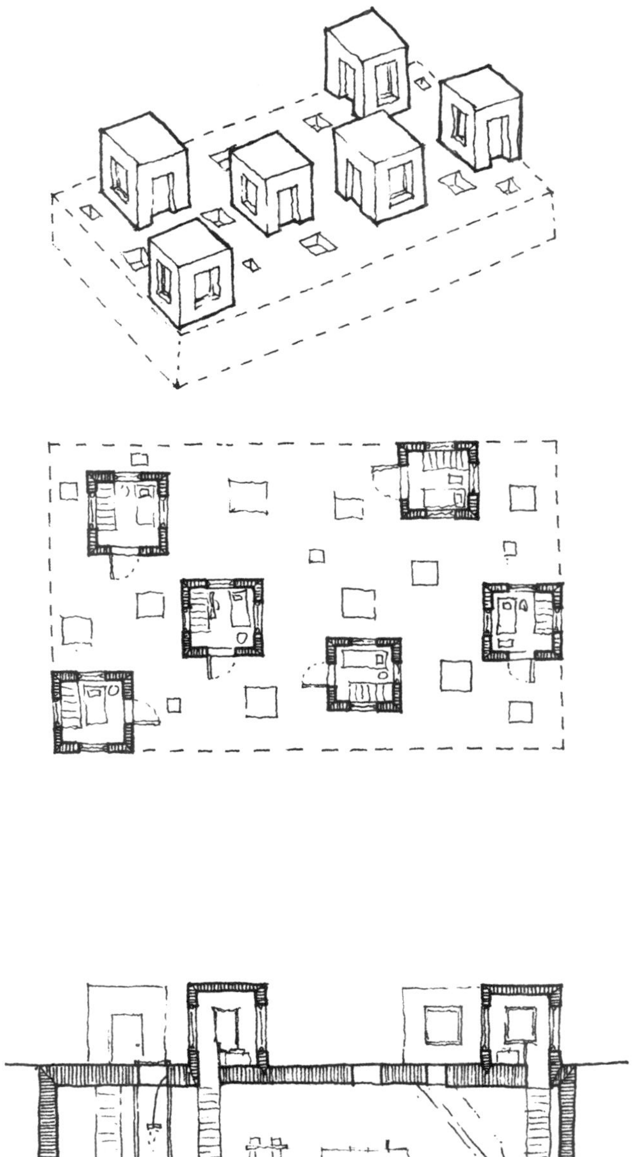

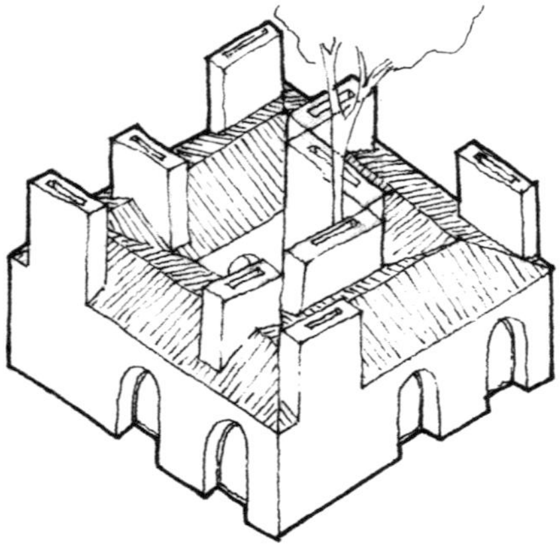

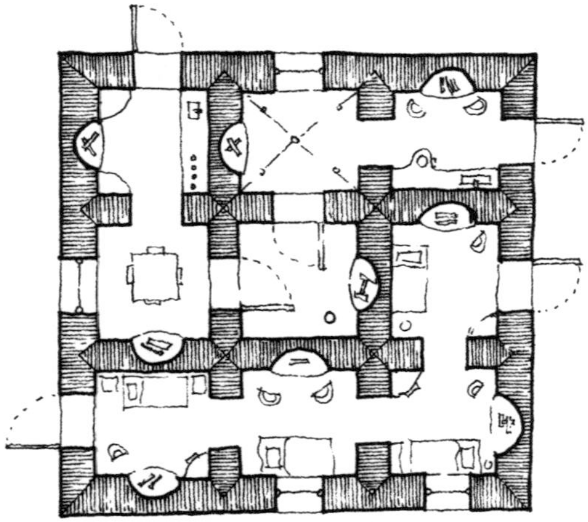

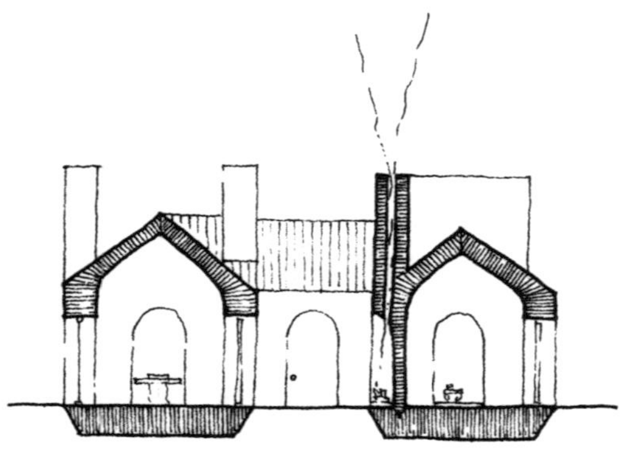

no.088

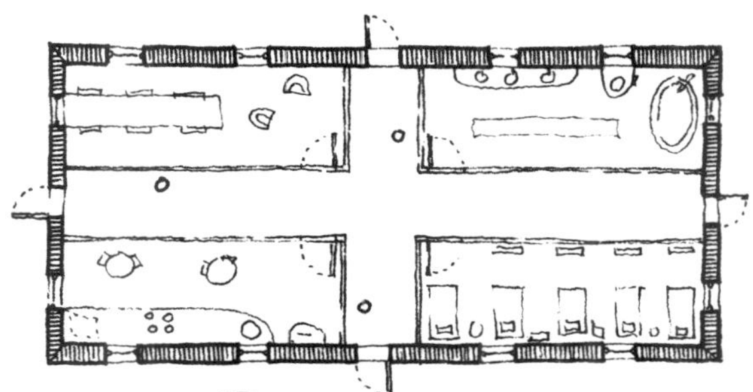

no.089

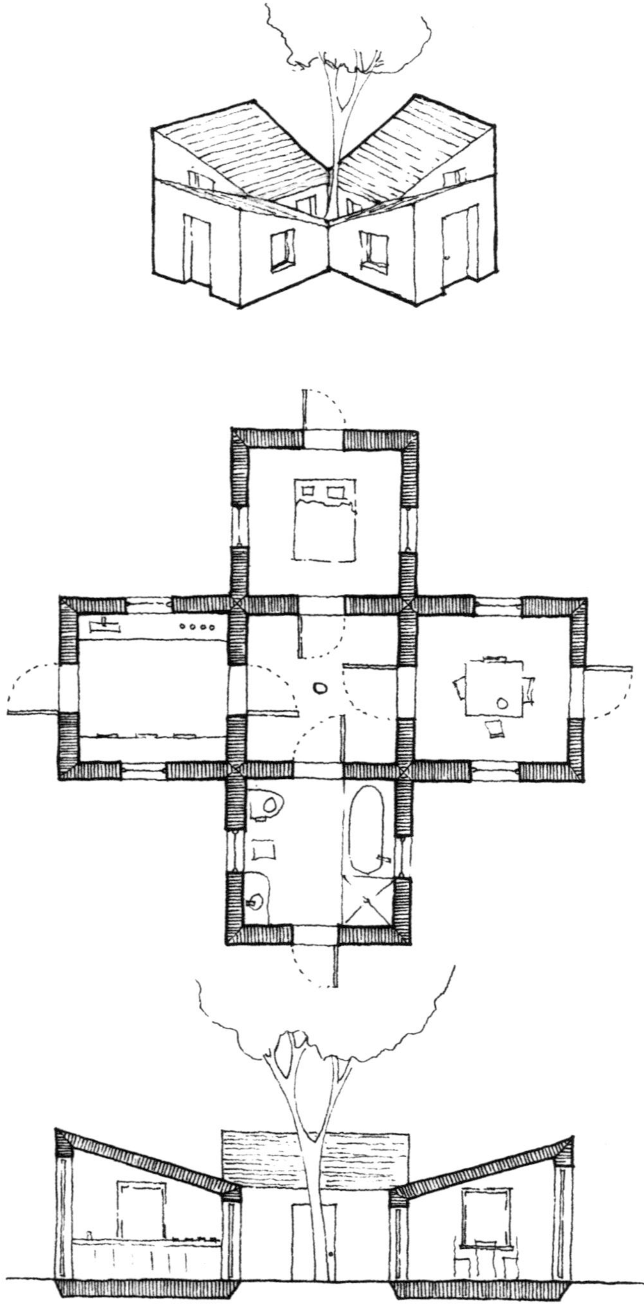

no.090

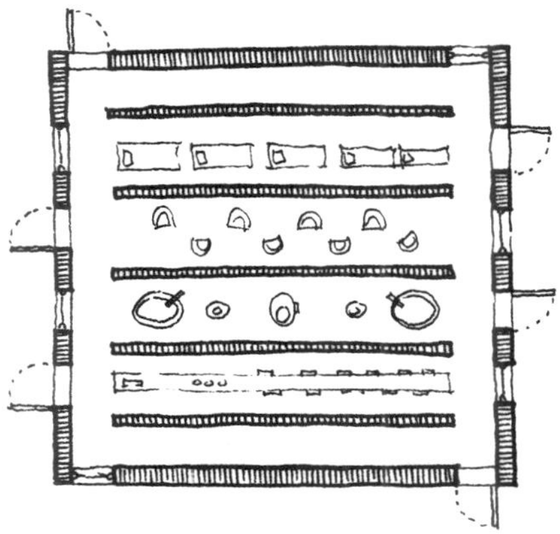

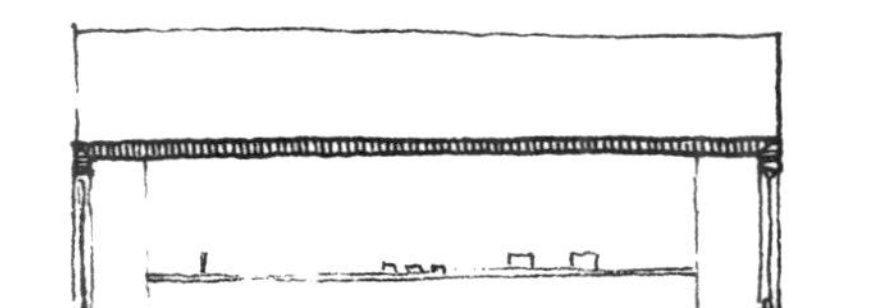

no.091

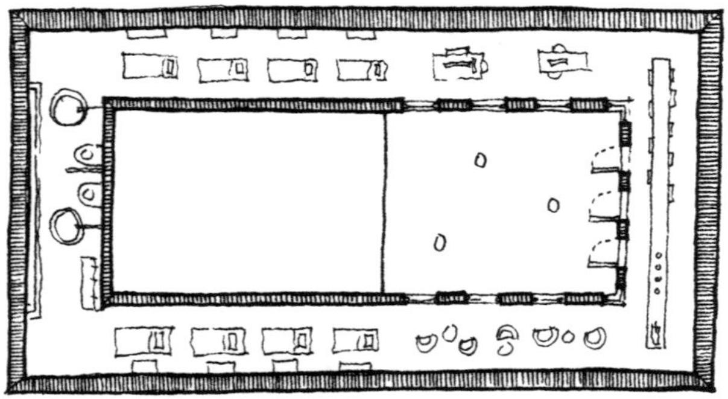

no.092

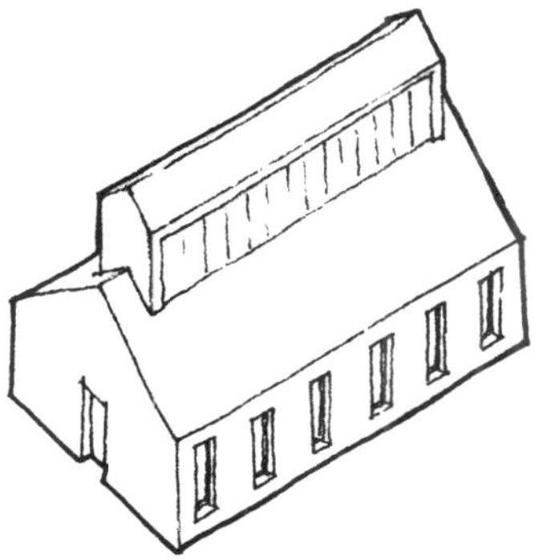

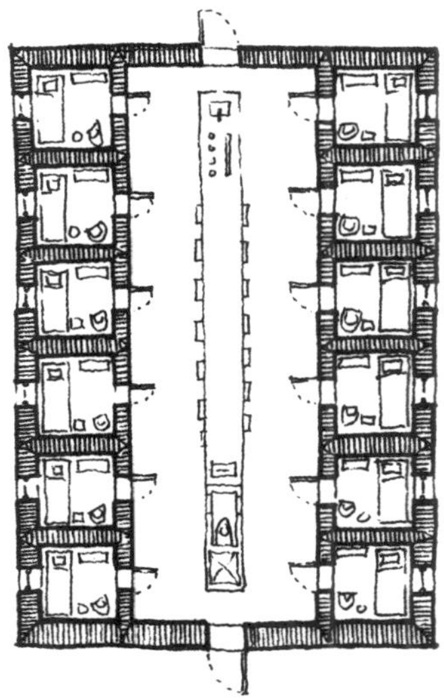

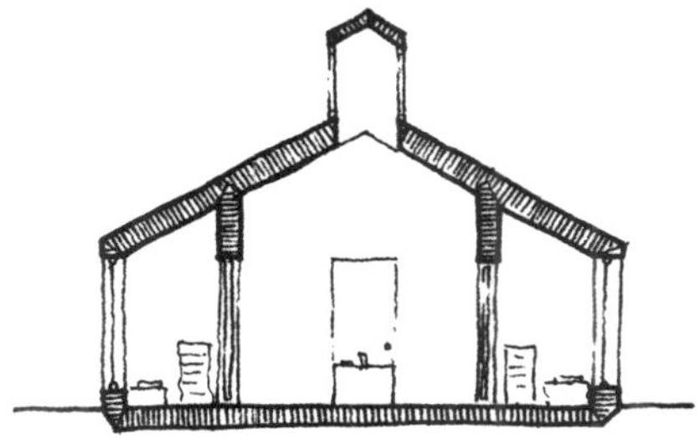

no.093

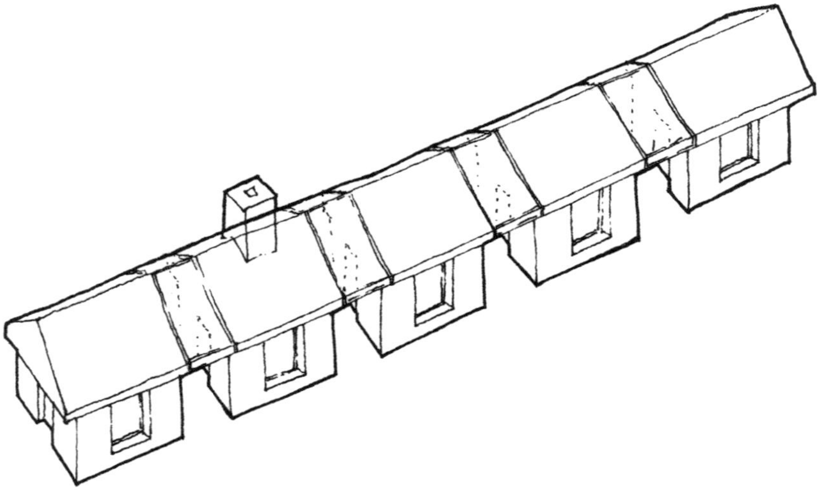

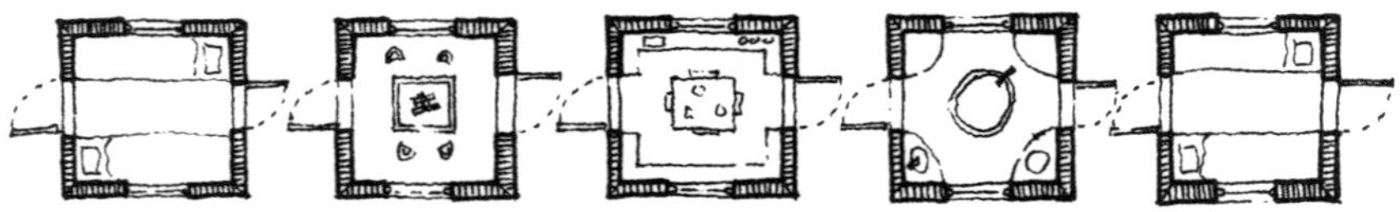

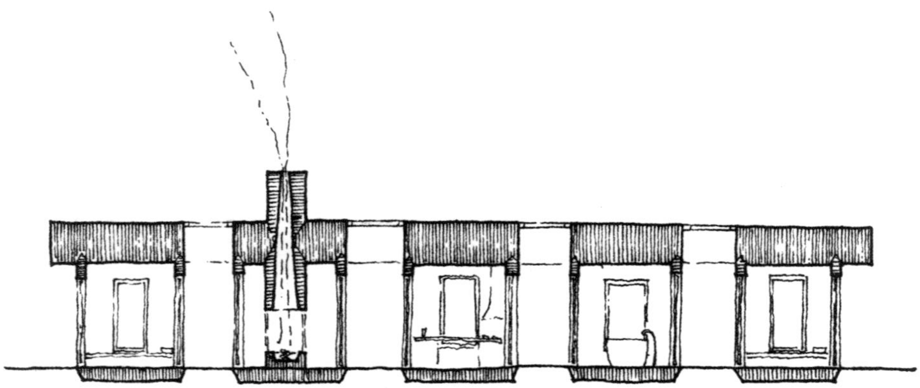

no.094

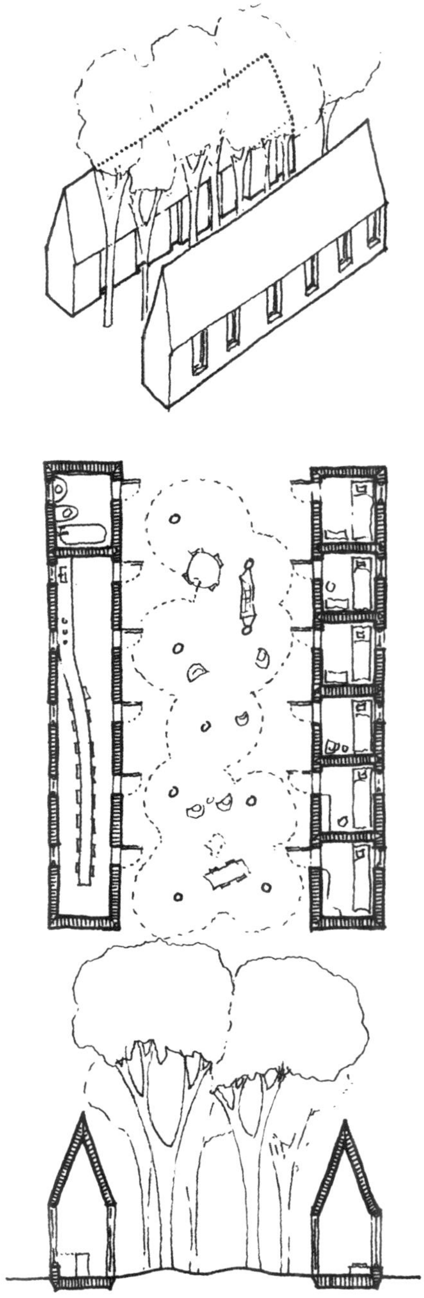

no.095

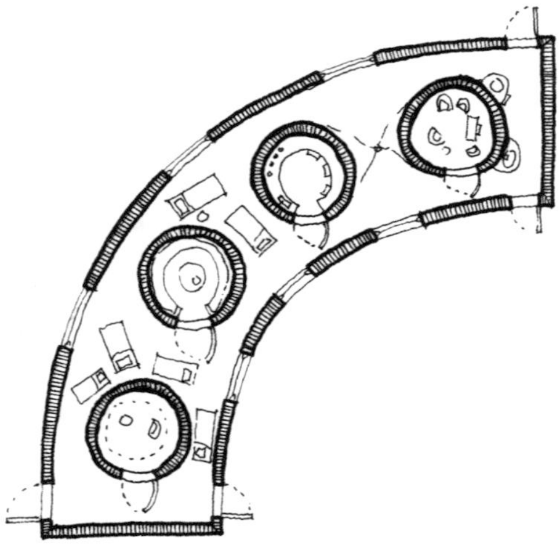

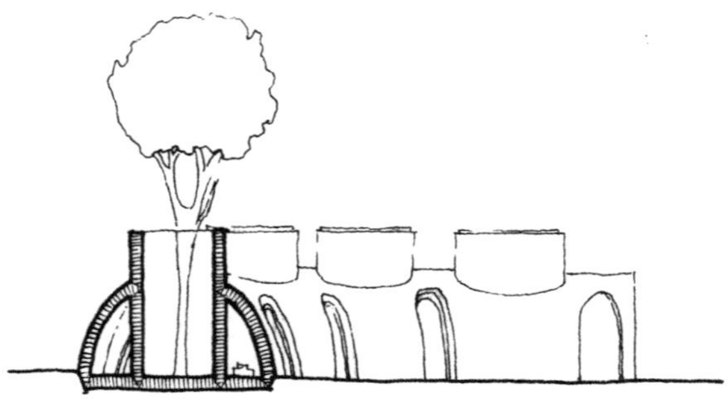

no.096

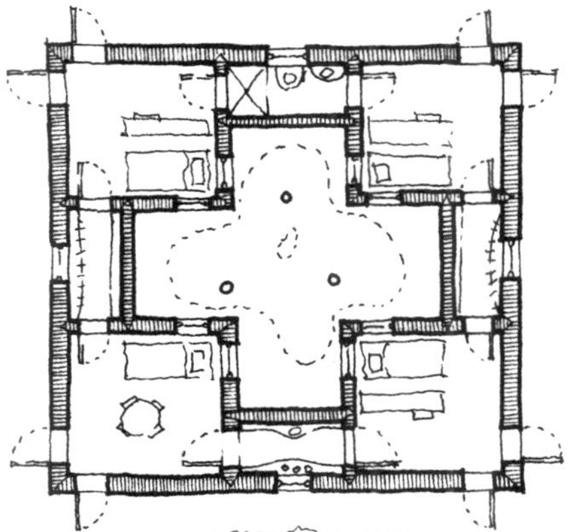

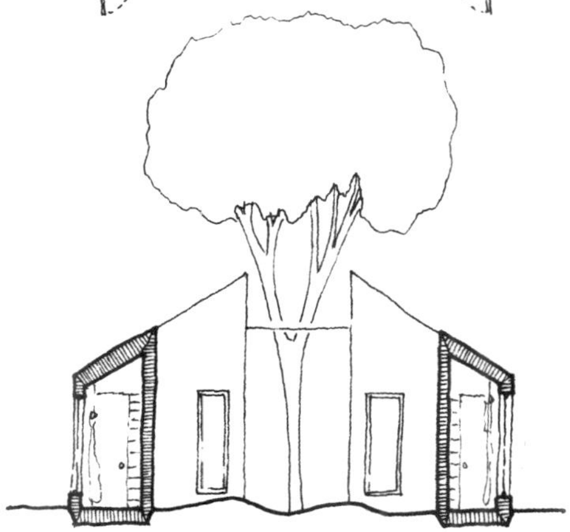

no.097

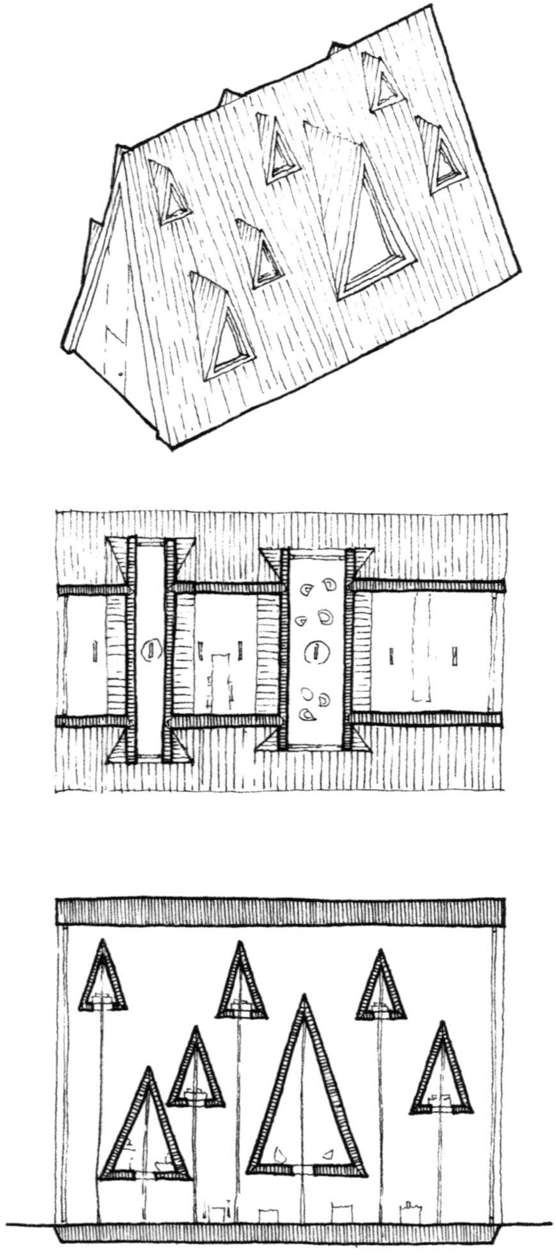

no.098

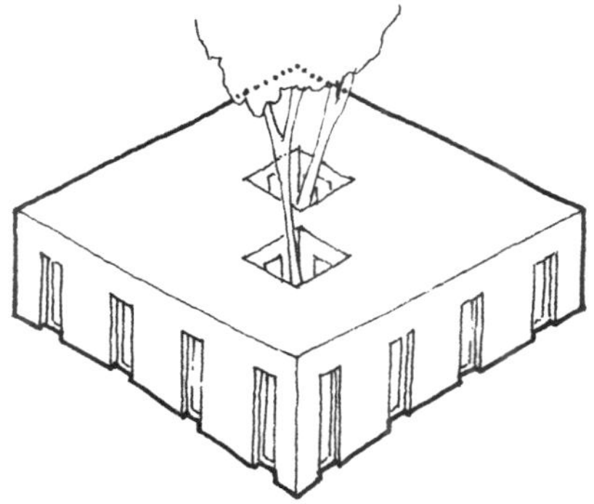

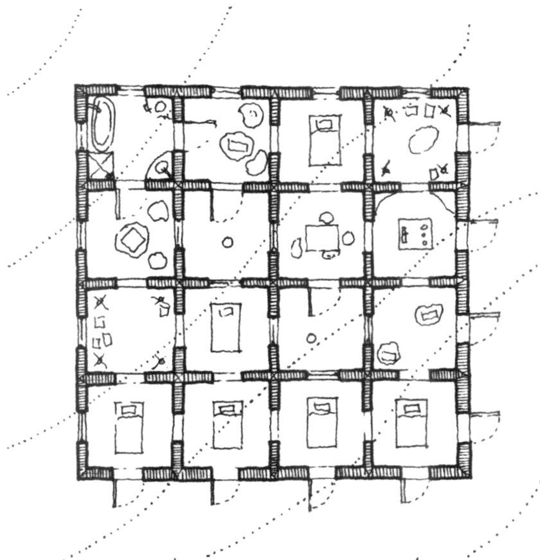

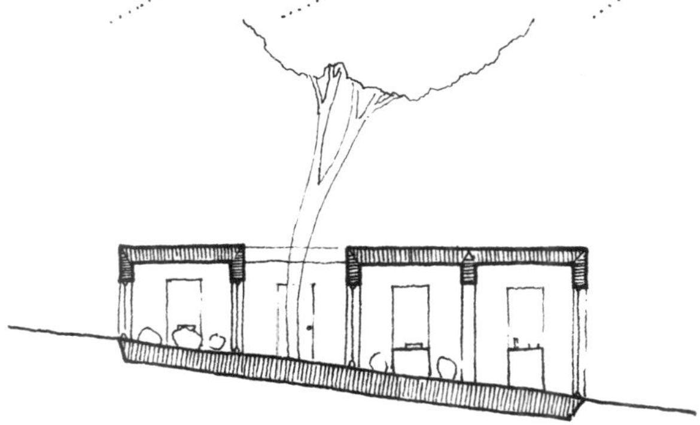

no.099

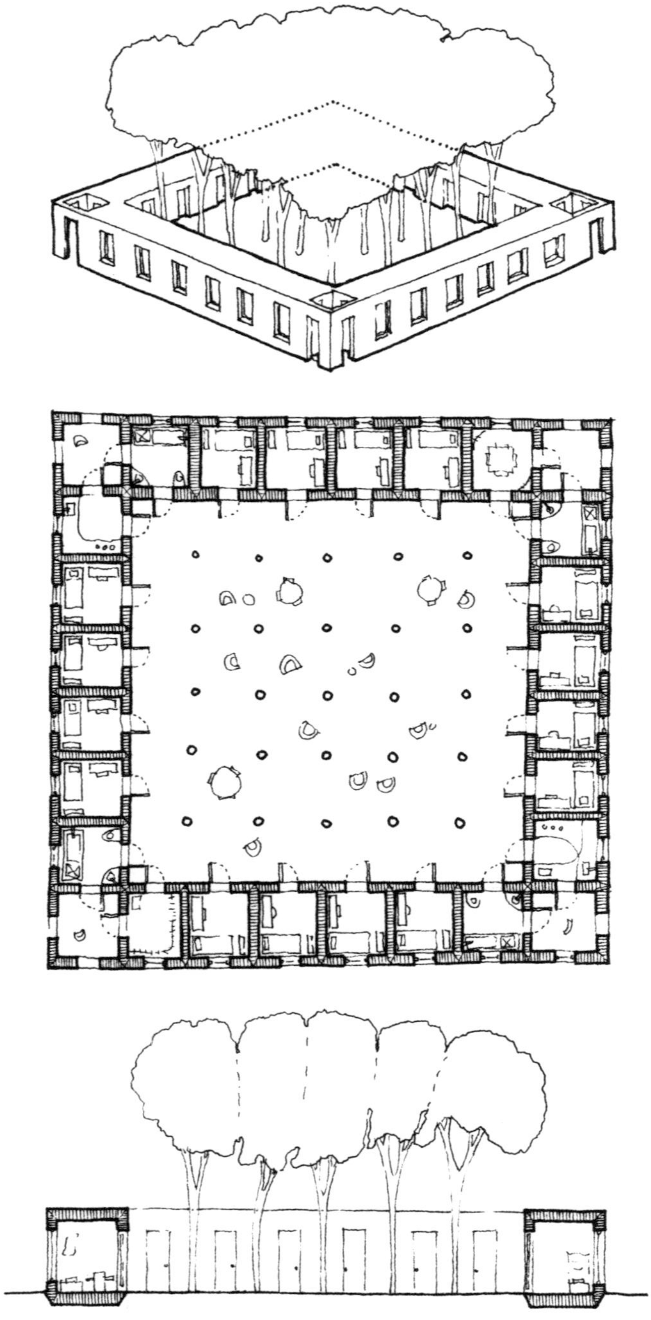

no.100

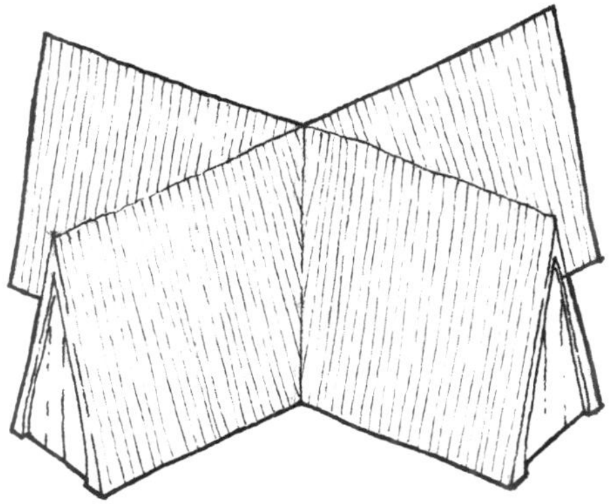

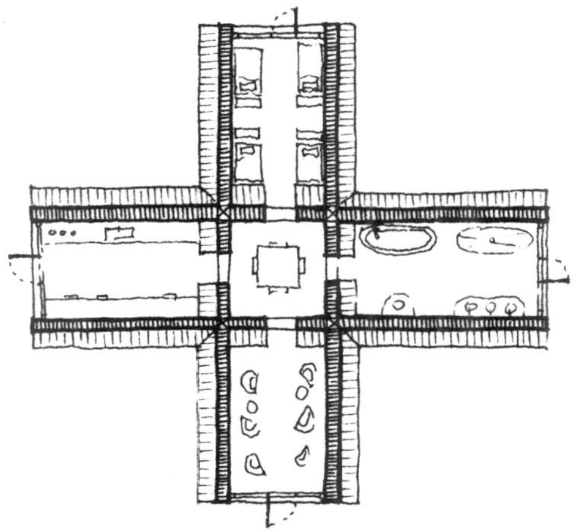

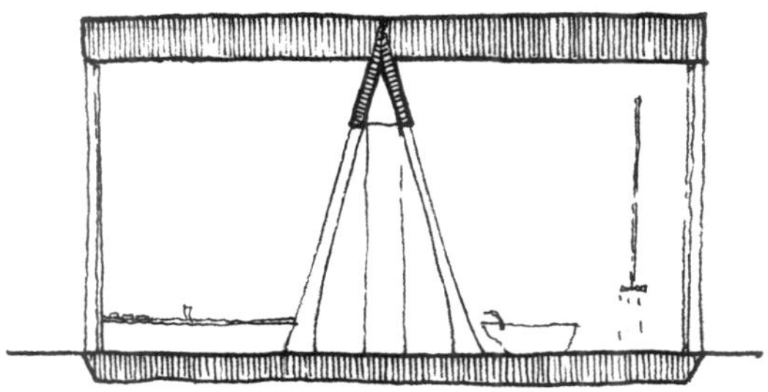

no.101

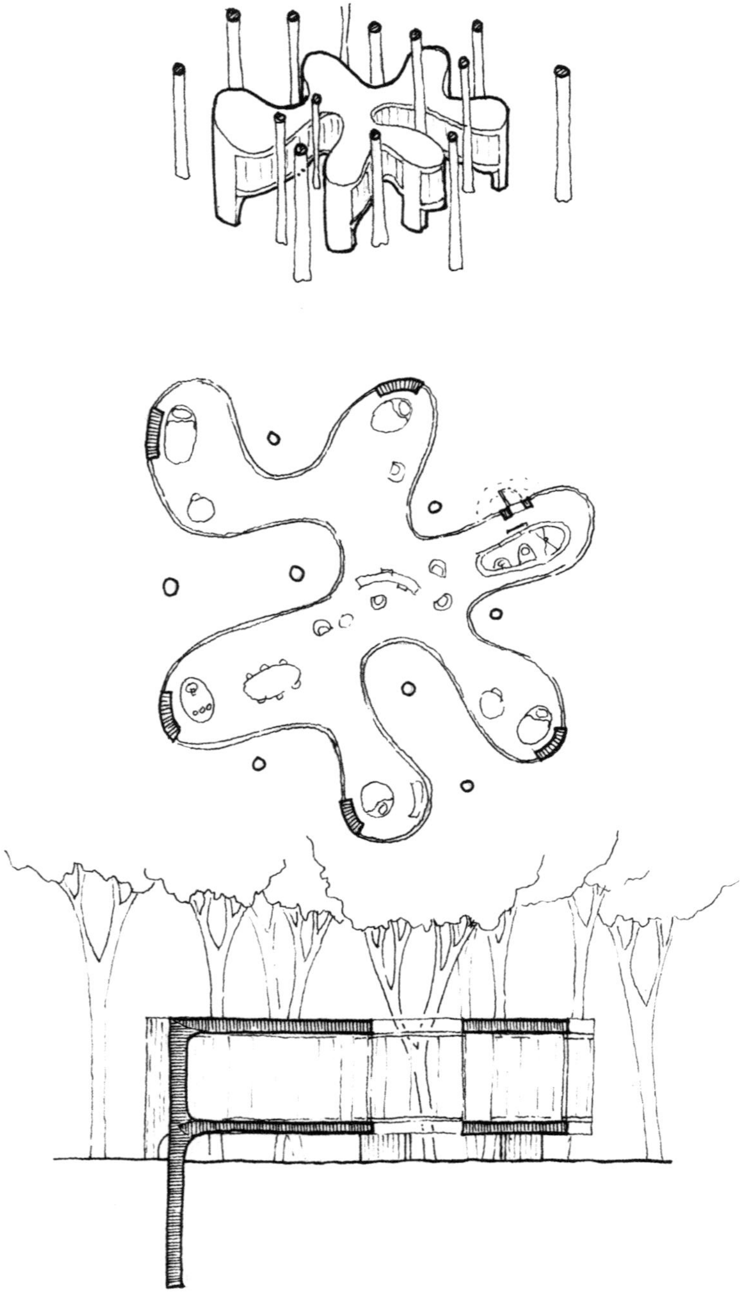

no.102

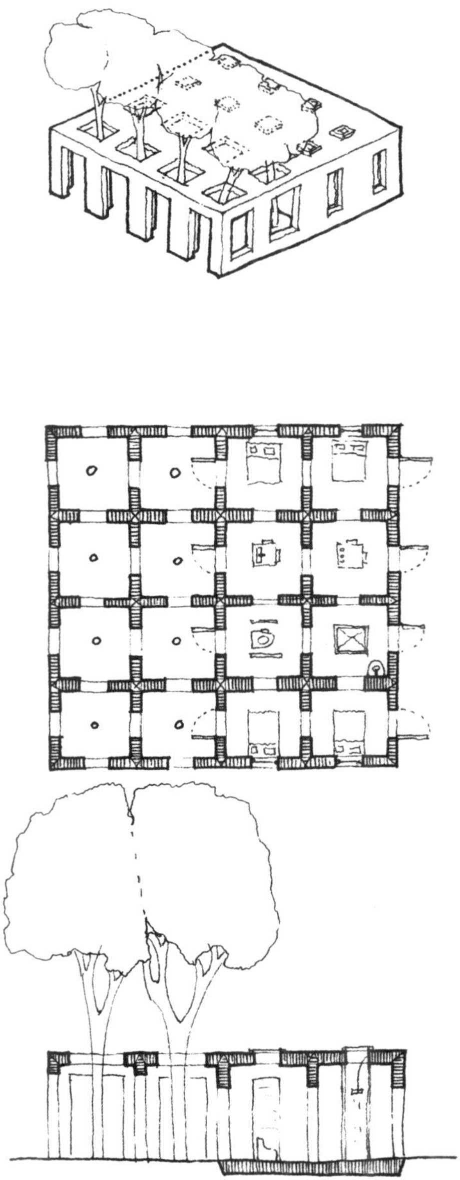

no.103

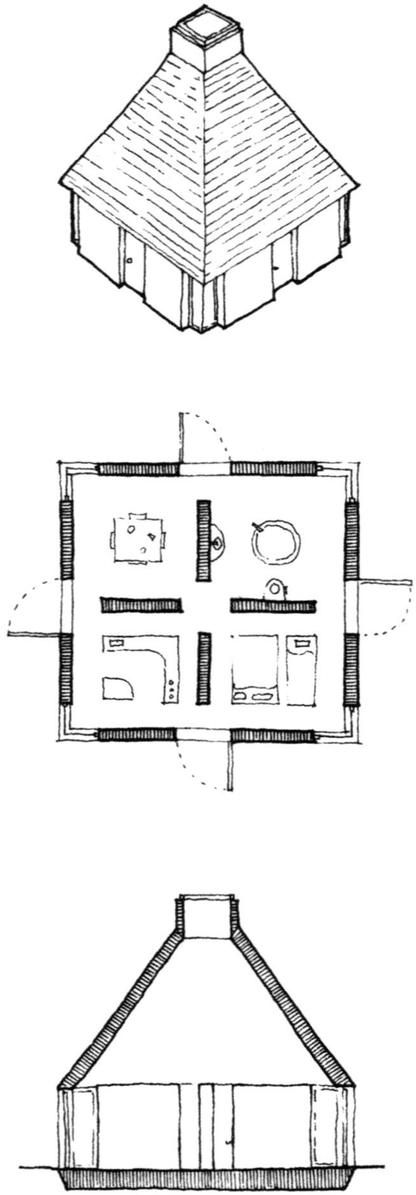

no.104

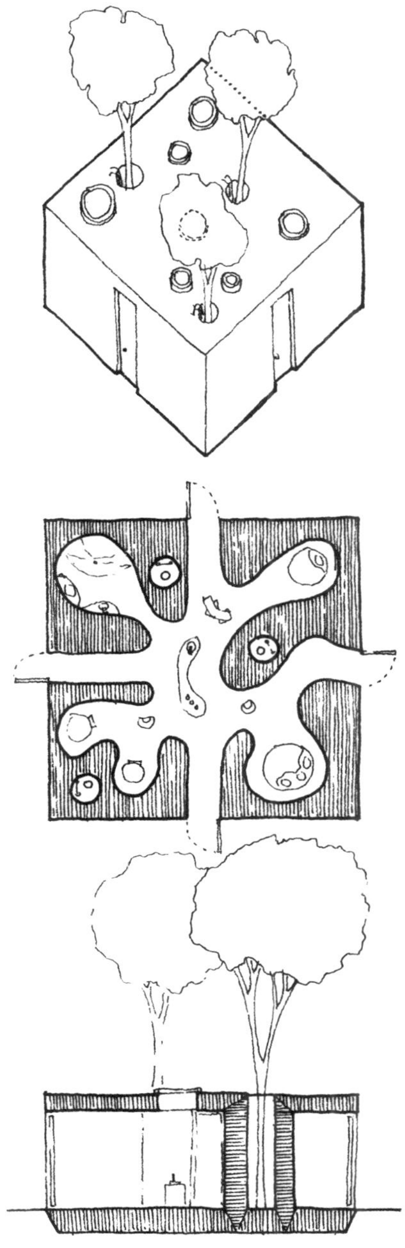

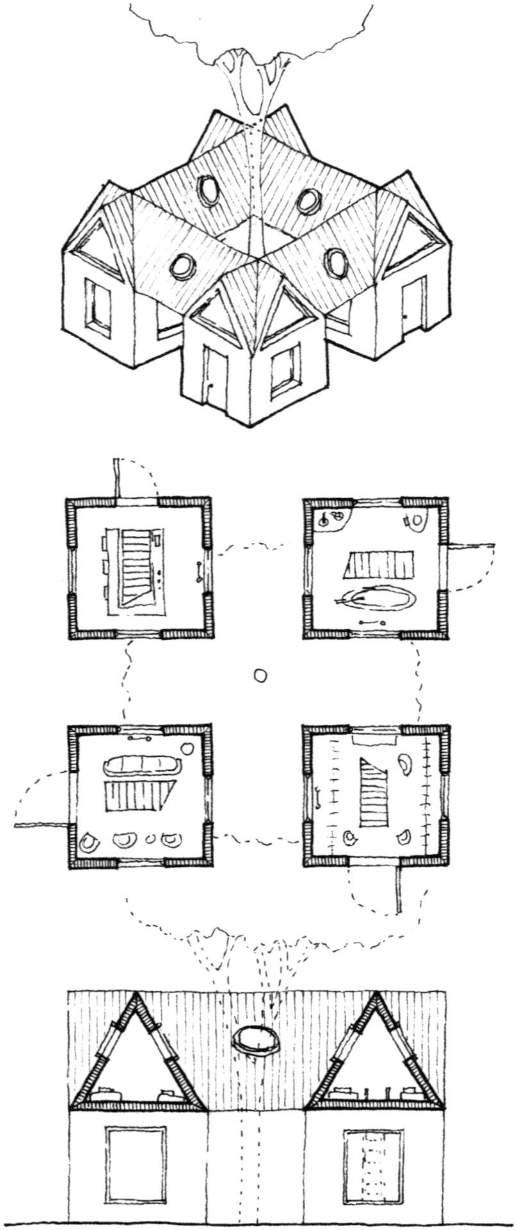

no.106

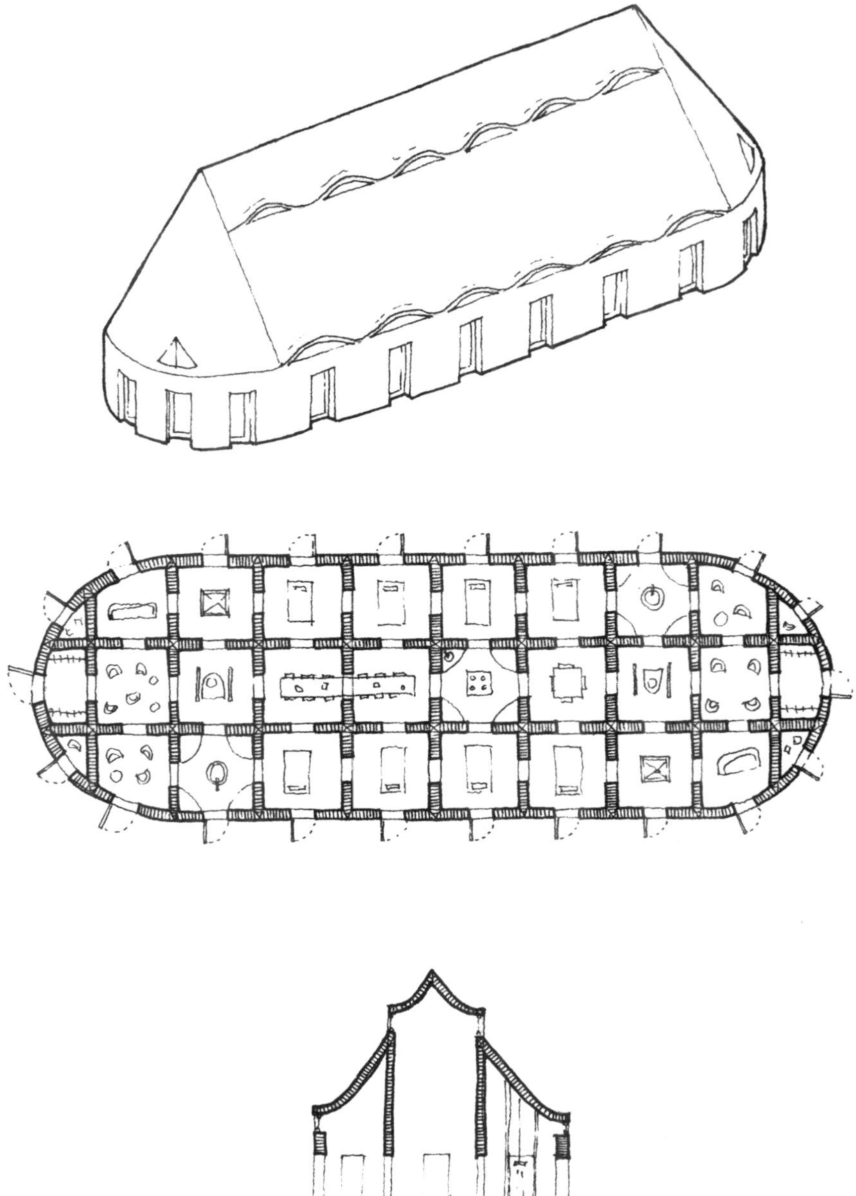

no.107

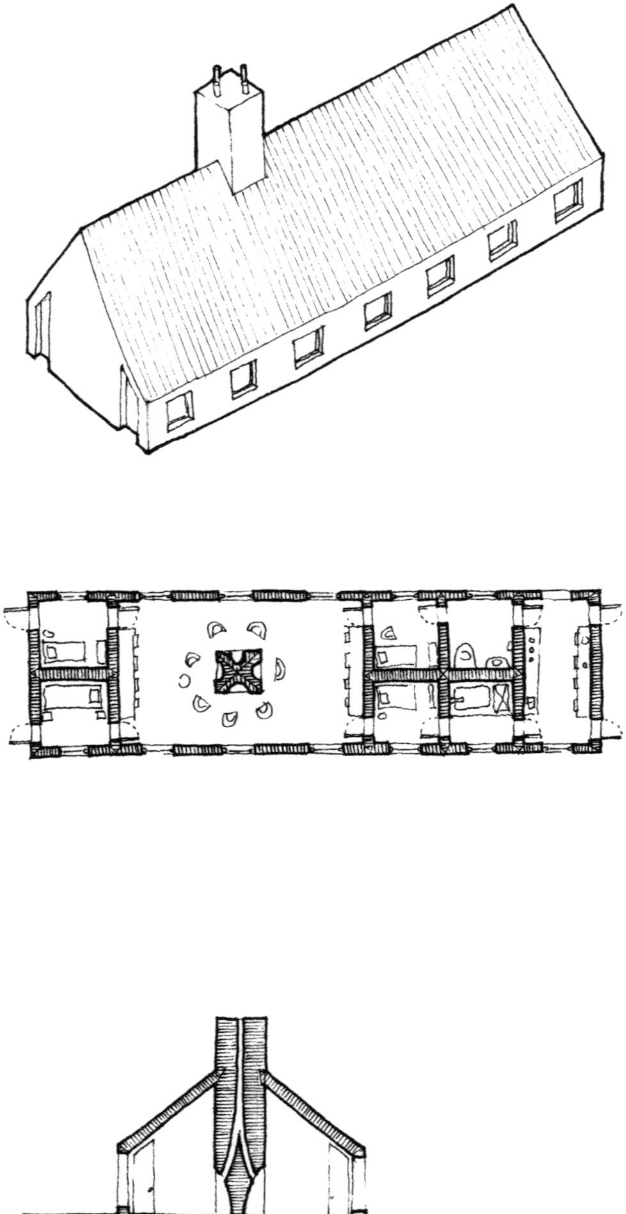

no.108

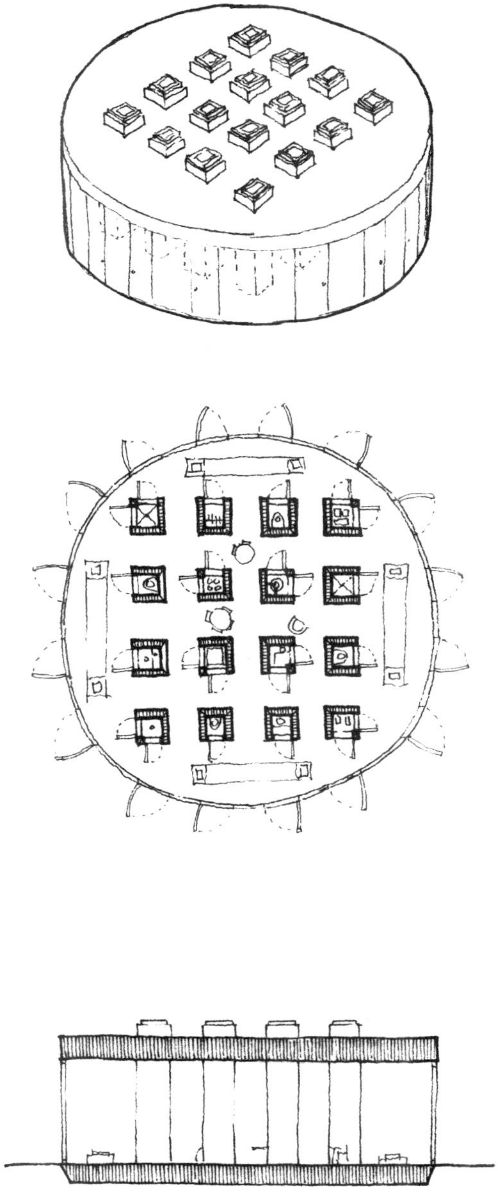

no.109

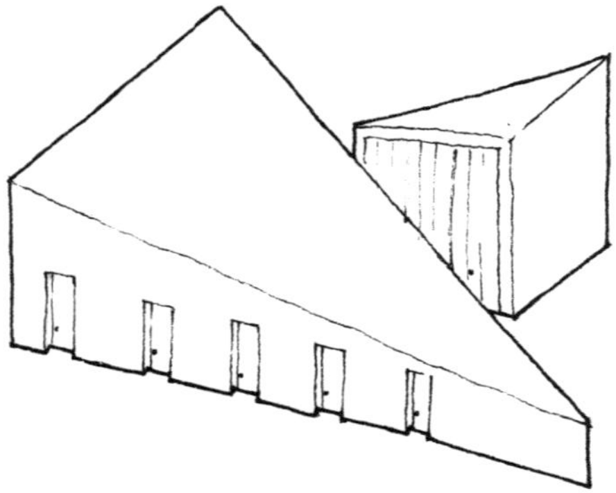

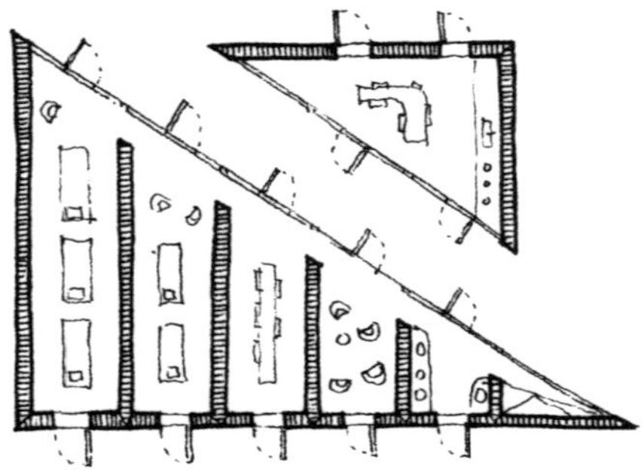

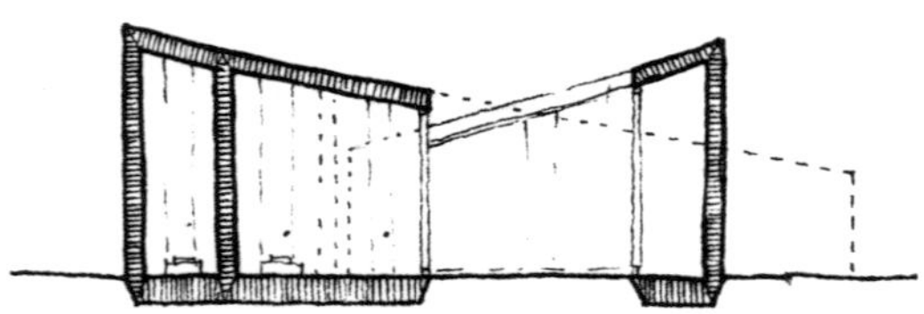

no.110

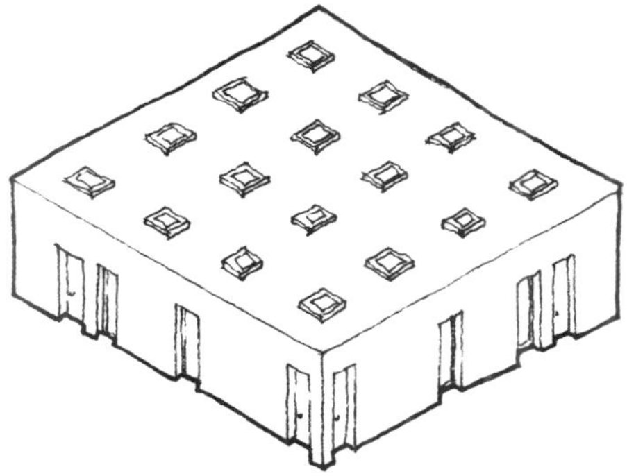

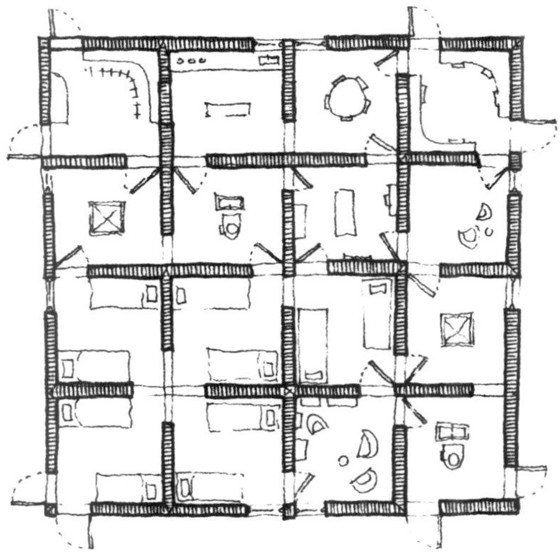

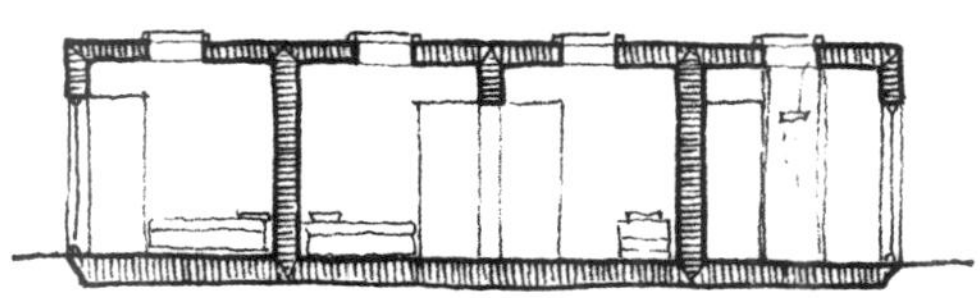

no.111

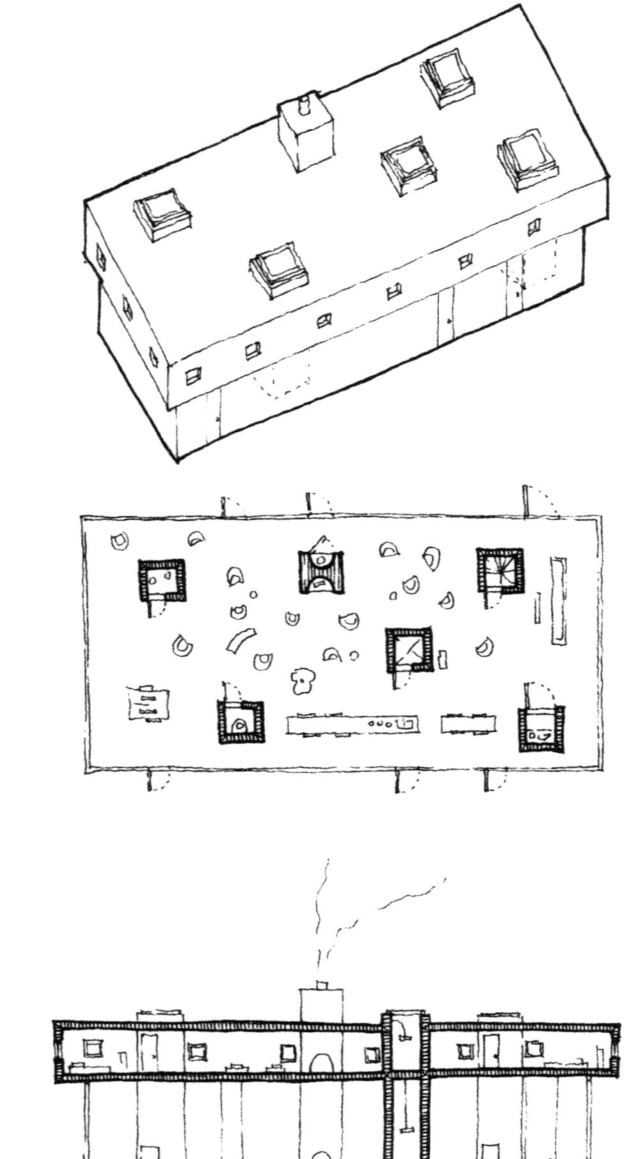

no.112

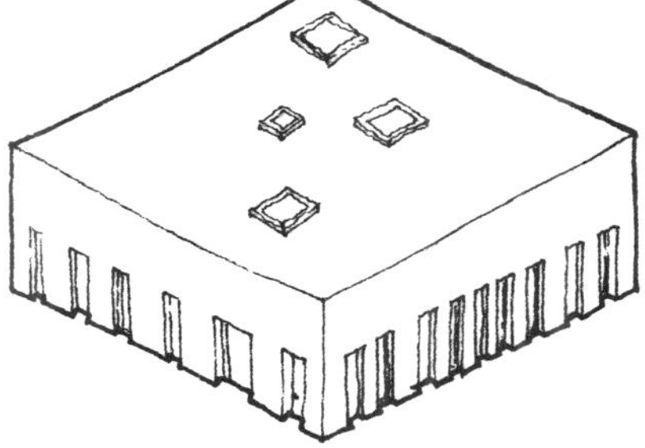

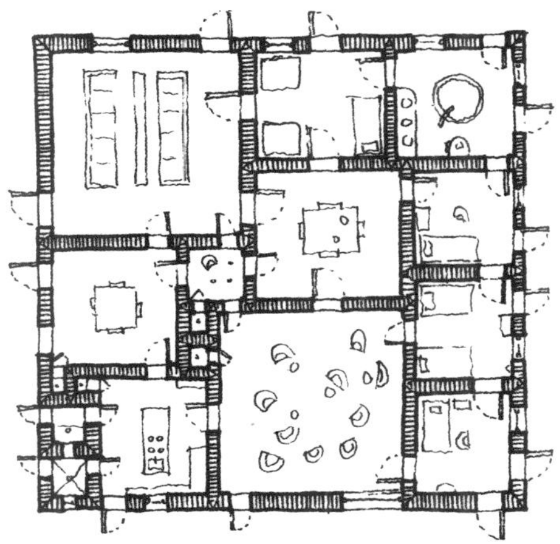

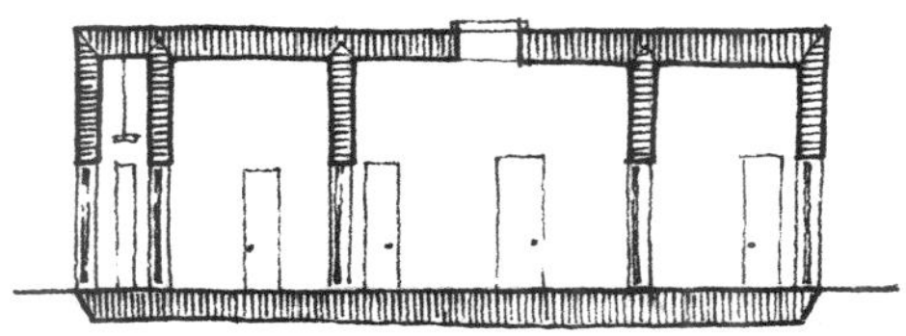

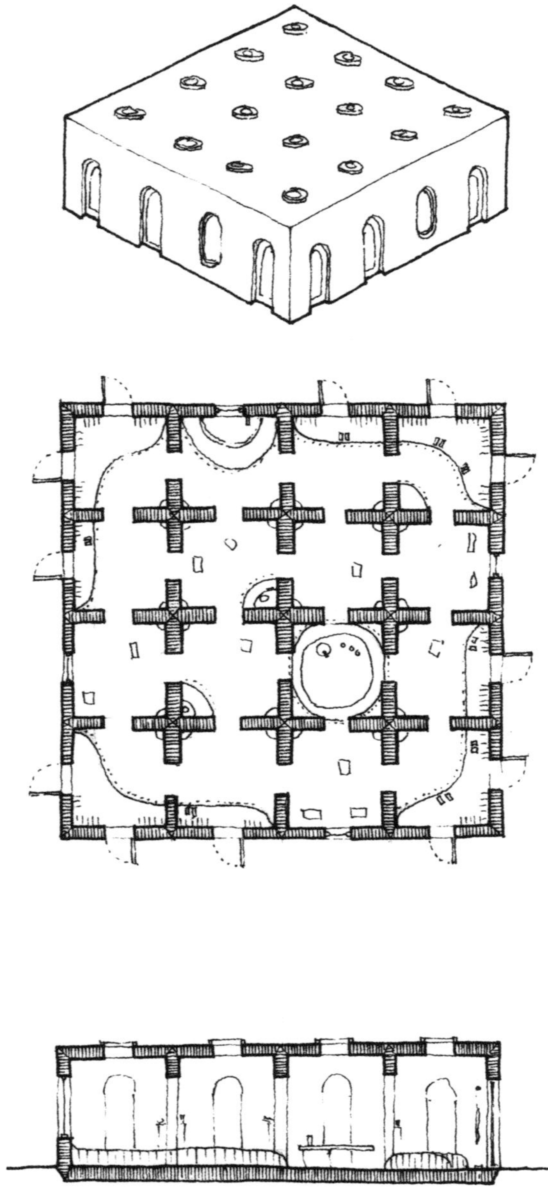

no.114

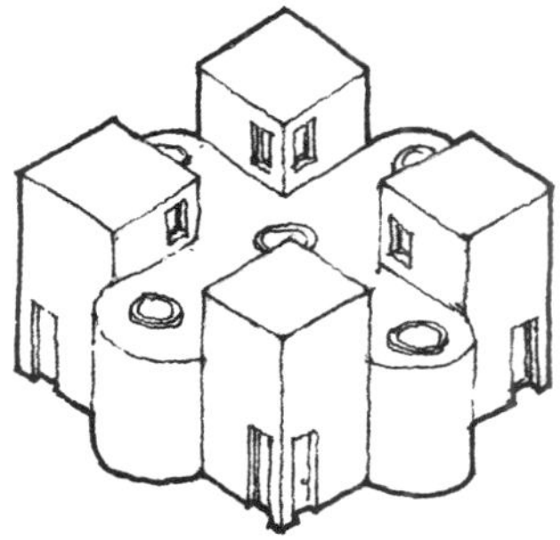

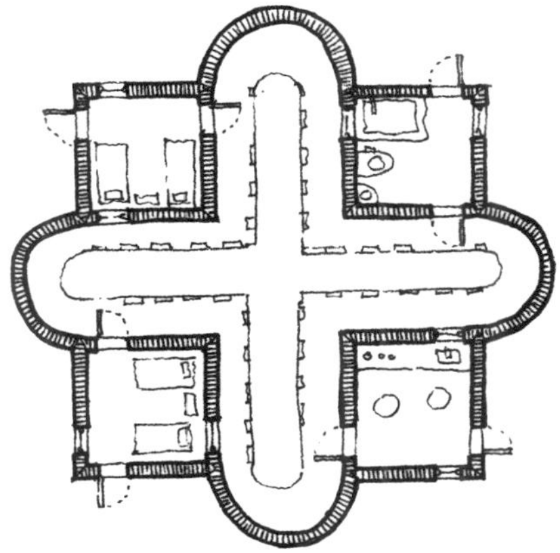

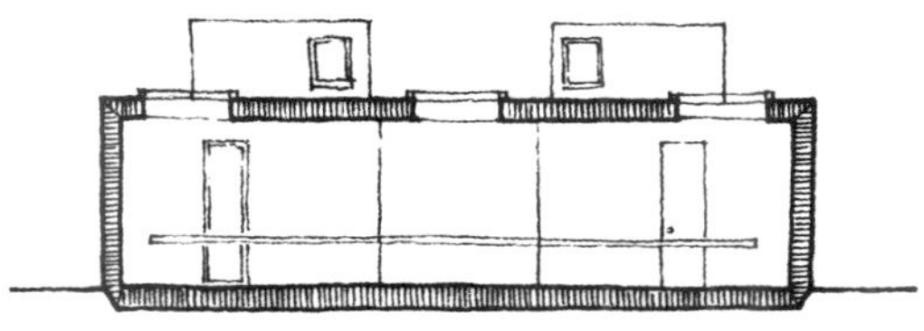

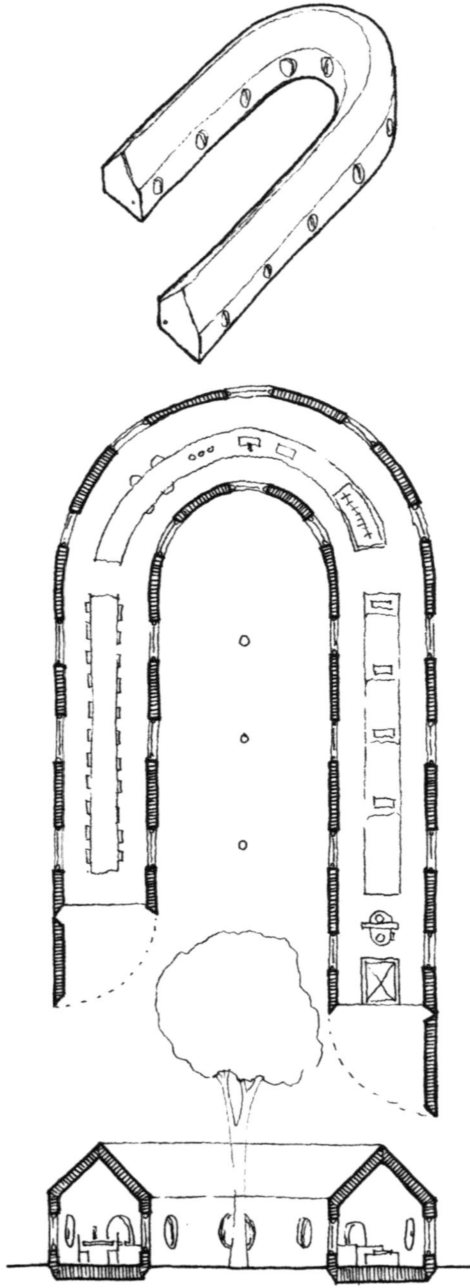

no.116

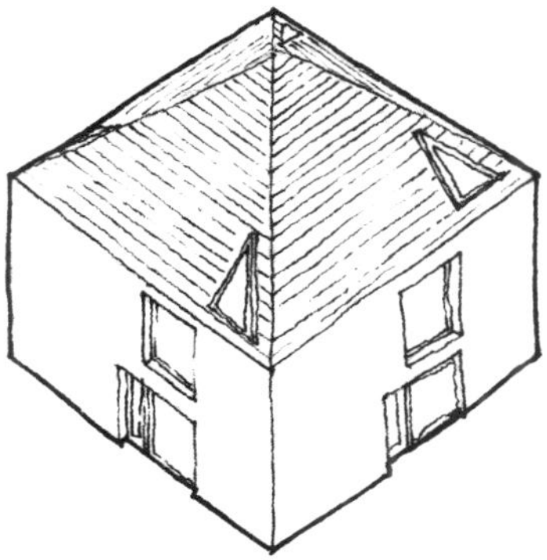

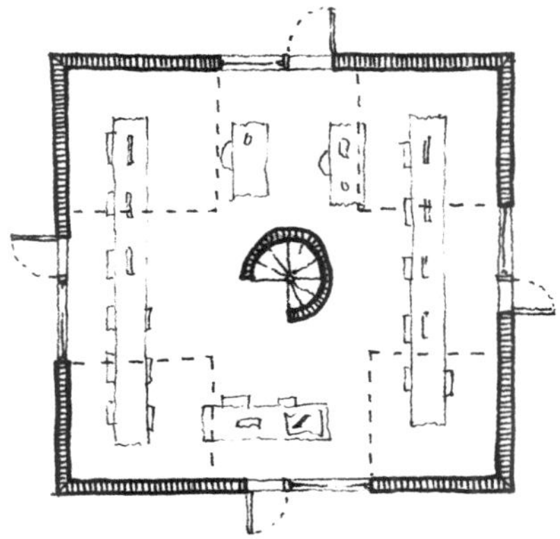

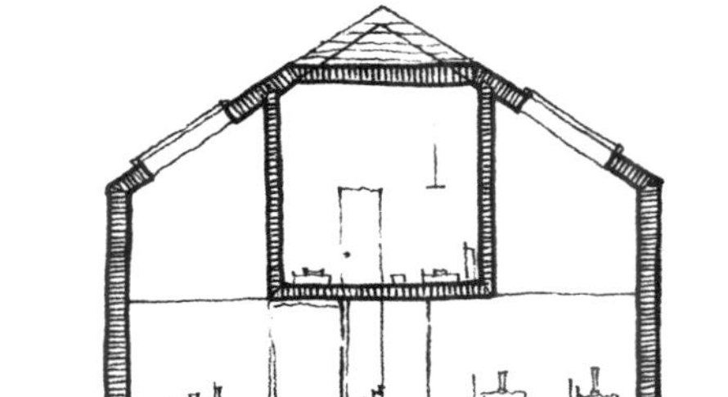

no.117

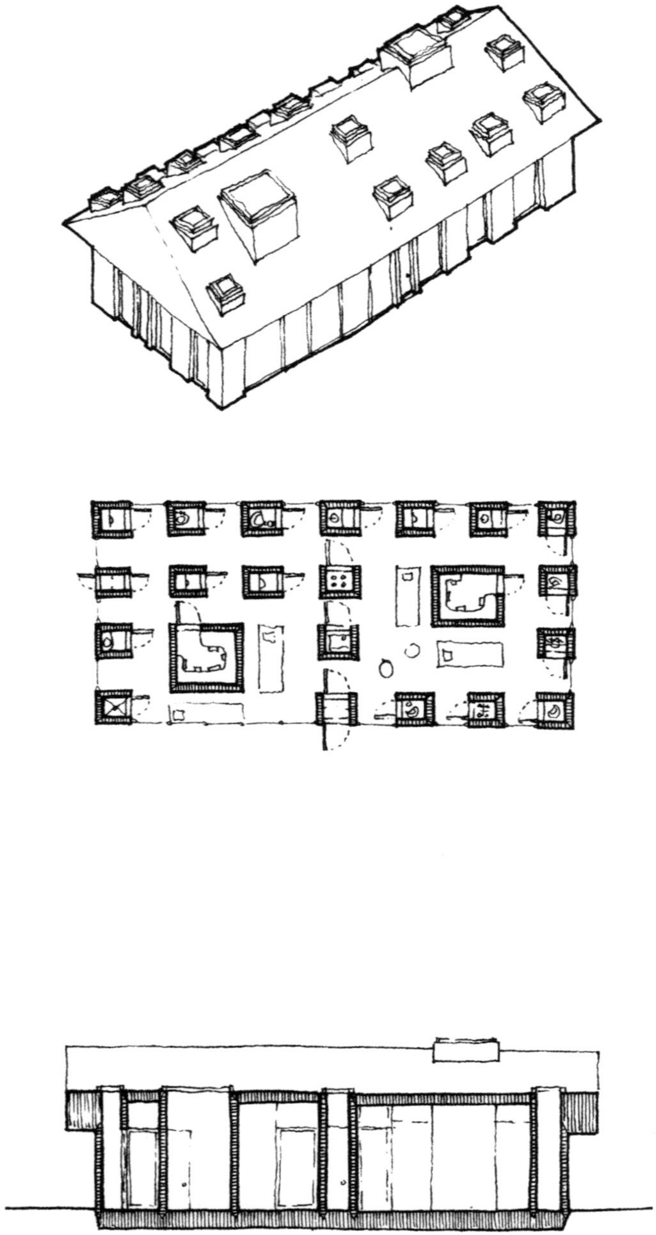

no.118

no.119

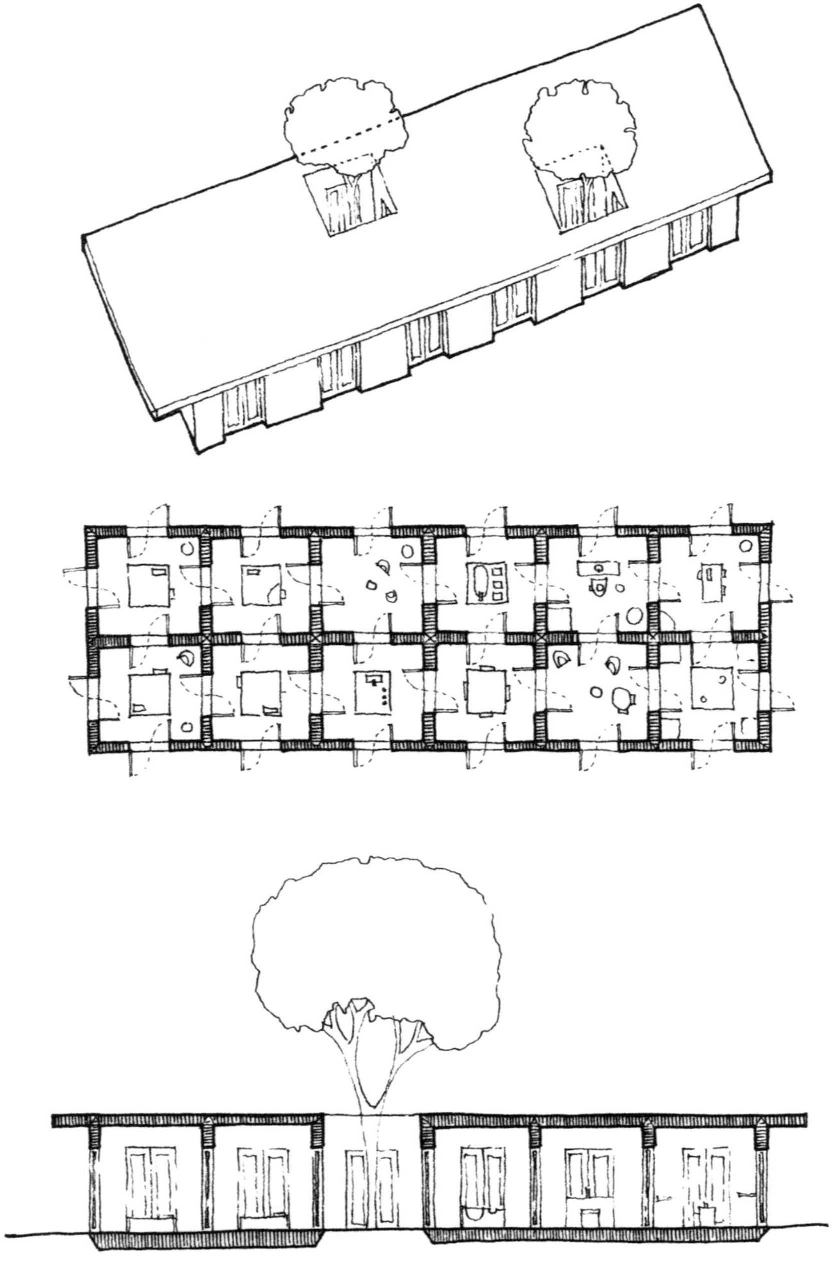

no.120

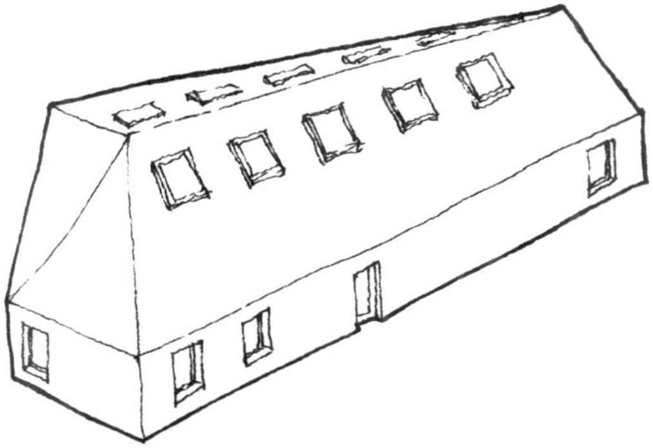

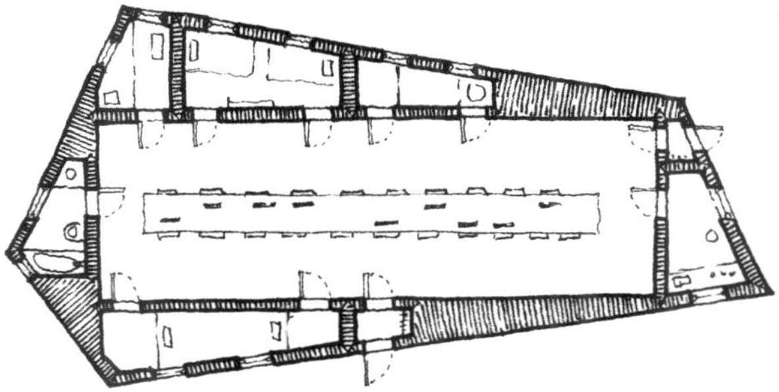

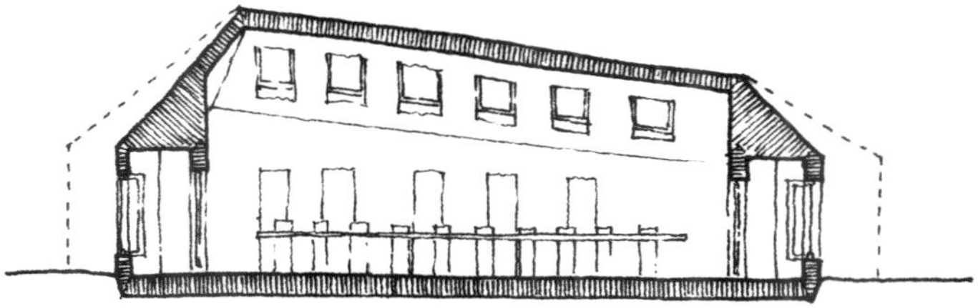

no.121

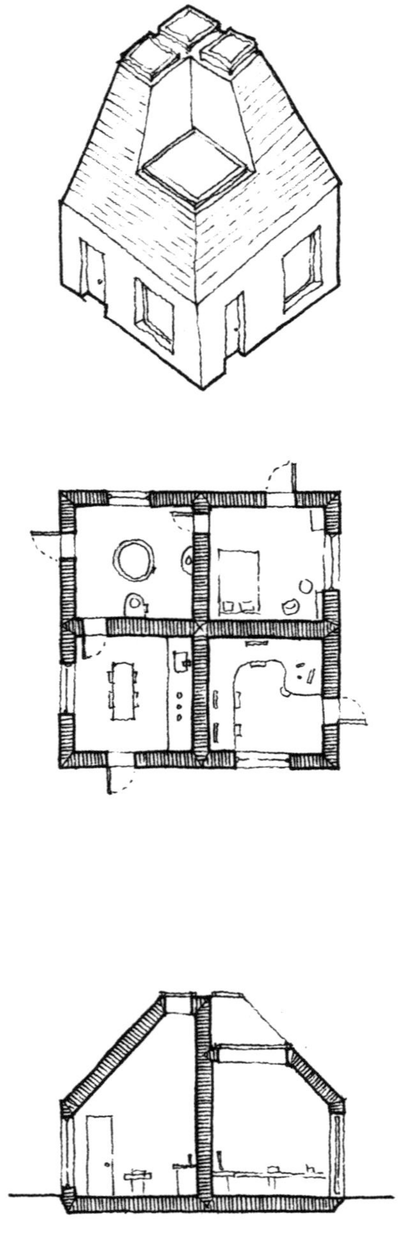

no.122

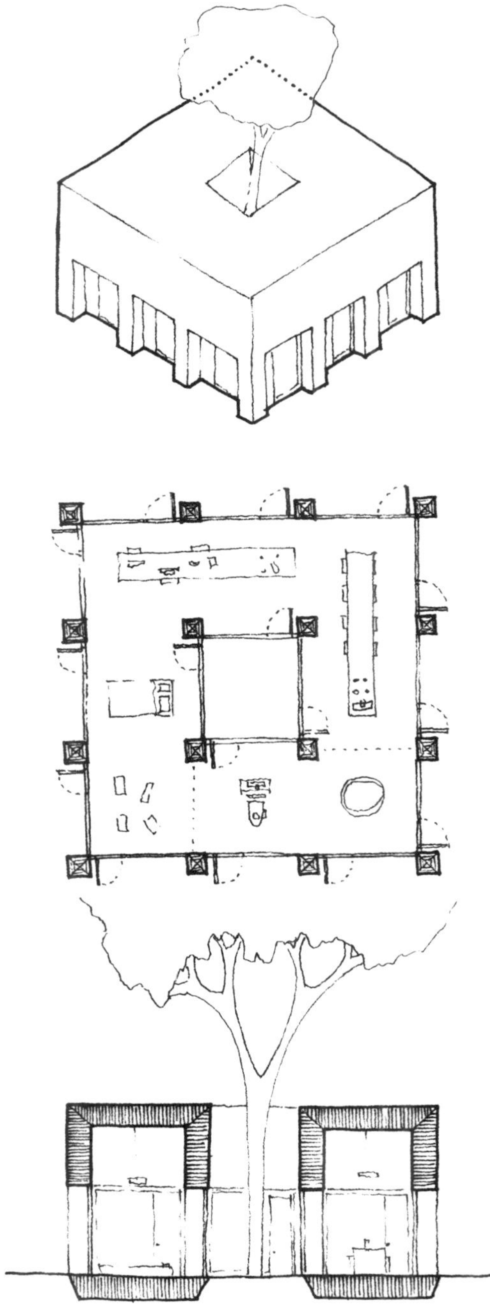

no.123

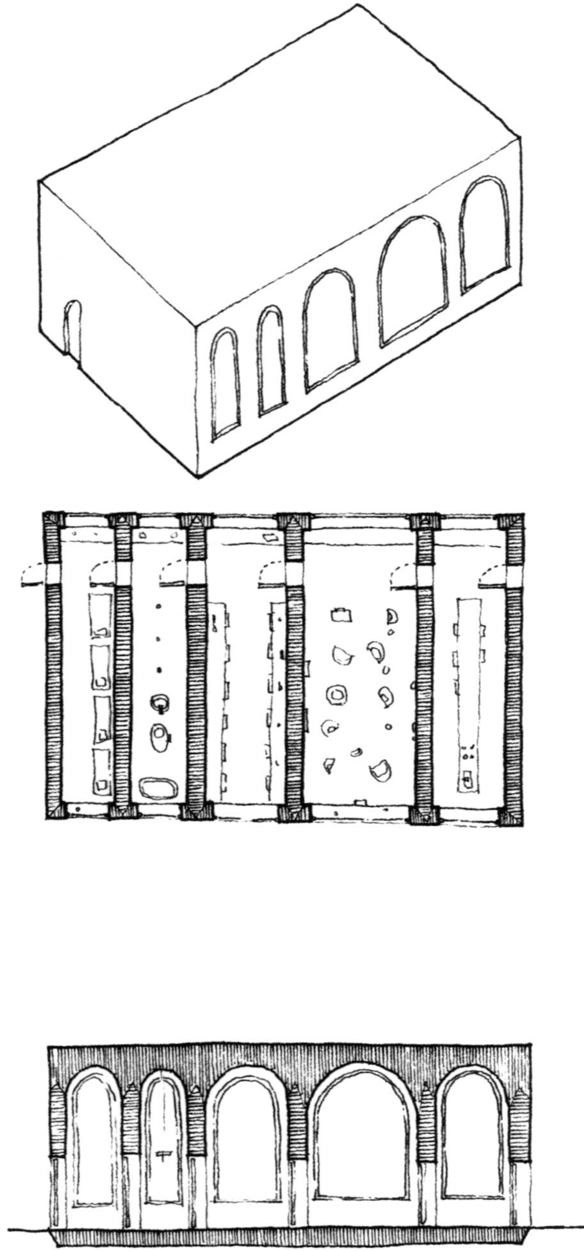

no.124

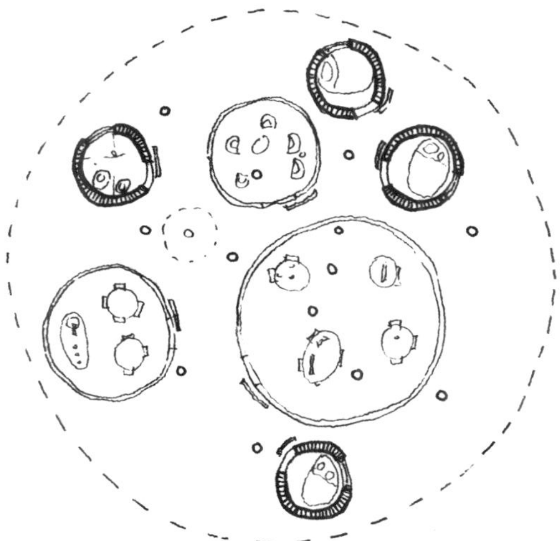

no.125

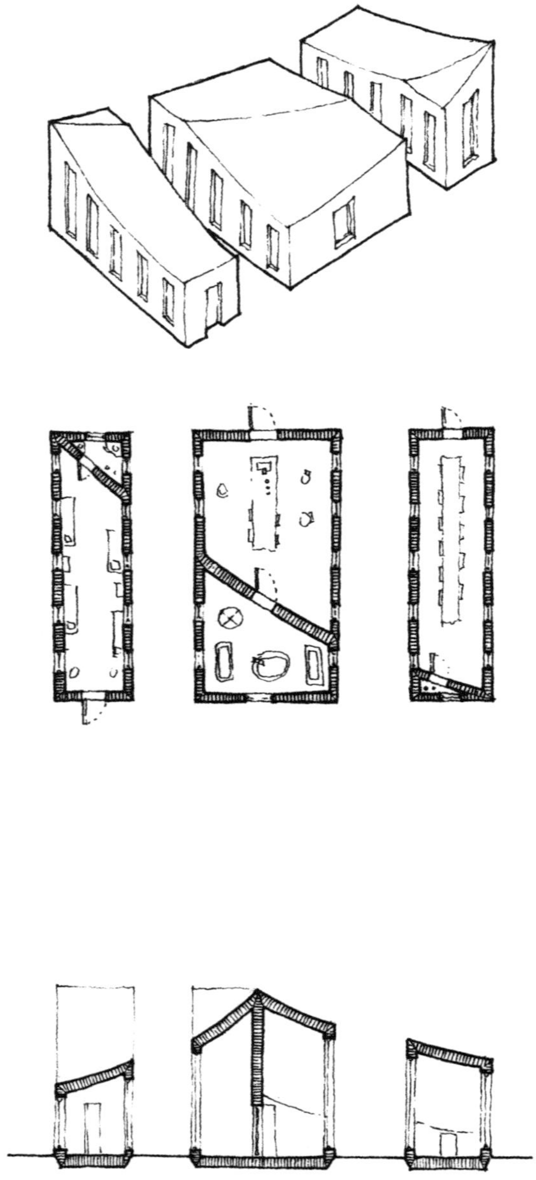

no.126

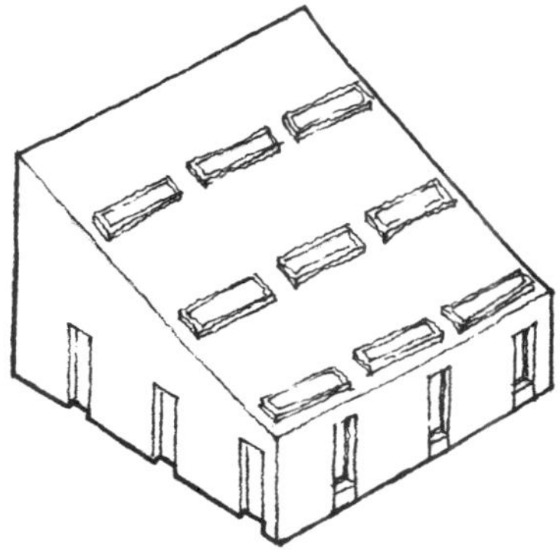

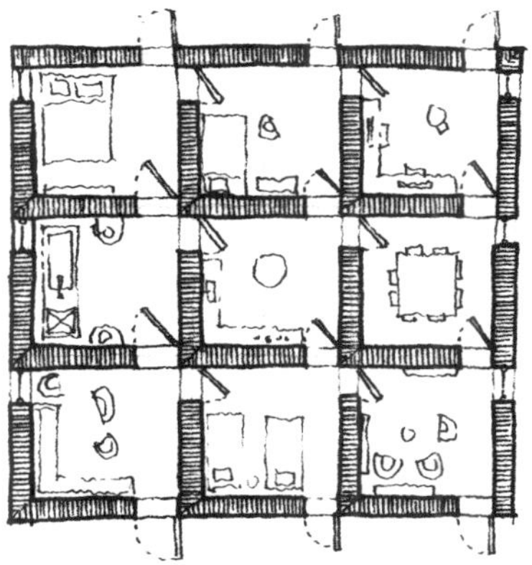

no.127

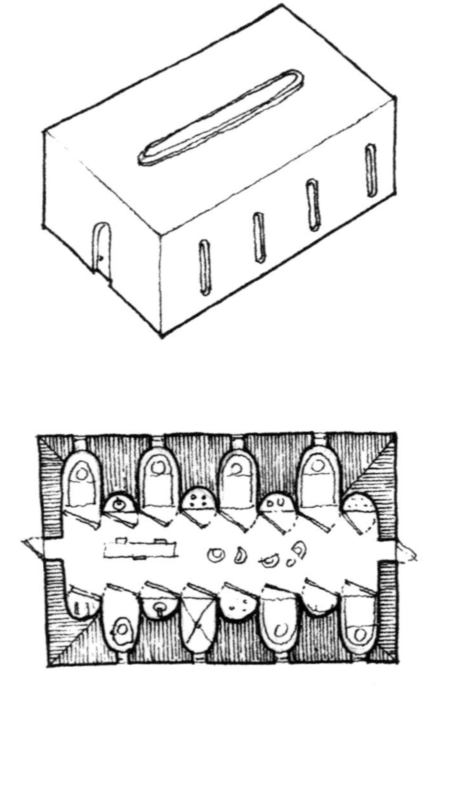

no.128

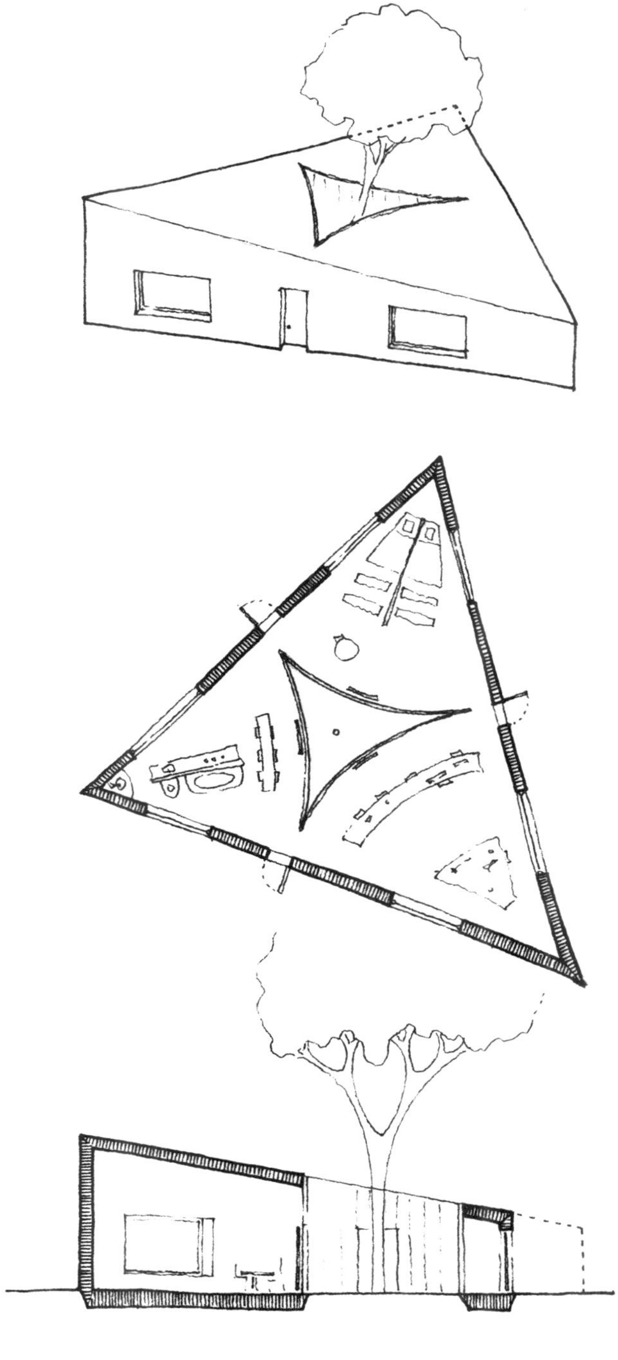

no.129

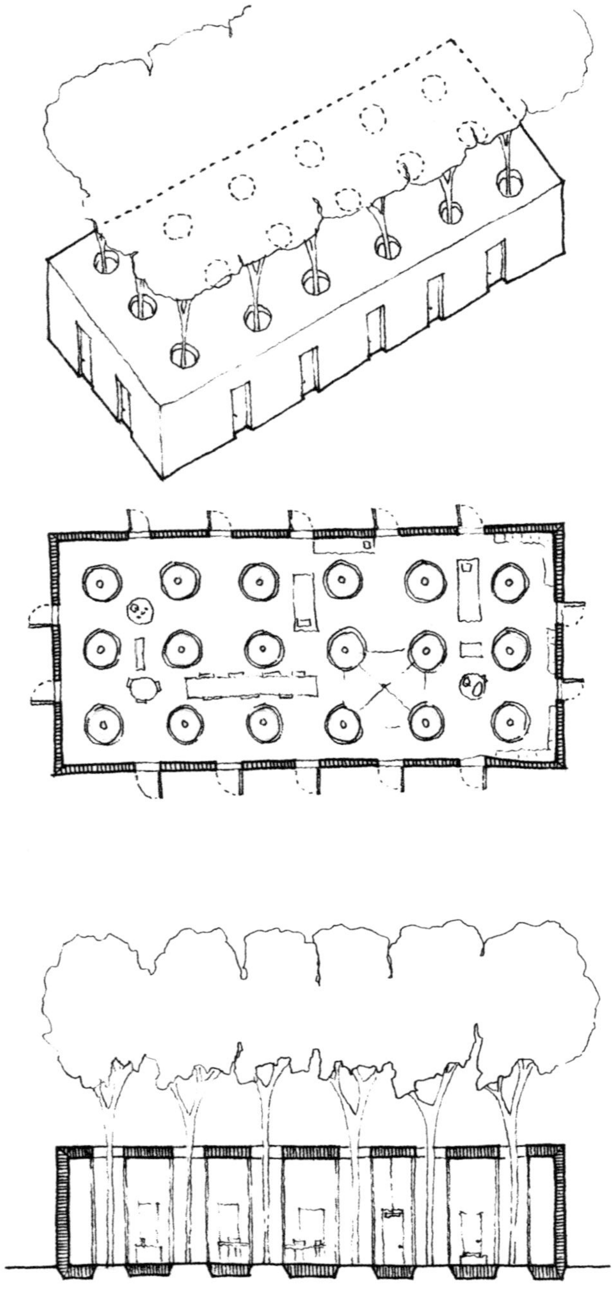

no.130

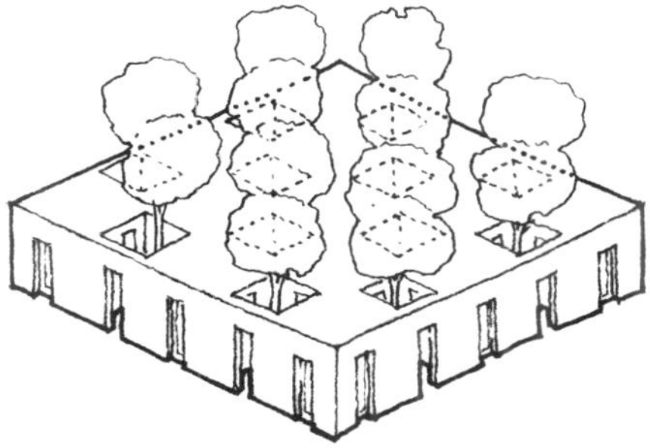

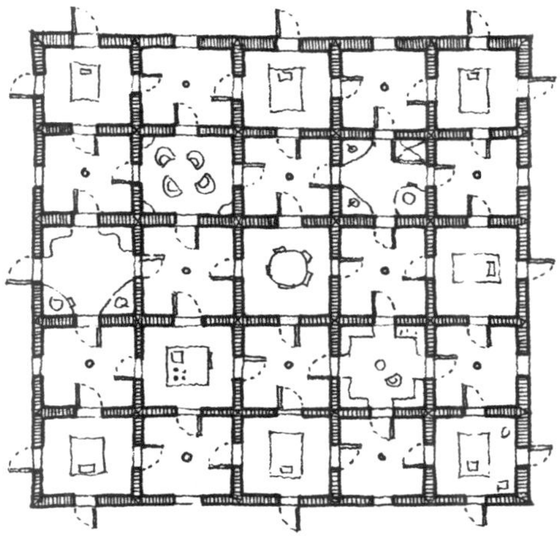

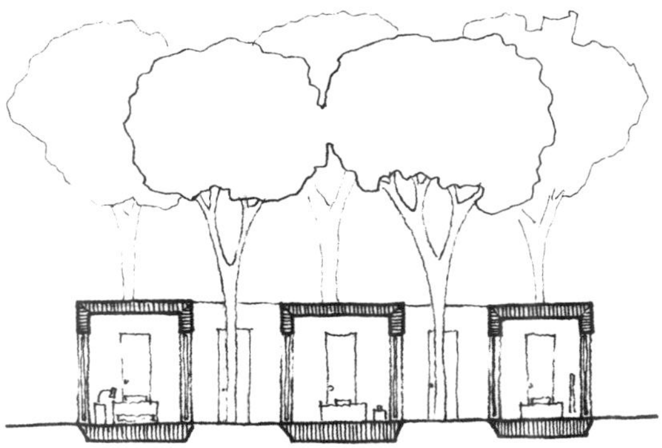

no.131

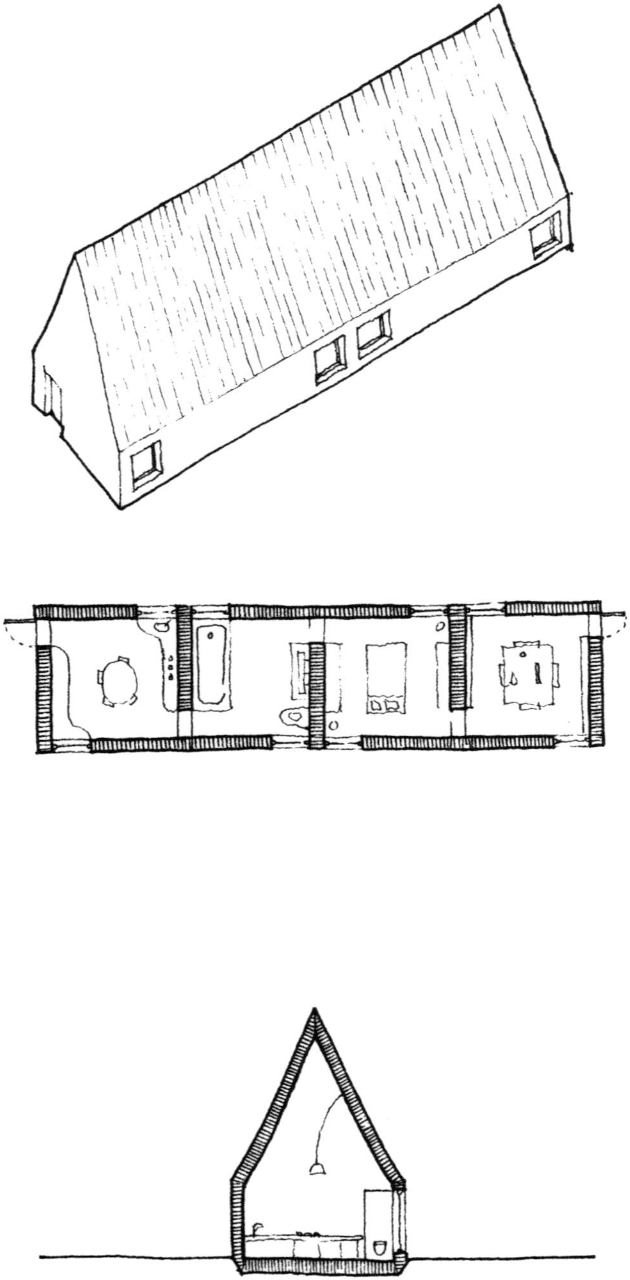

no.132

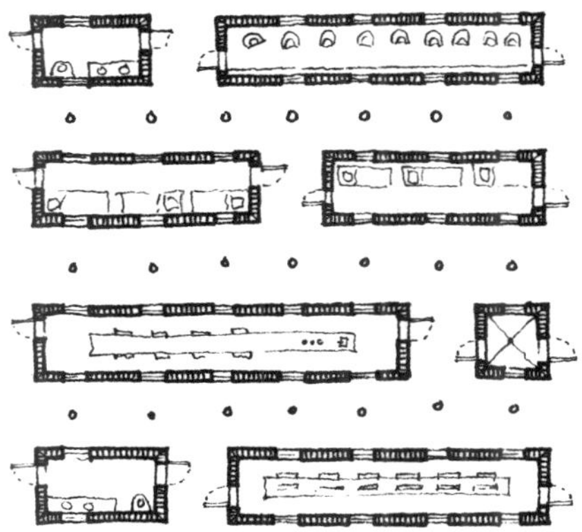

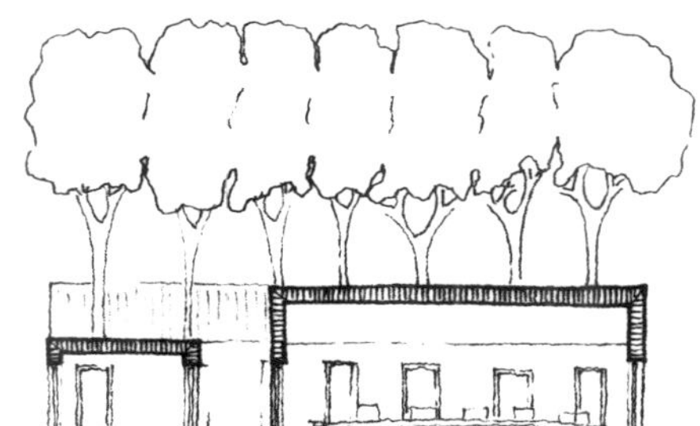

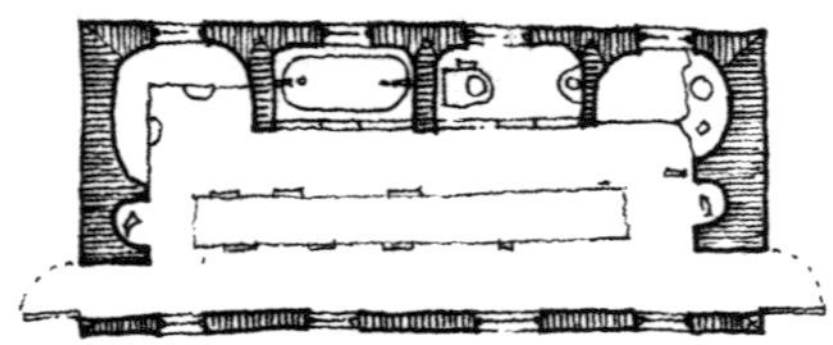

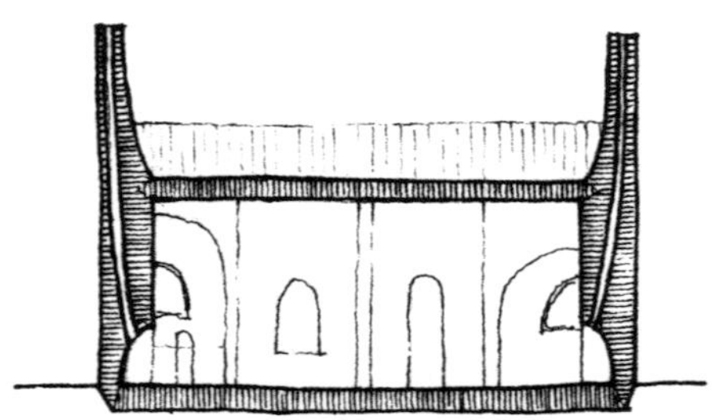

no.134

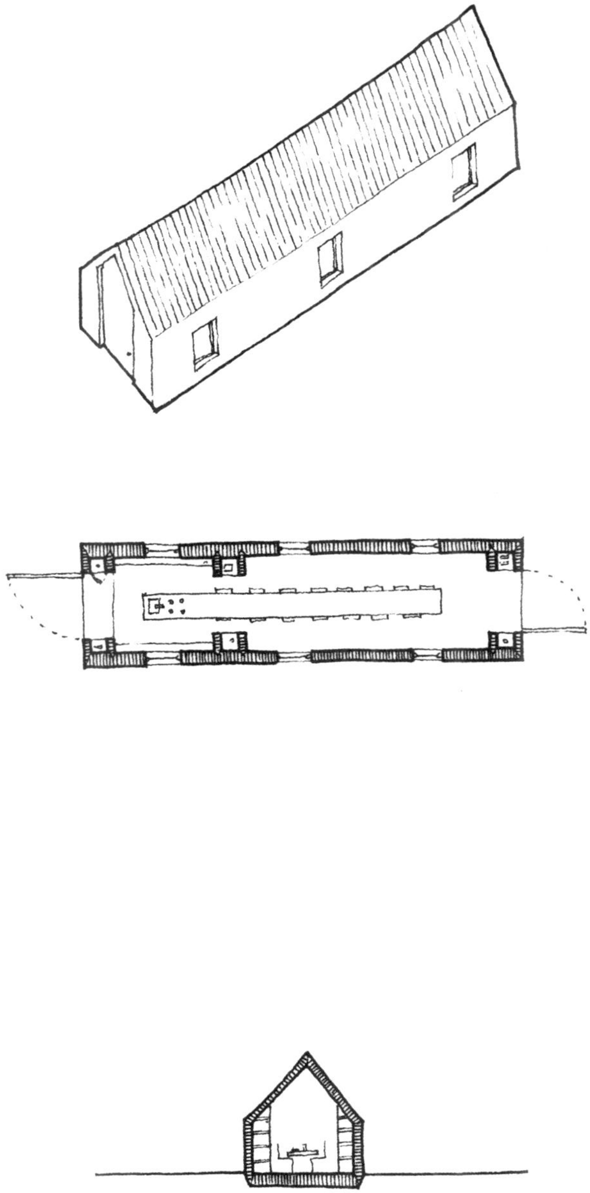

no.135

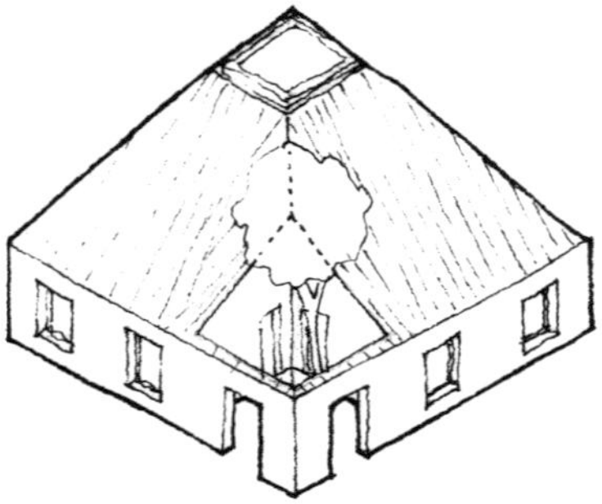

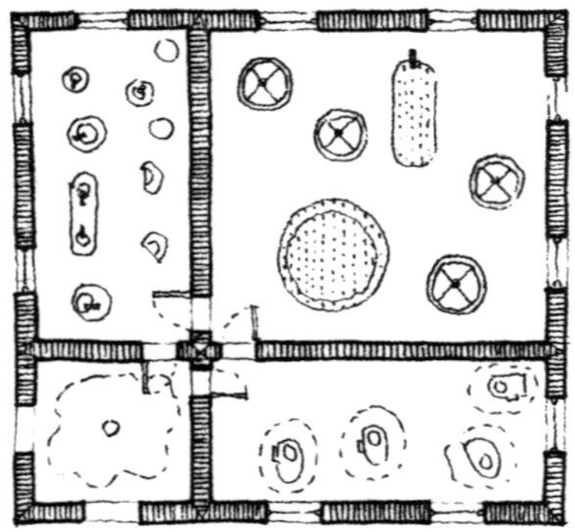

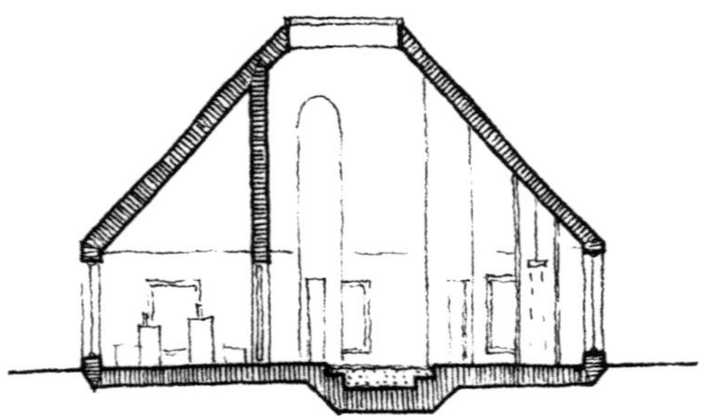

no.136

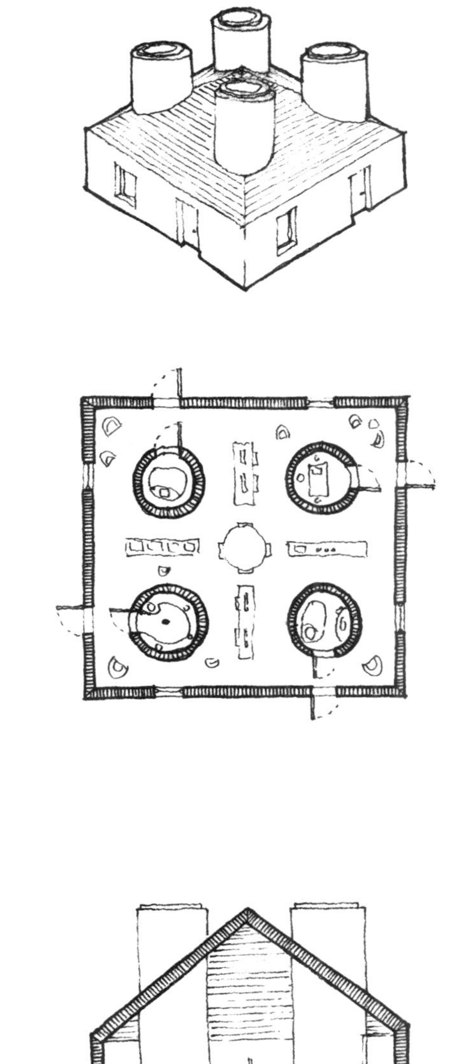

no.137

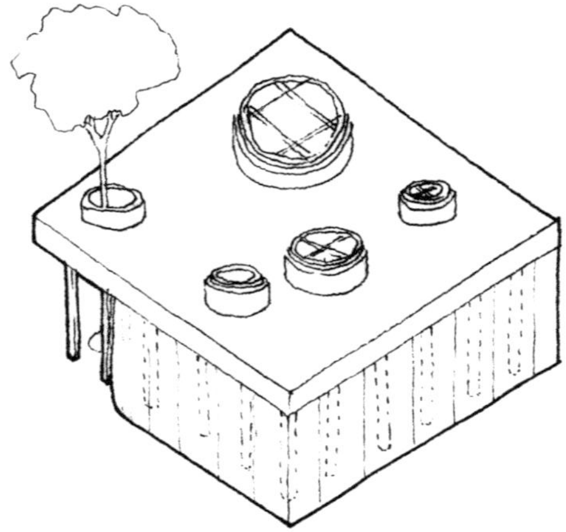

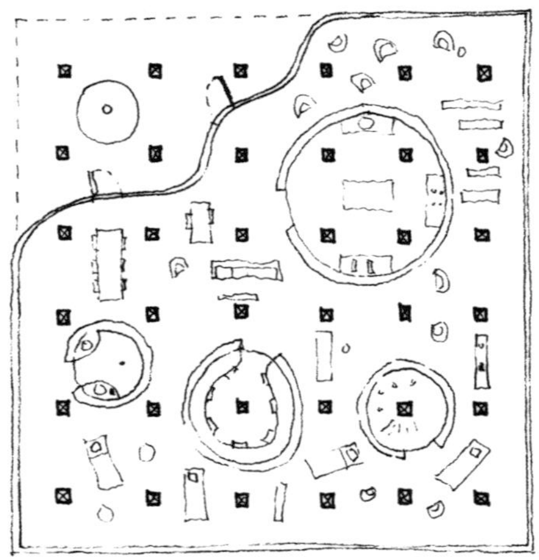

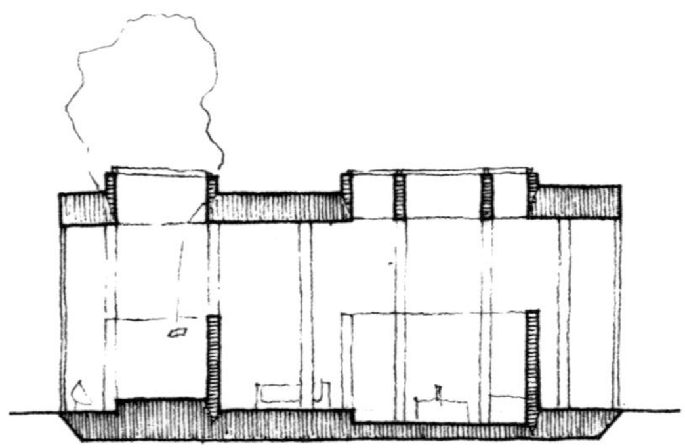

no.138

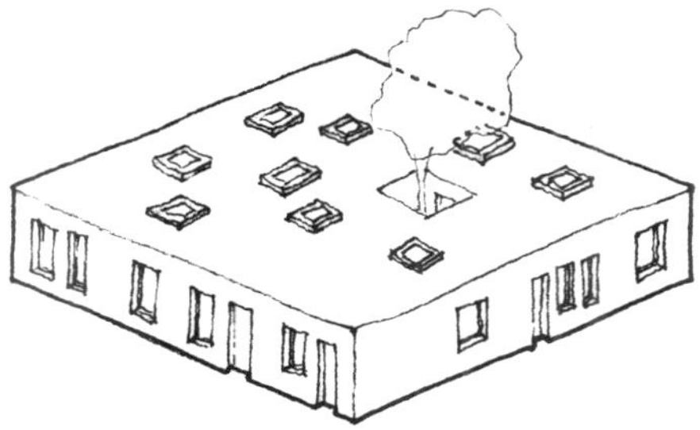

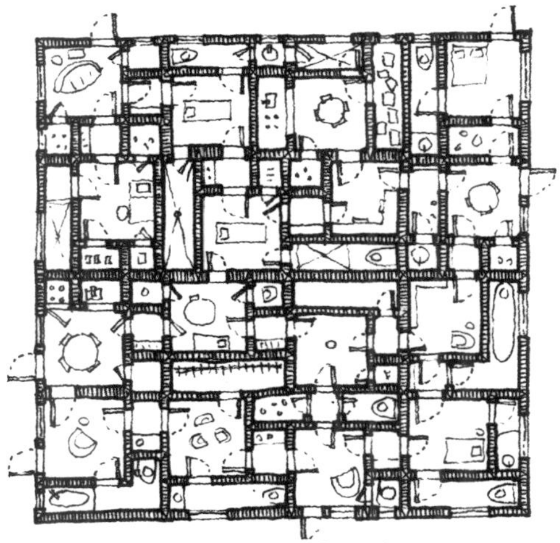

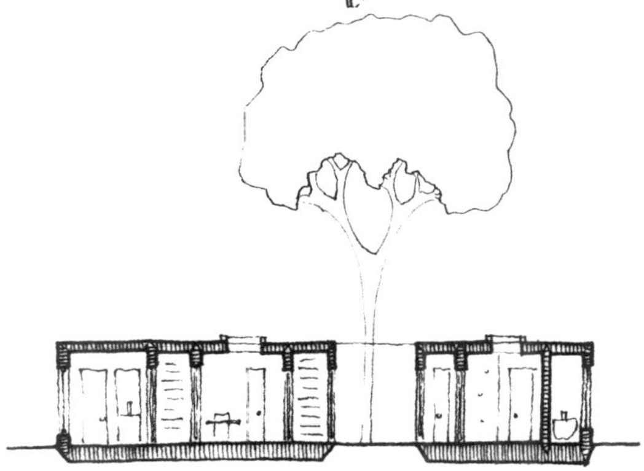

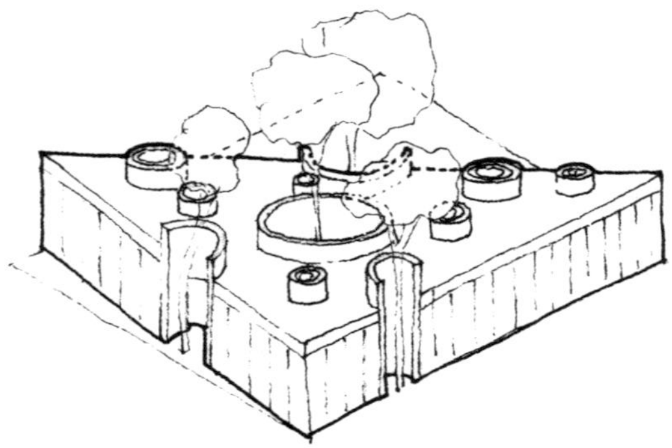

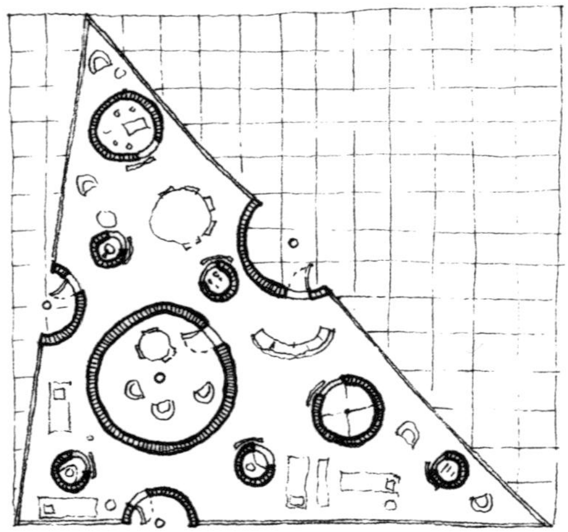

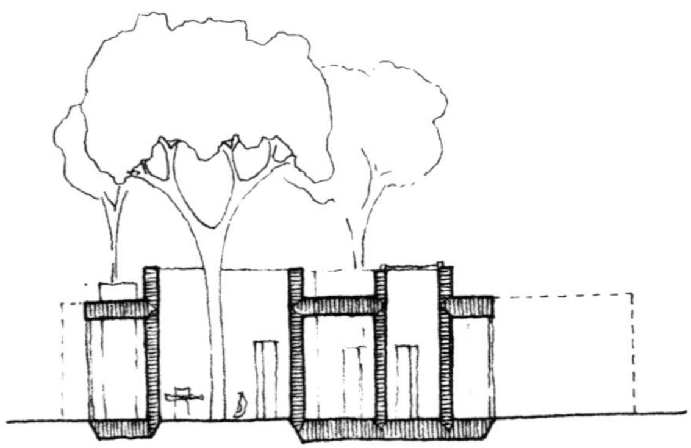

no.140

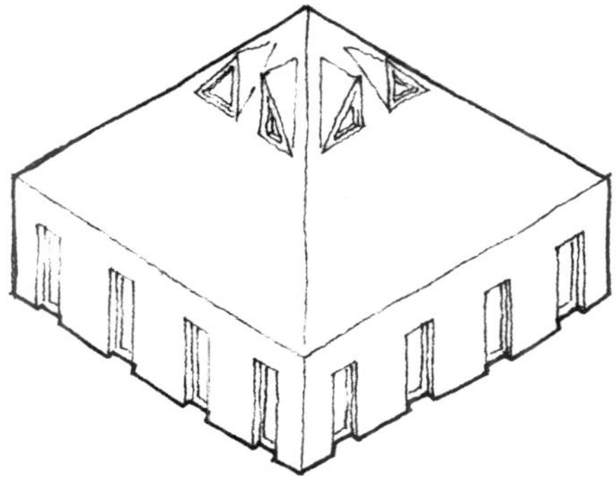

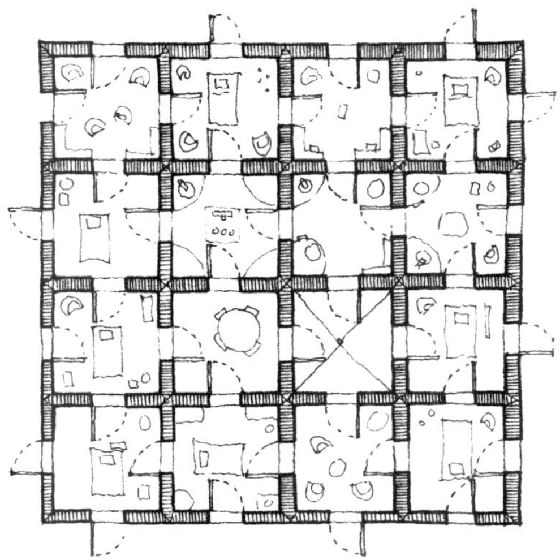

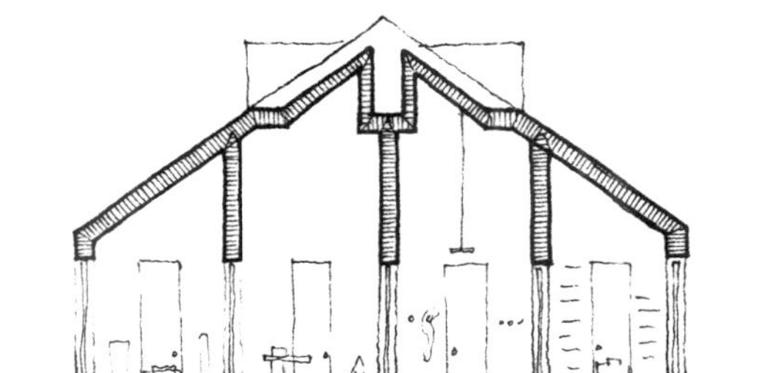

no.141

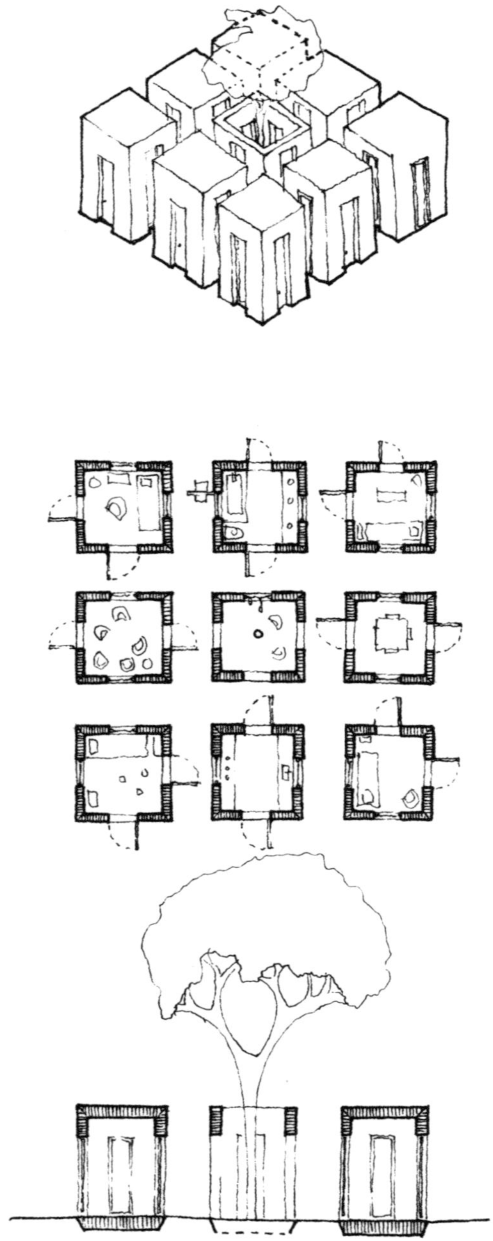

no.142

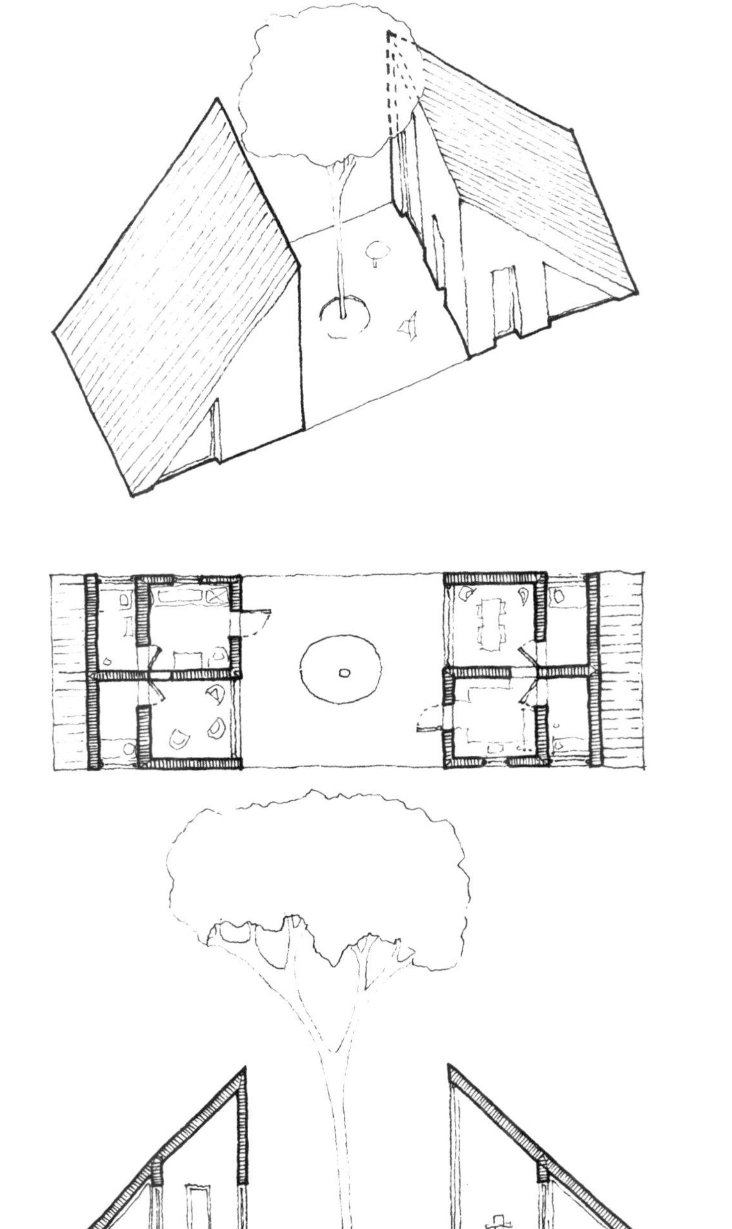

no.143

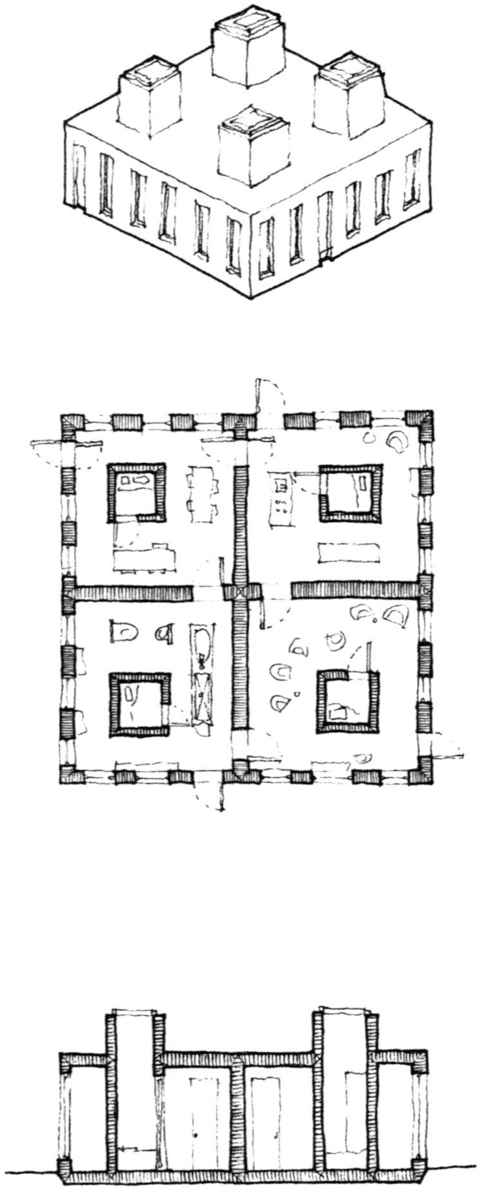

no.144

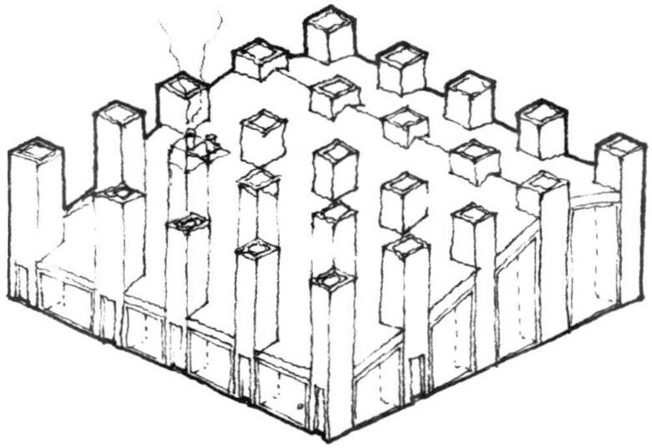

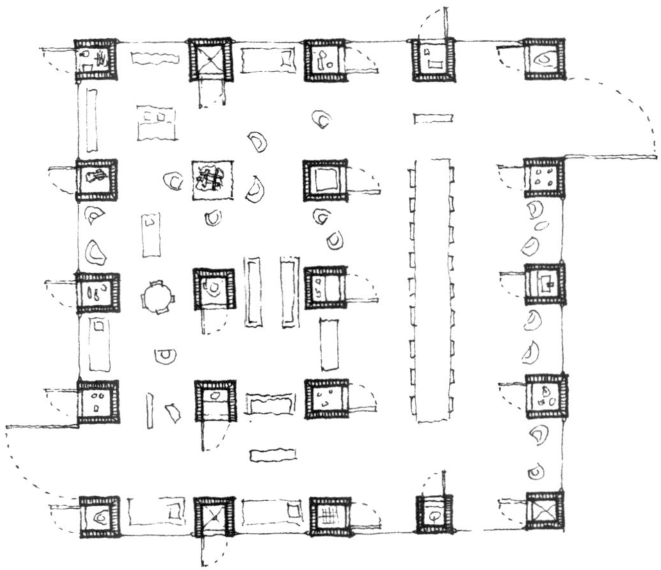

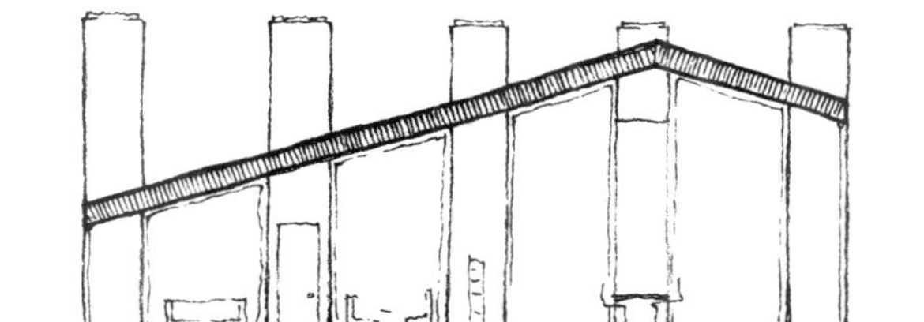

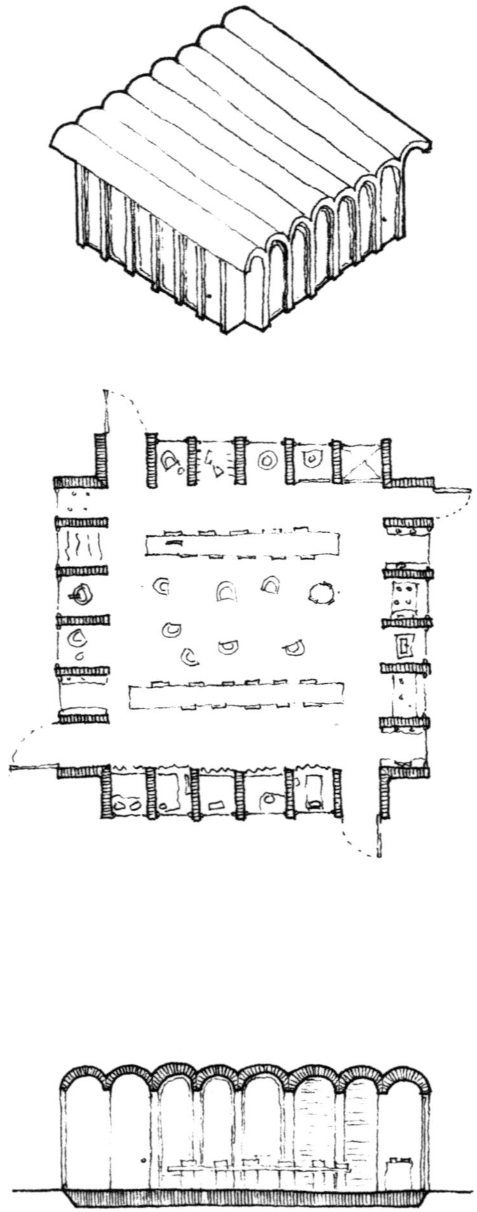

no.146

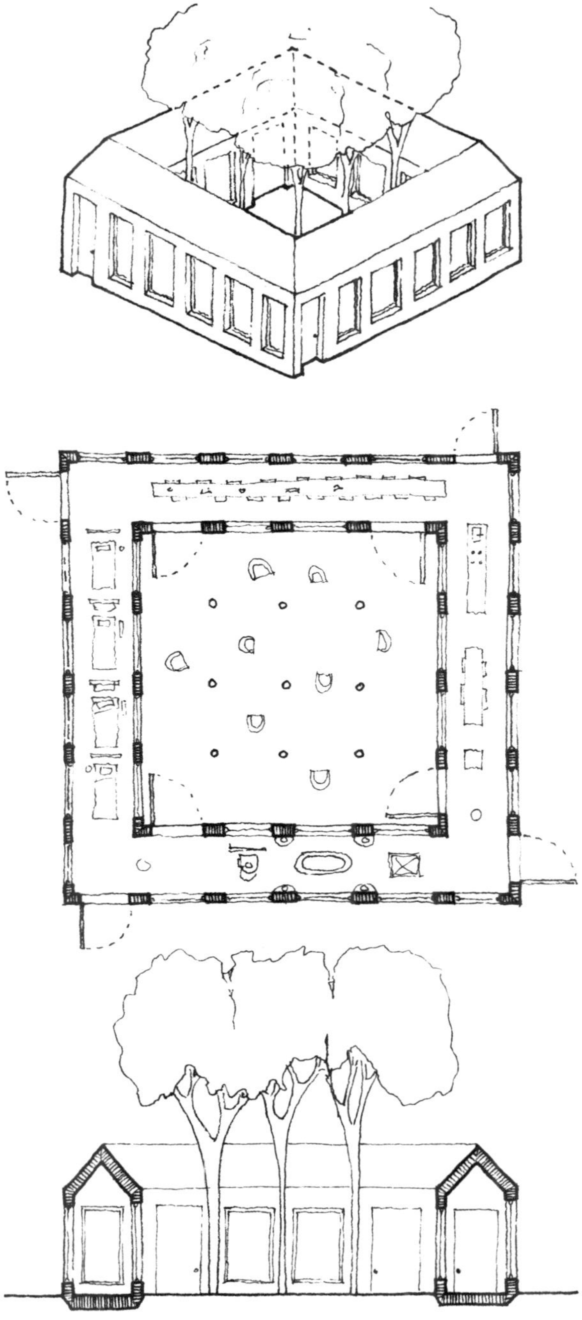

no.147

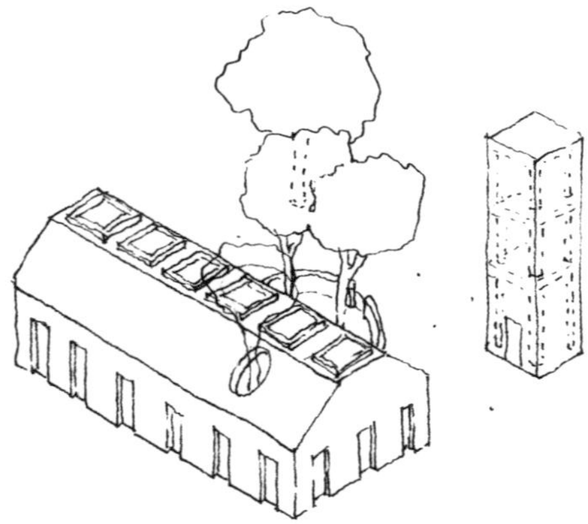

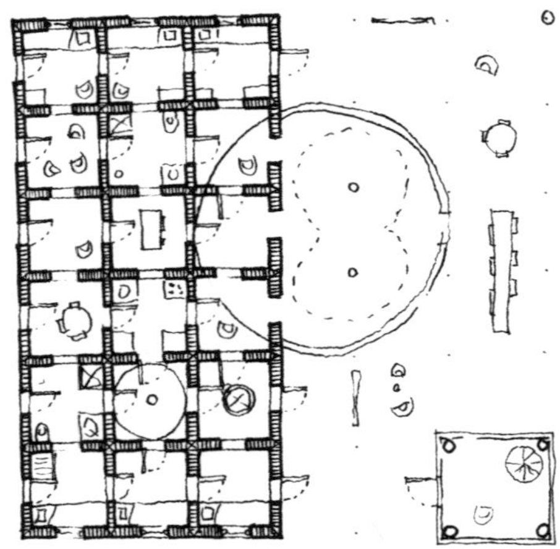

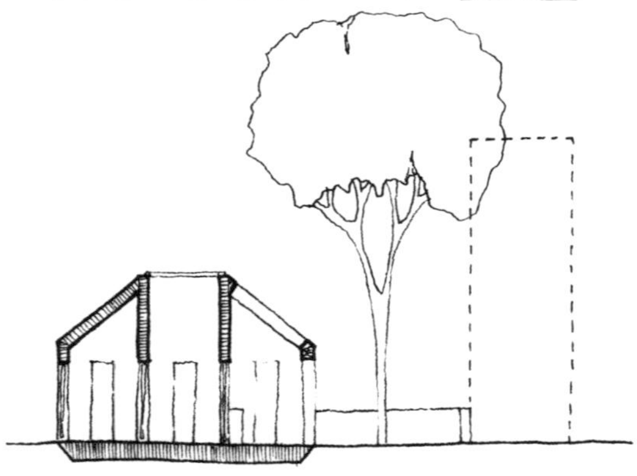

no.148

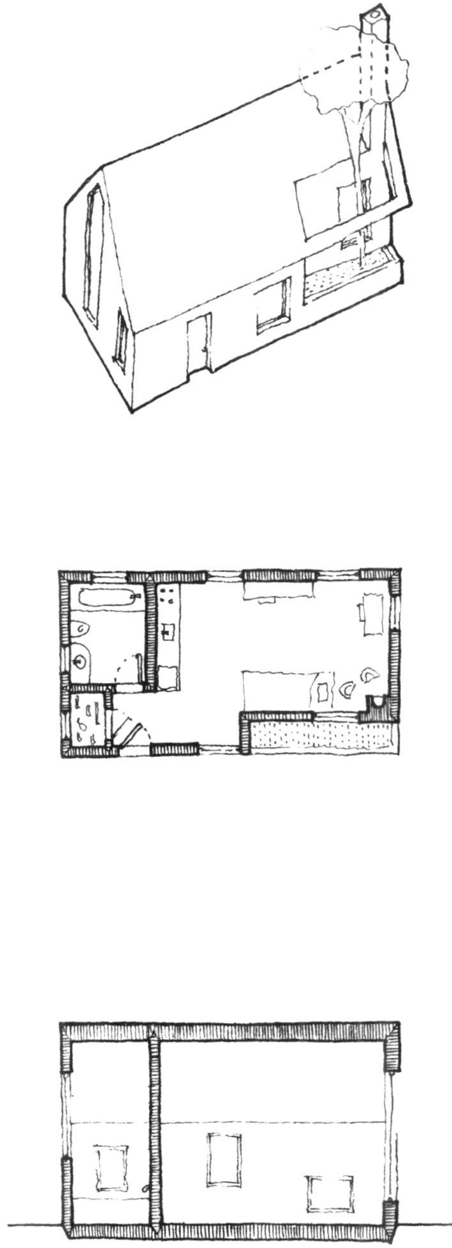

no.149

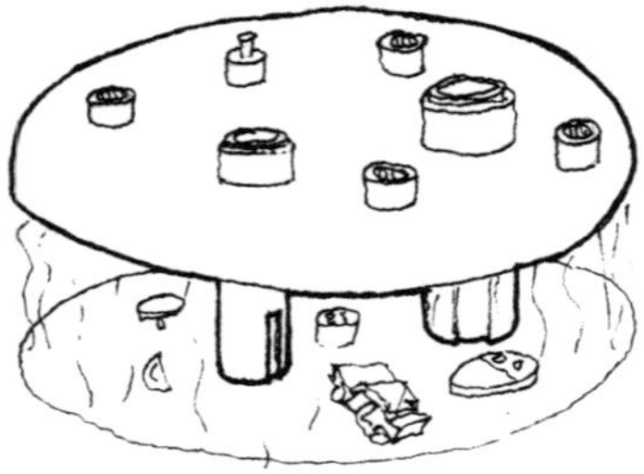

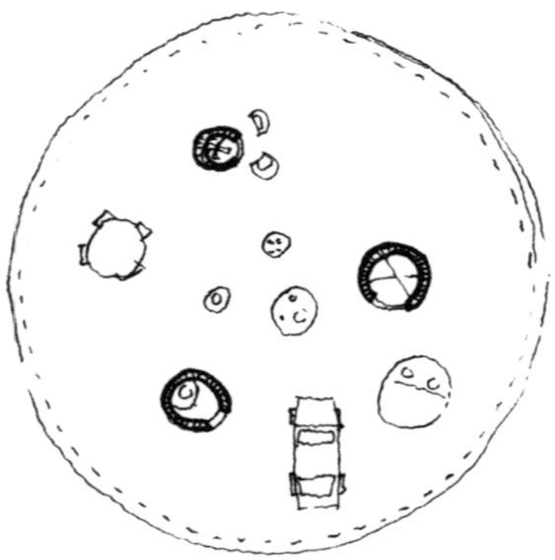

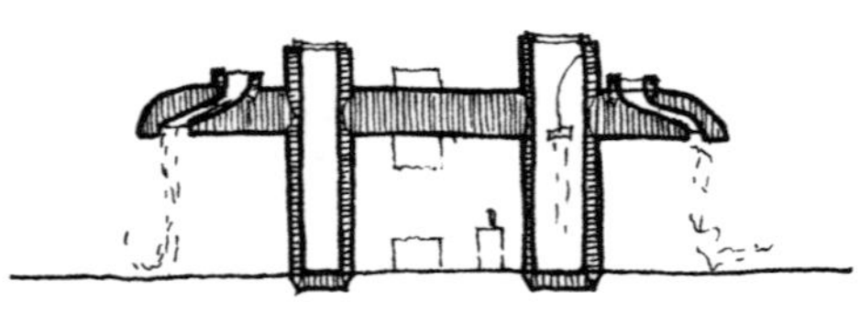

no.150

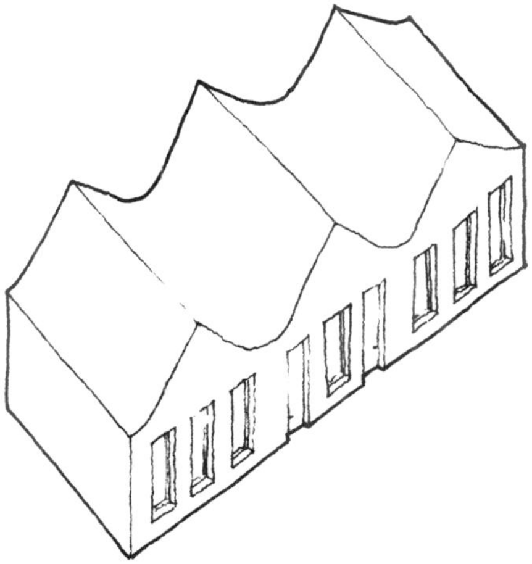

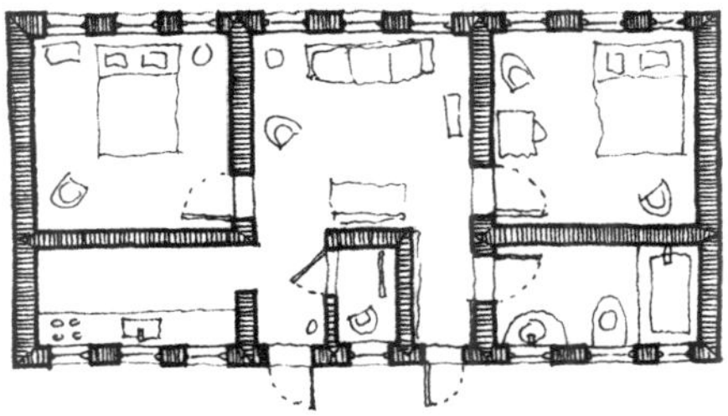

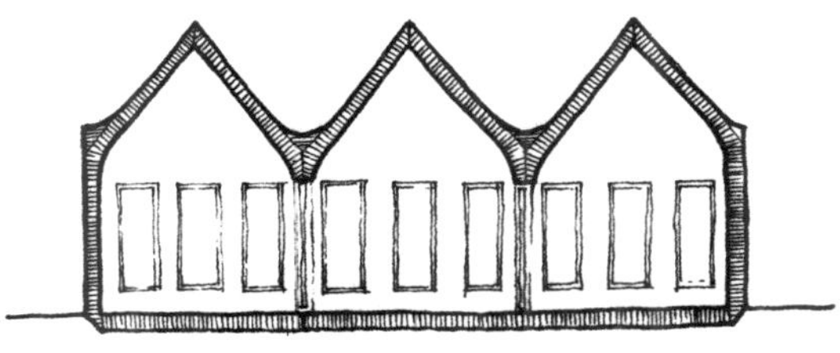

no.151

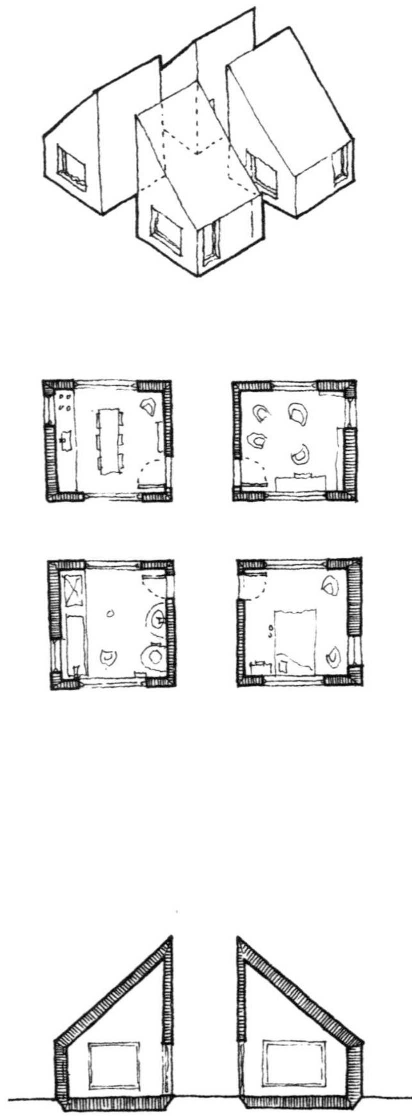

no.152

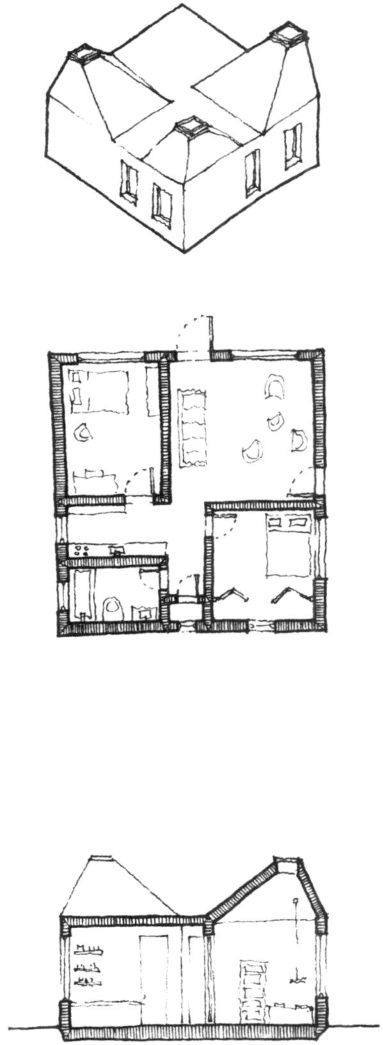

no.153

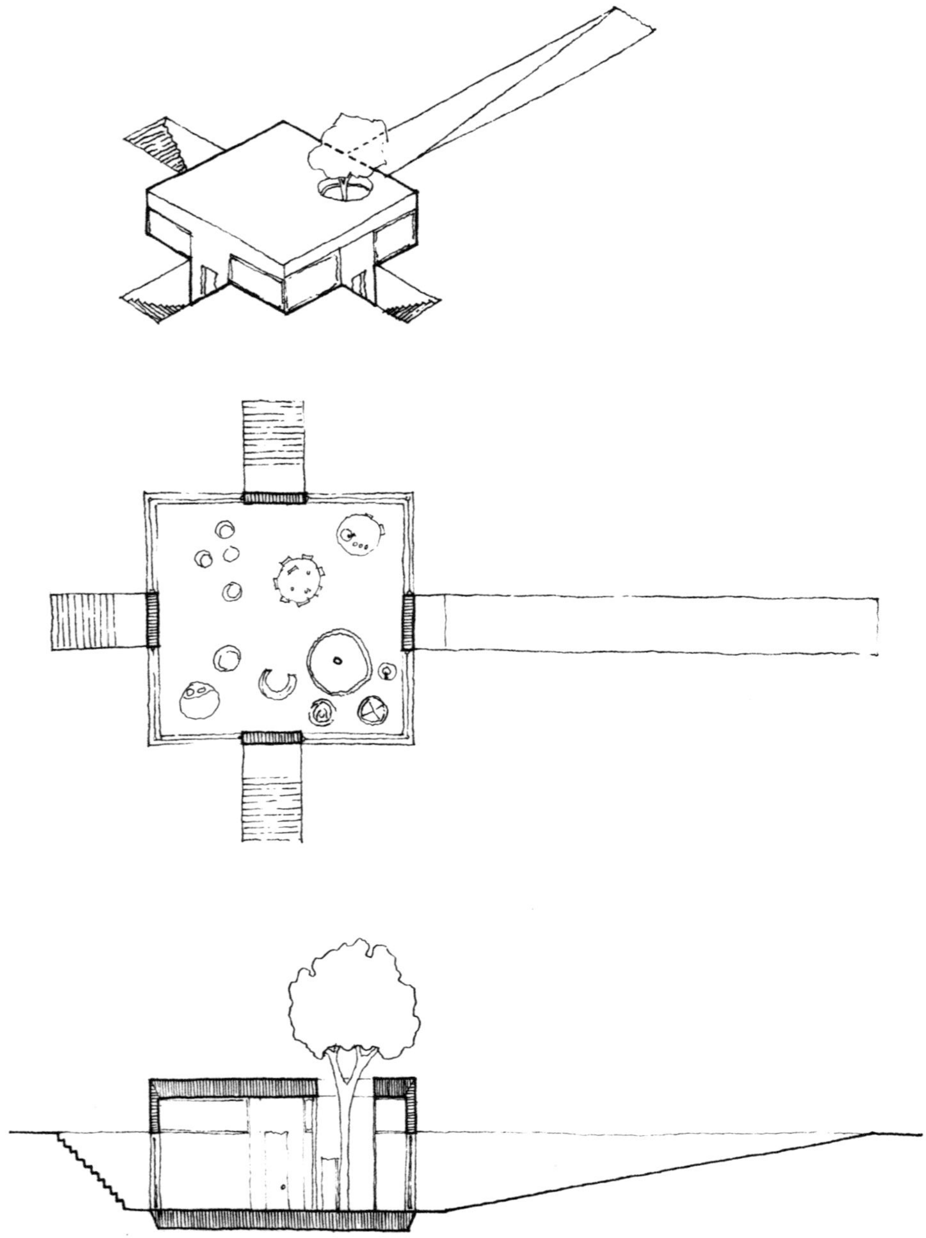

no.154

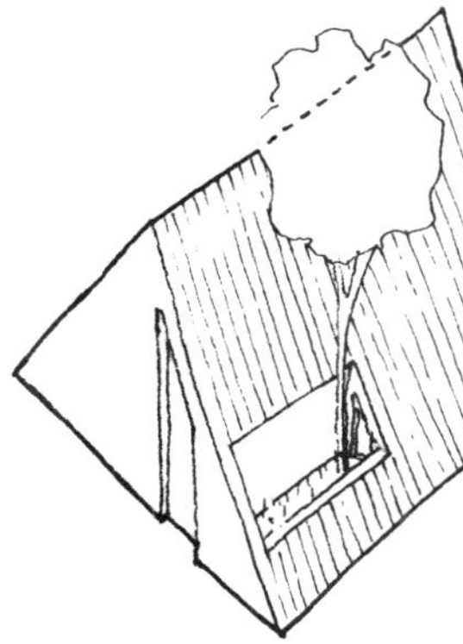

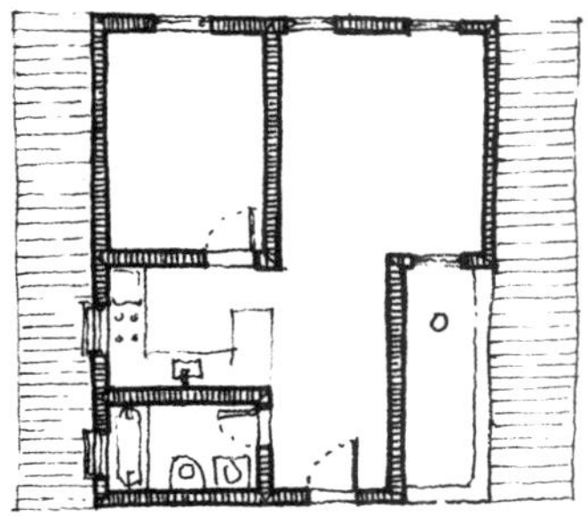

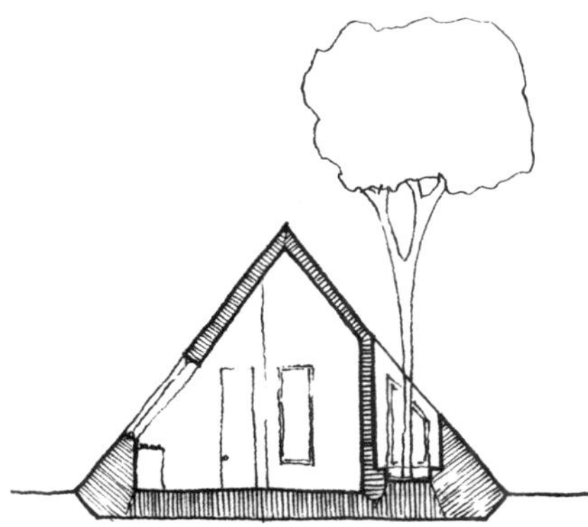

no.155

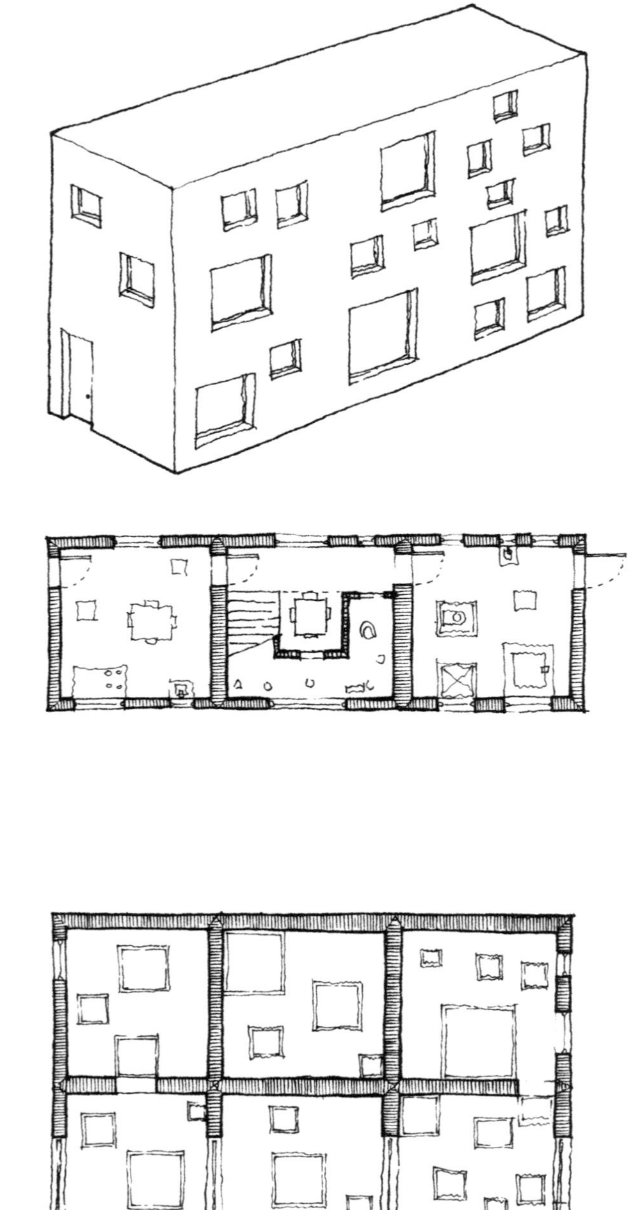

no.156

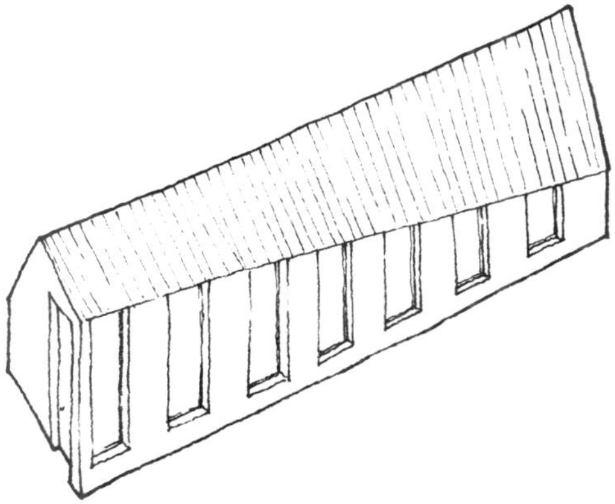

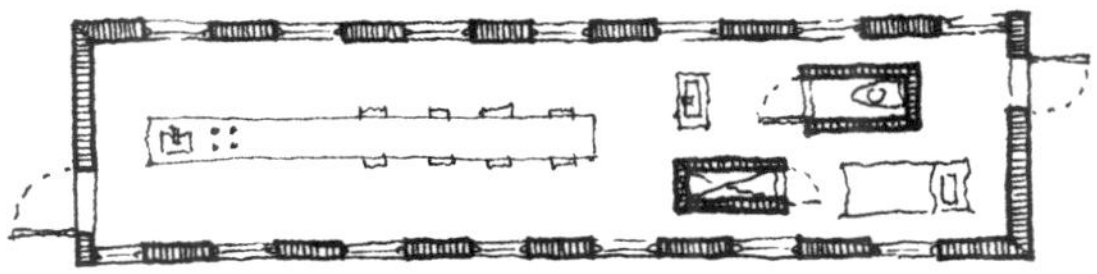

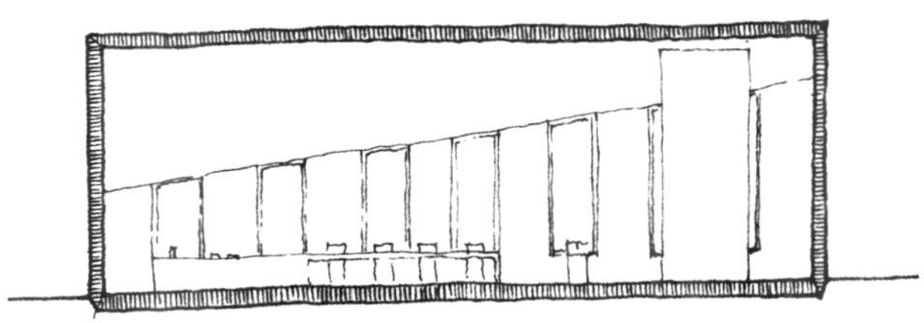

no.157

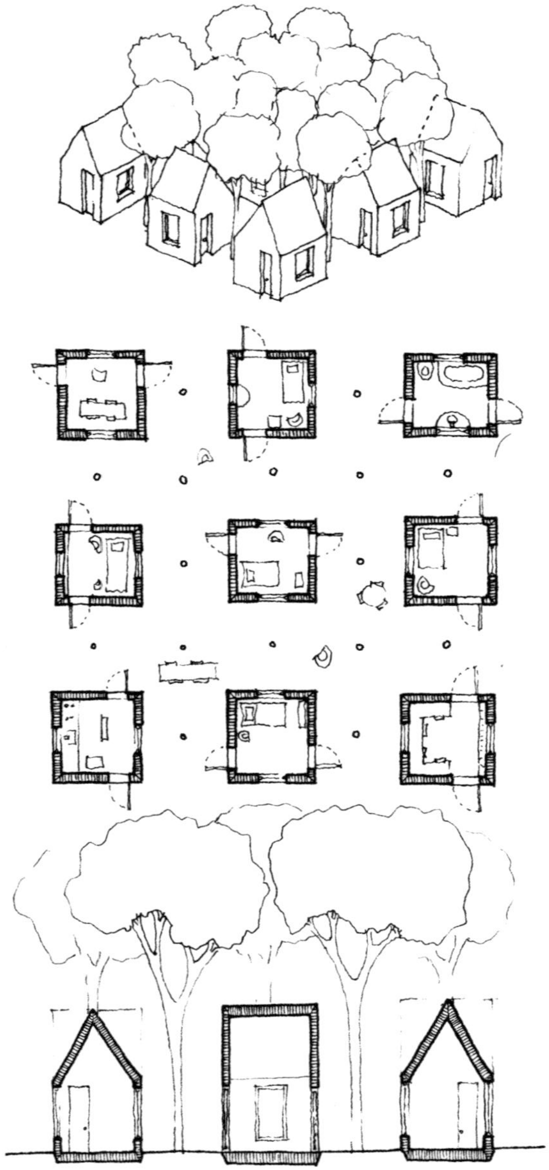

no.158

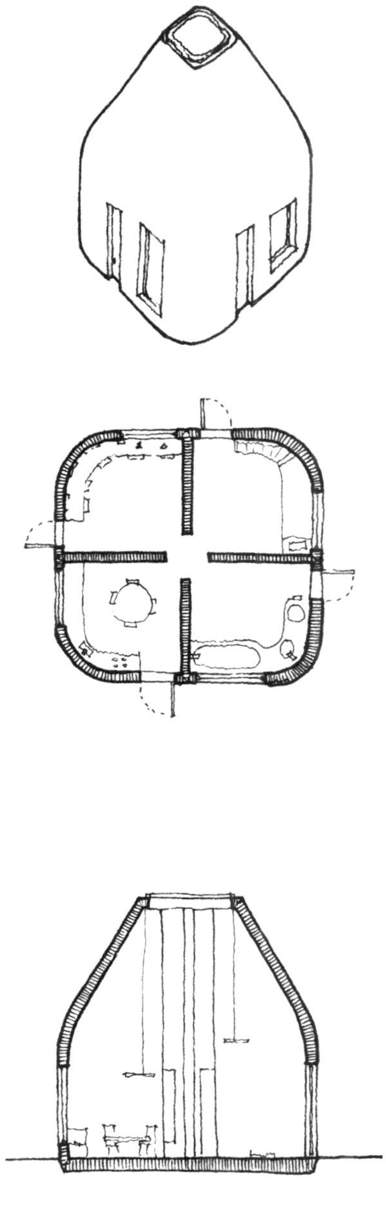

no.159

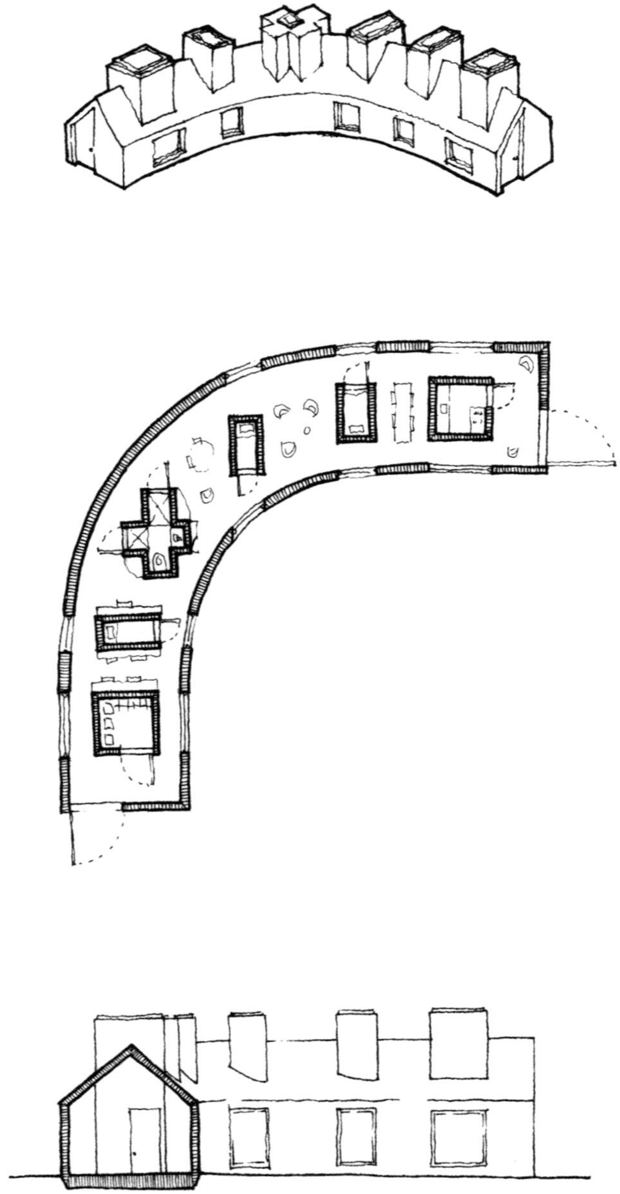

no.160

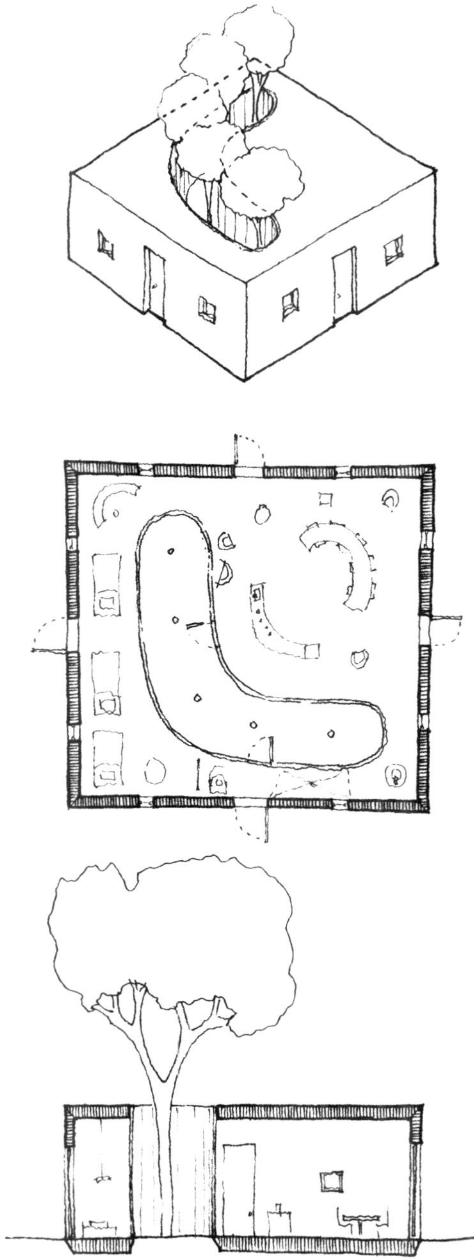

no.161

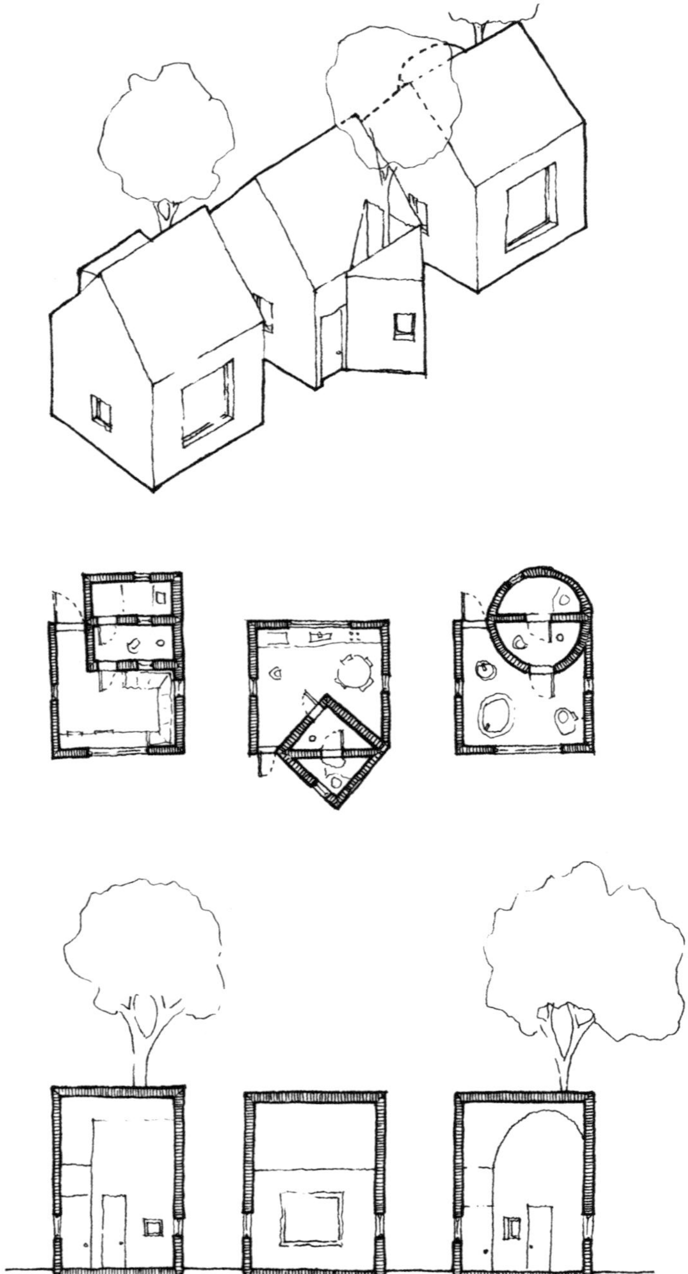

no.162

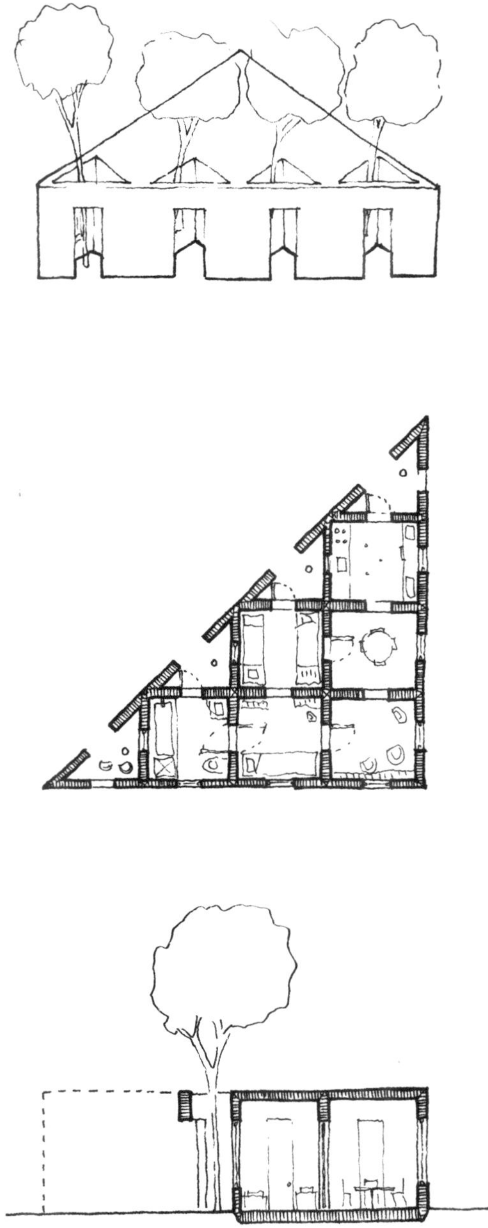

no.163

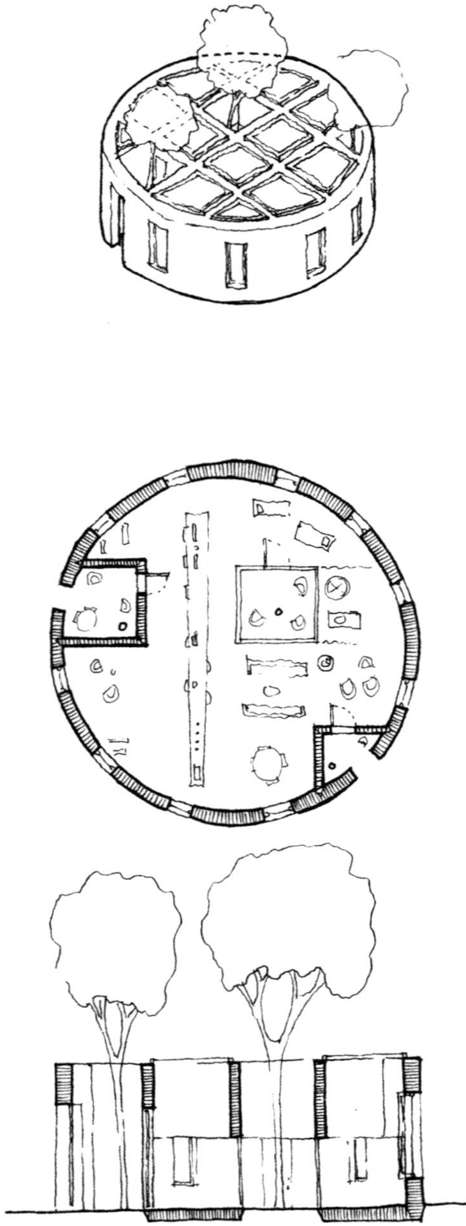

no.164

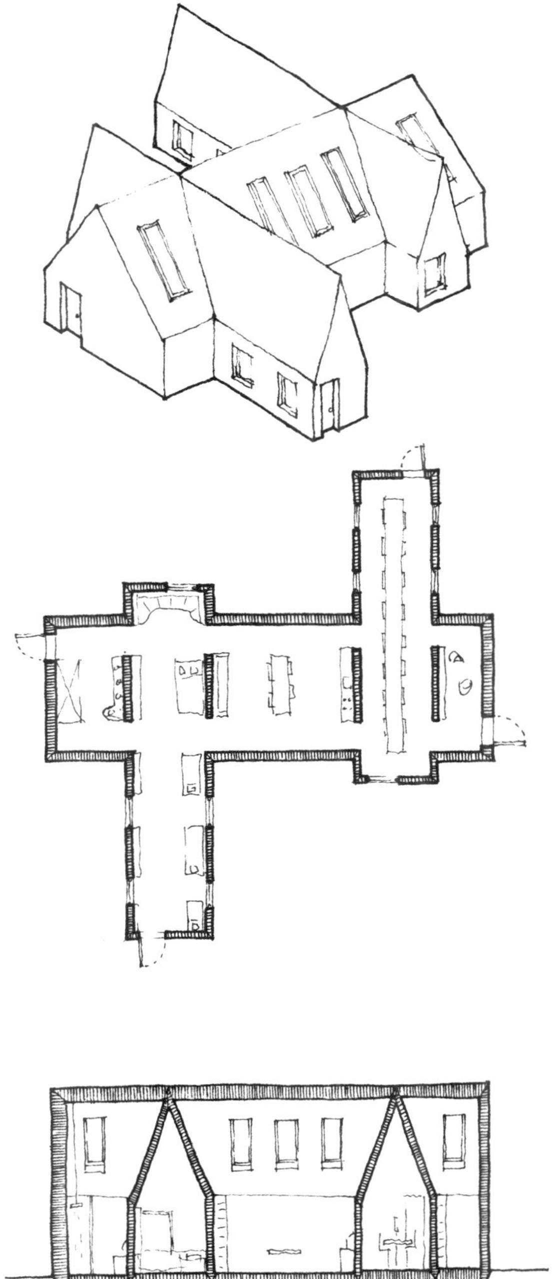

no.165

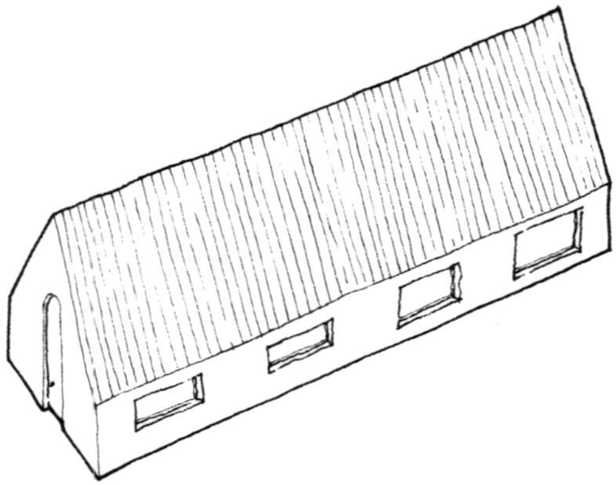

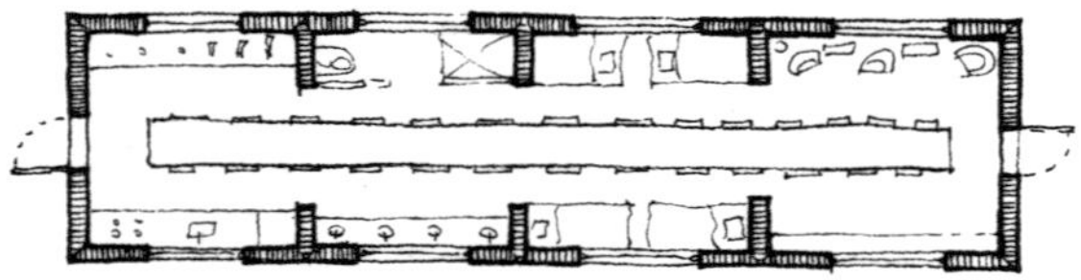

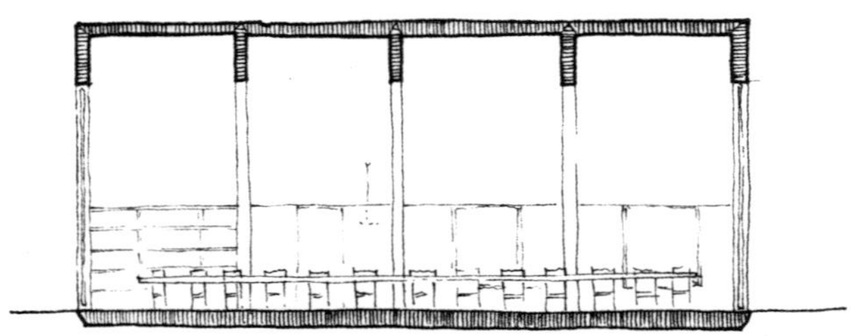

no.166

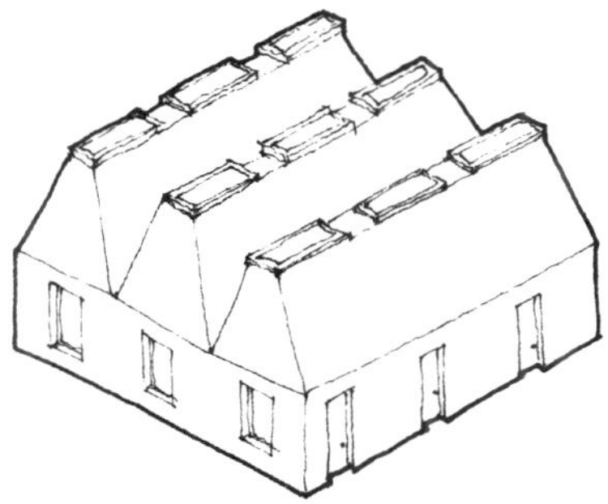

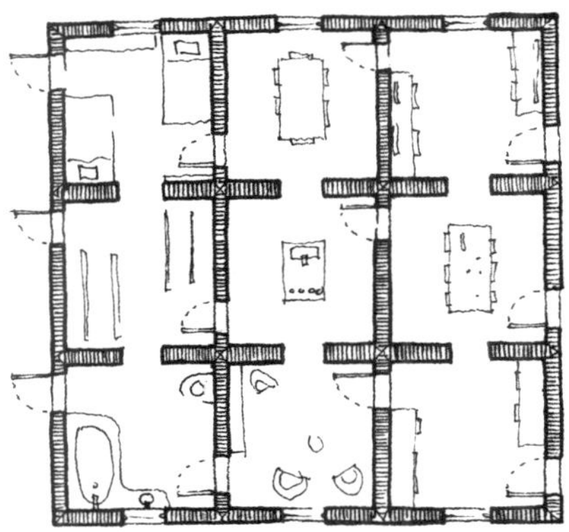

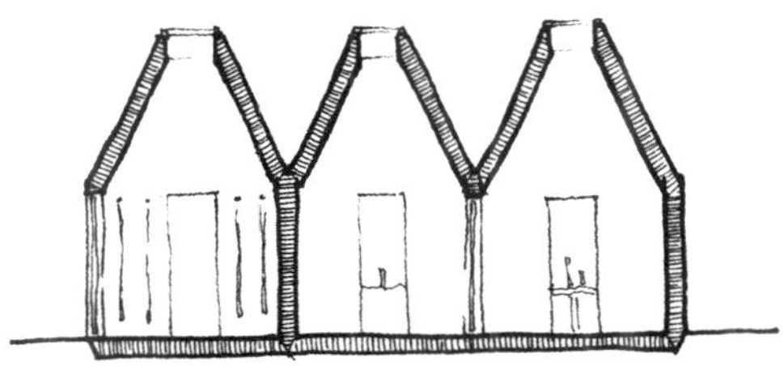

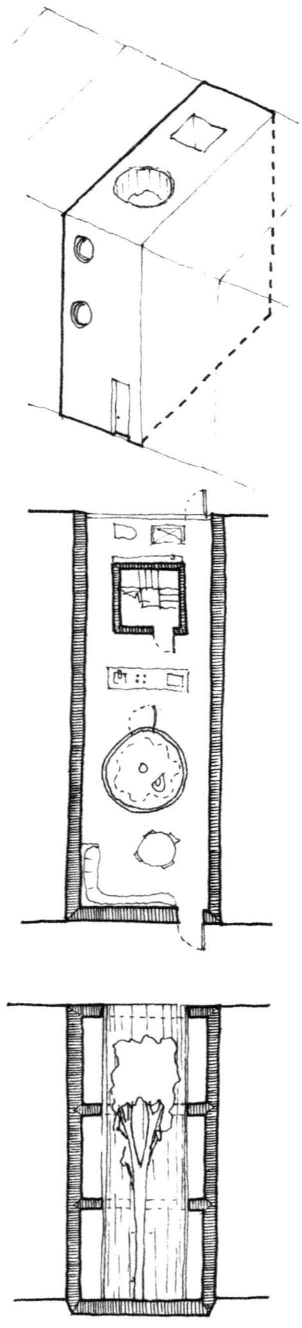

no.168

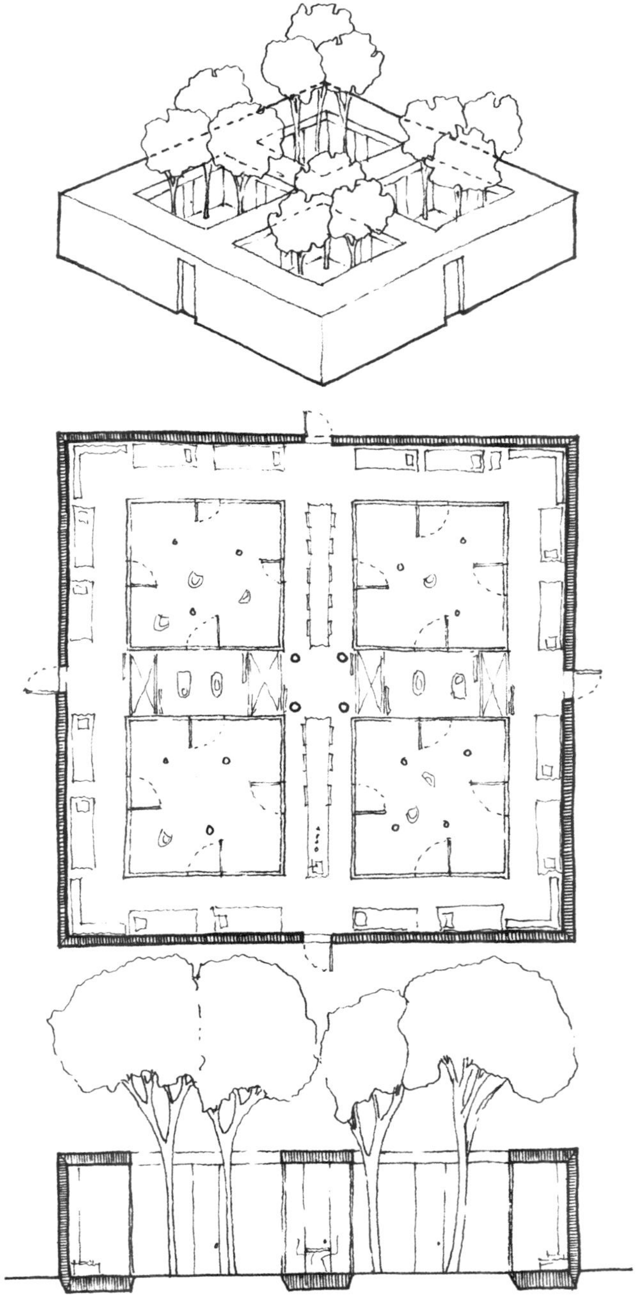

no.169

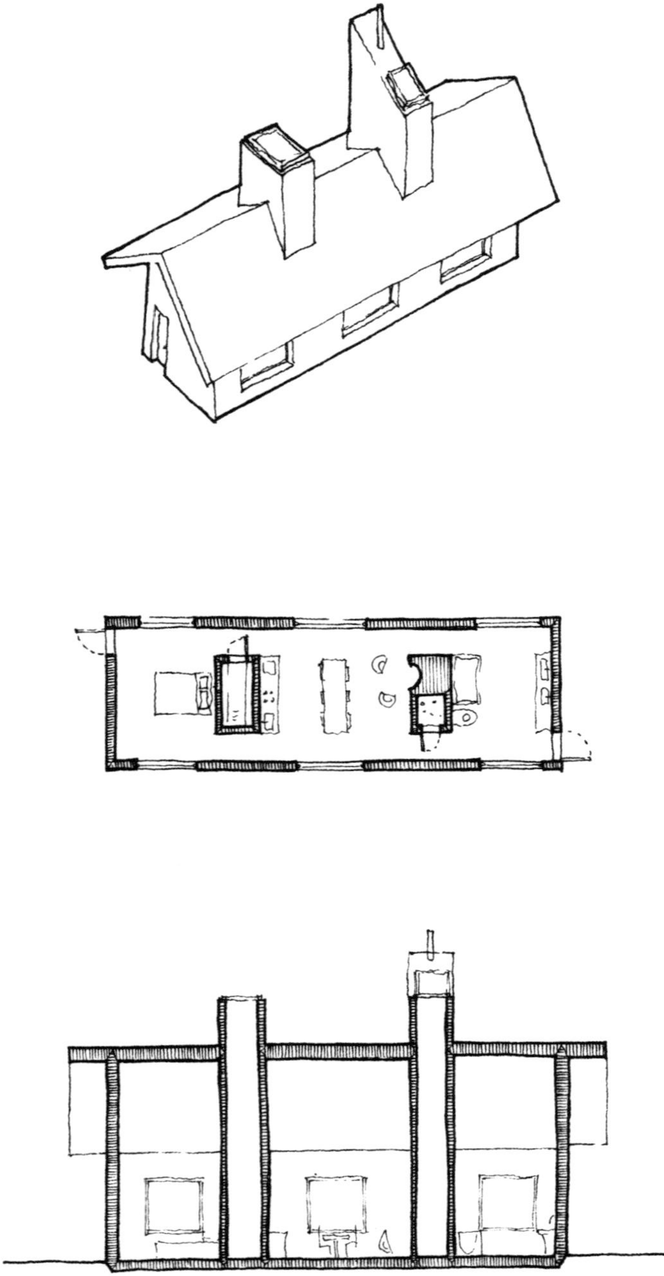

no.170

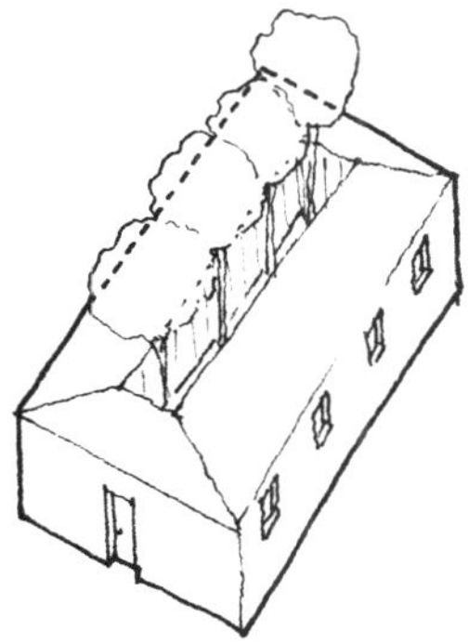

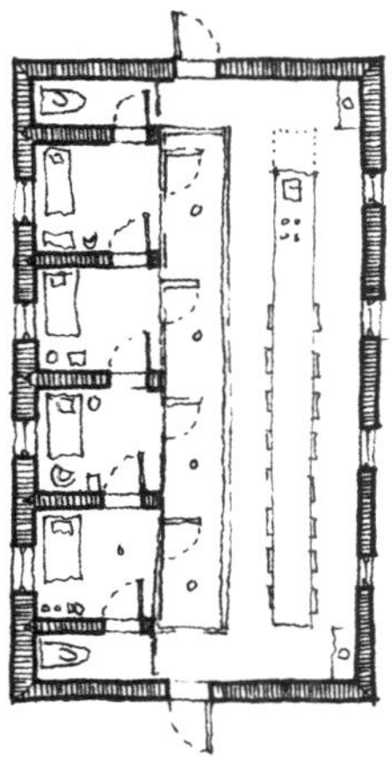

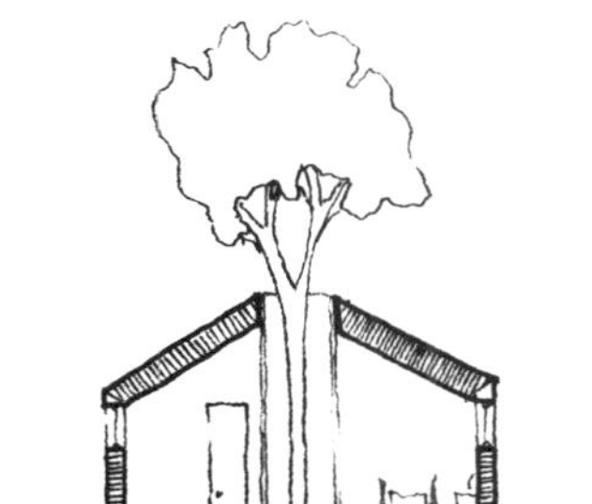

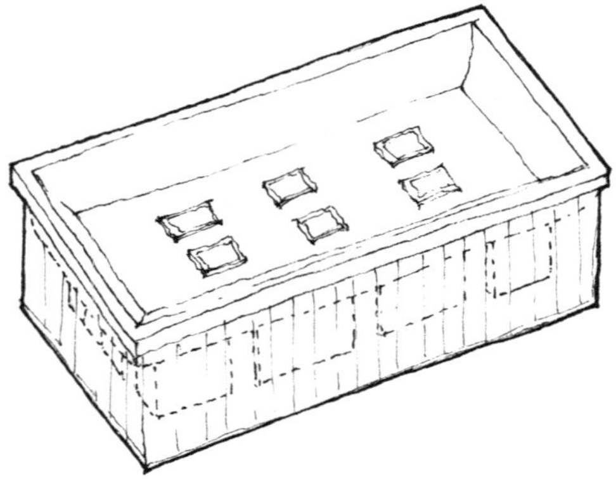

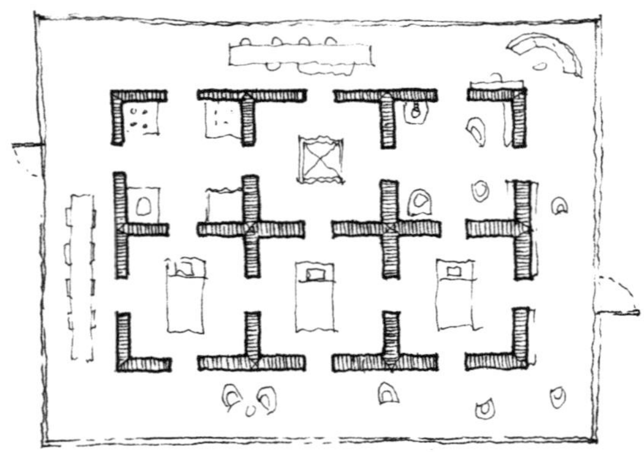

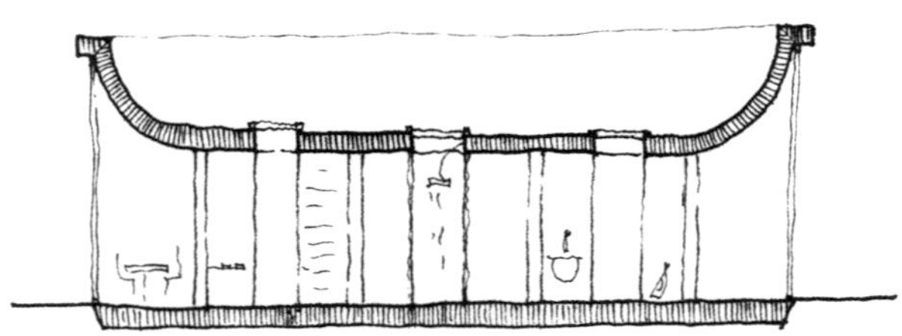

no.172

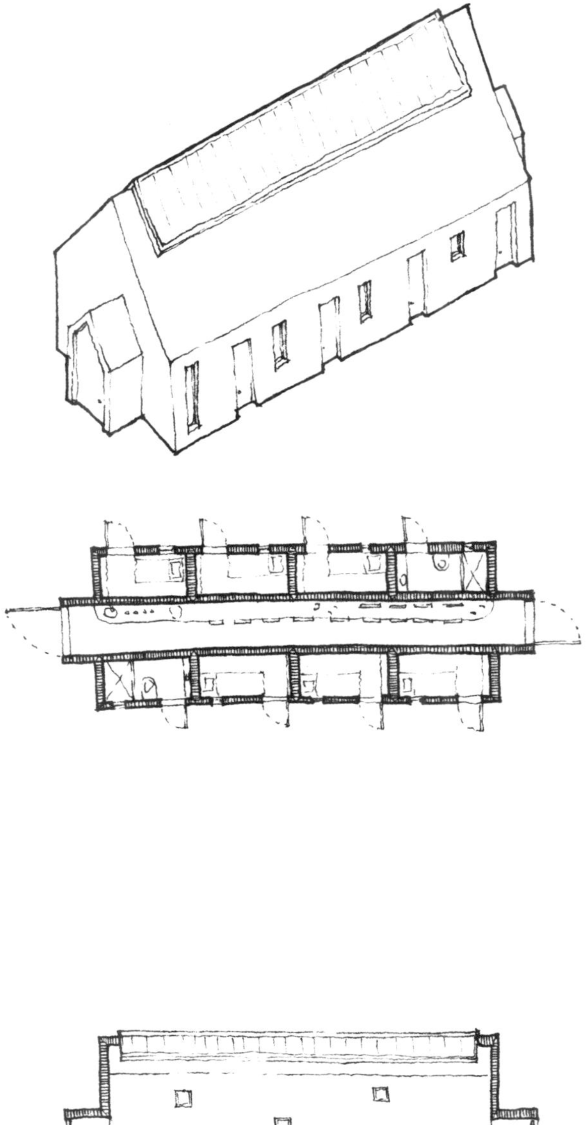

no.173

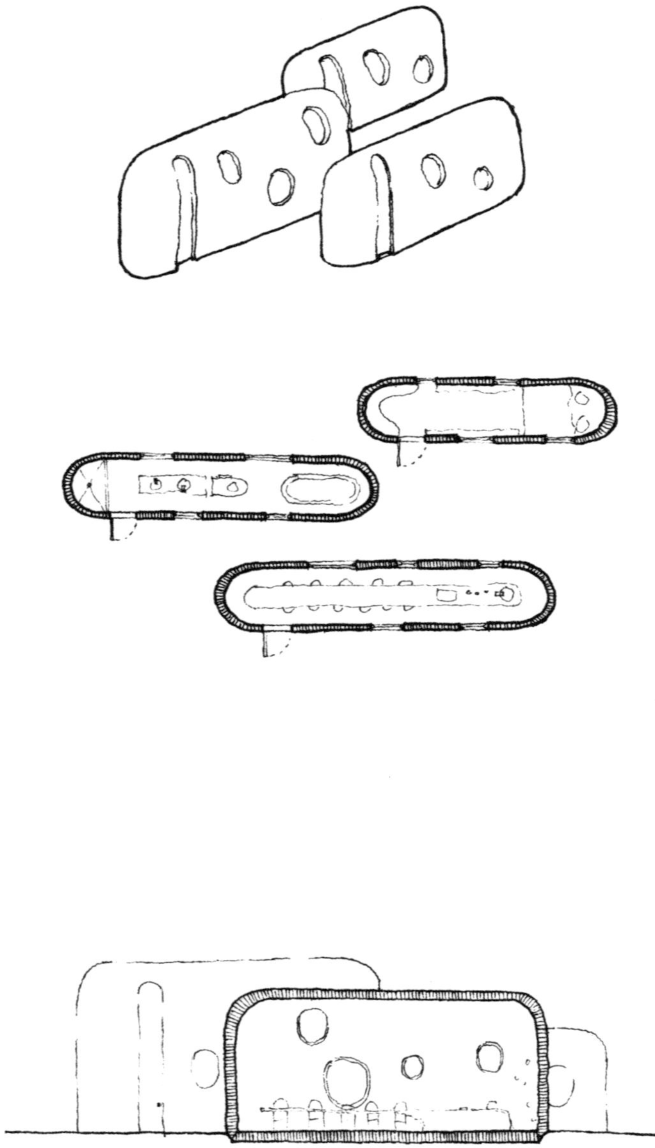

no.174

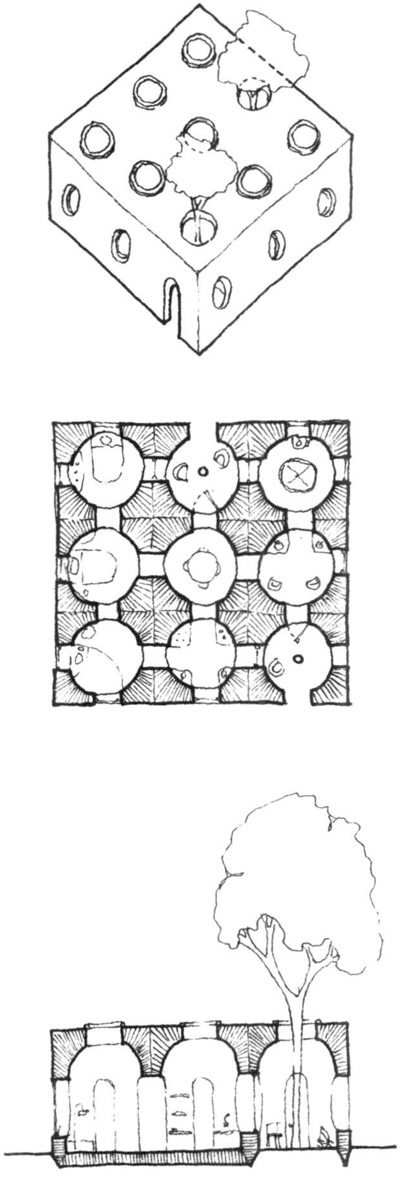

no.175

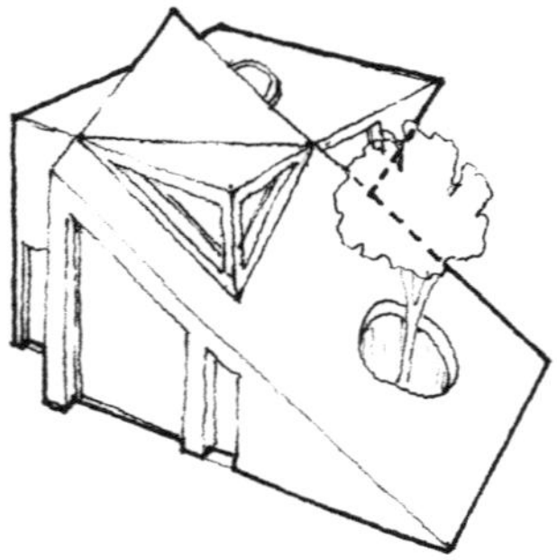

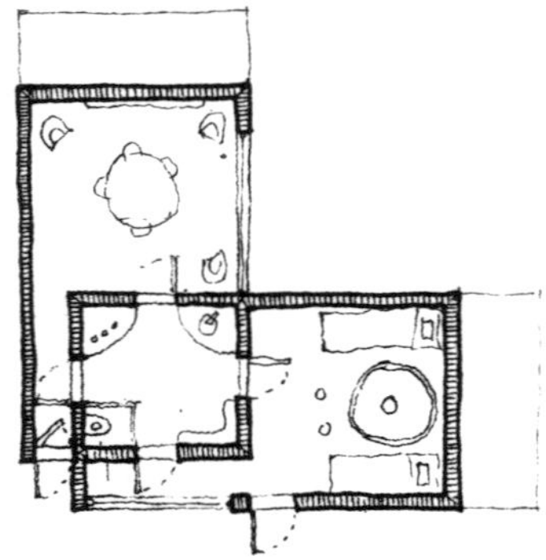

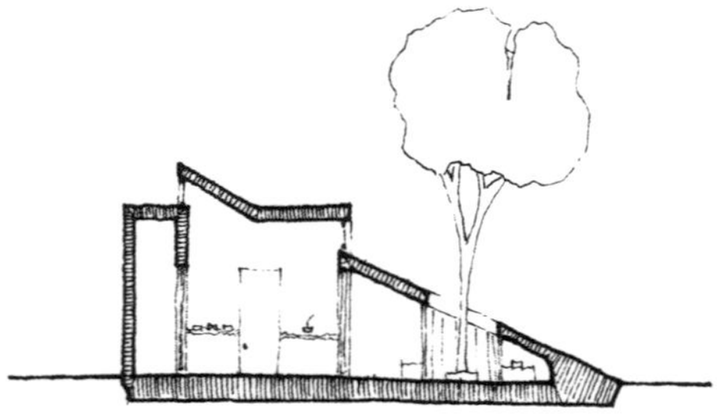

no.176

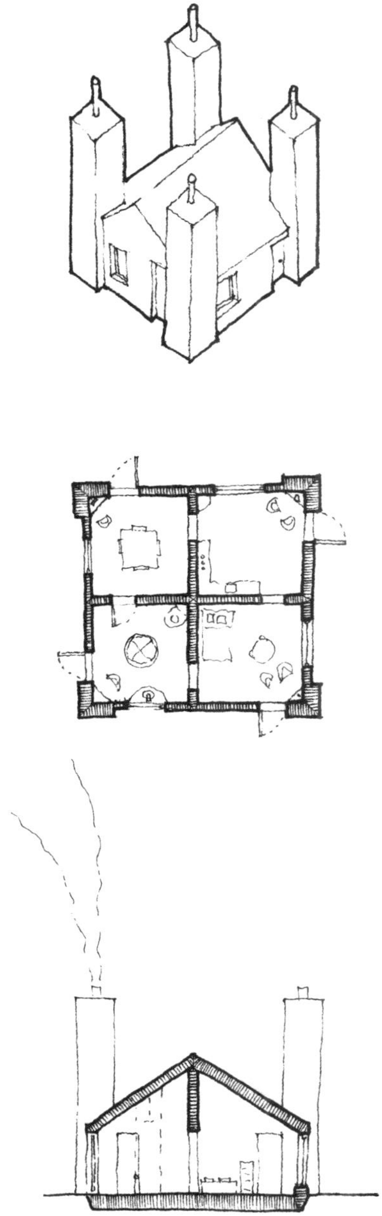

no.177

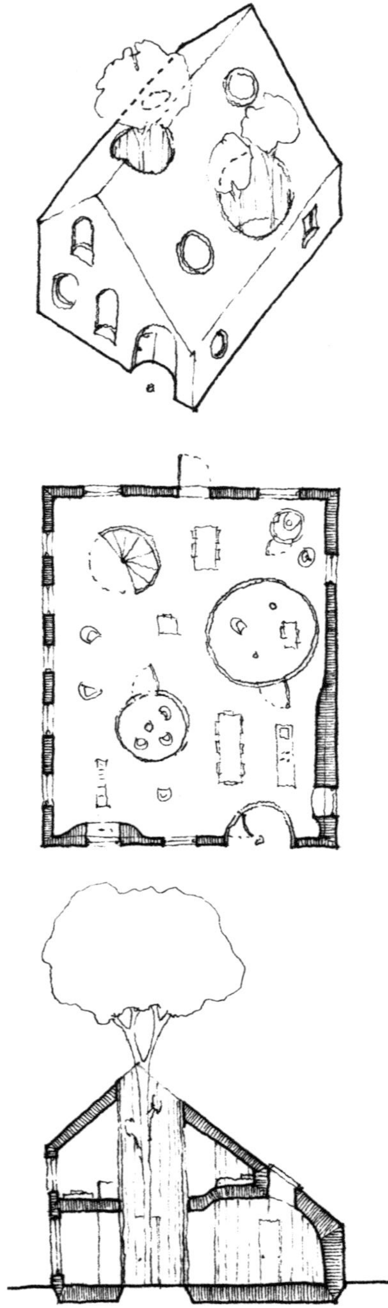

no.178

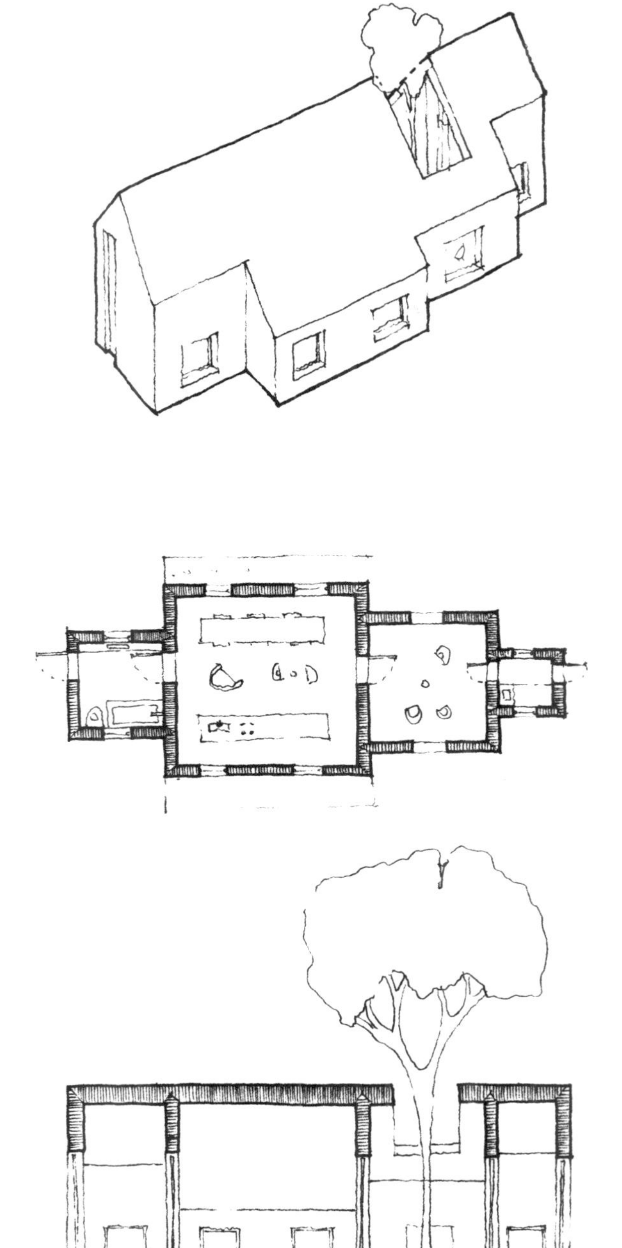

no.179

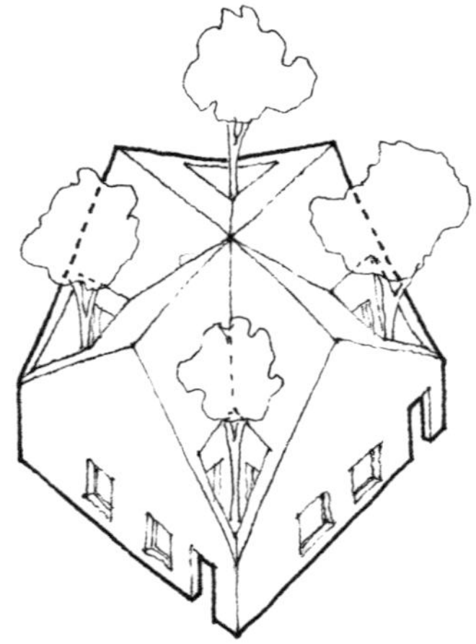

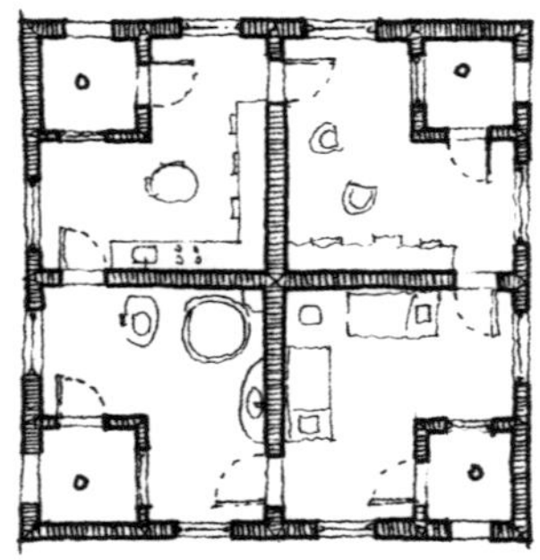

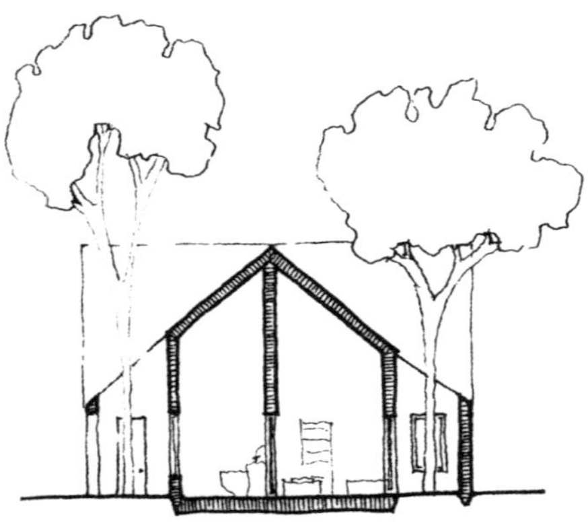

no.180

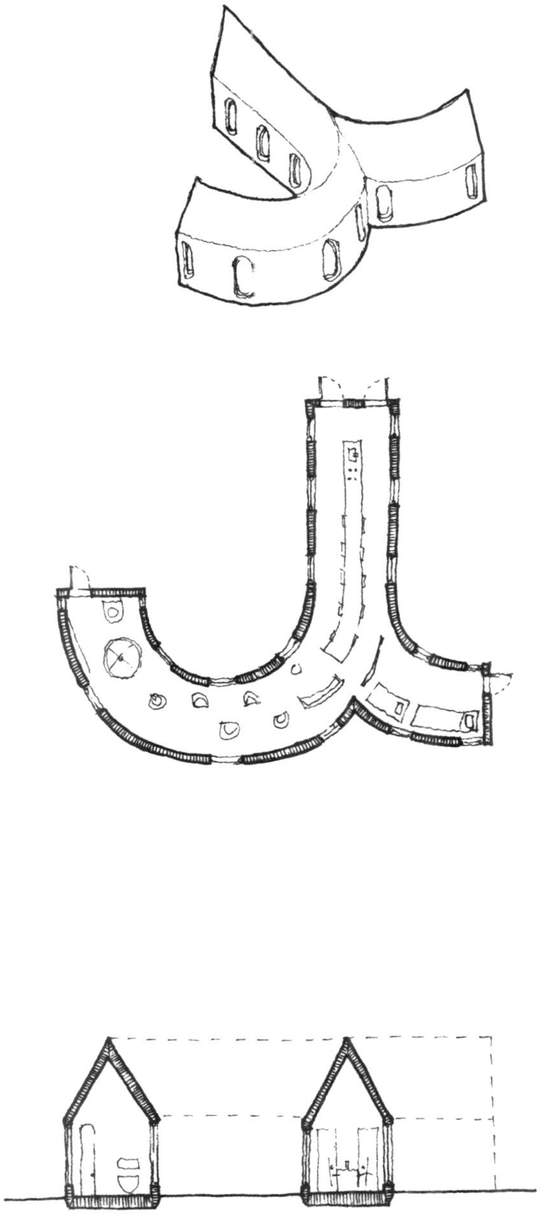

no.181

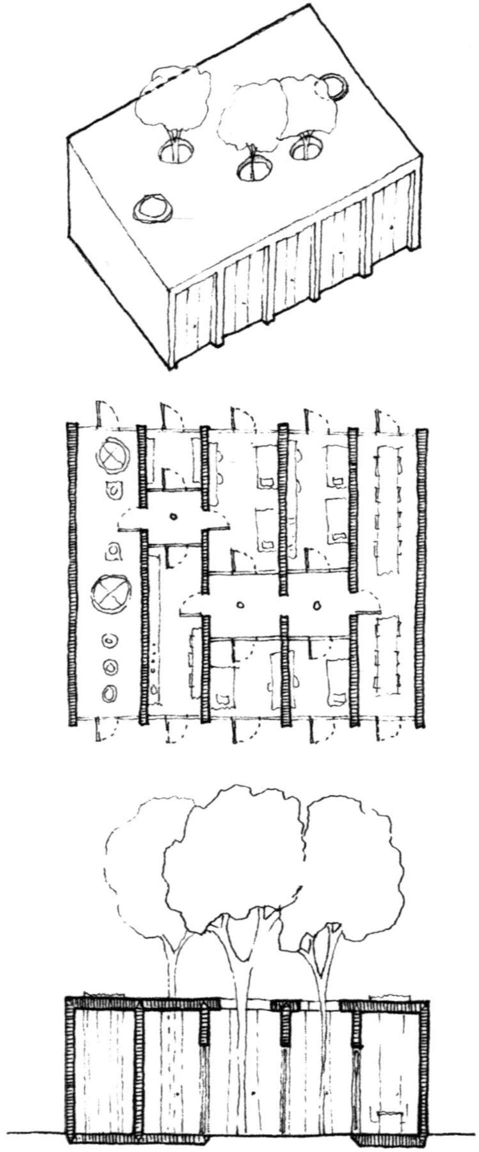

no.182

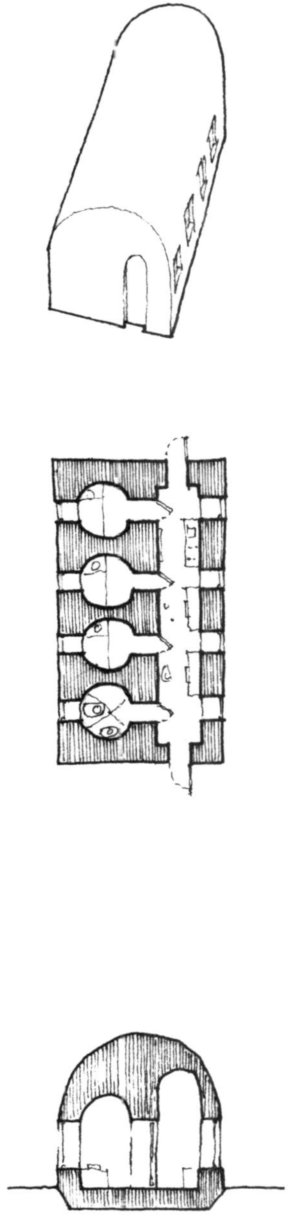

no.183

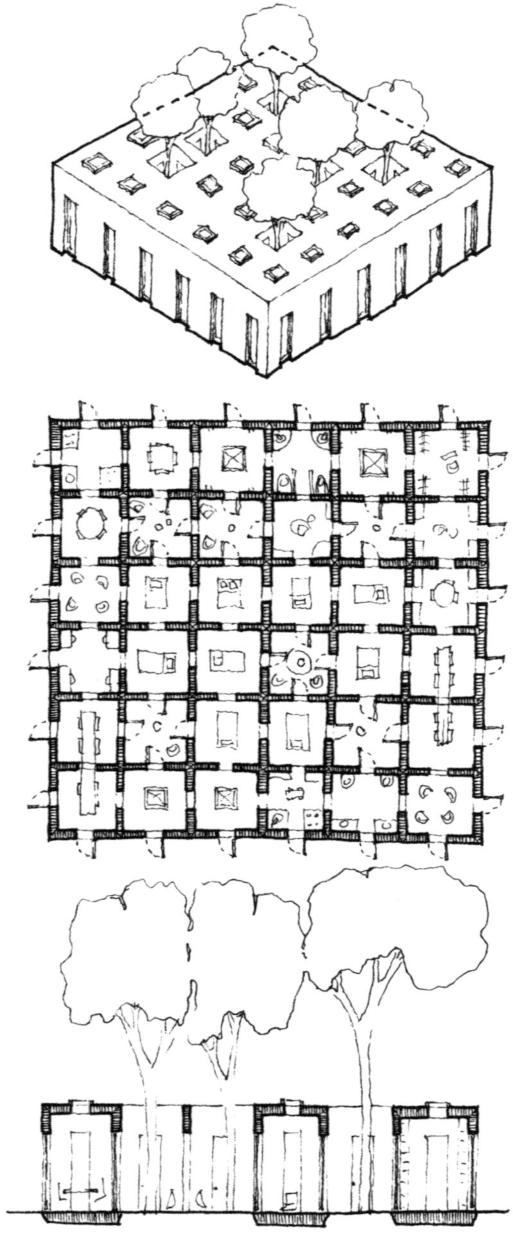

no.184

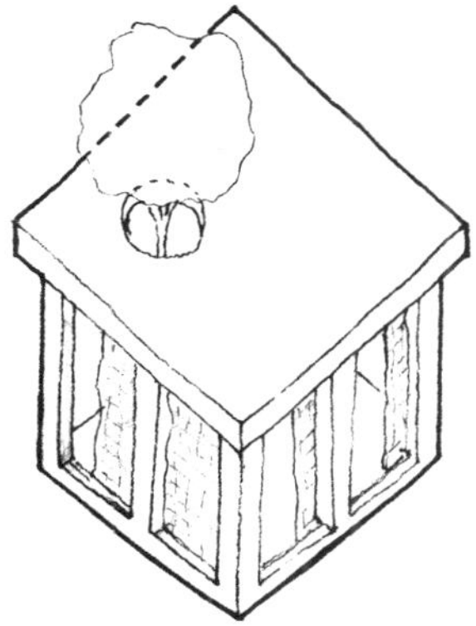

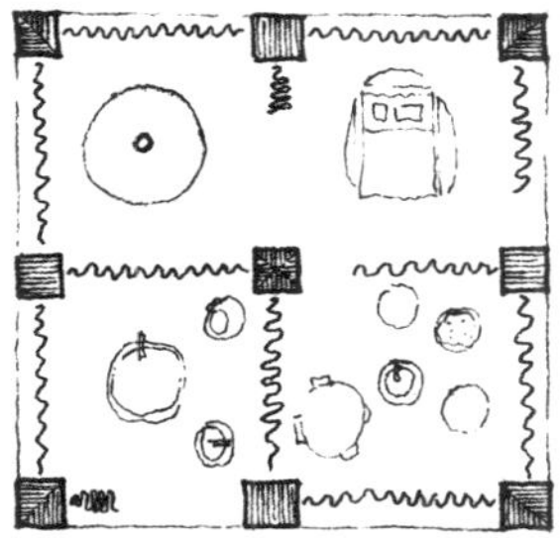

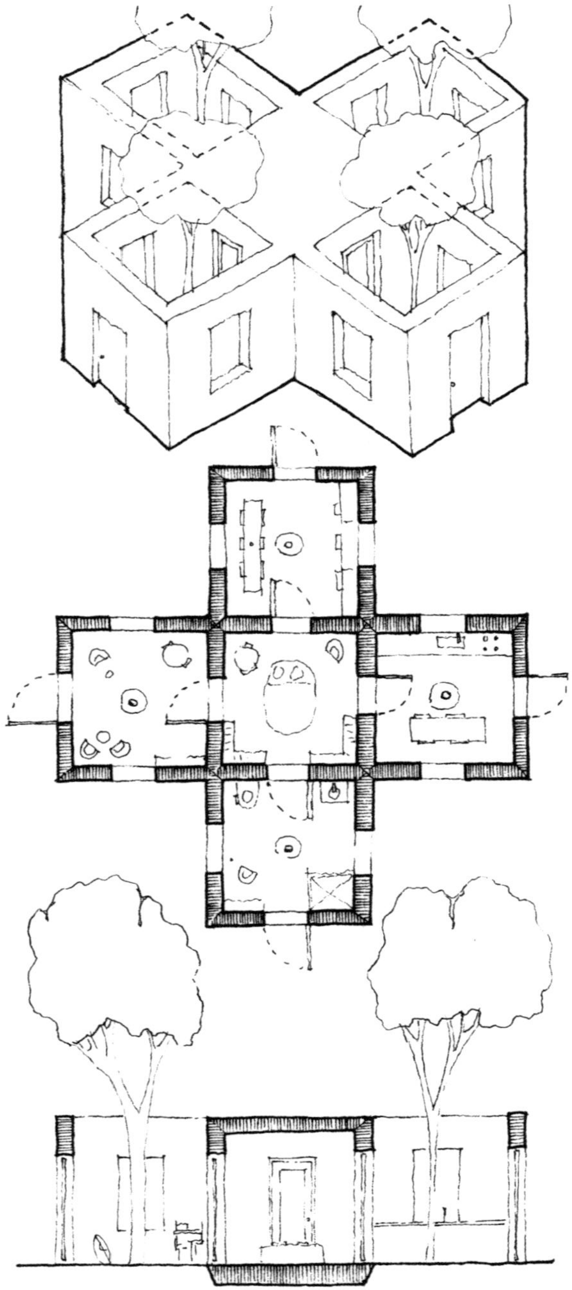

no.186

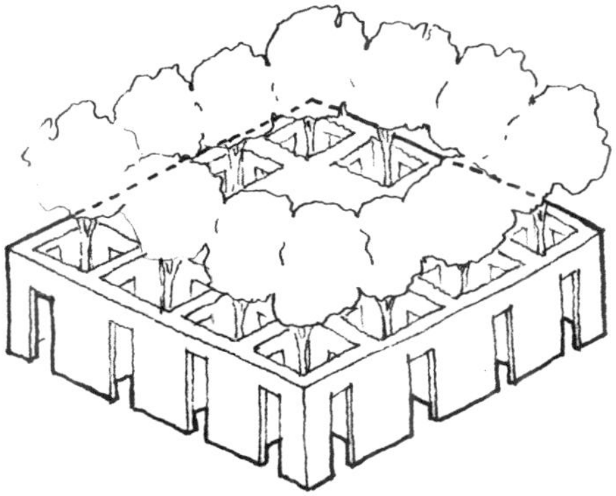

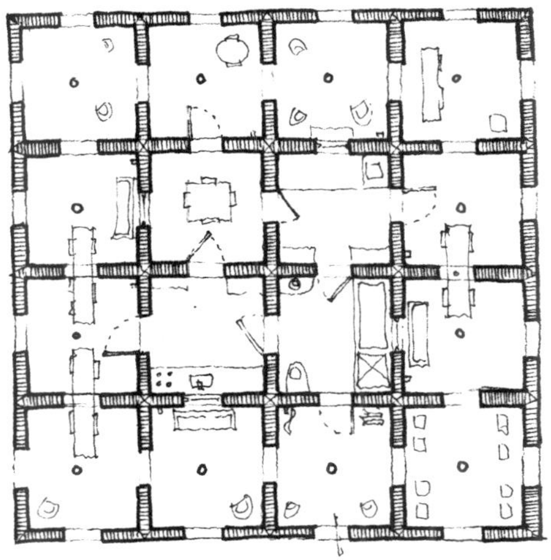

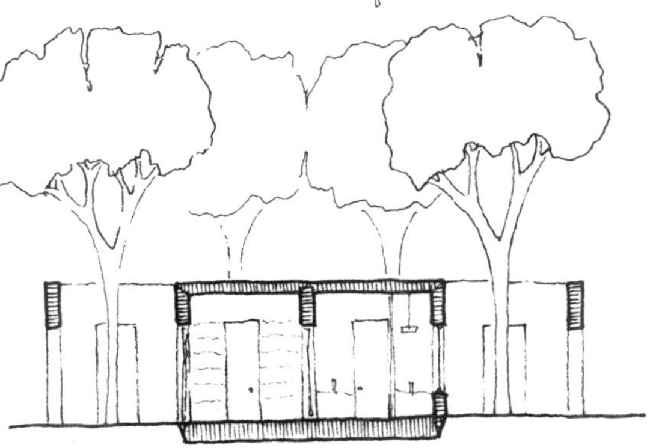

no.187

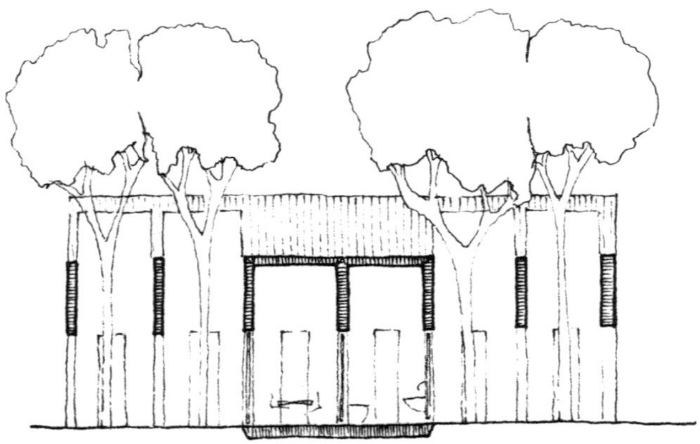

no.188

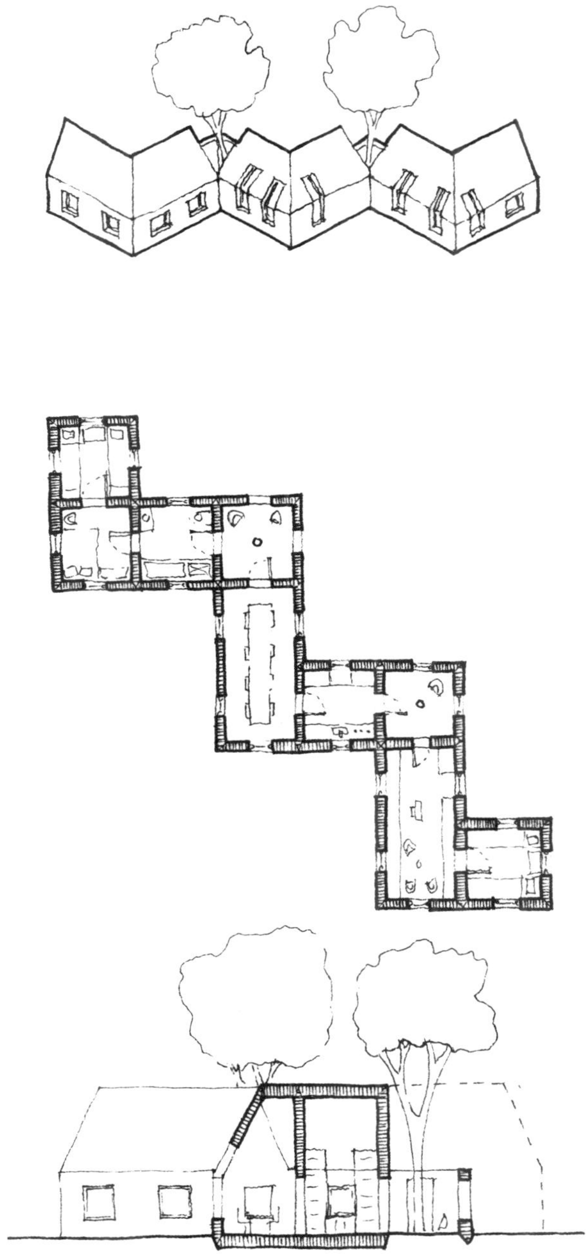

no.189

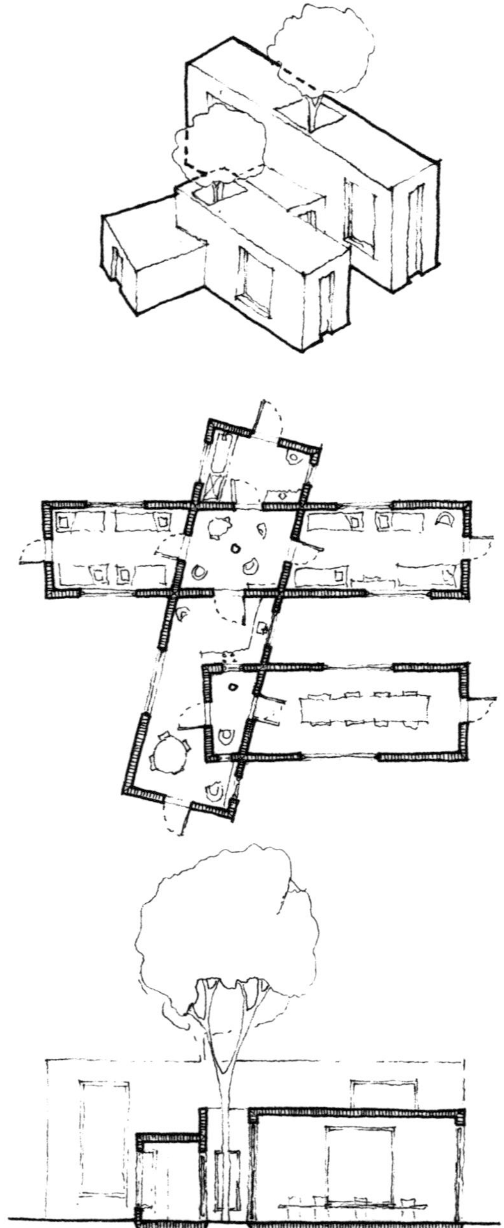

no.190

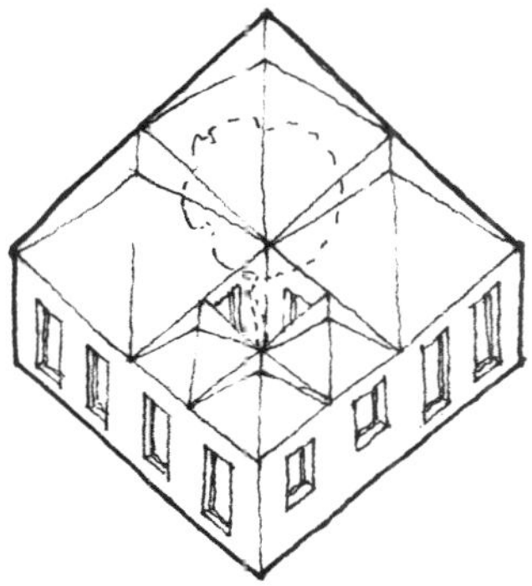

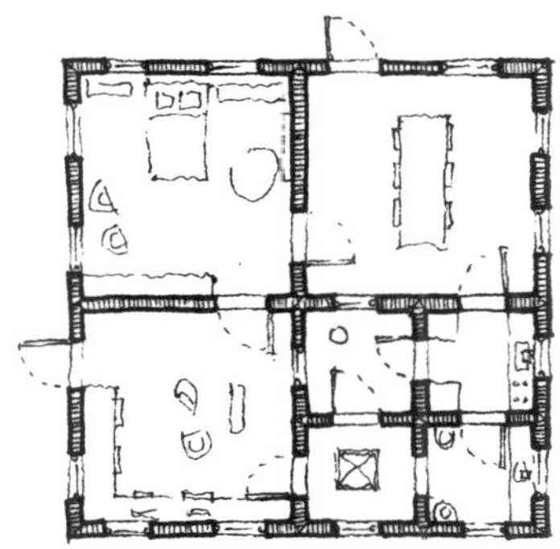

no.191

no.192

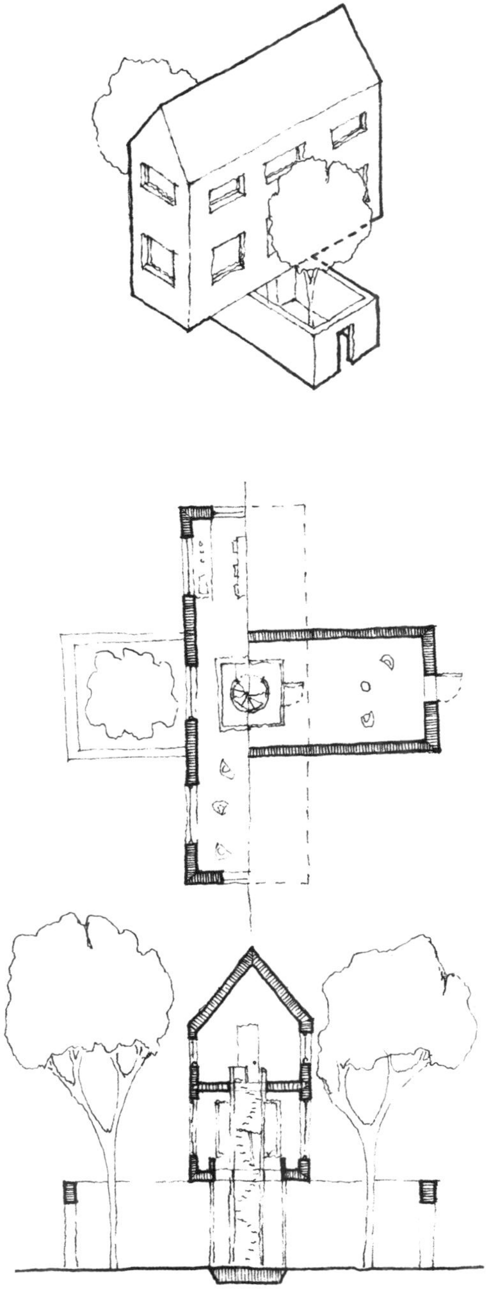

no.193

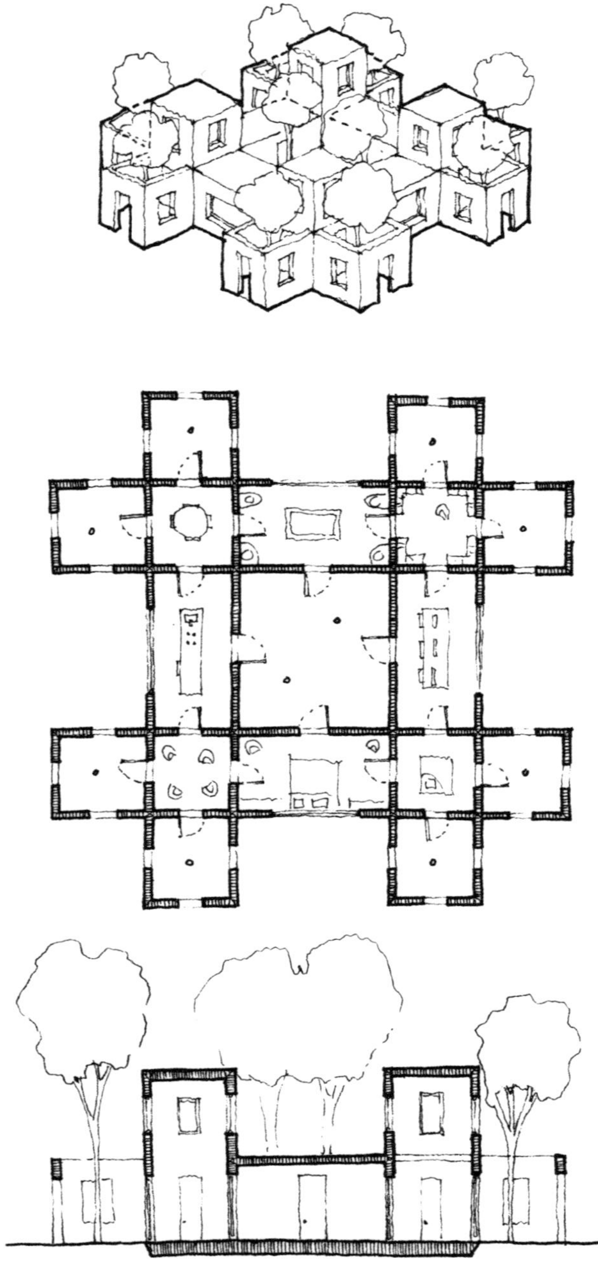

no.194

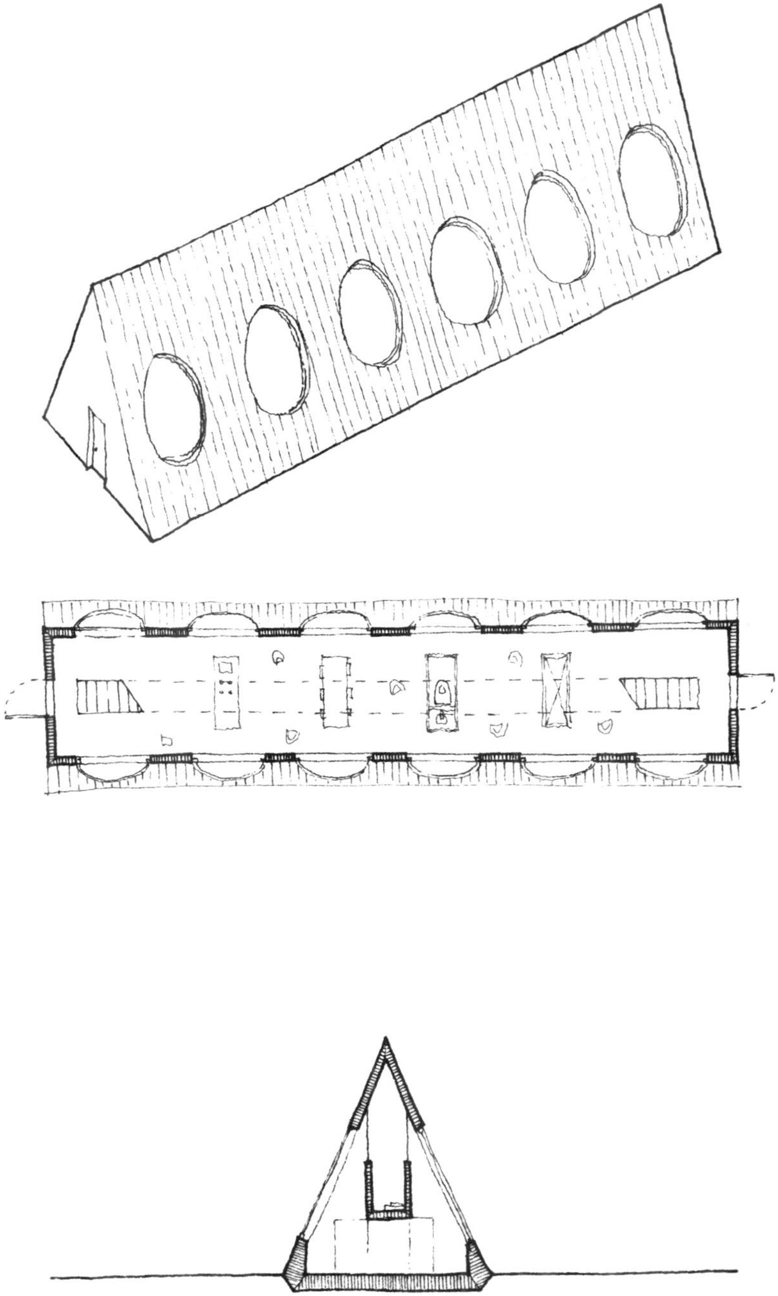

no.195

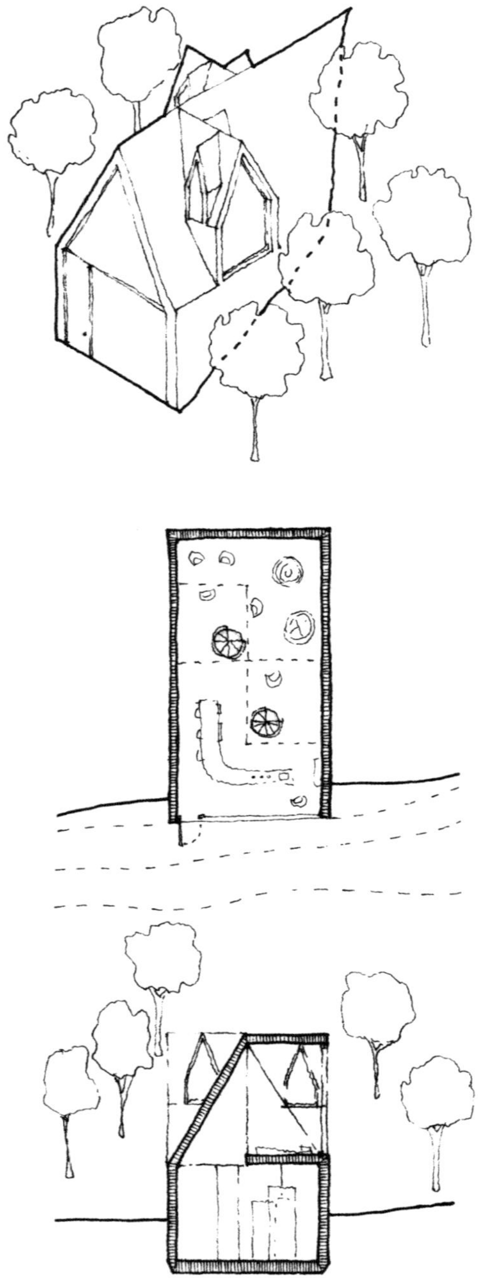

no.196

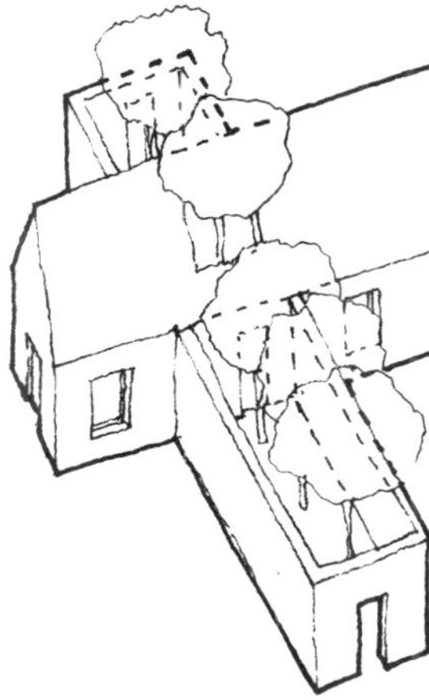

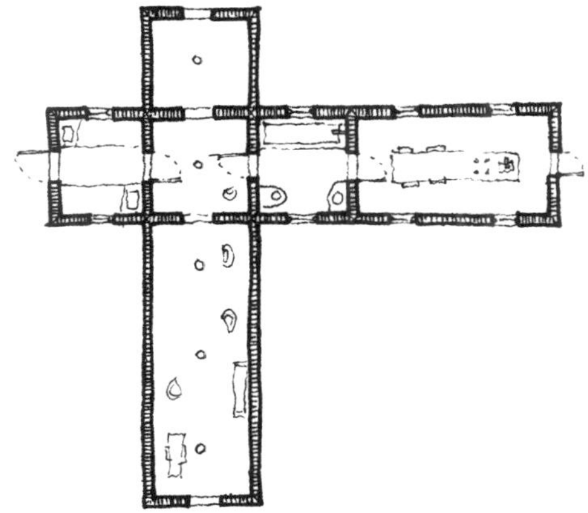

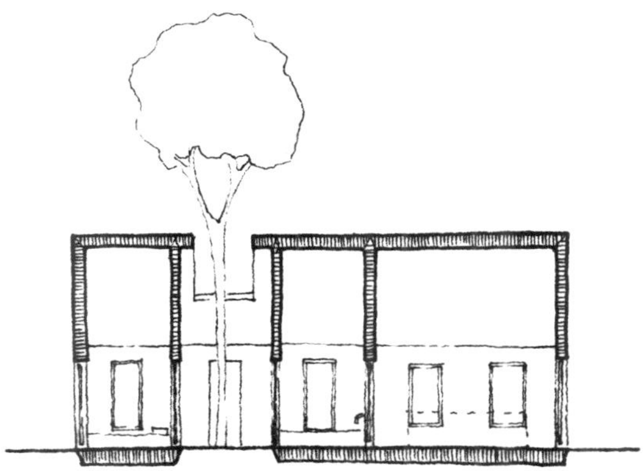

no.197

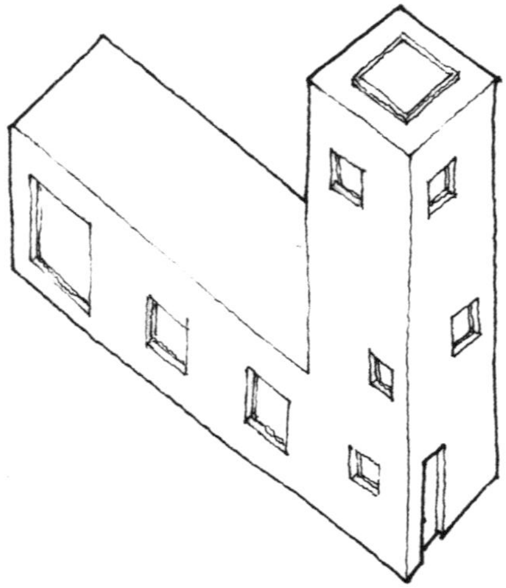

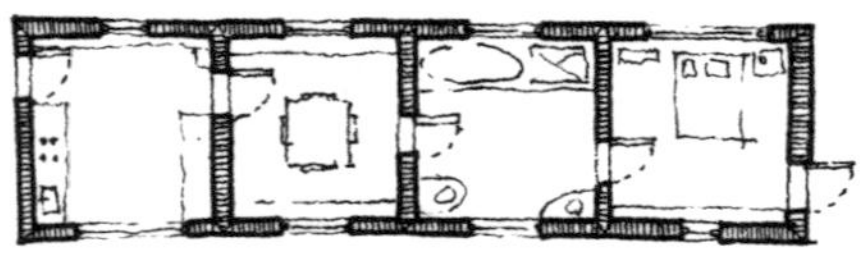

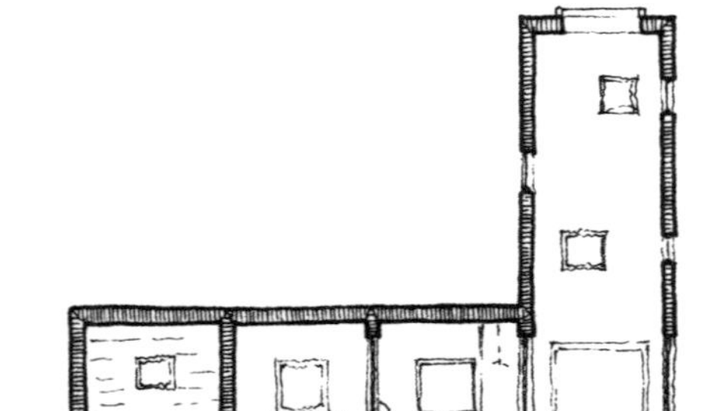

no.198

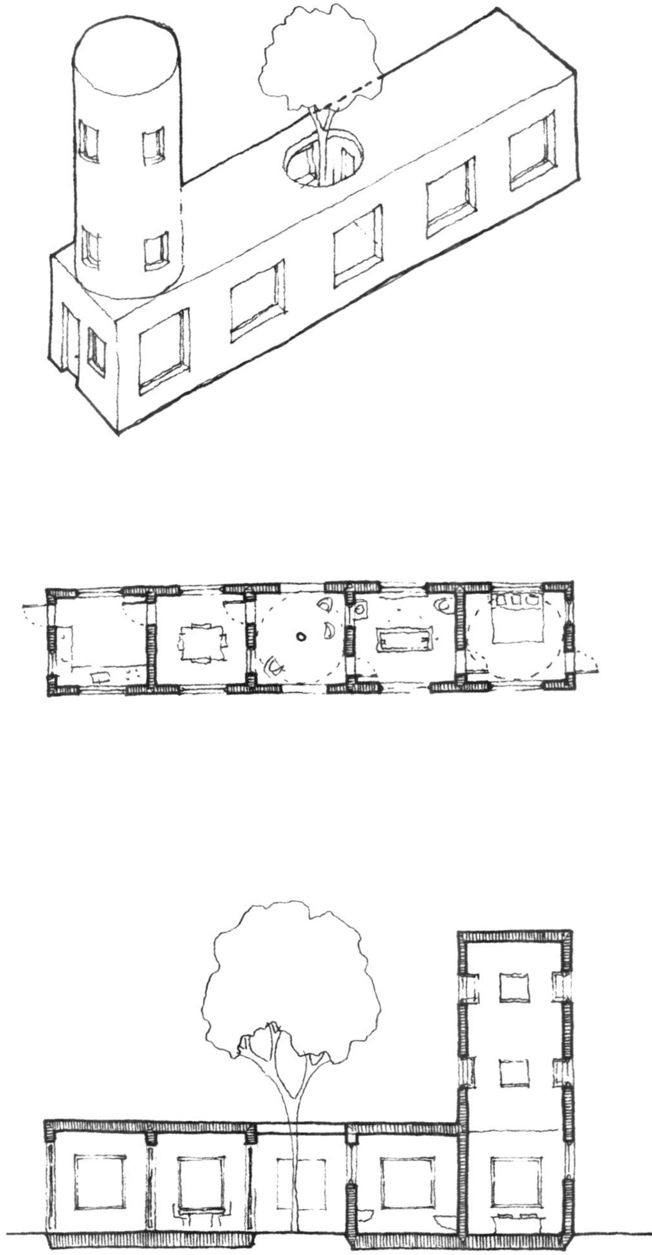

no.199

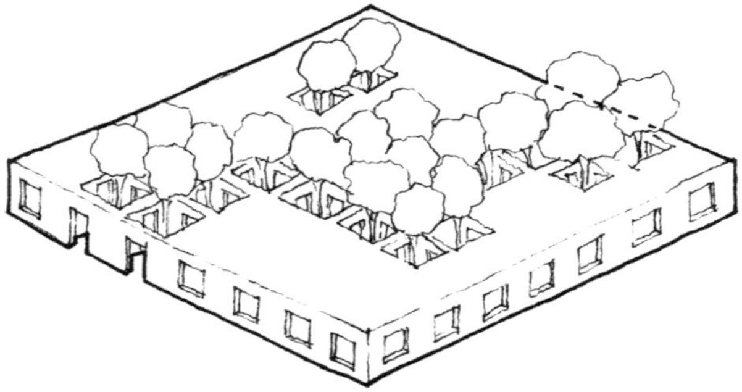

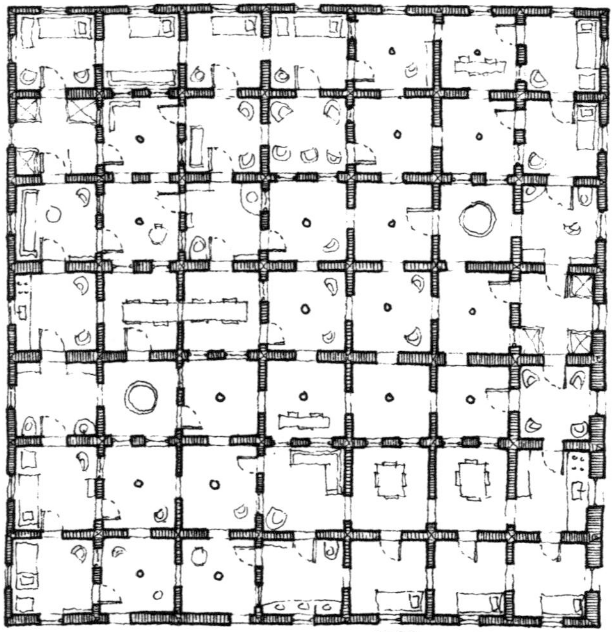

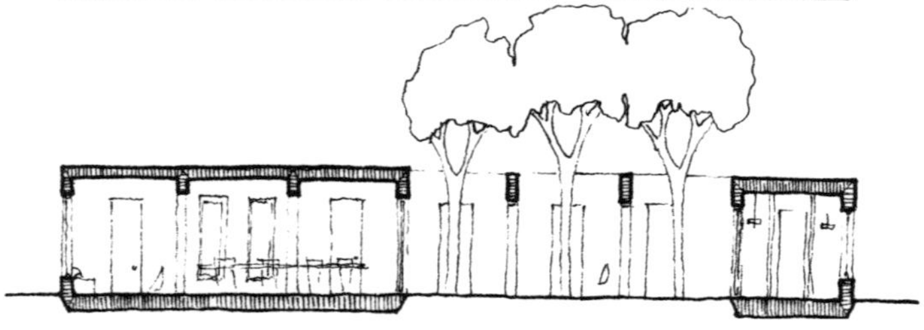

no.200

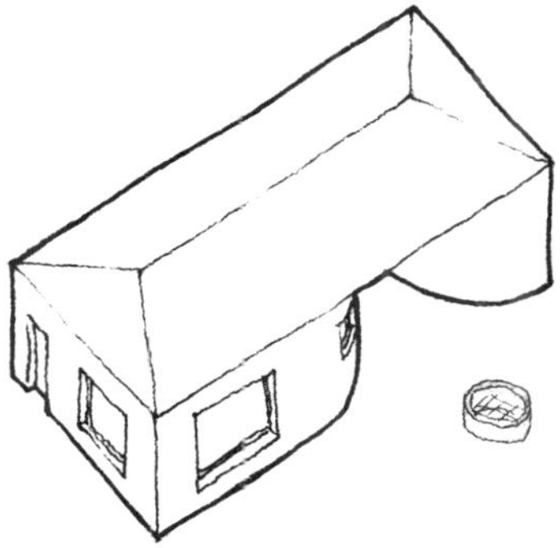

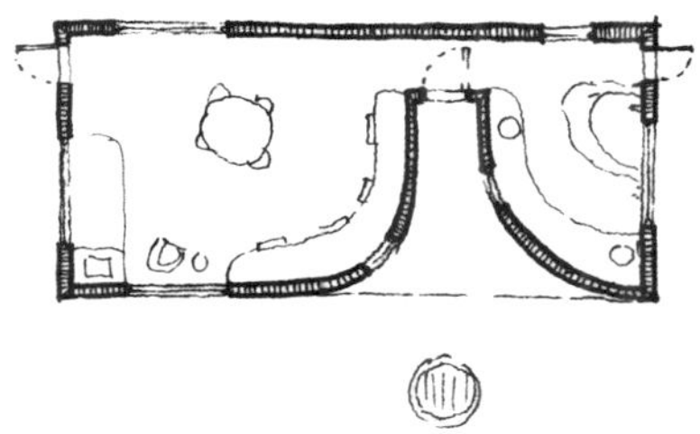

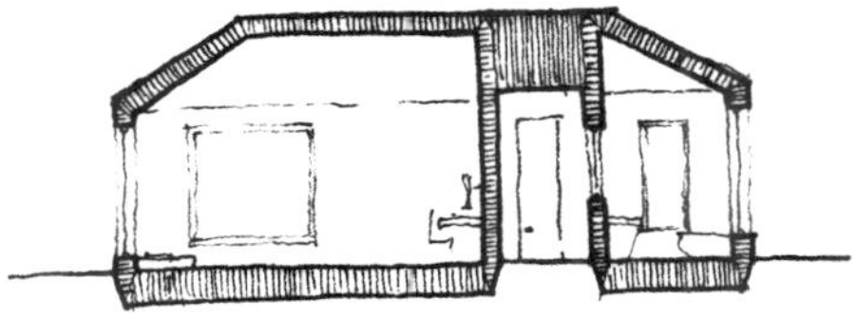

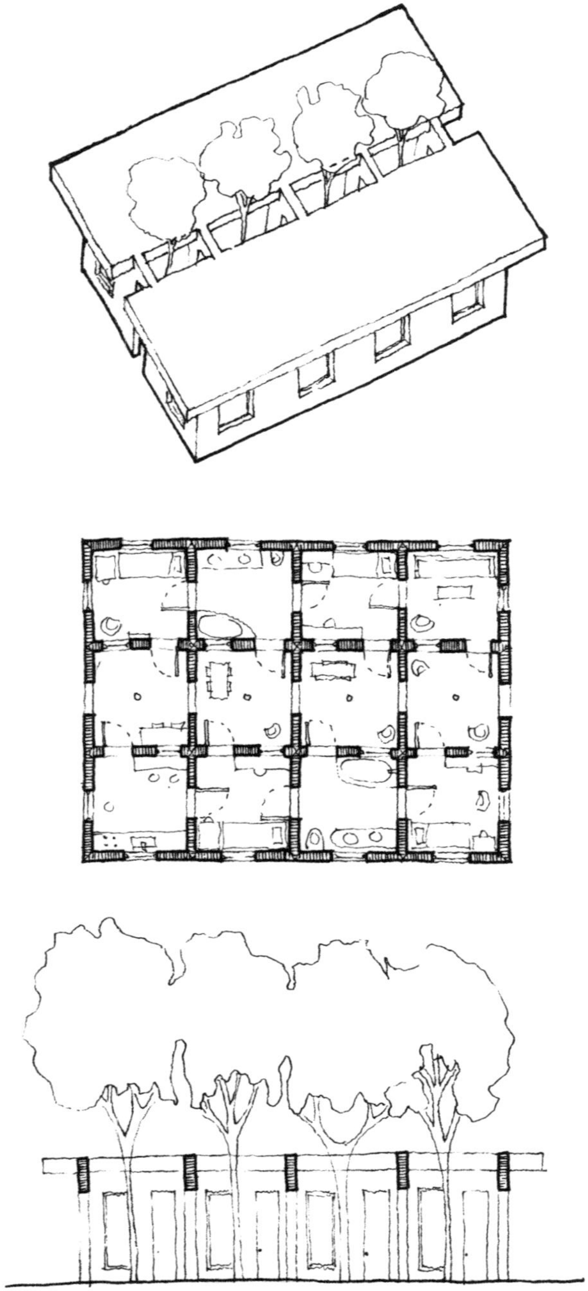

no.202

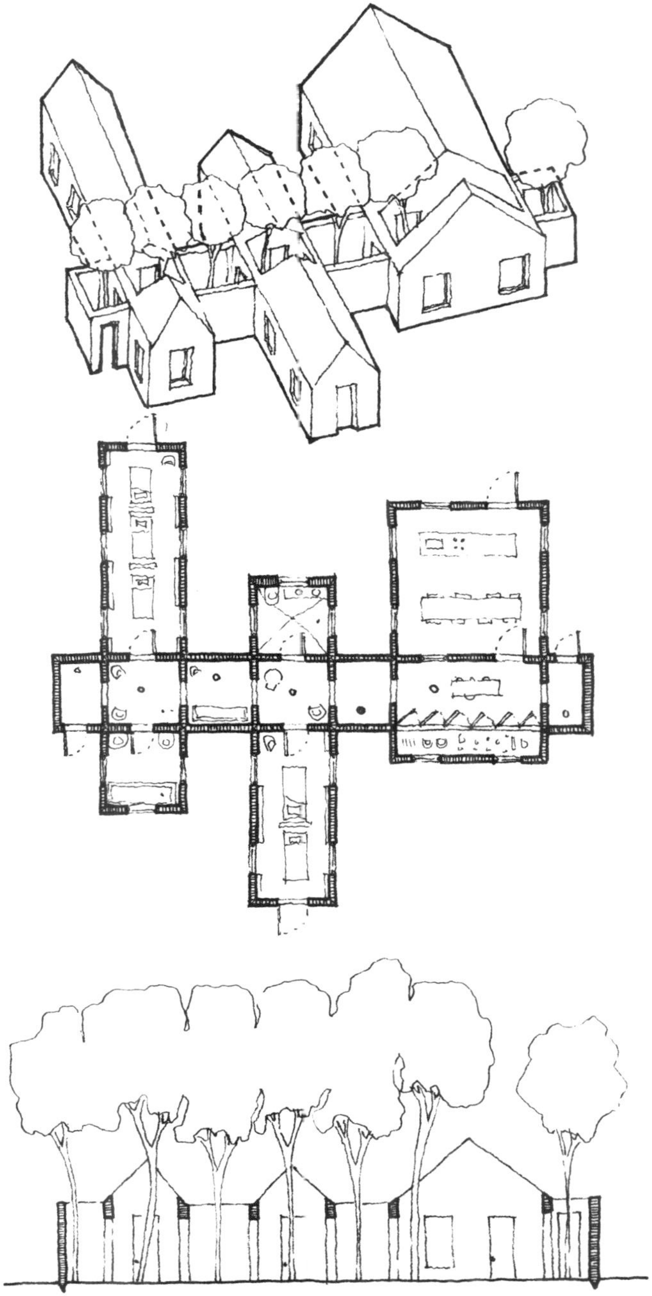

no.203

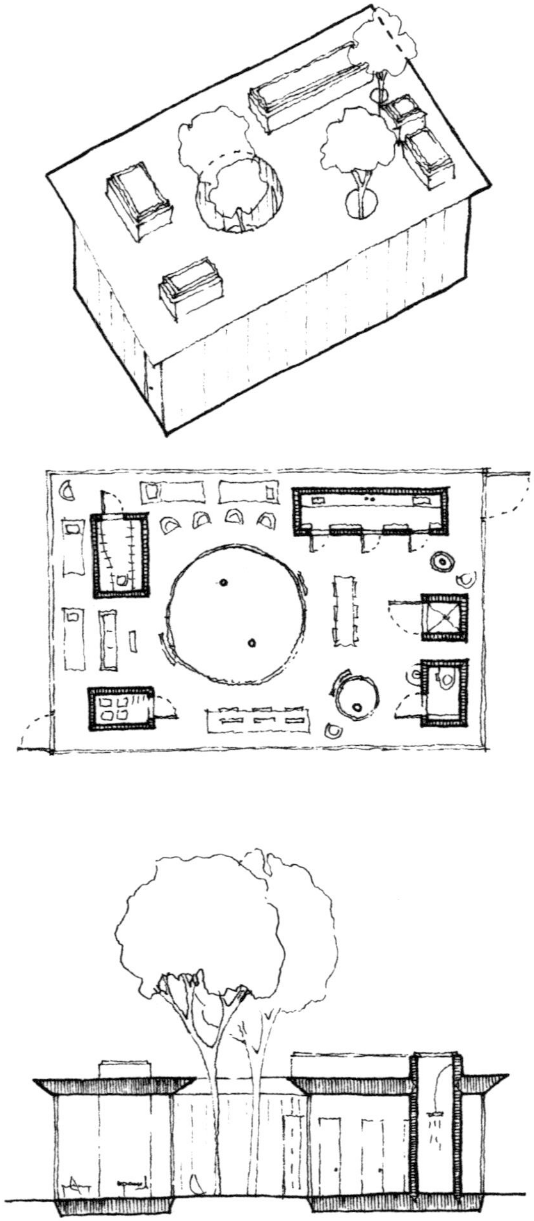

no.204

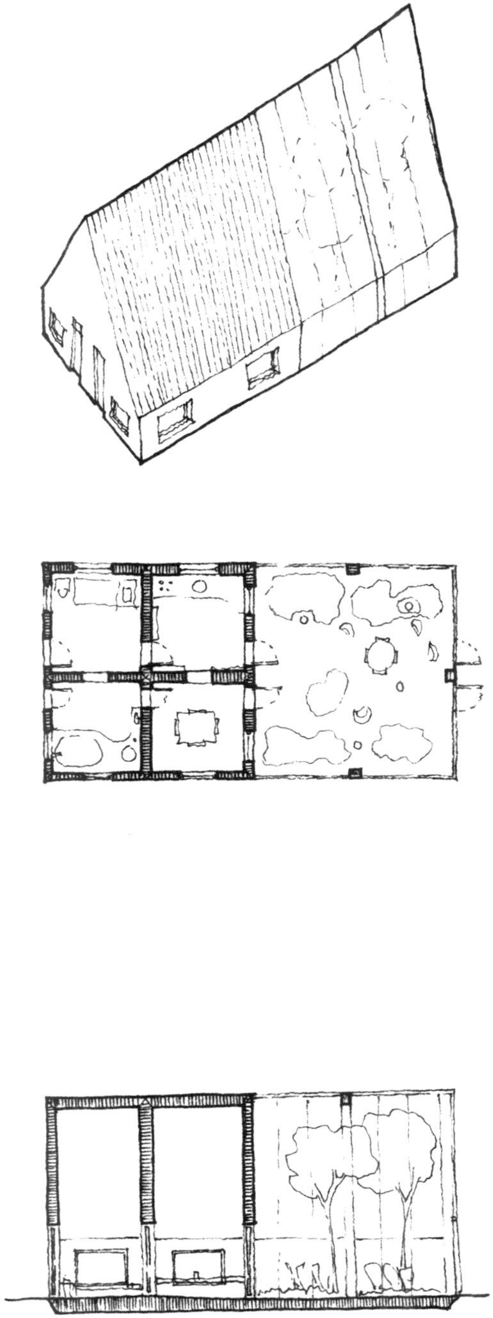

no.205

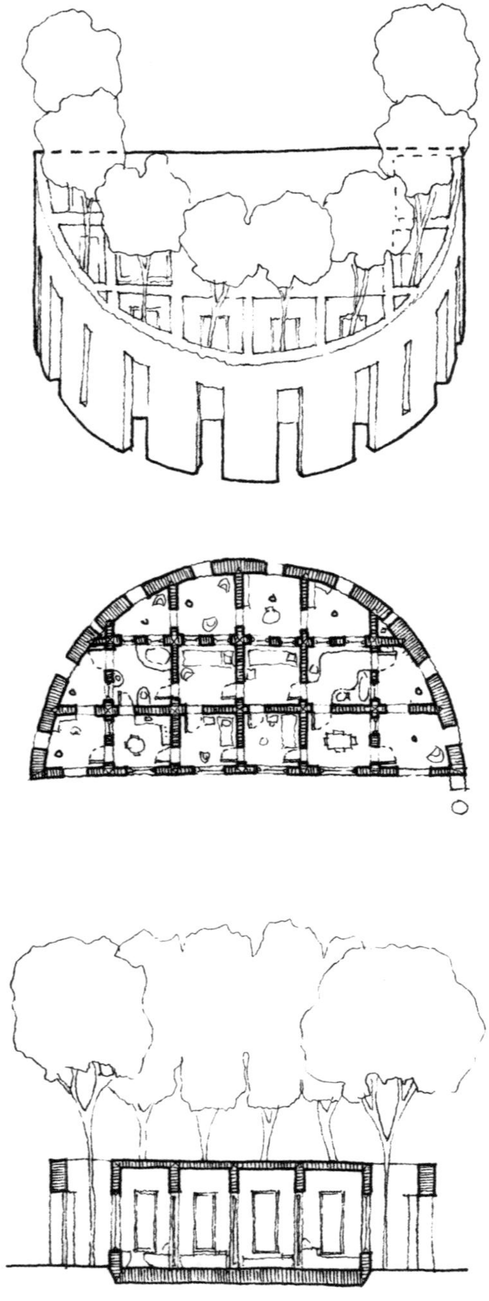

no.206

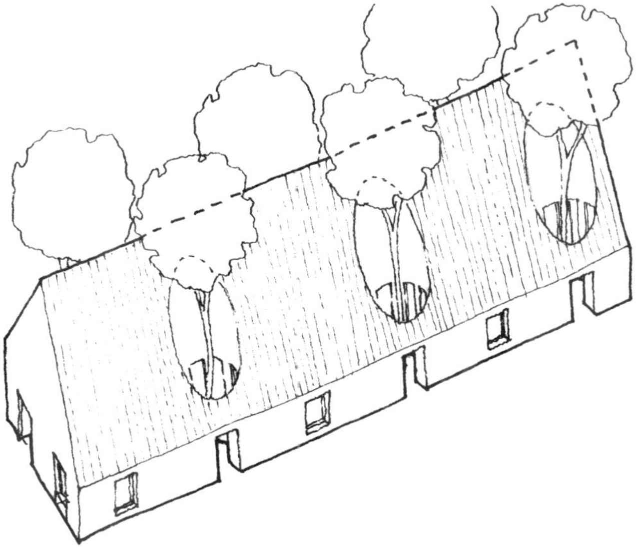

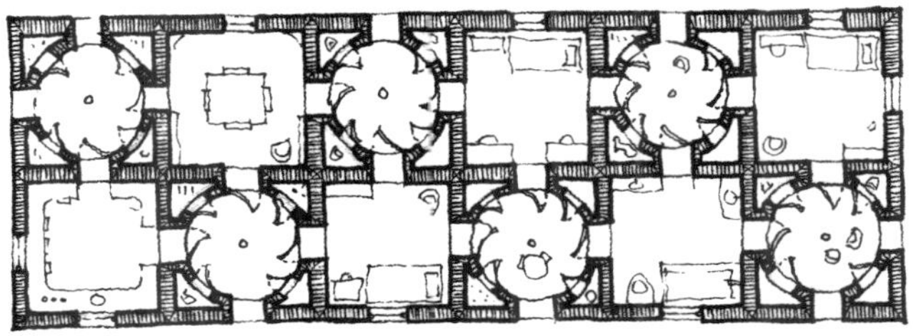

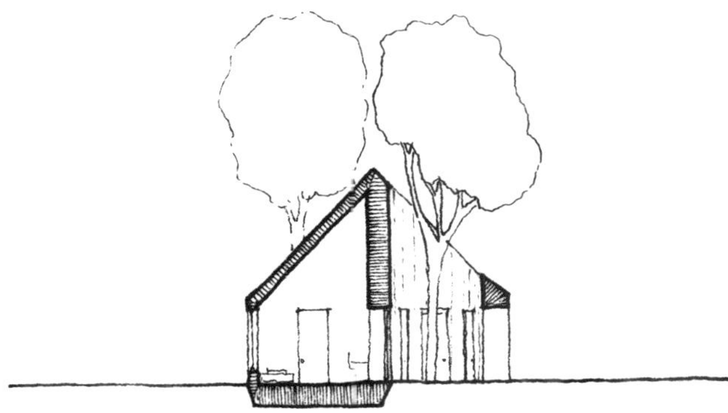

no.207

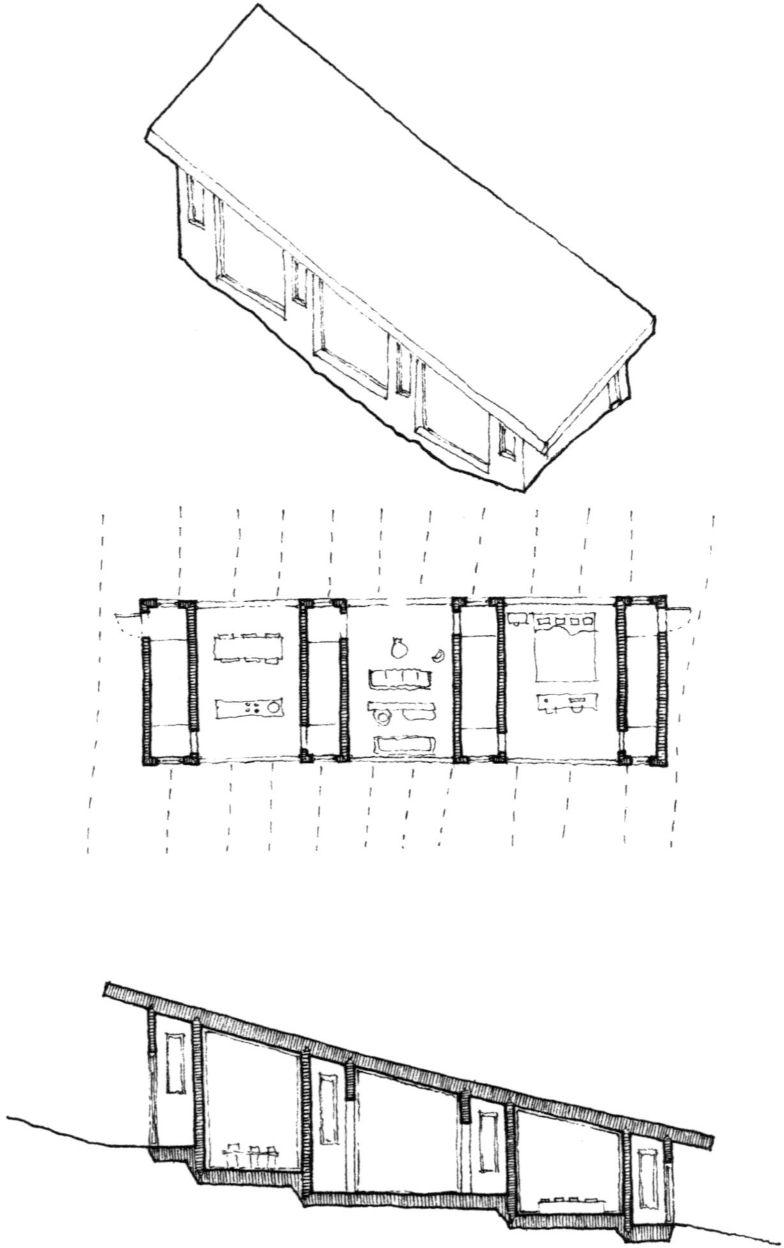

no.208

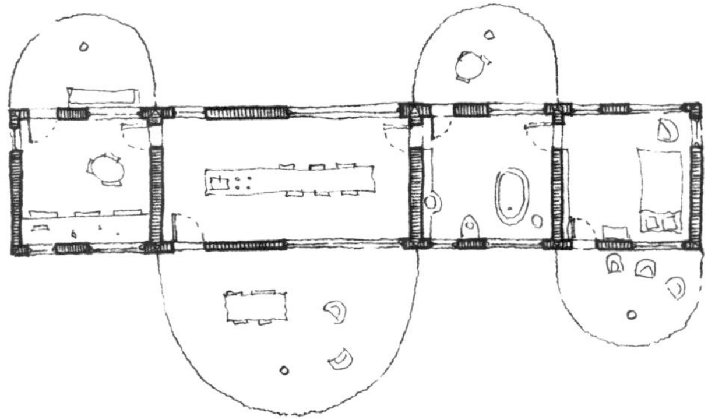

no.209

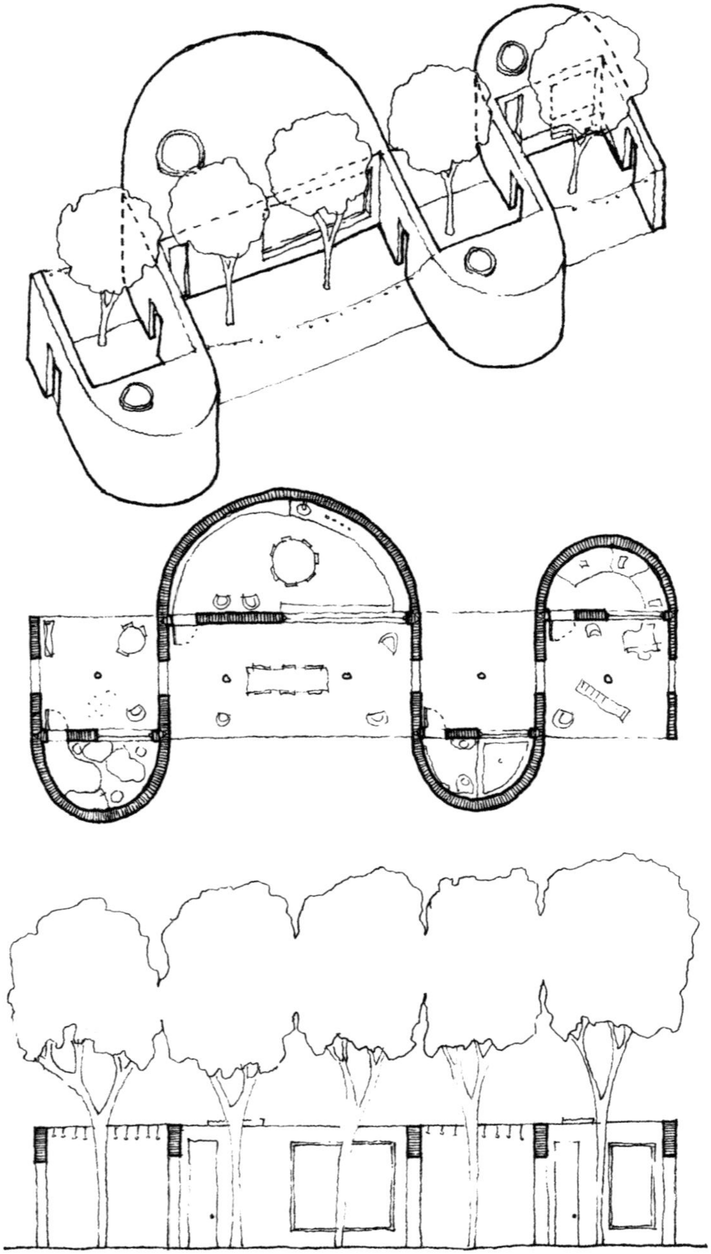

no.210

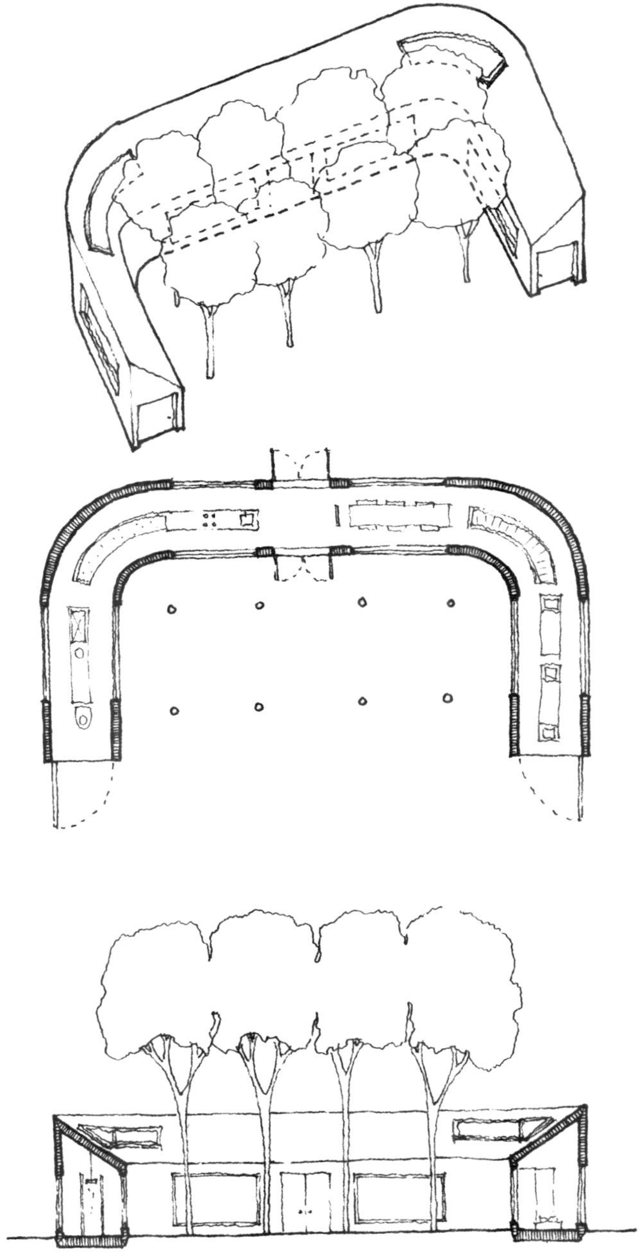

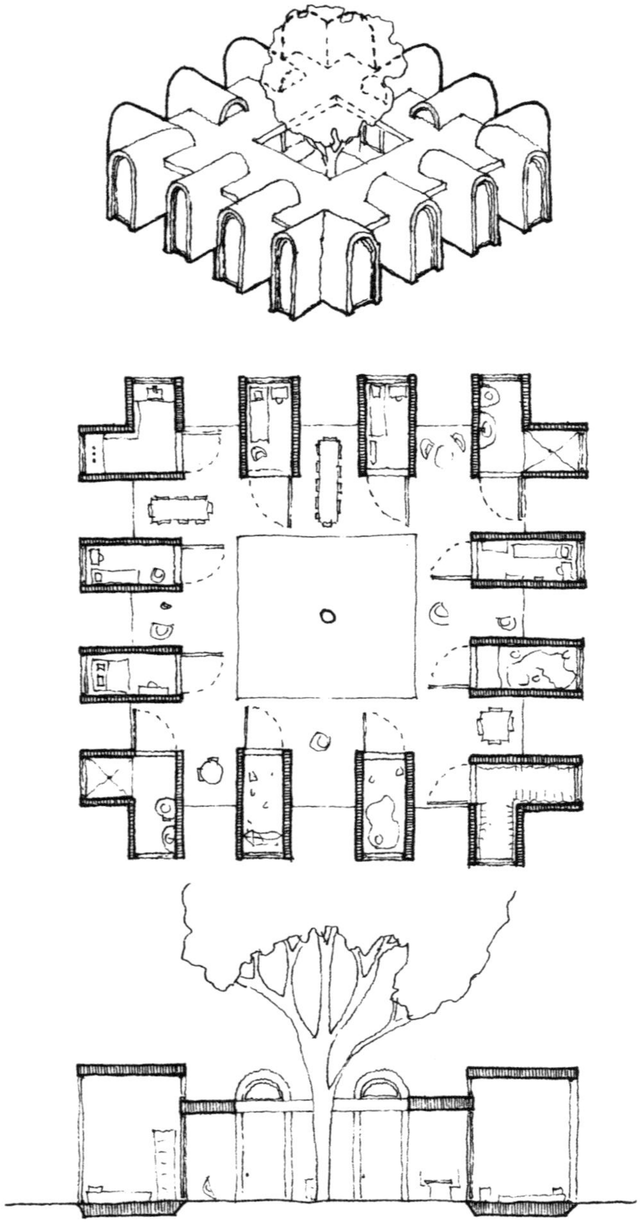

no.212

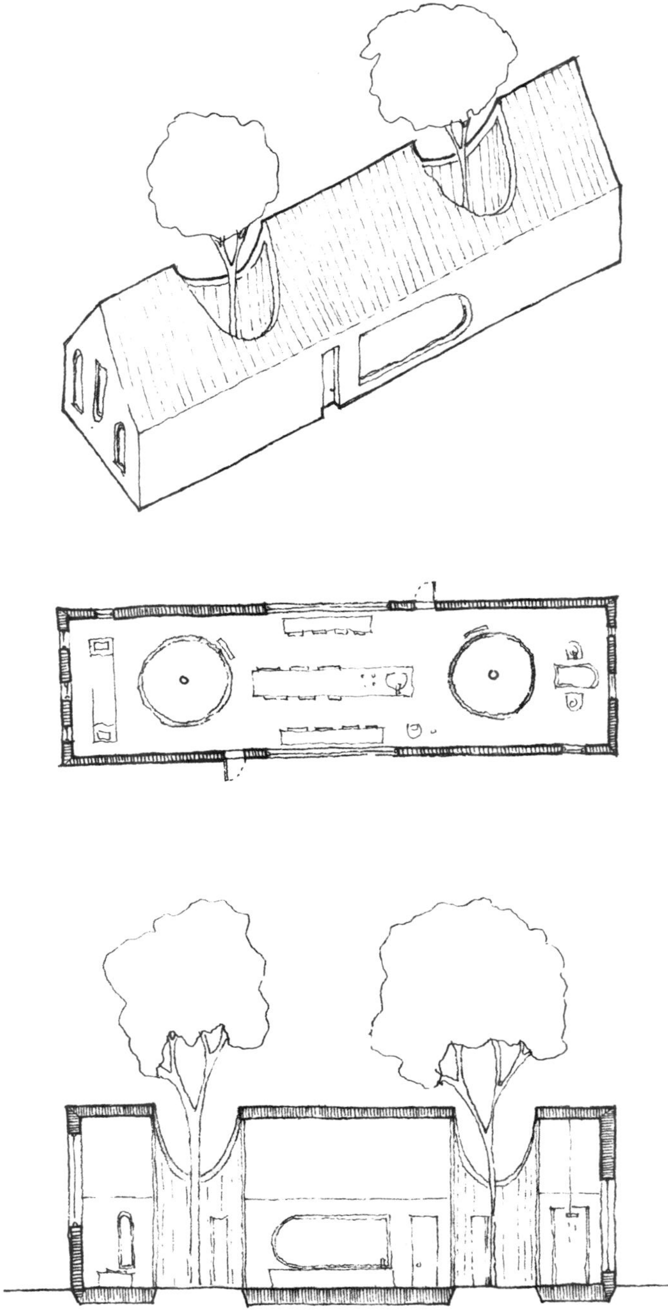

no.213

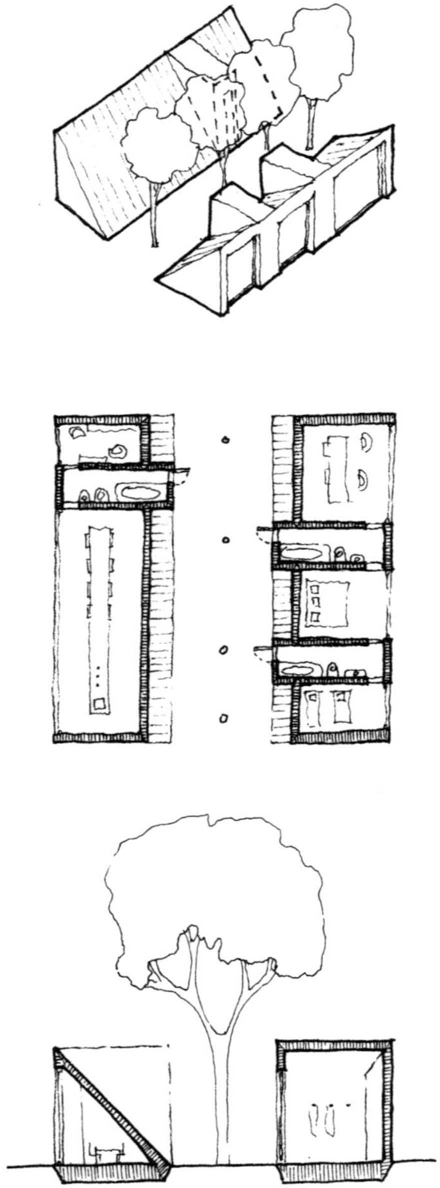

no.214

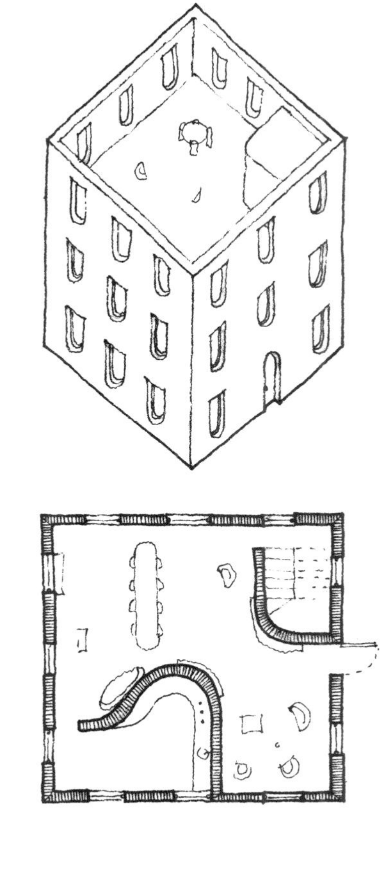

no.215

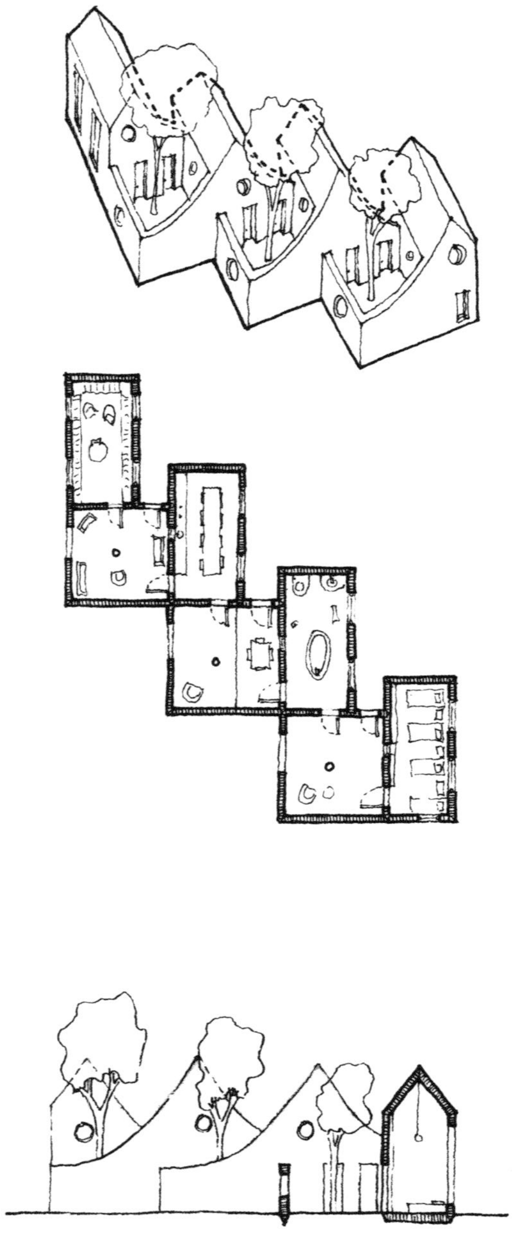

no.216

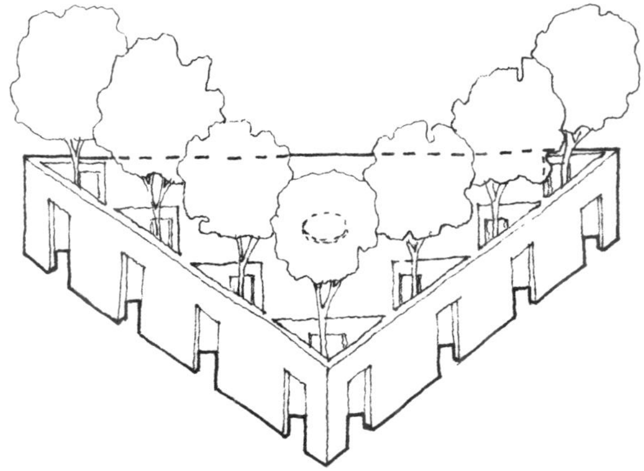

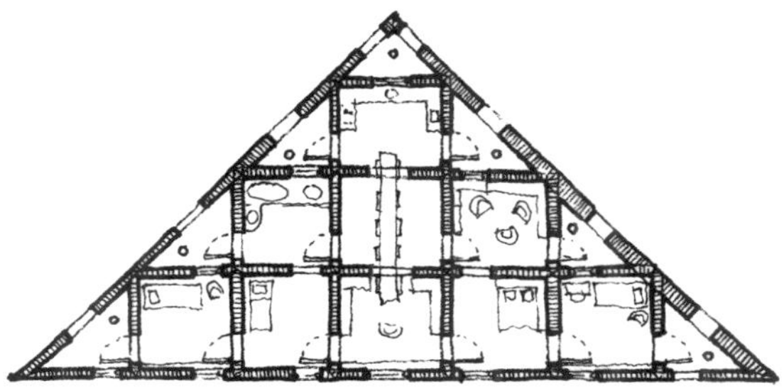

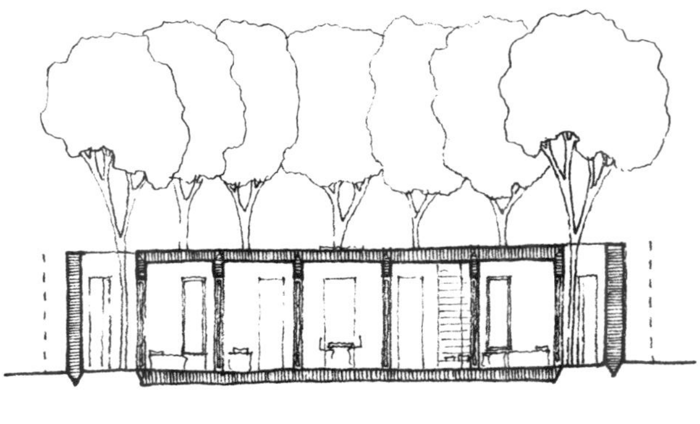

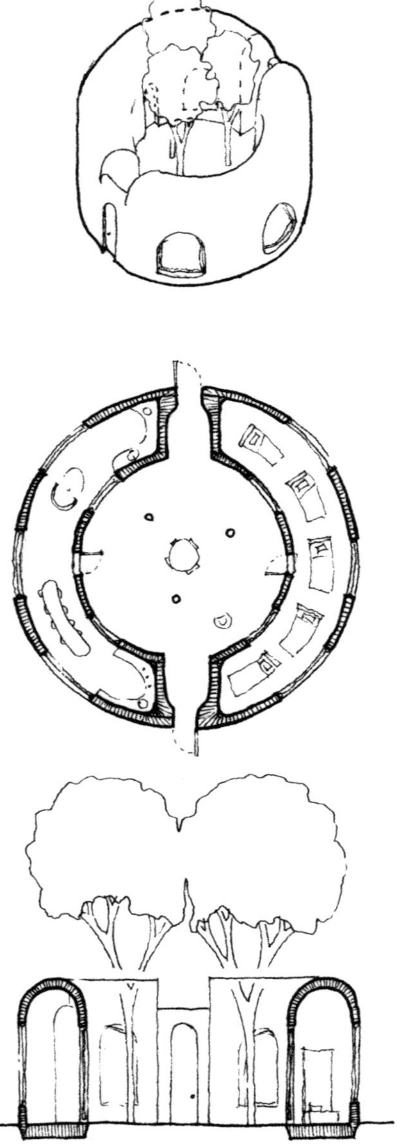

no.218

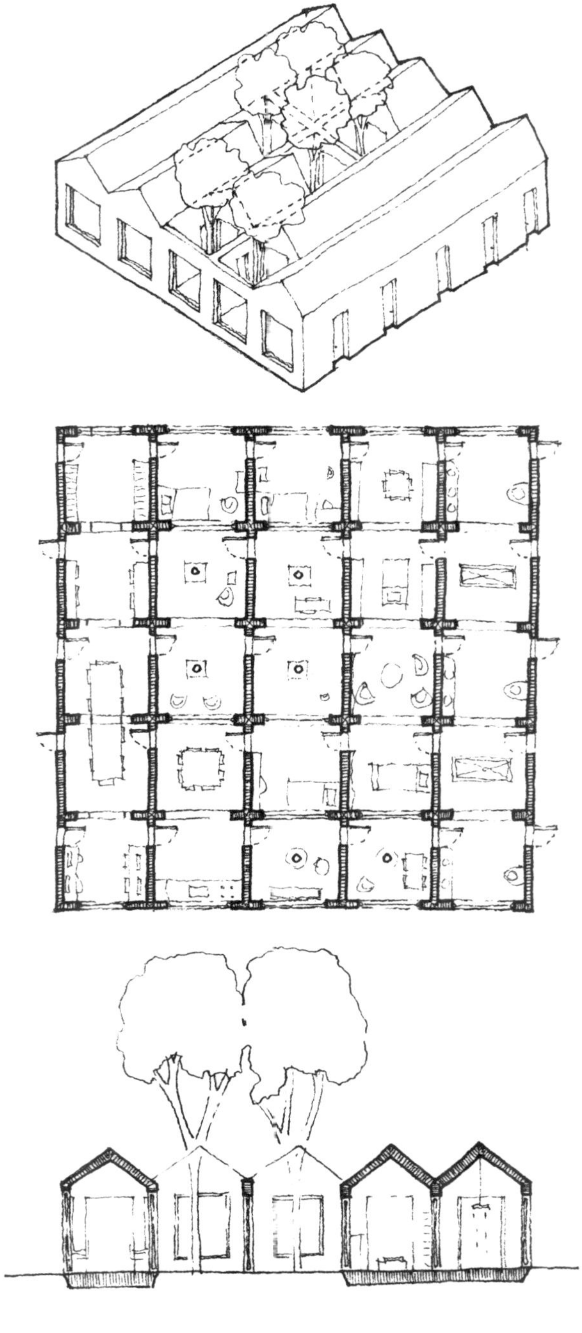

no.219

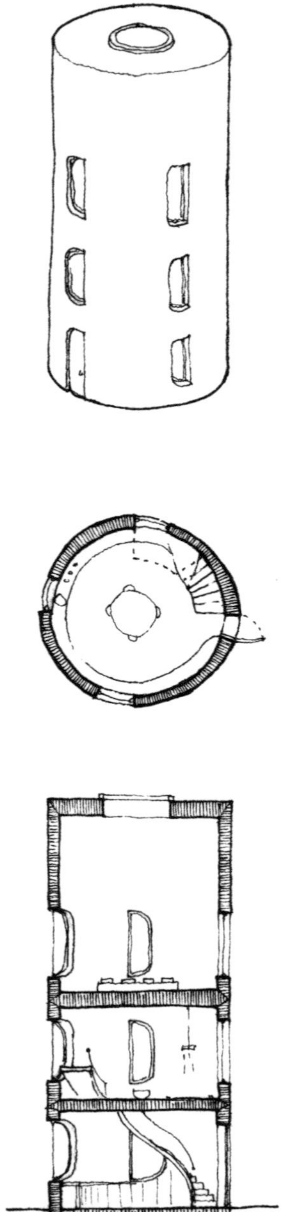

no.220

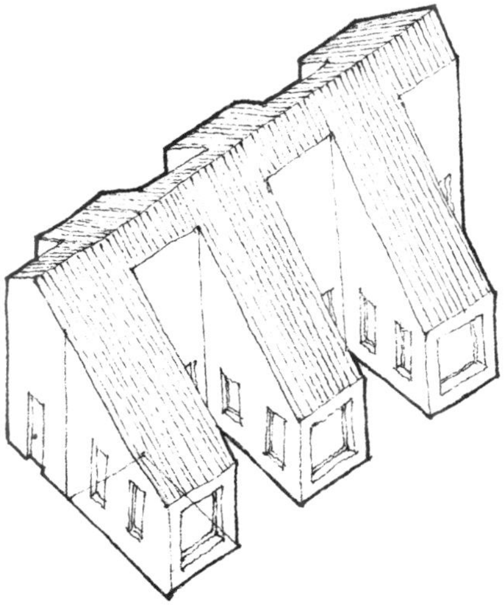

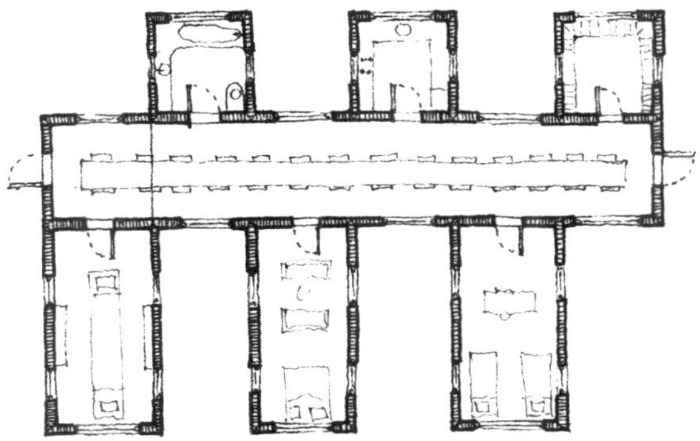

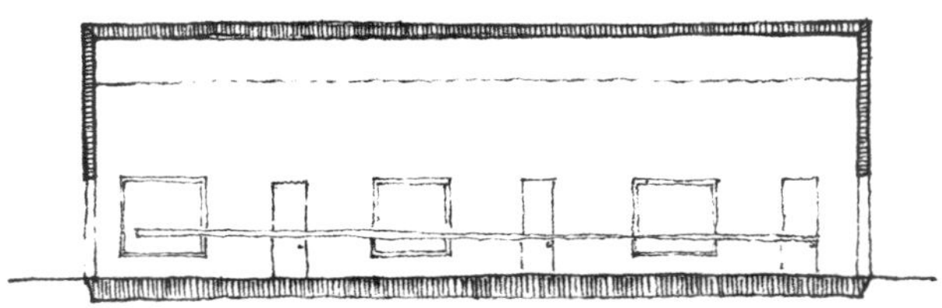

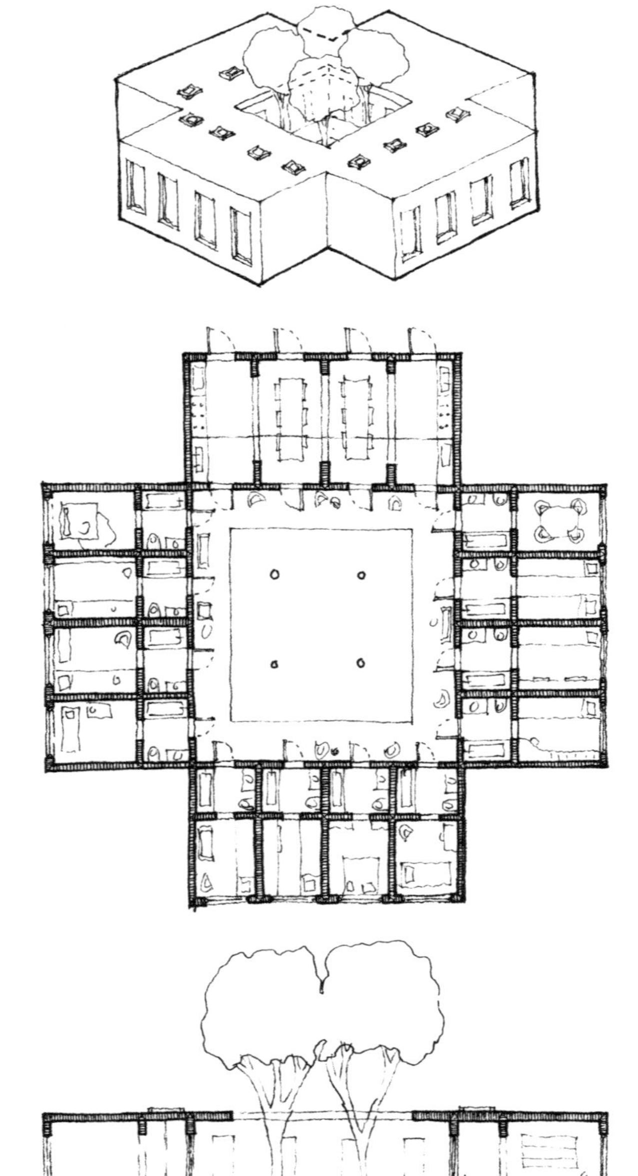

no.222

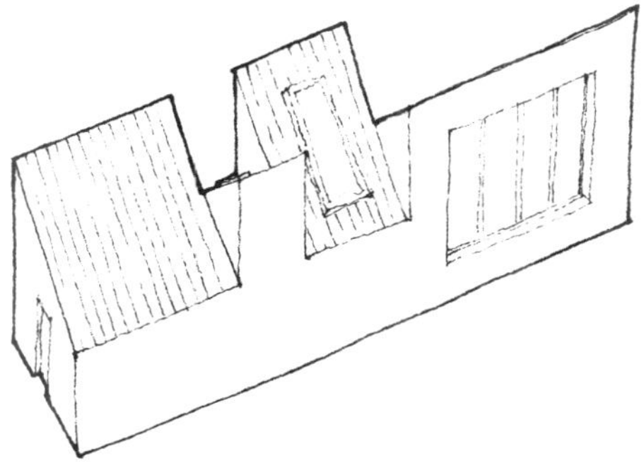

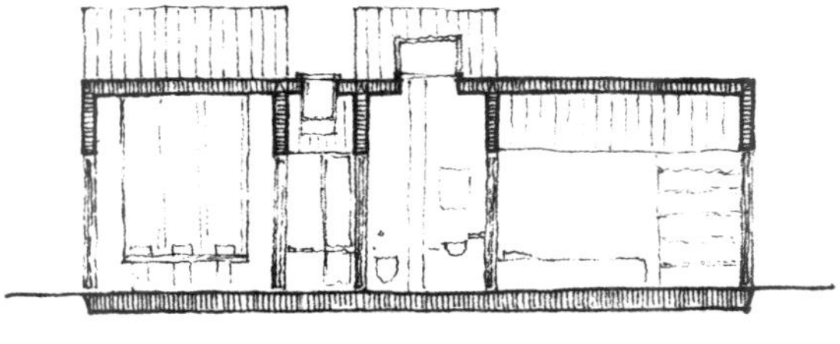

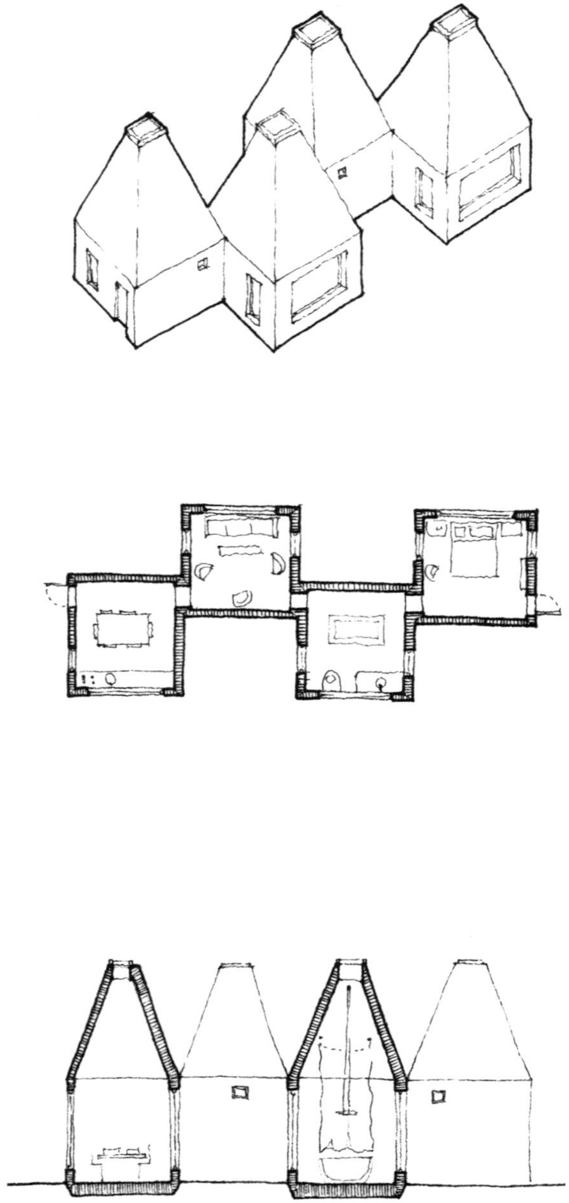

no.224

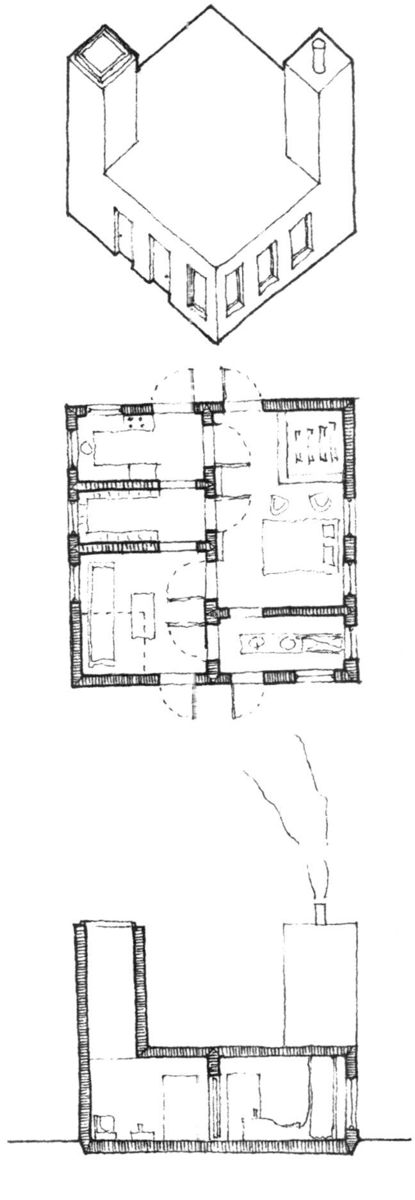

no.225

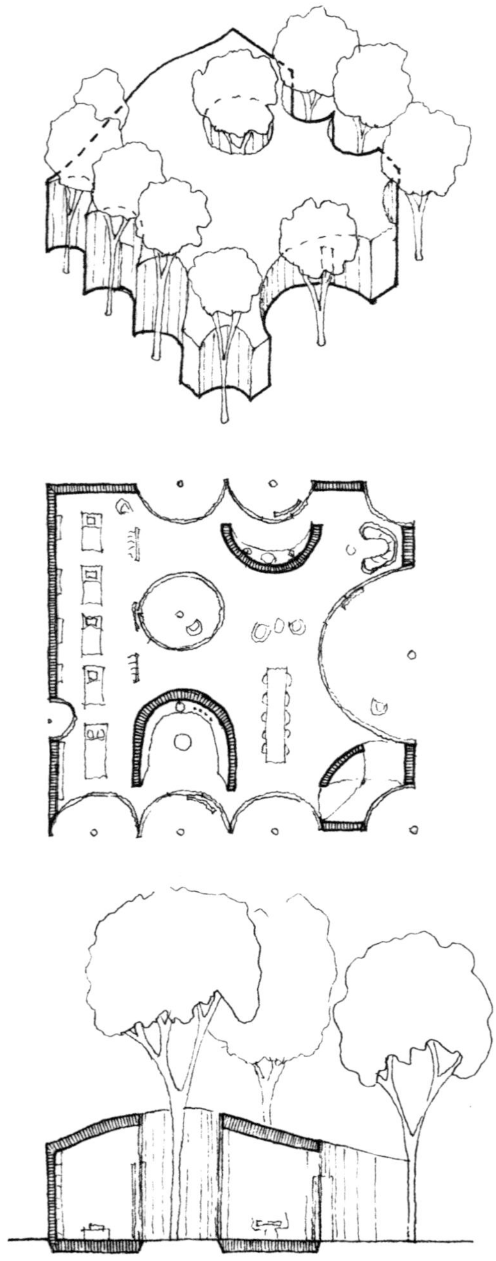

no.226

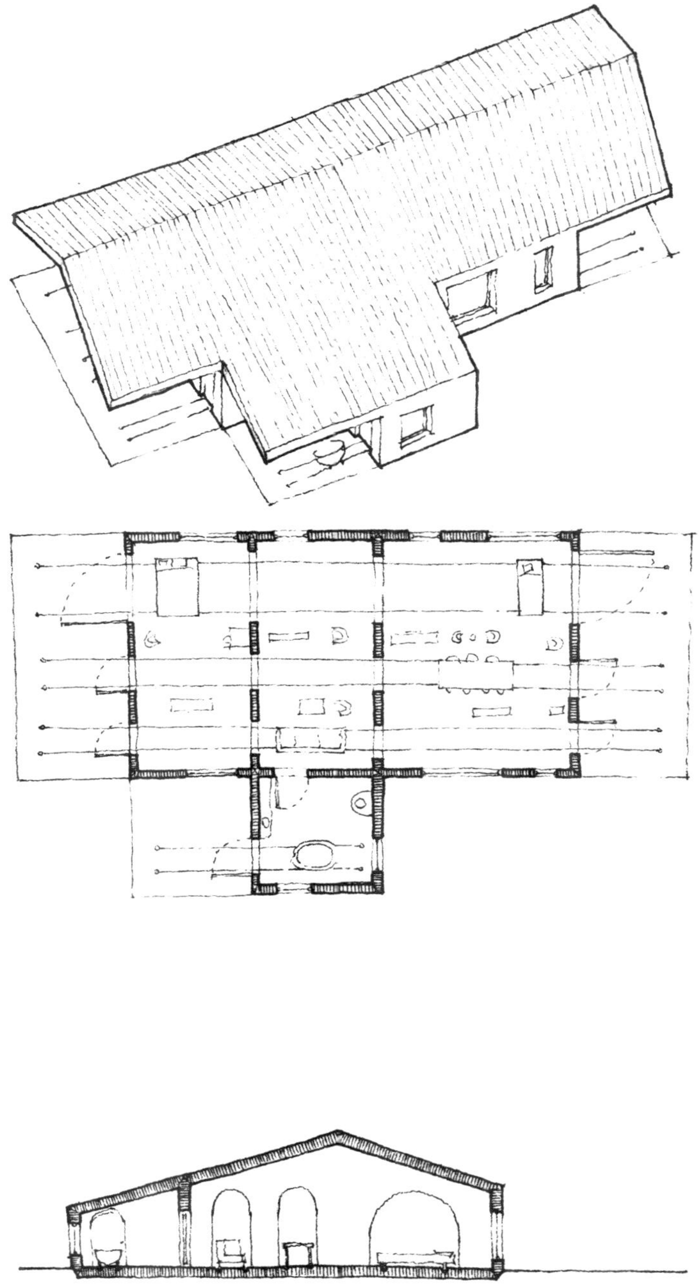

no.227

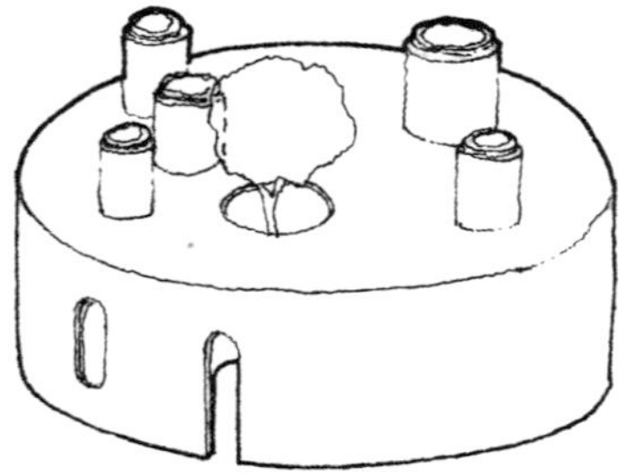

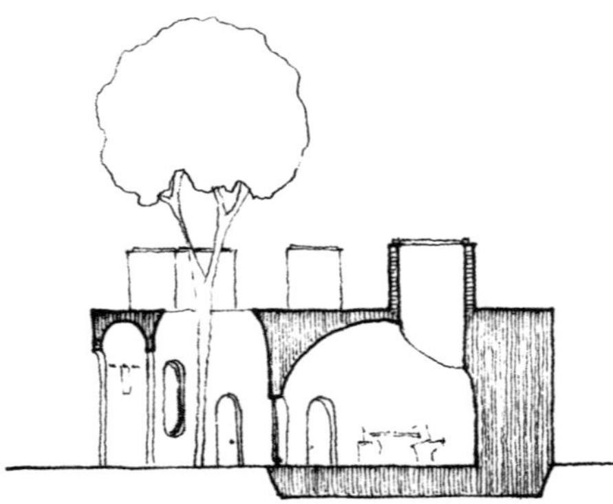

no.228

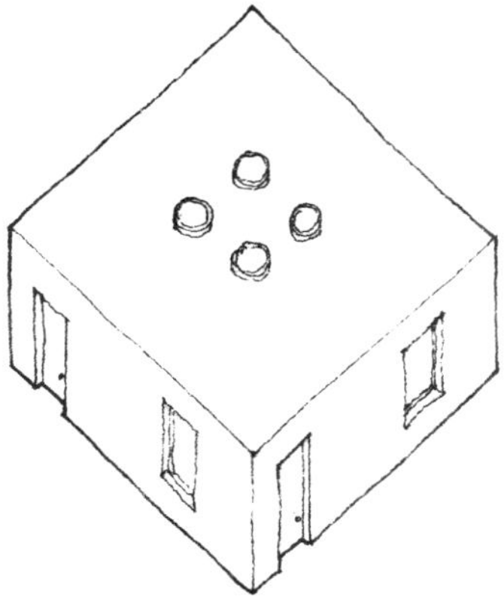

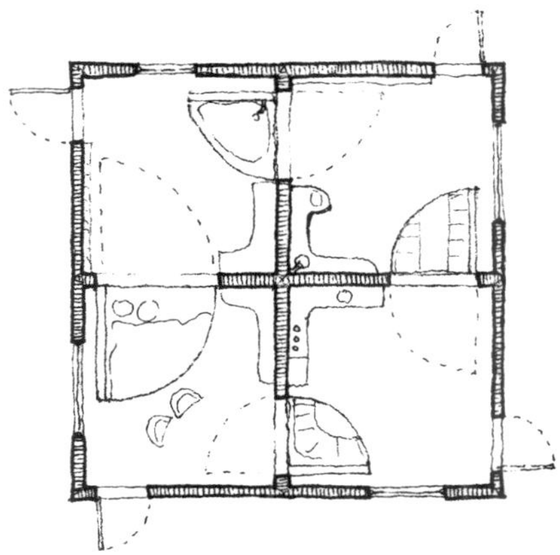

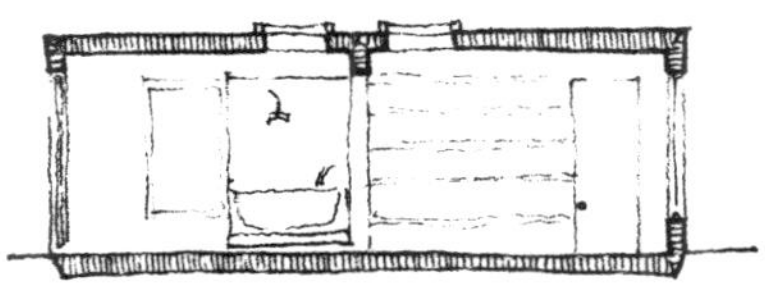

no.229

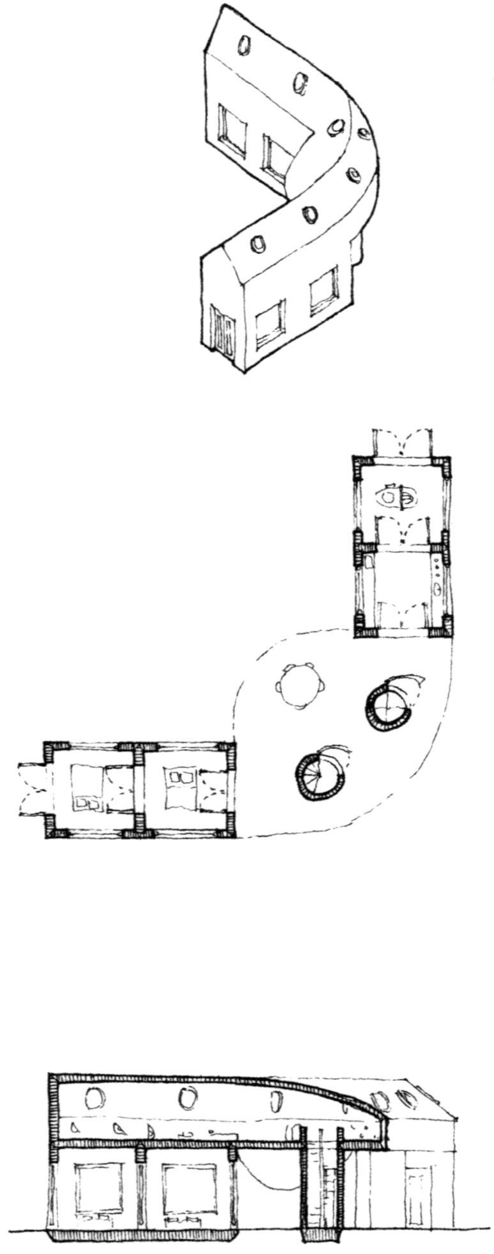

no.230

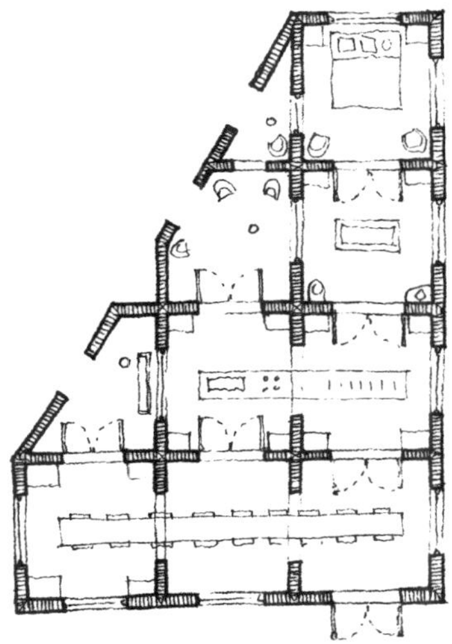

no.231

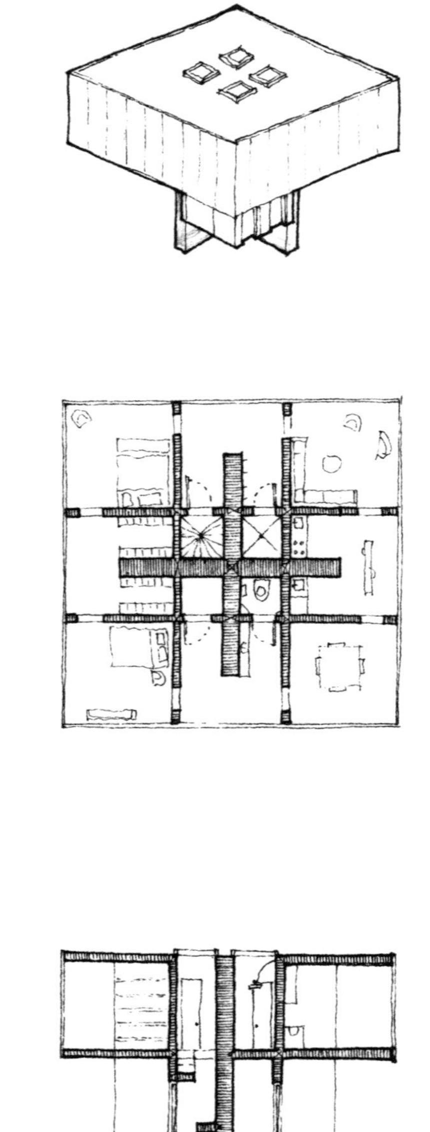

no.232

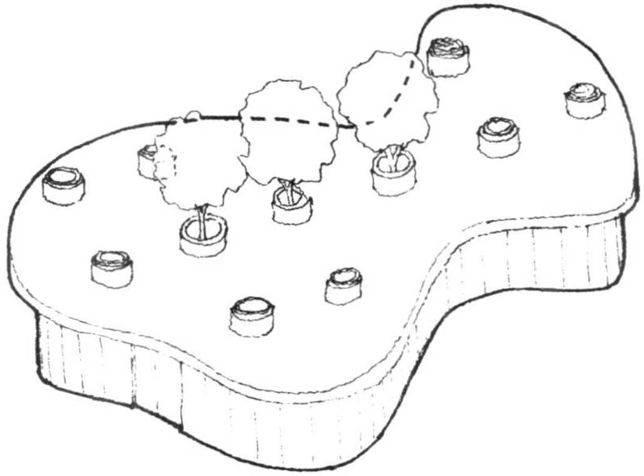

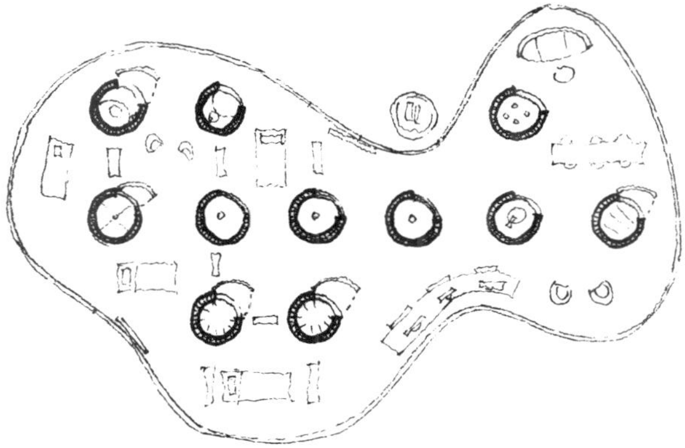

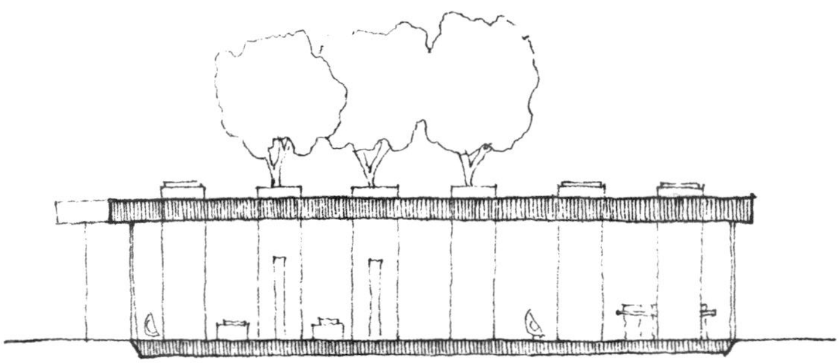

no.233

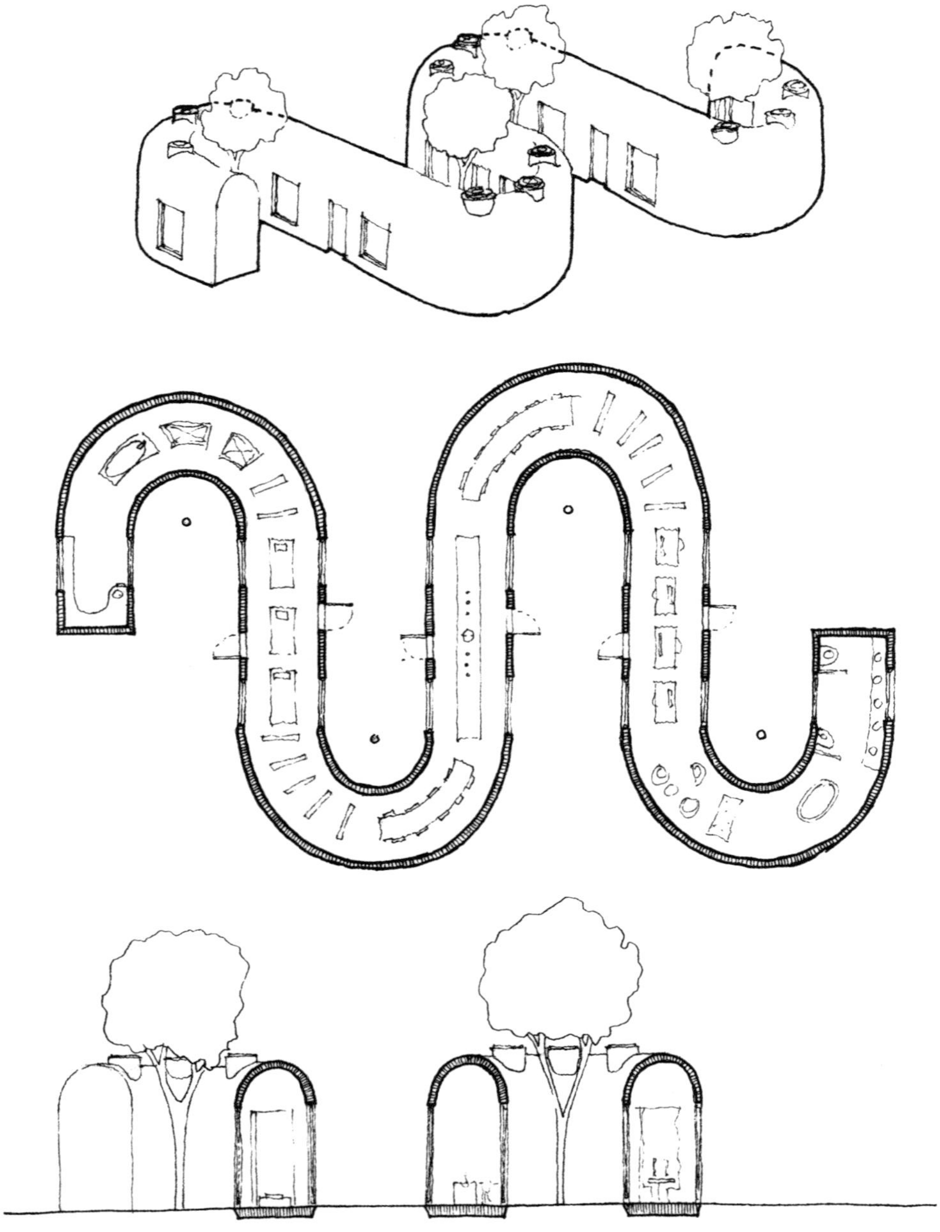

no.234

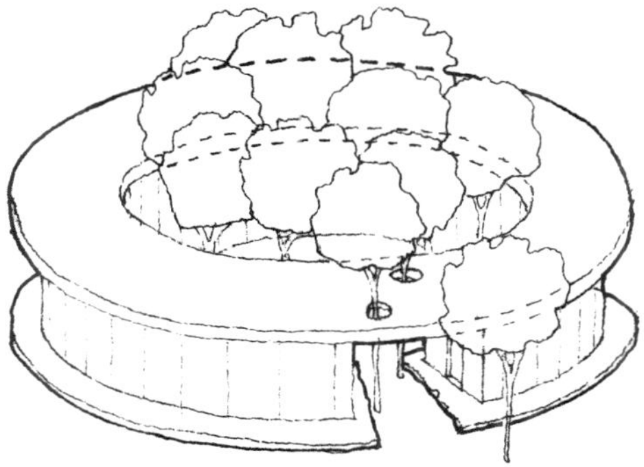

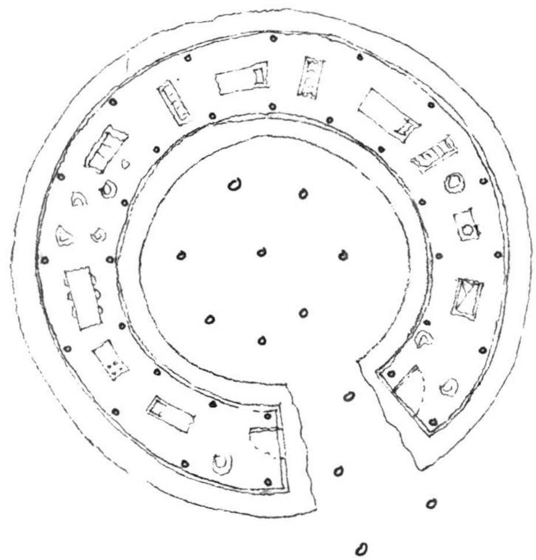

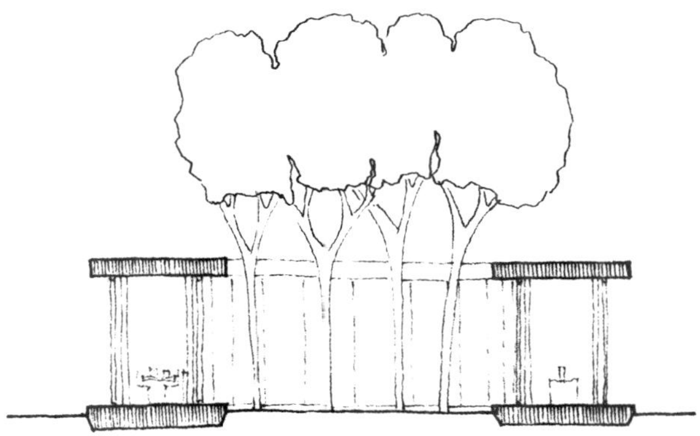

no.235

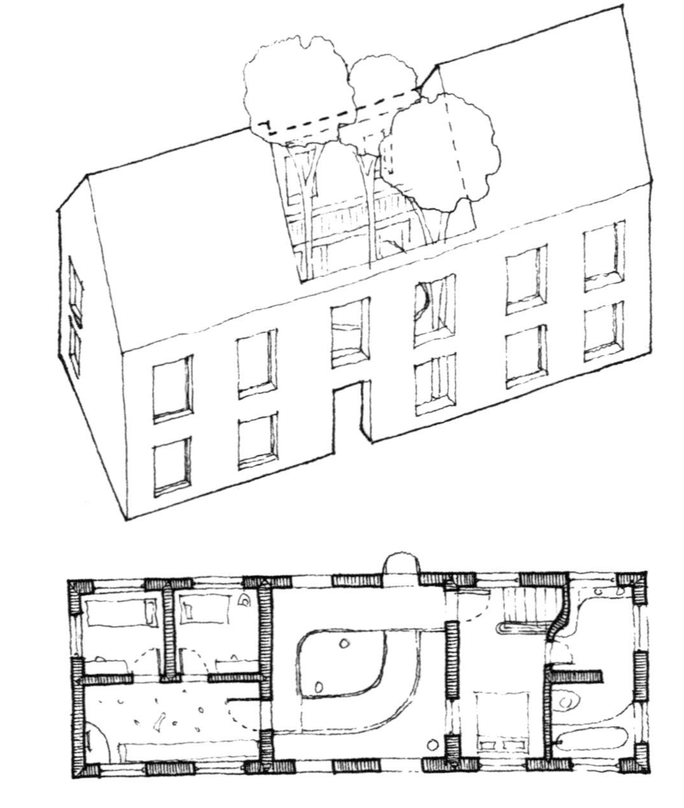

no.236

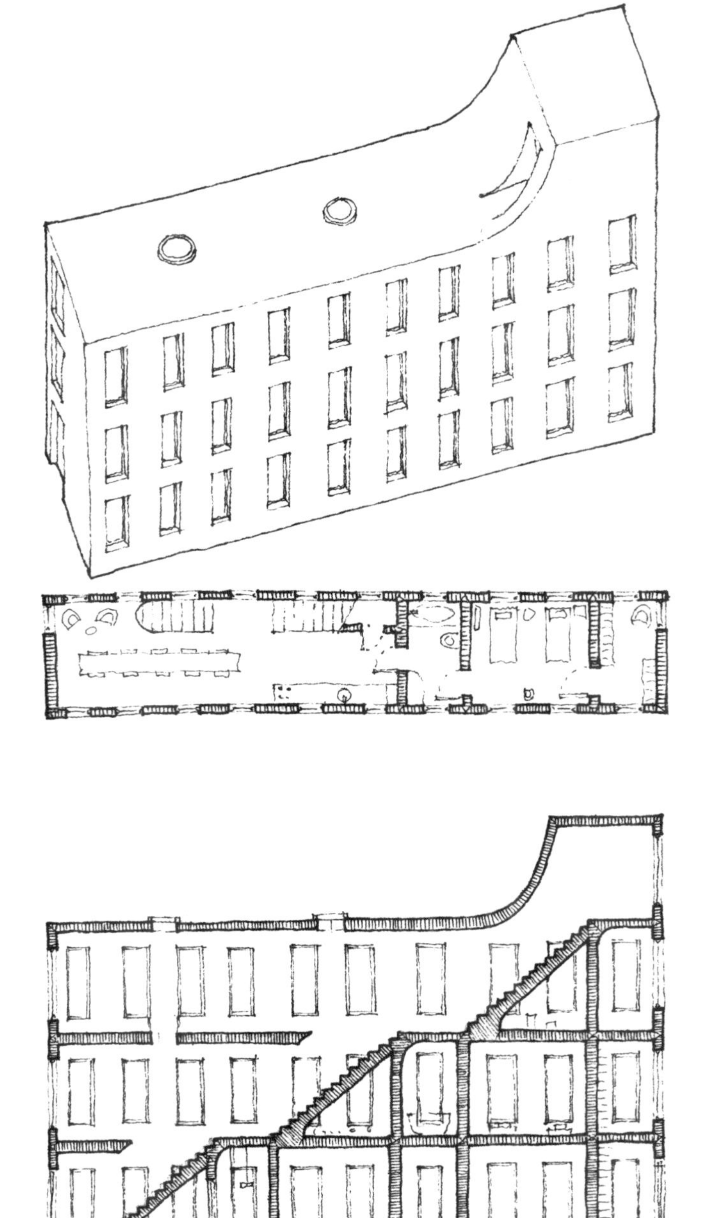

no.237

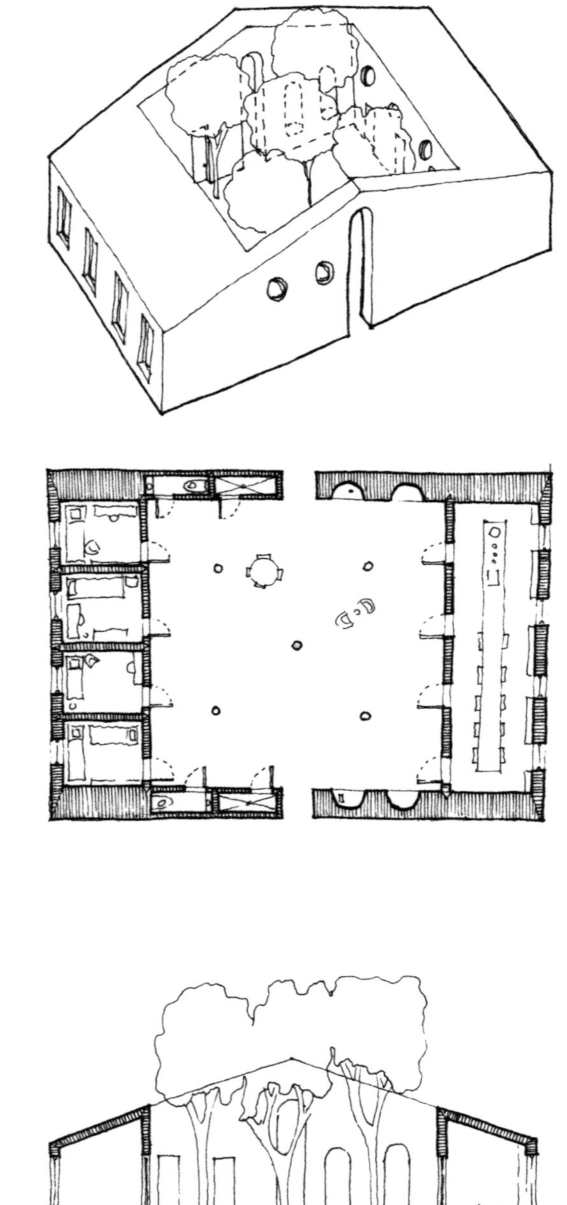

no.238

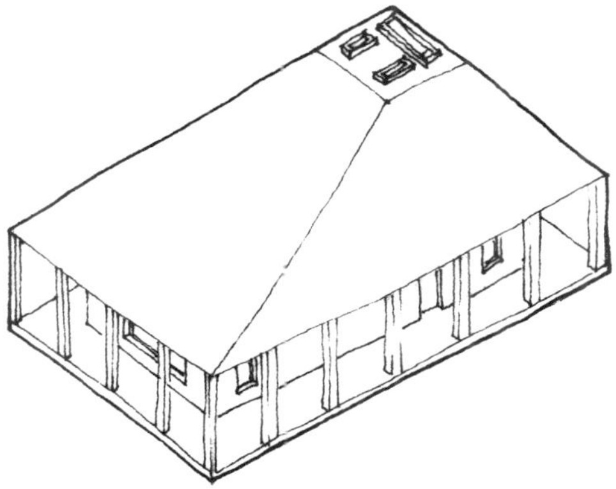

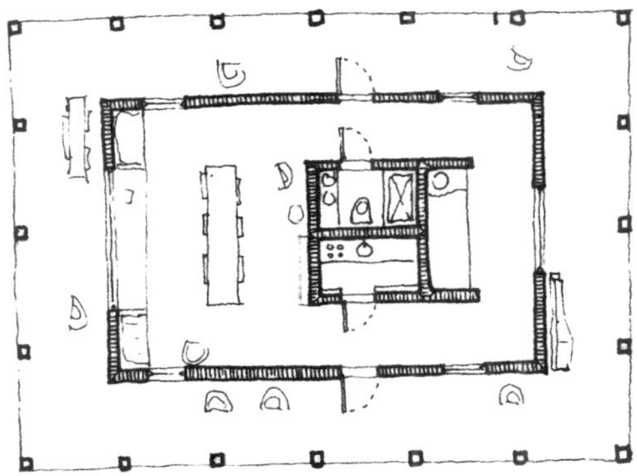

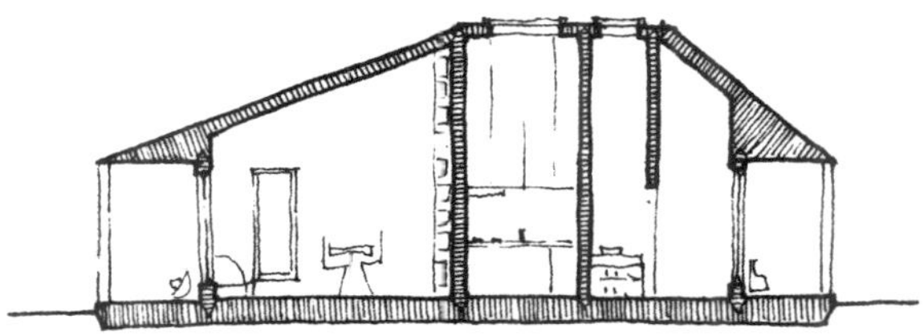

no.239

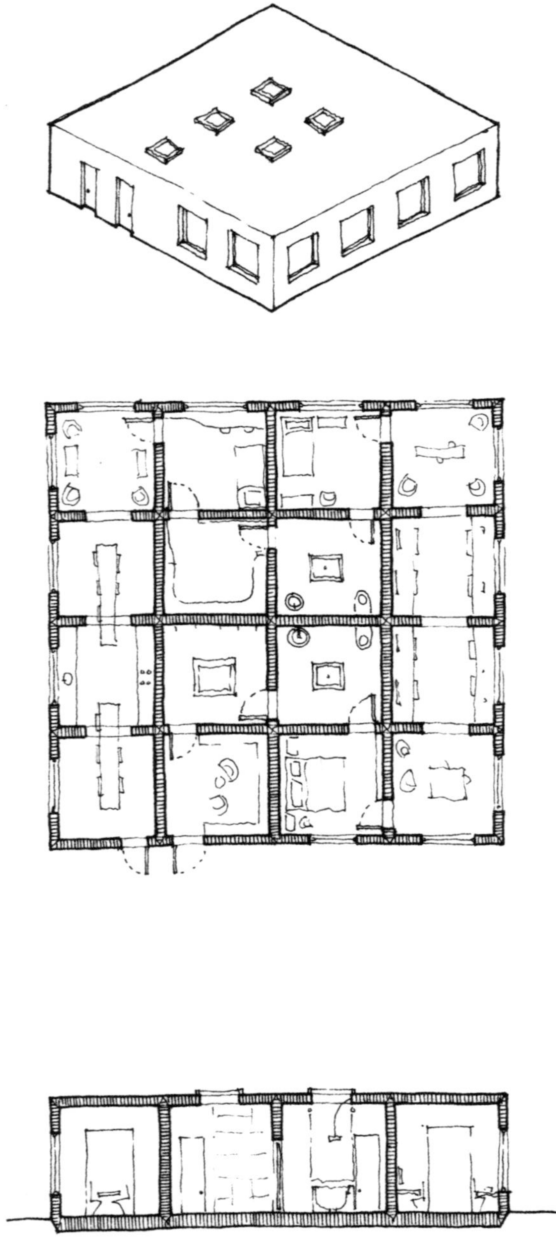

no.240

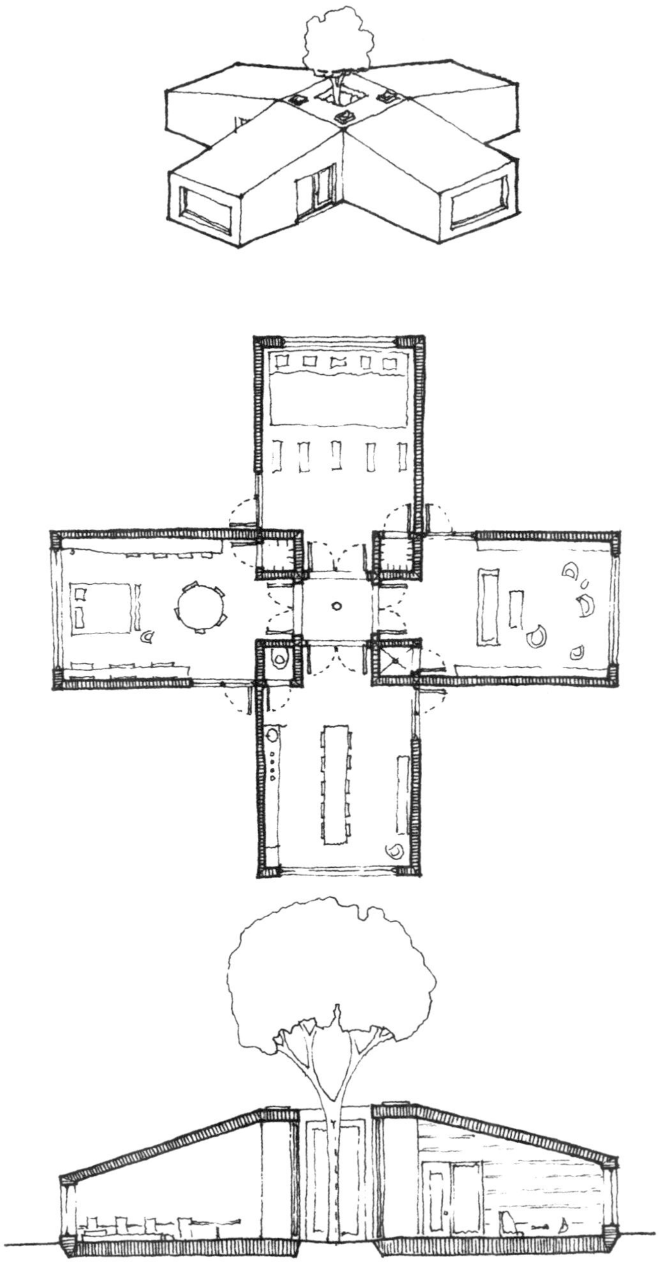

no.241

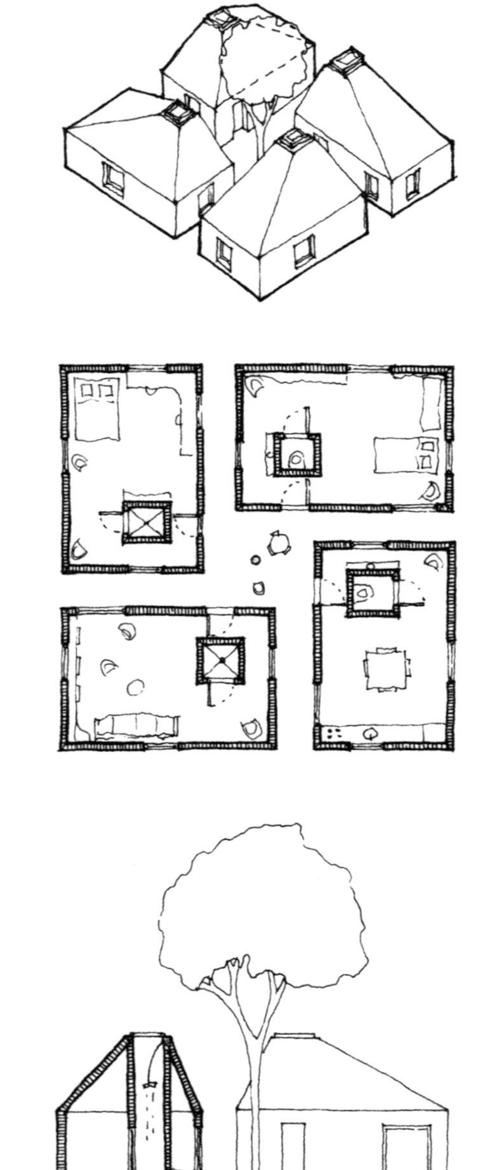

no.242

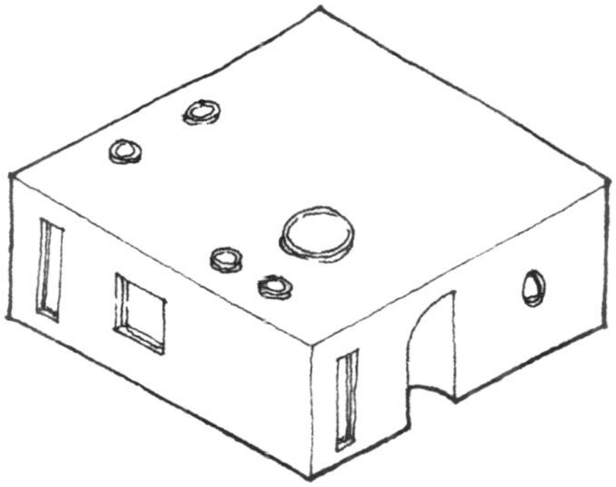

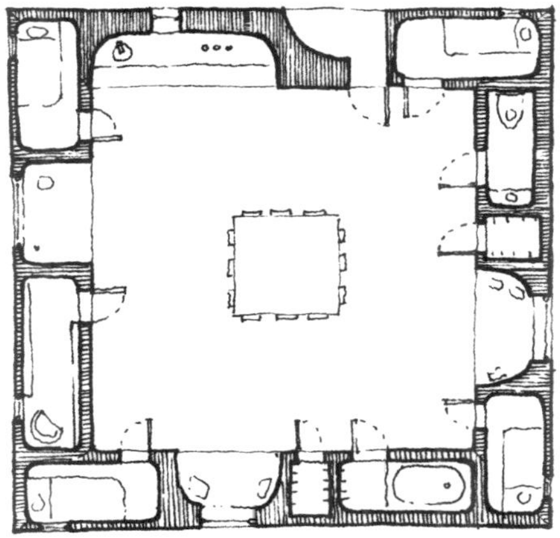

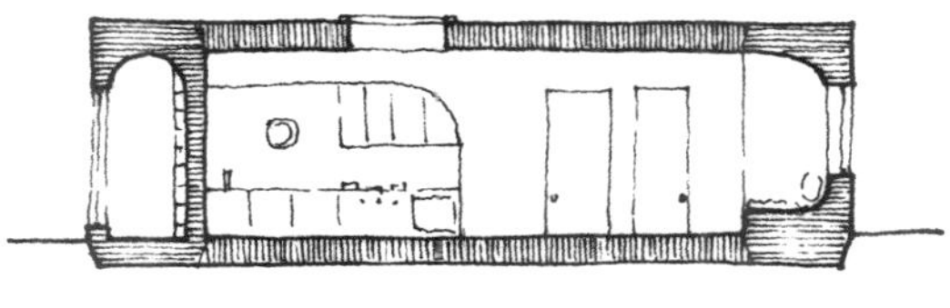

no.243

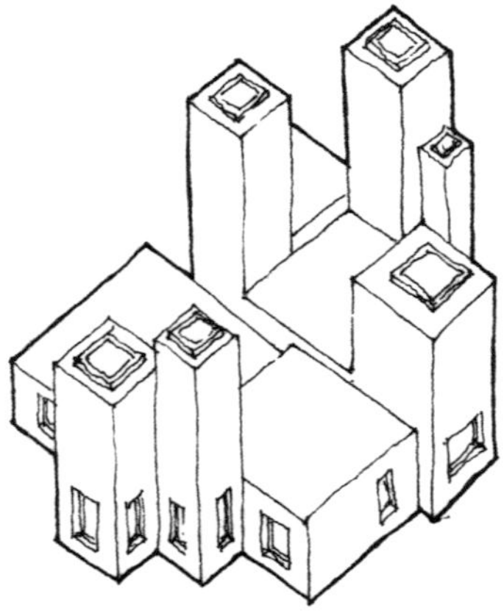

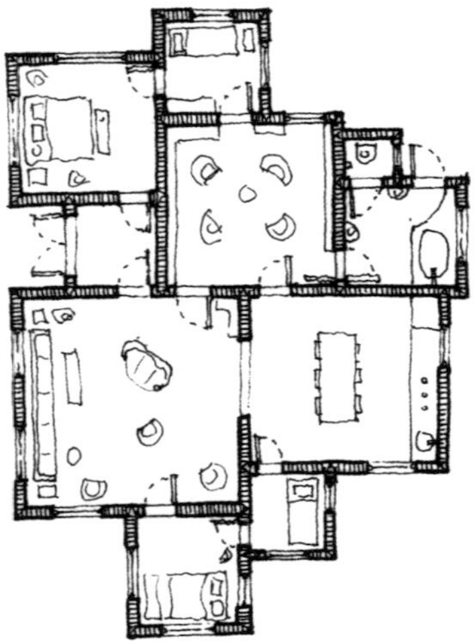

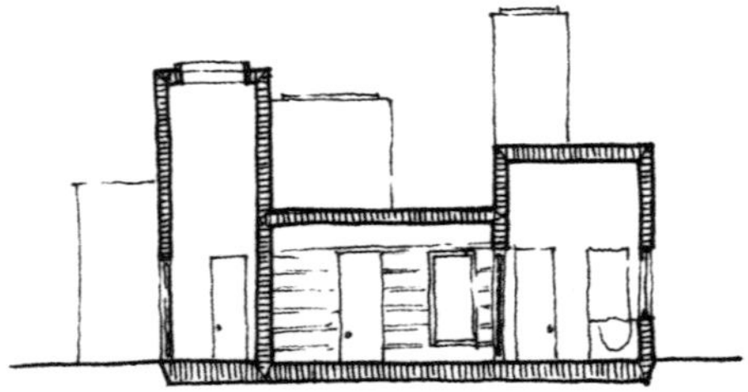

no.244

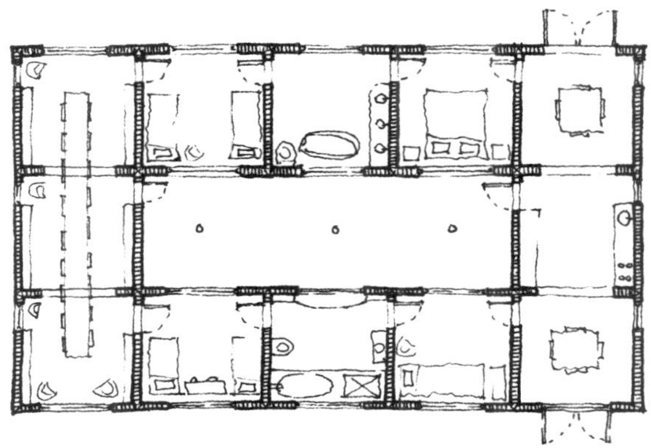

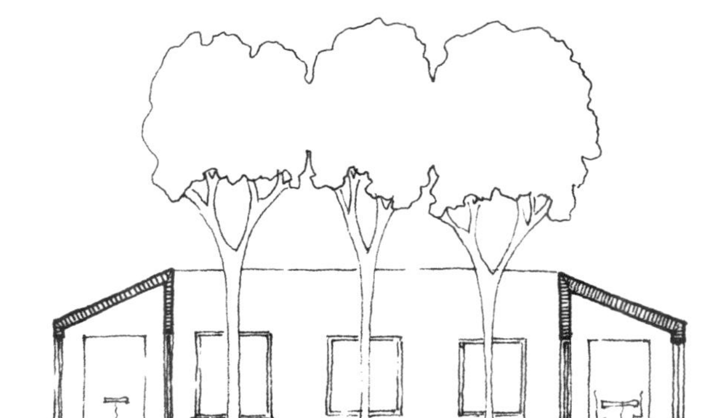

no.245

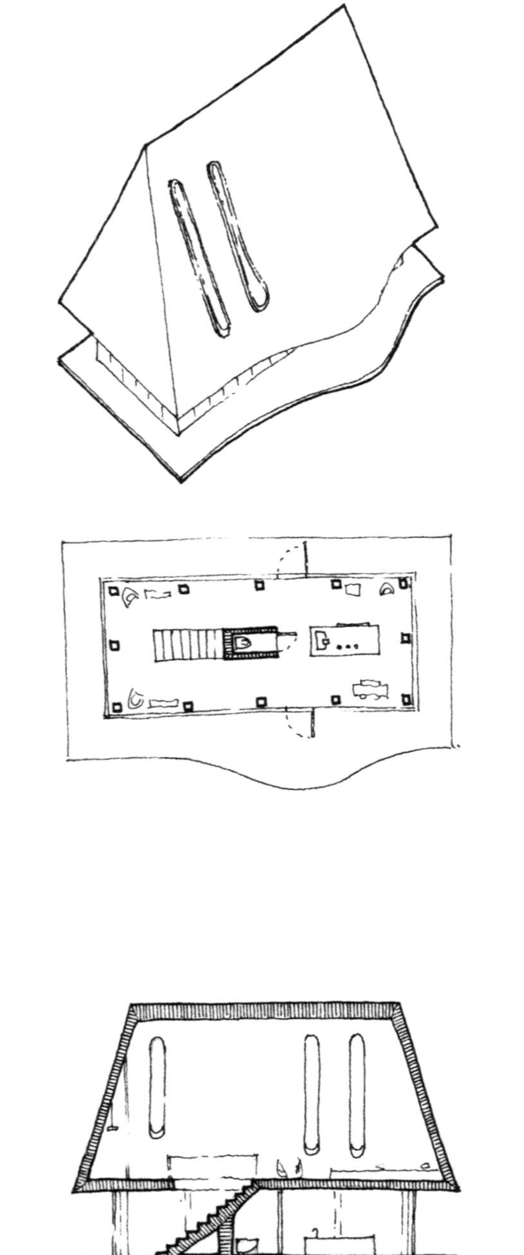

no.246

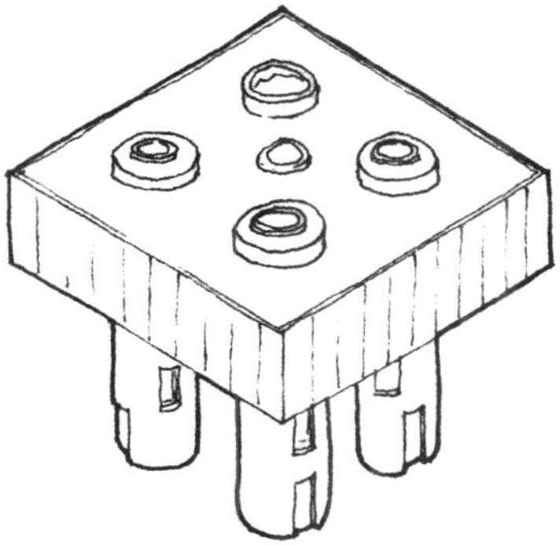

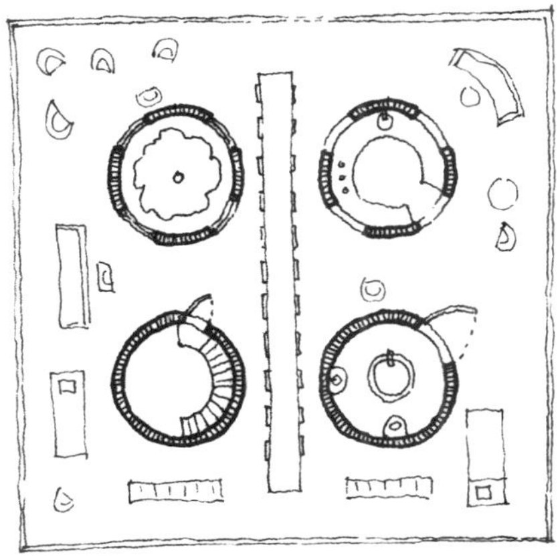

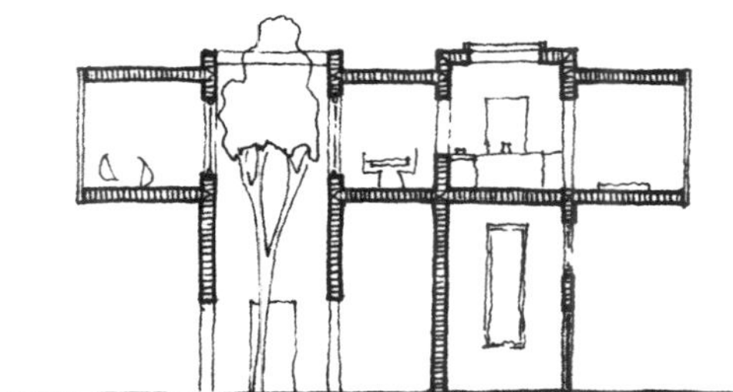

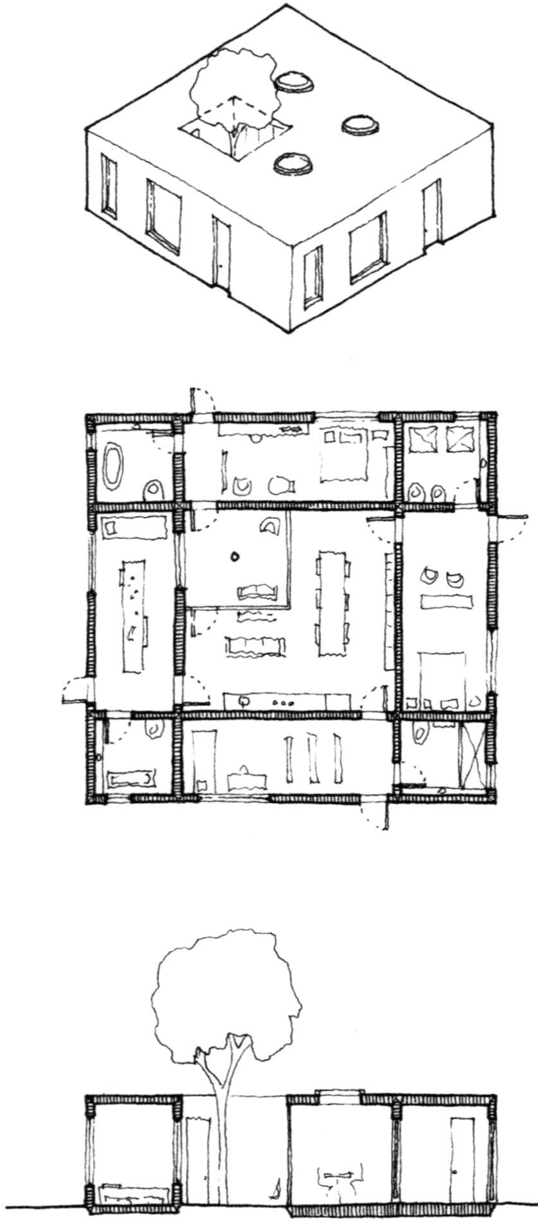

no.248

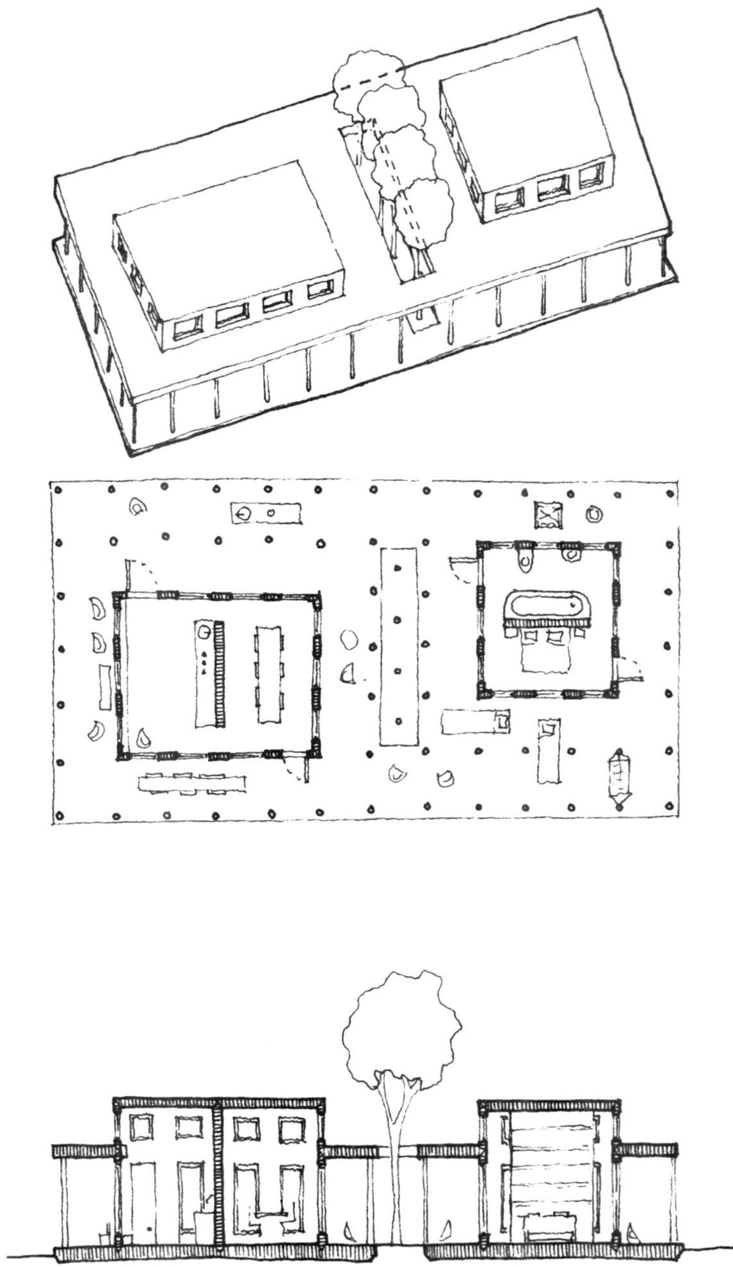

no.249

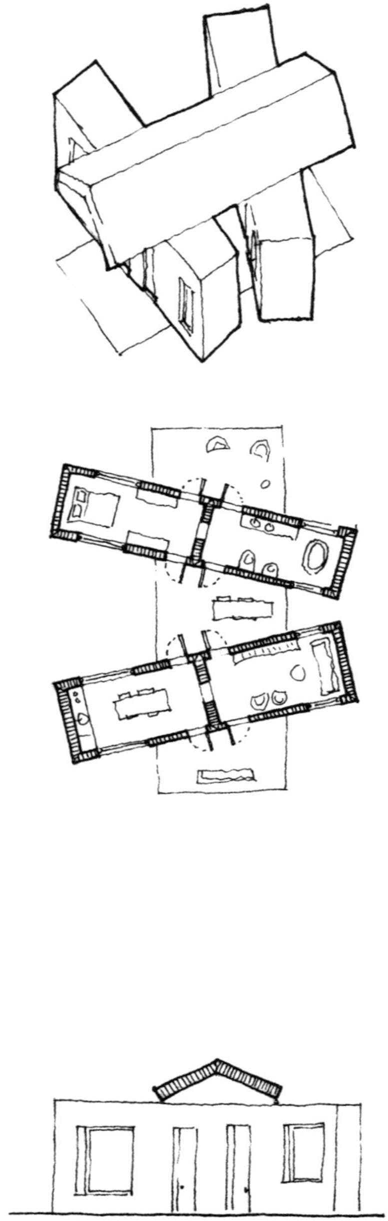

no.250

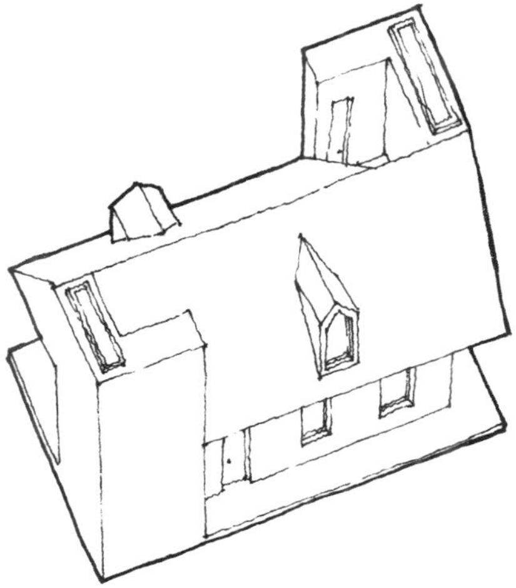

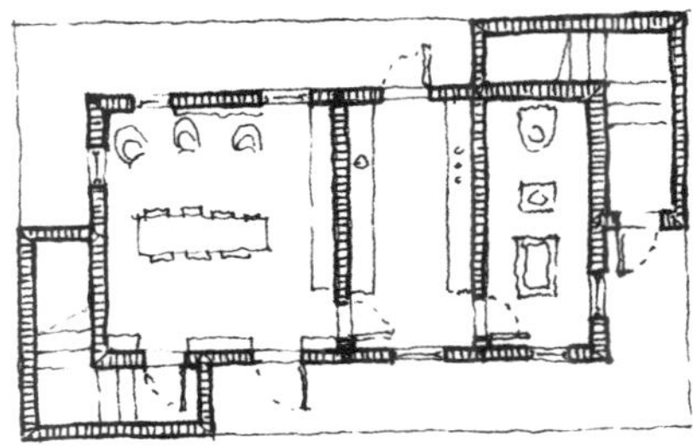

no.251

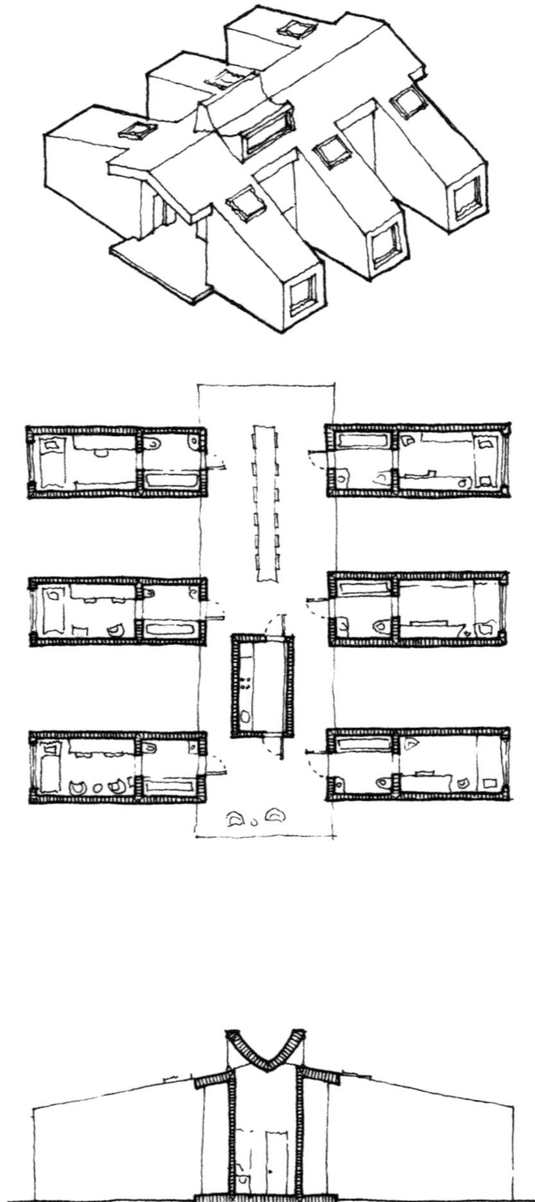

no.252

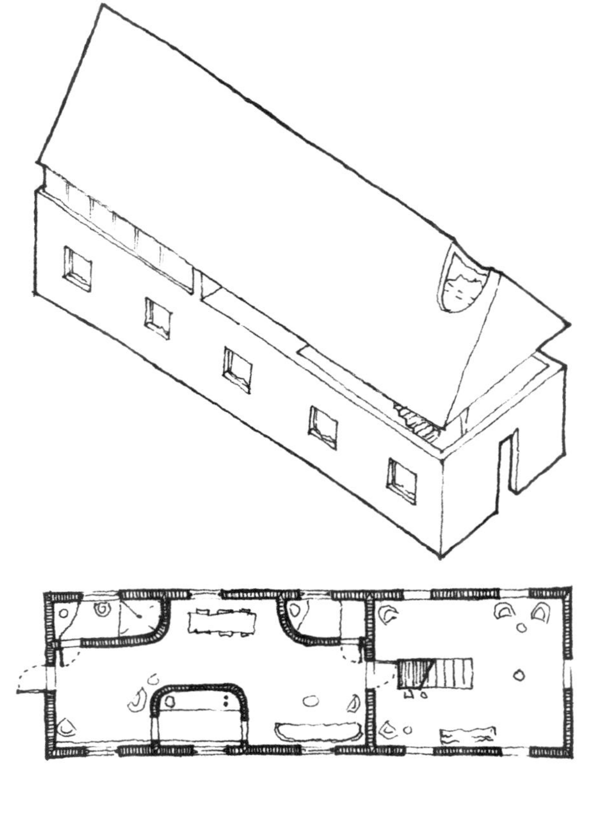

no.253

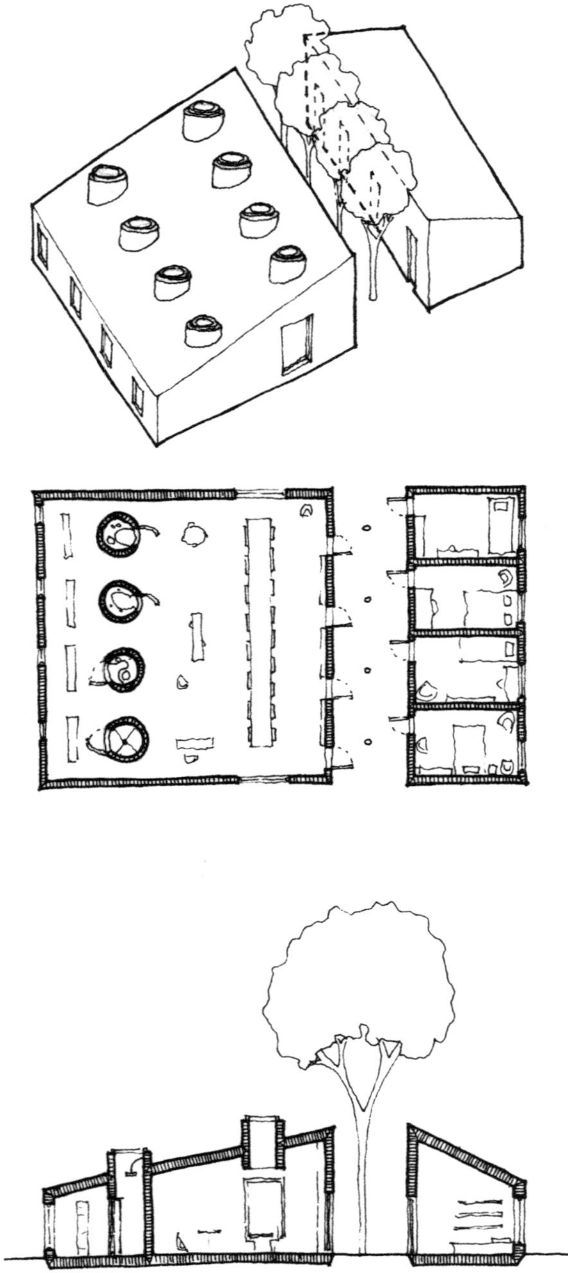

no.254

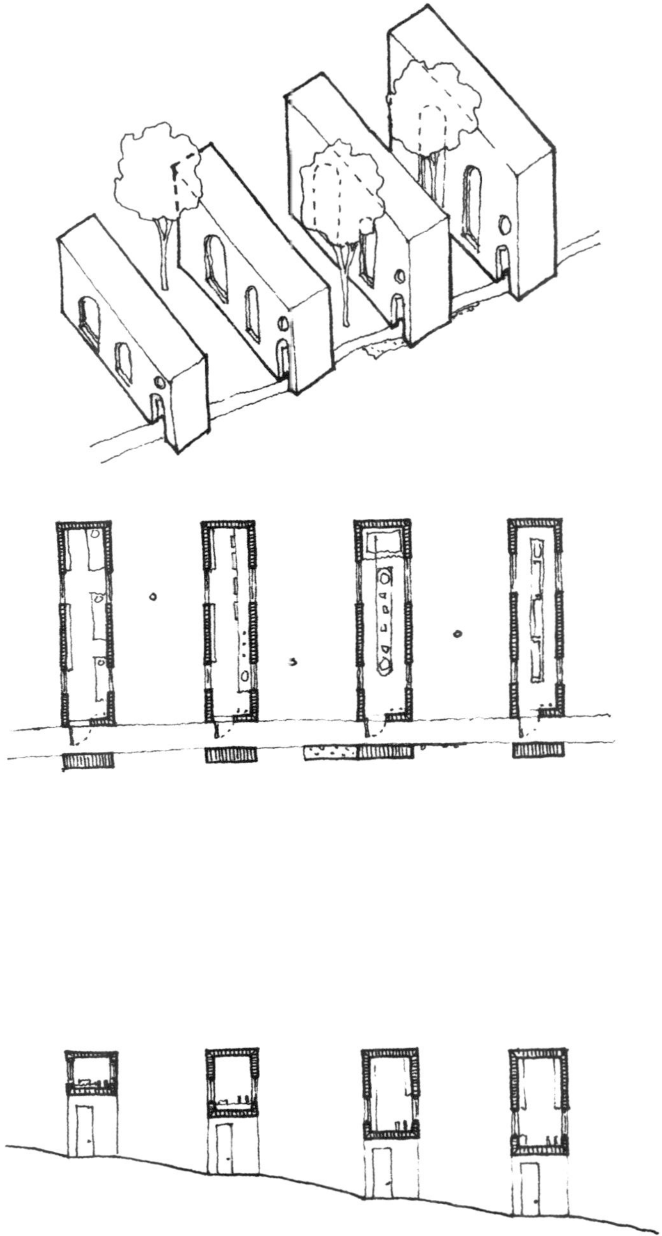

no.255

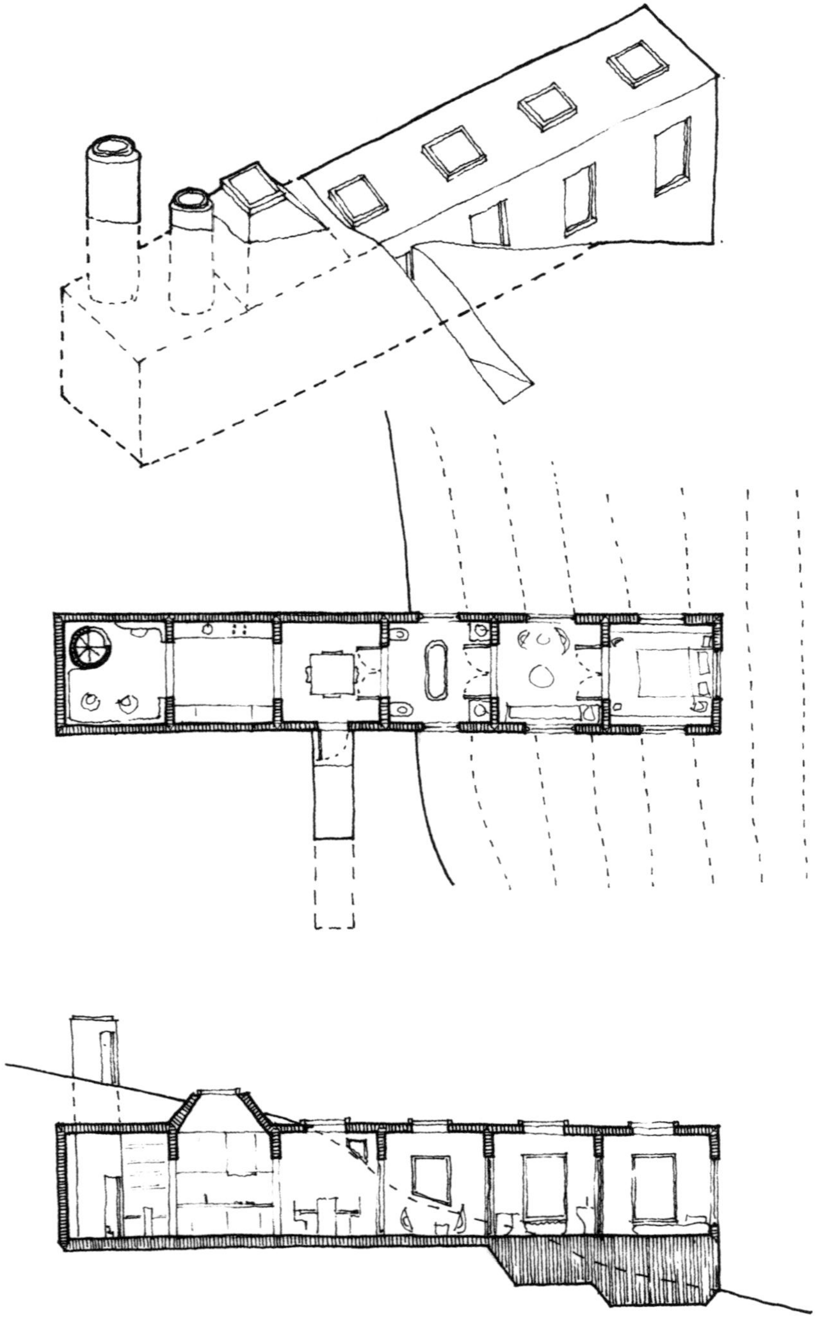

no.256

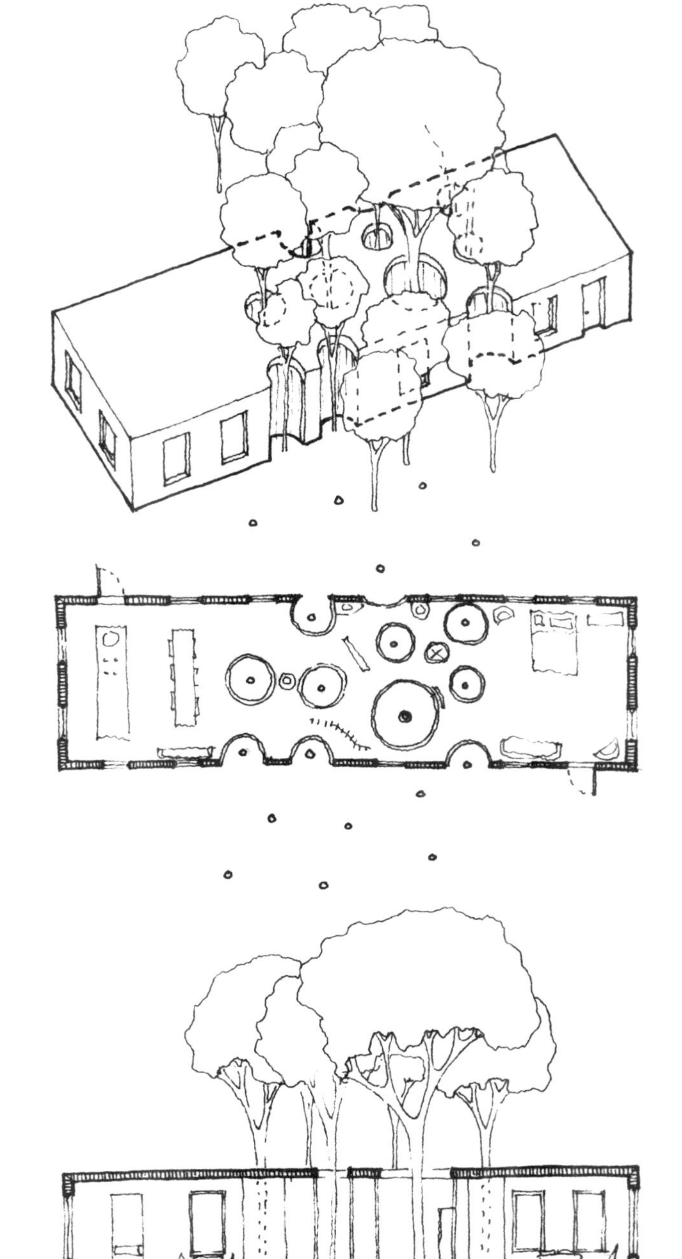

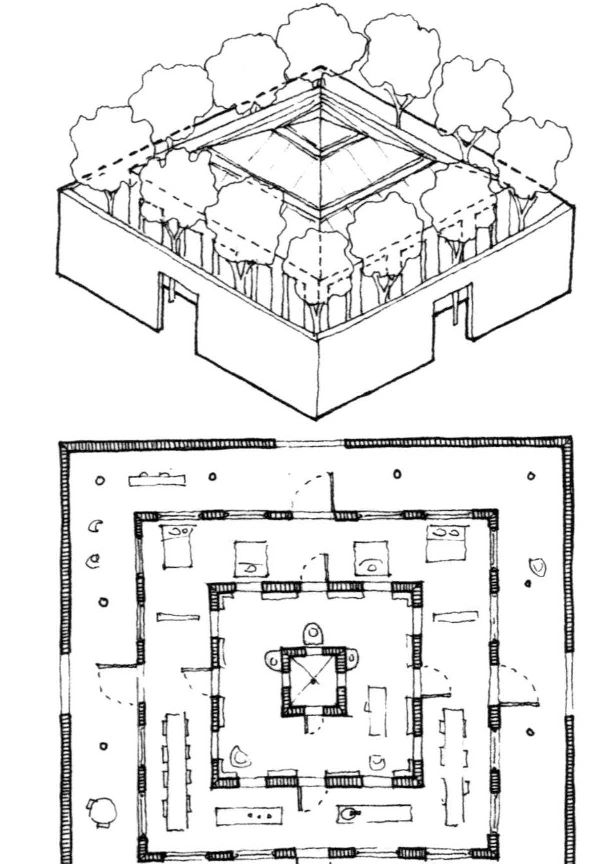

no.258

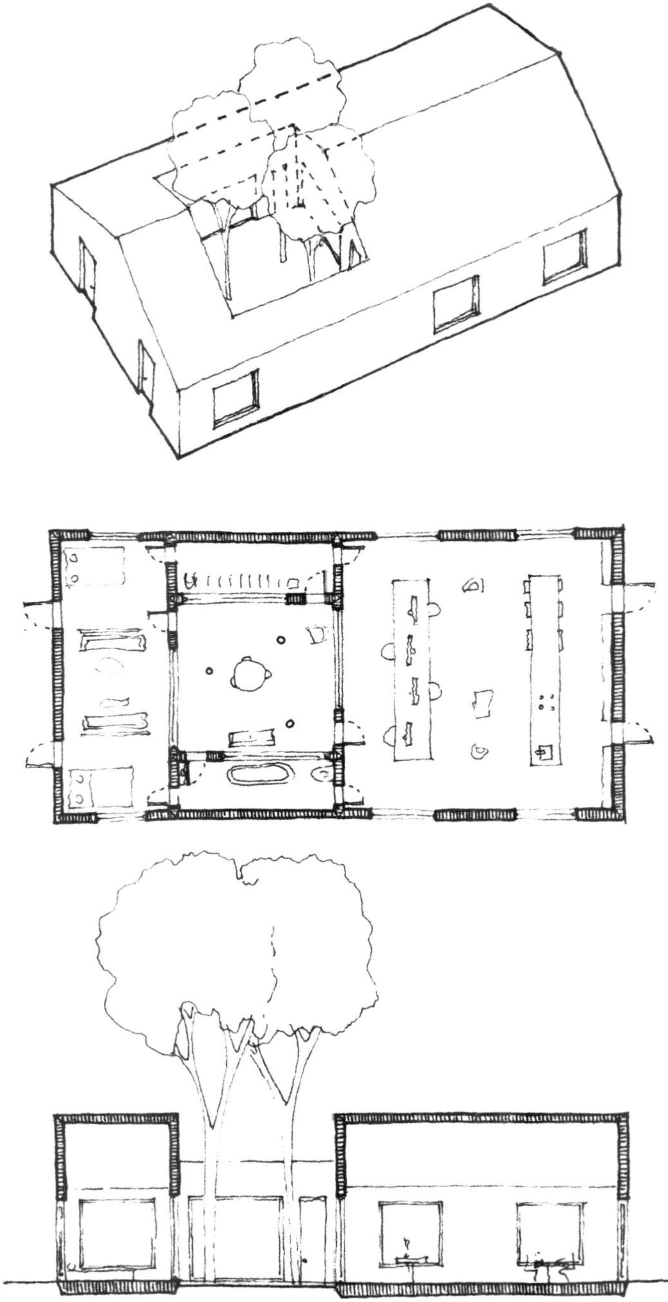

no.259

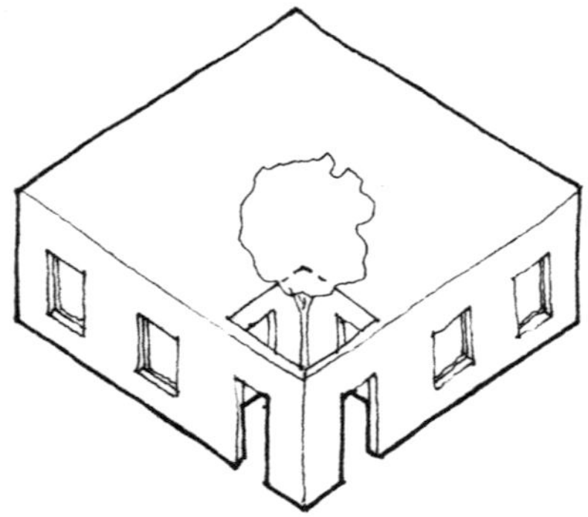

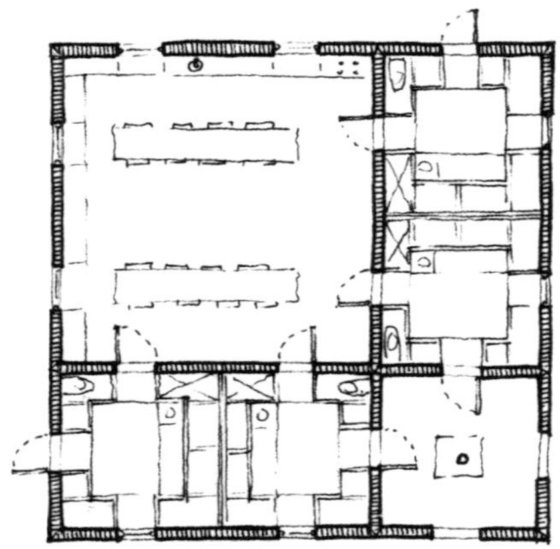

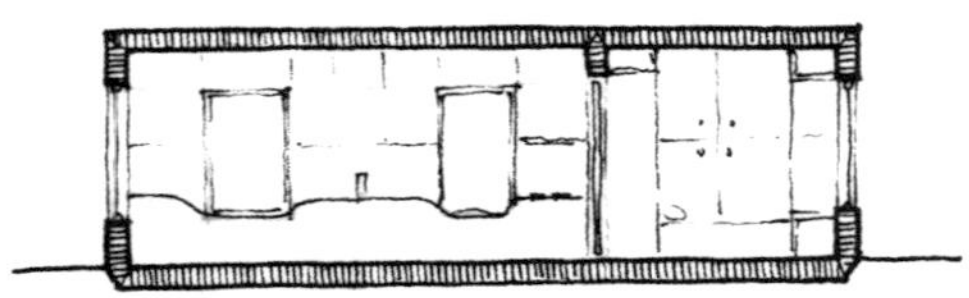

no.260

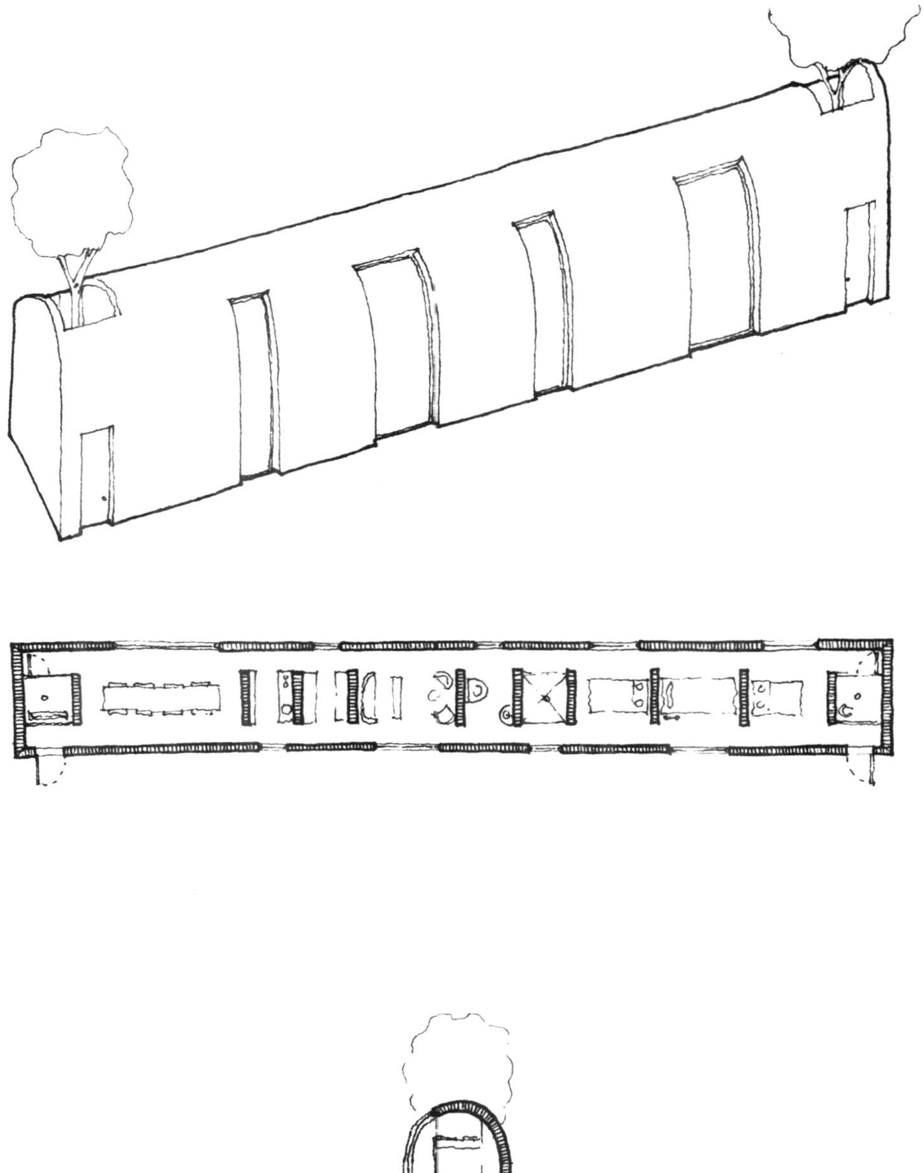

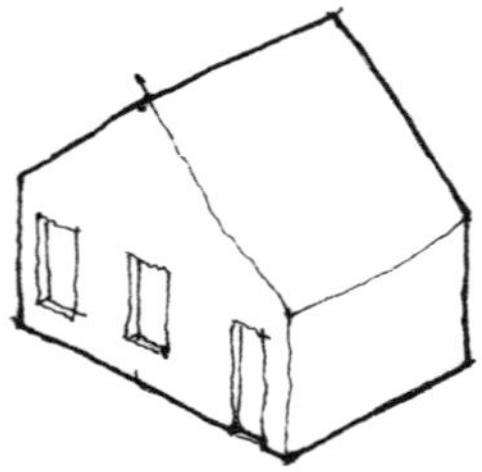

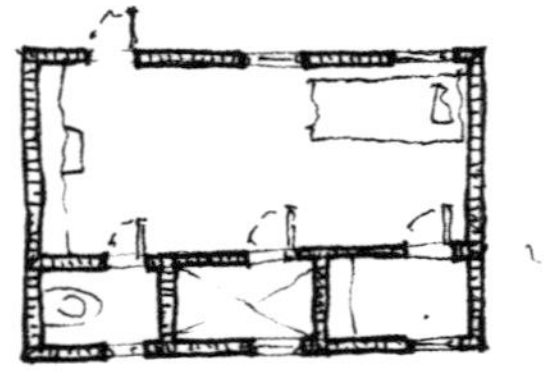

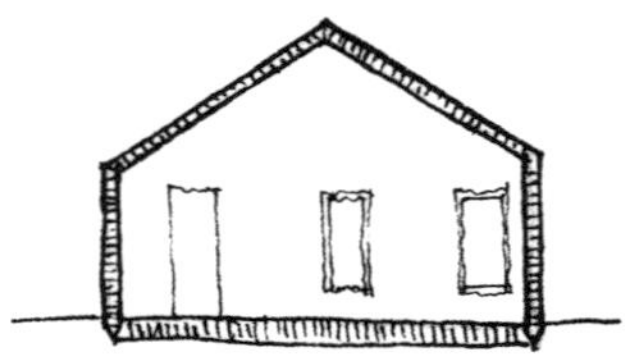

no.262

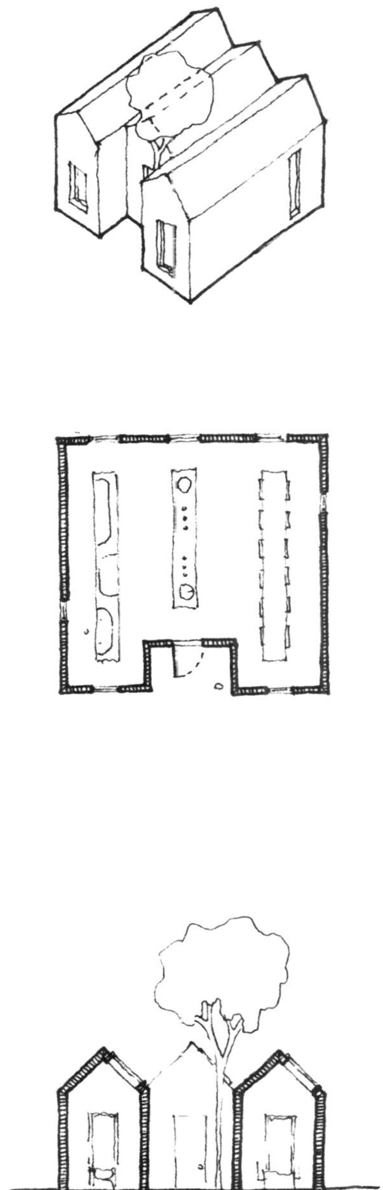

no.263

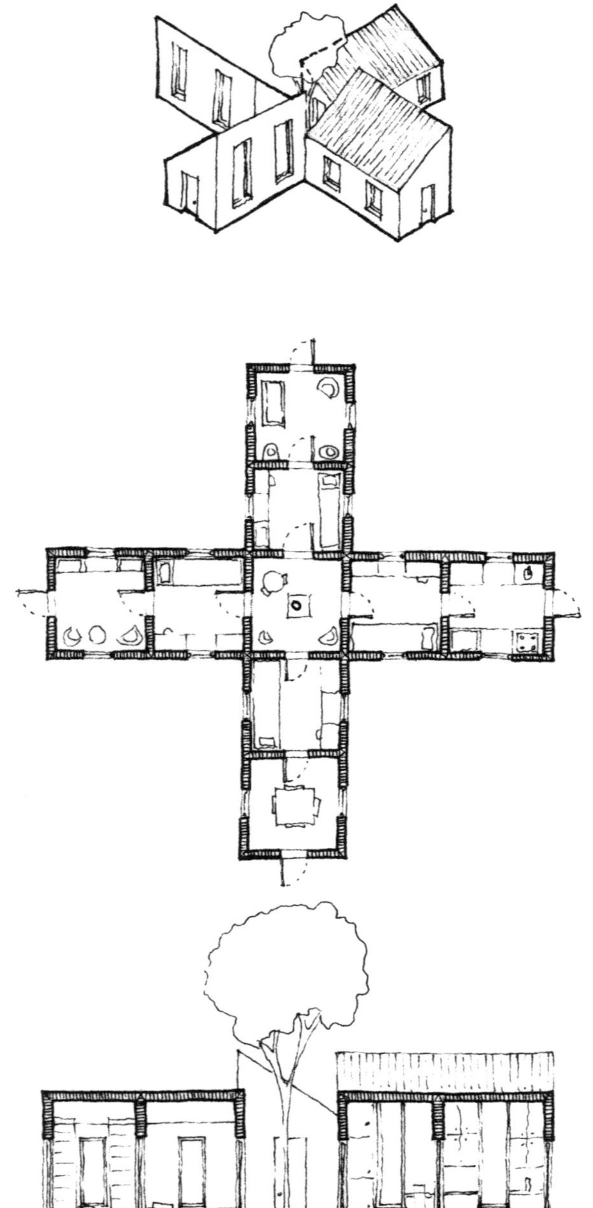

no.264

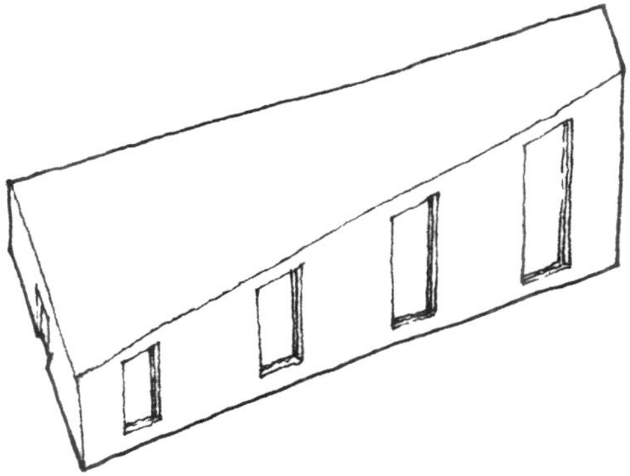

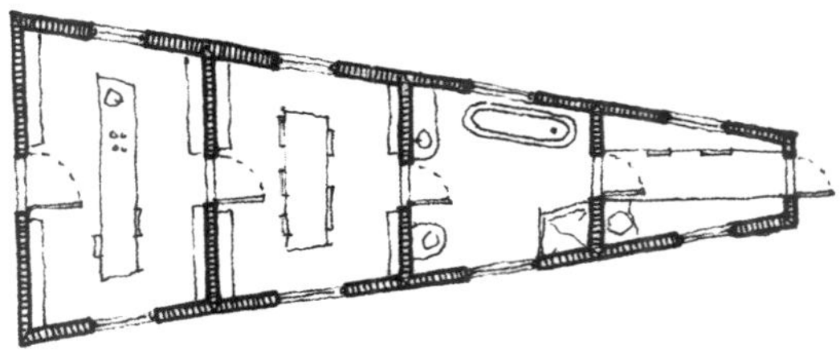

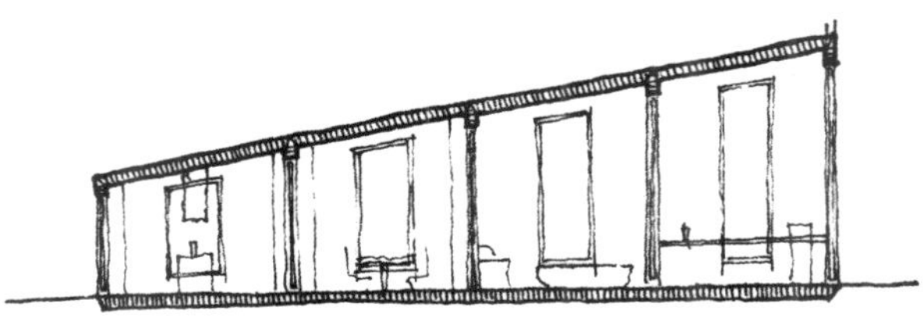

no.265

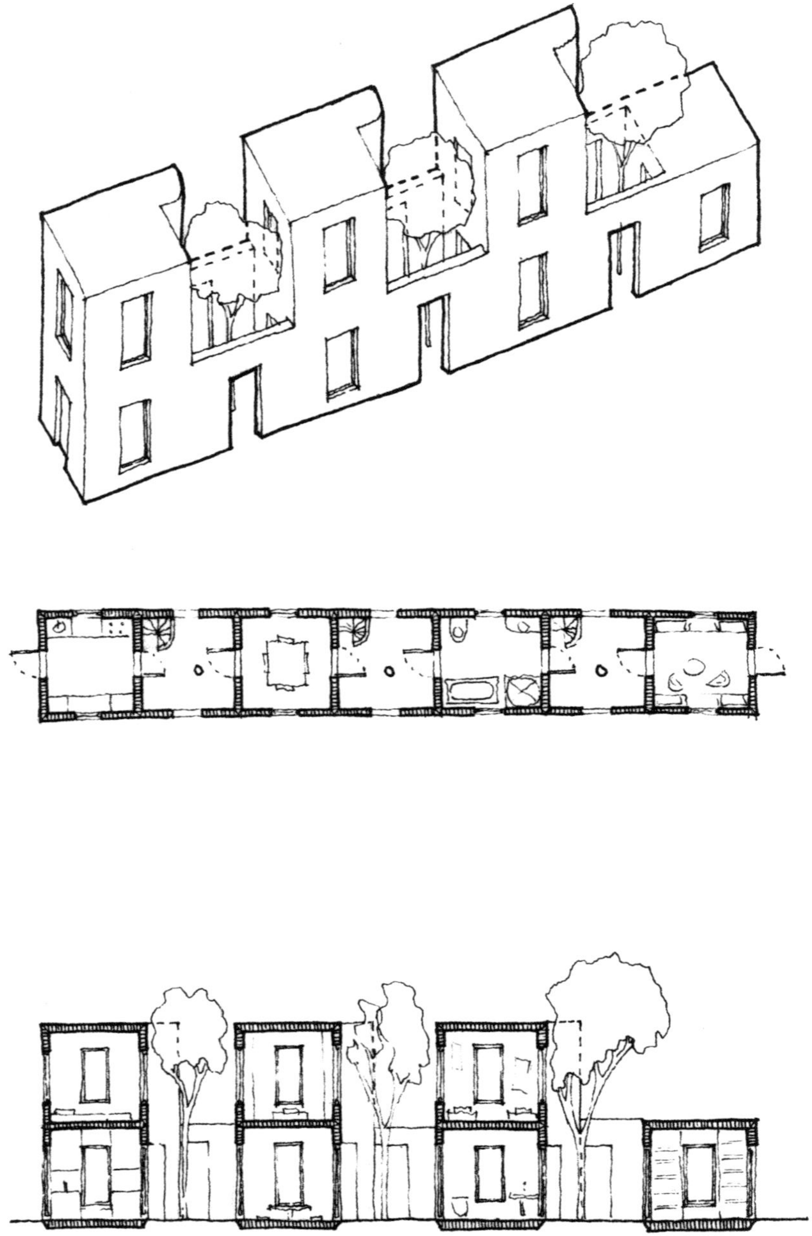

no.266

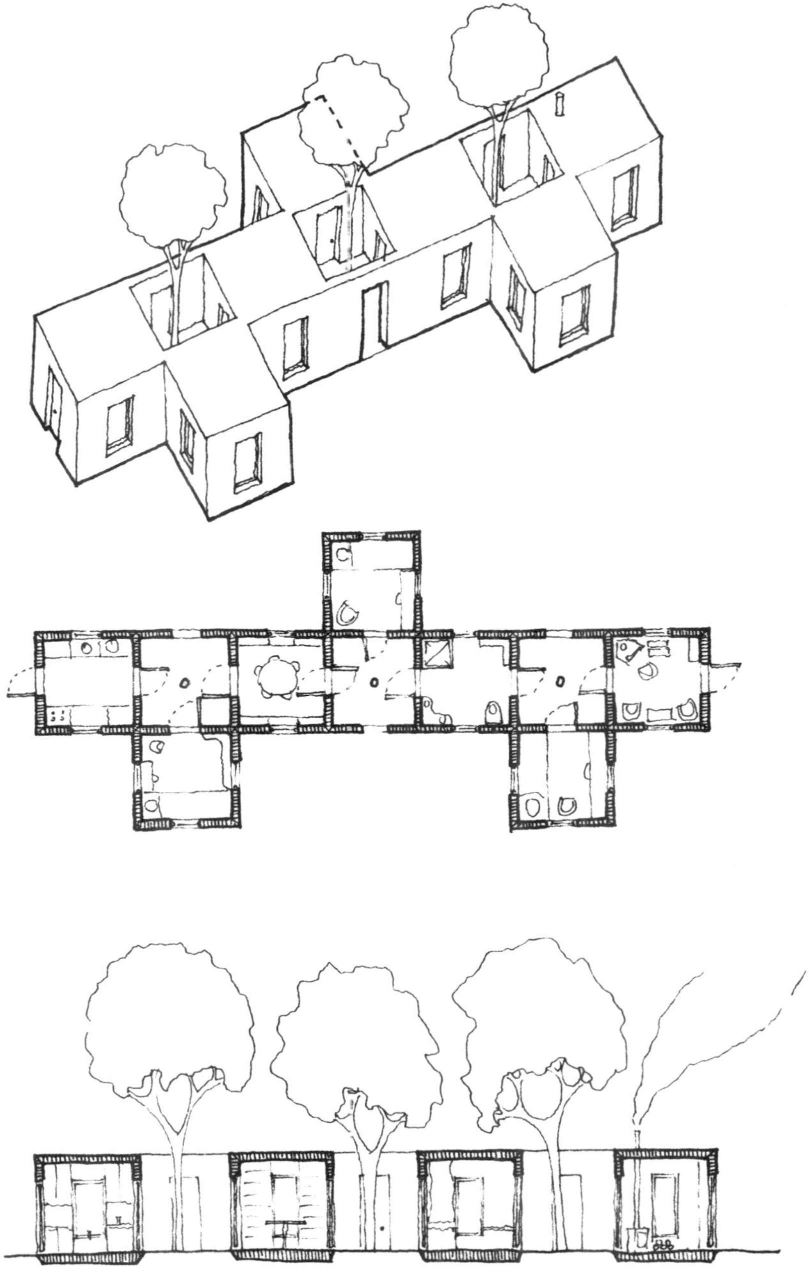

no.267

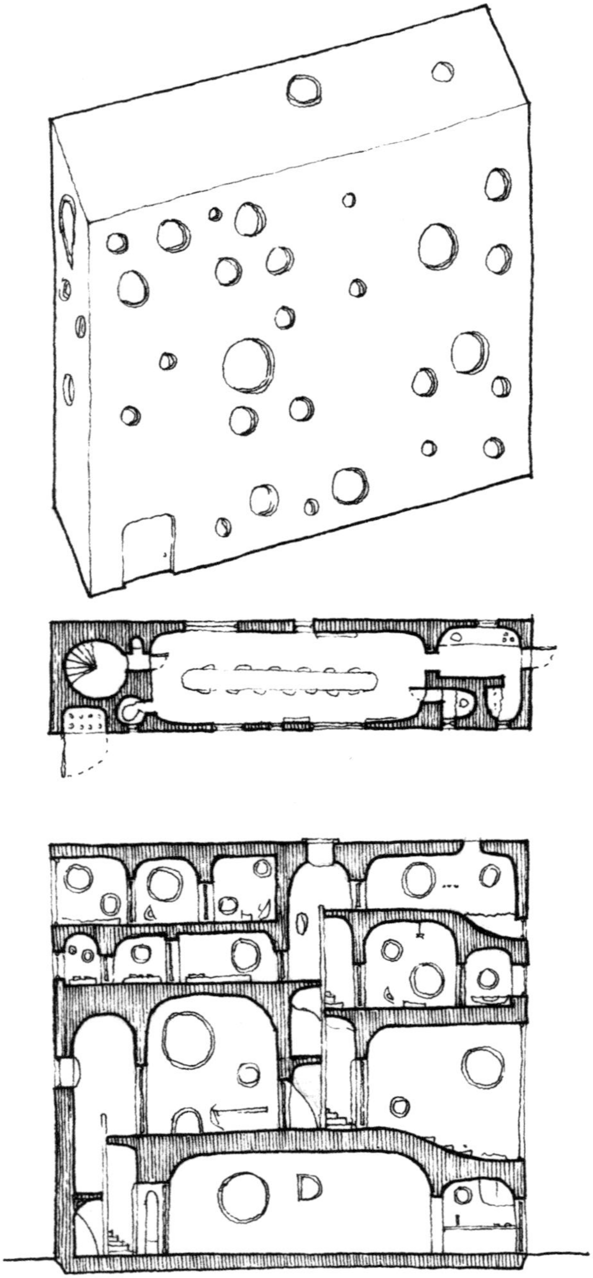

no.268

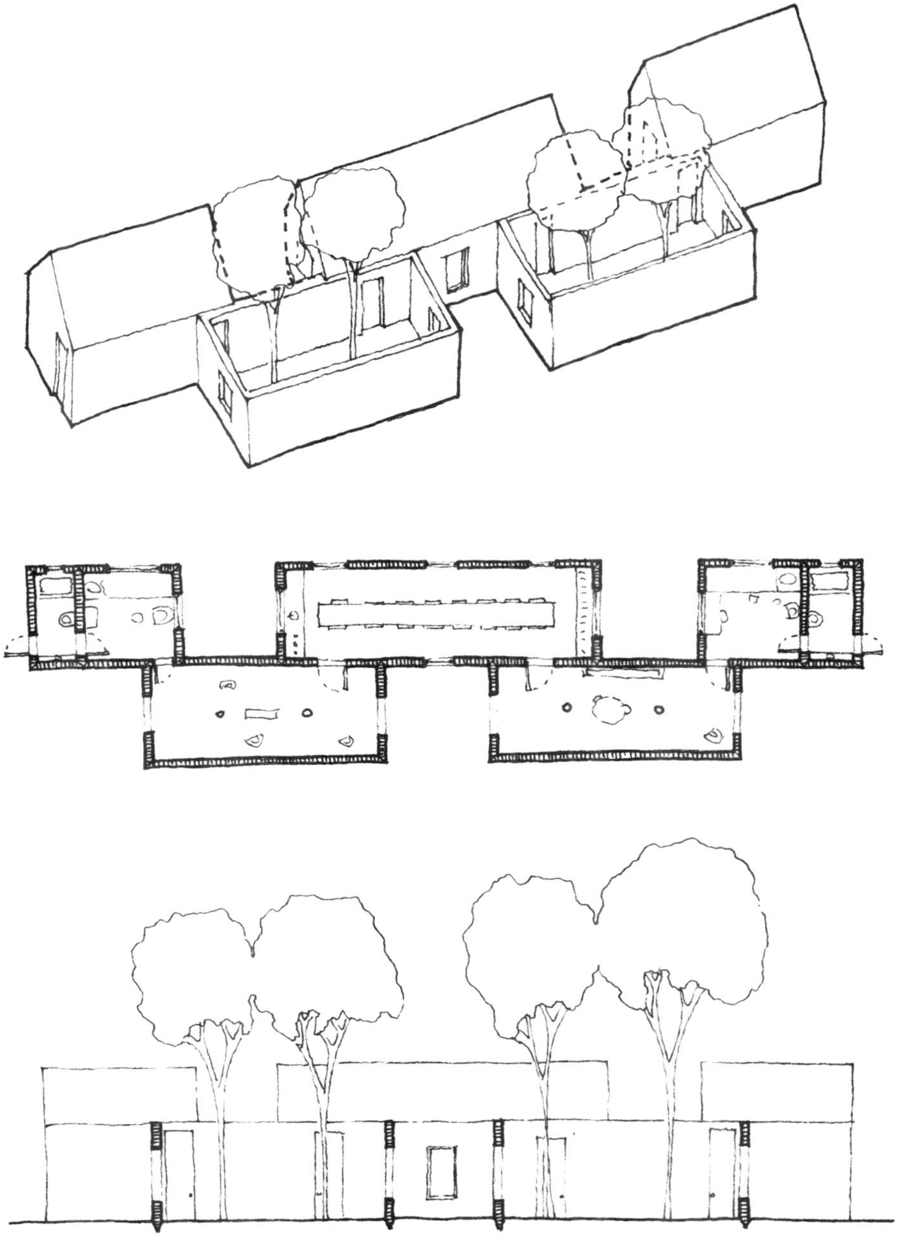

no.269

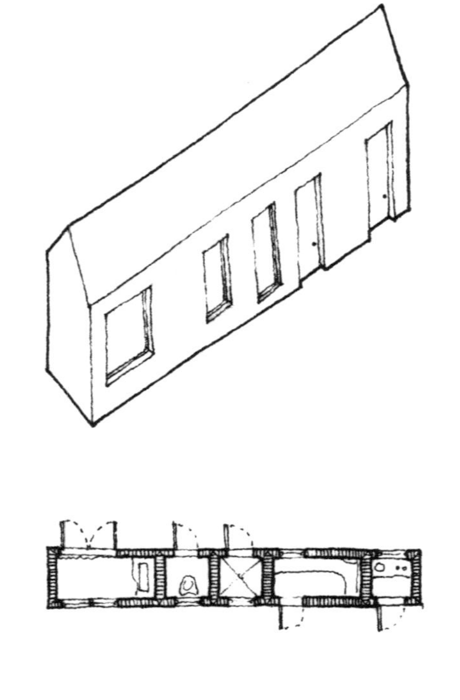

no.270

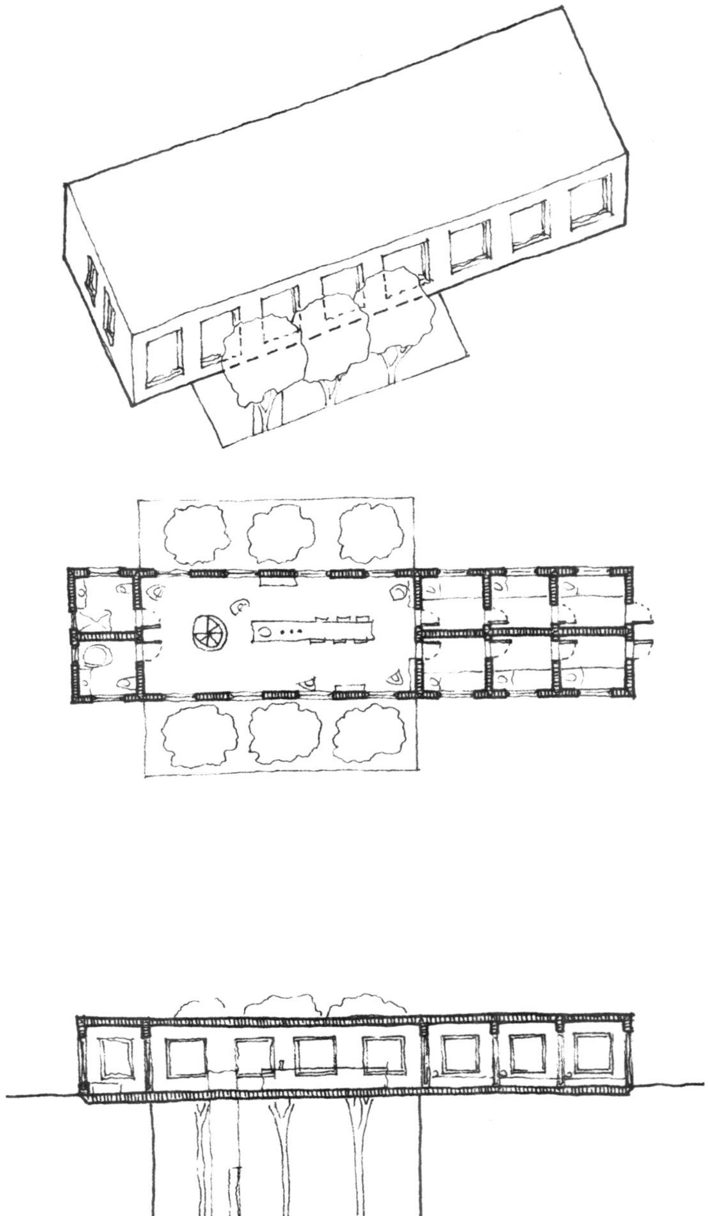

no.271

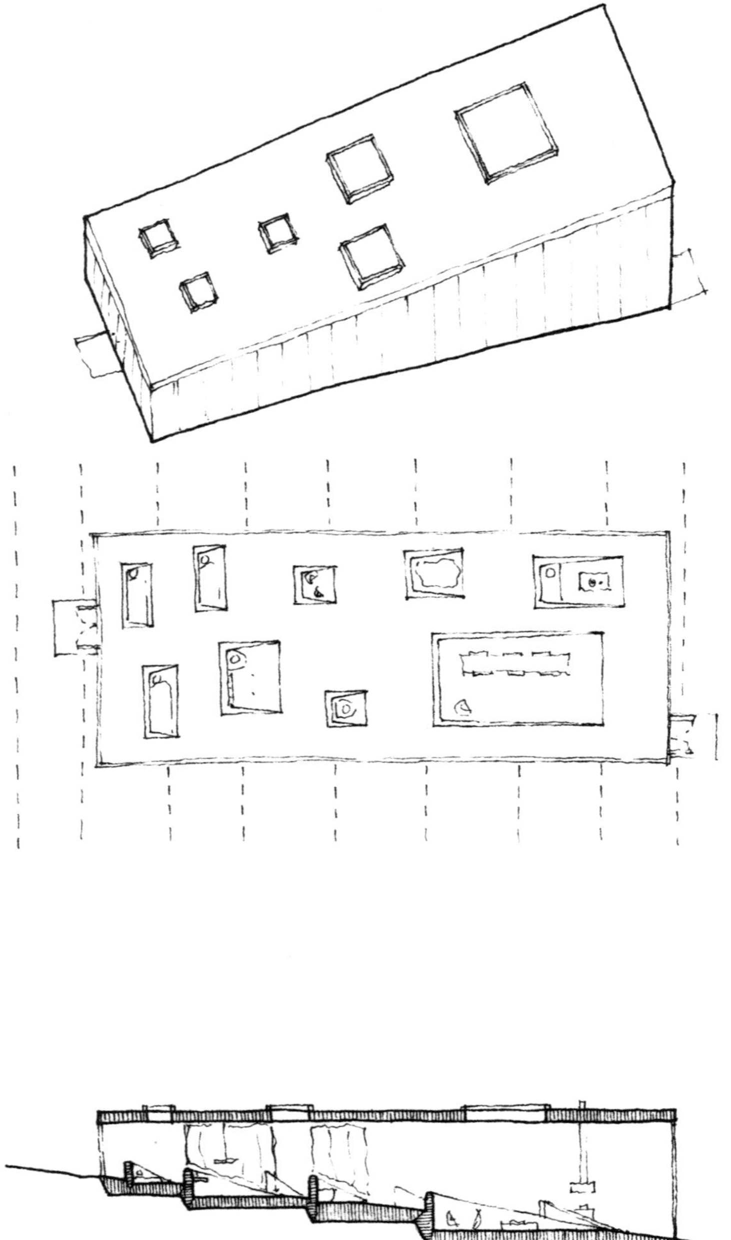

no.272

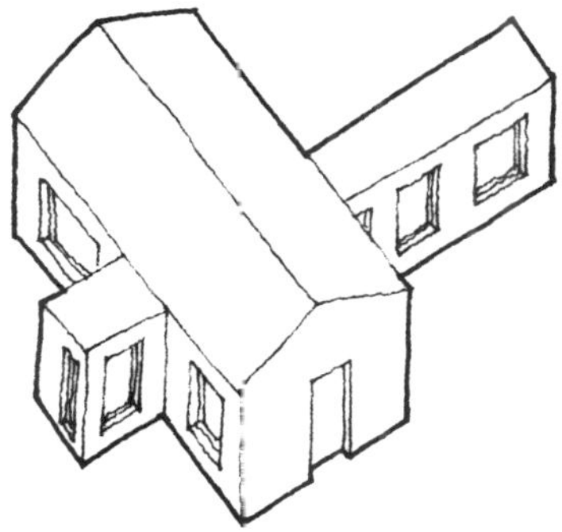

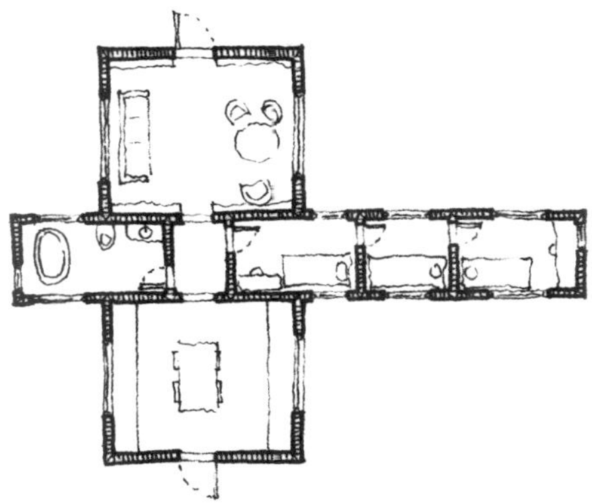

no.273

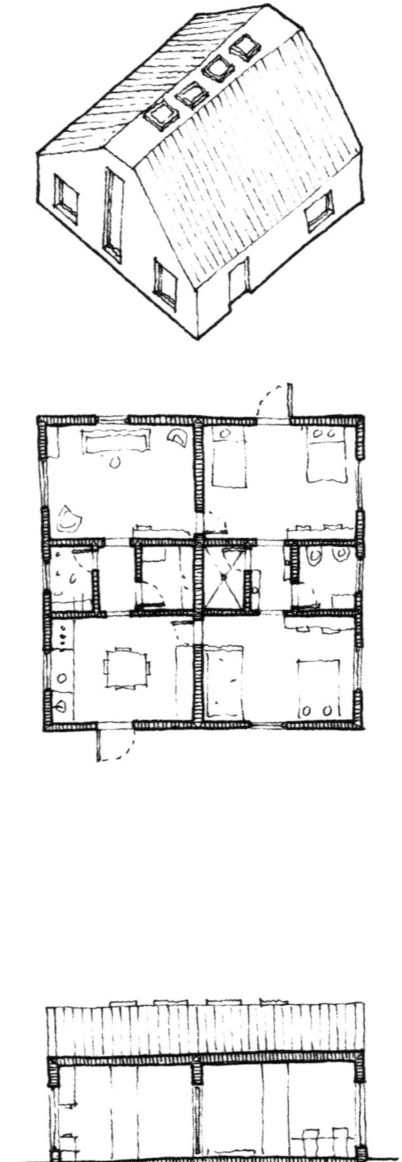

no.274

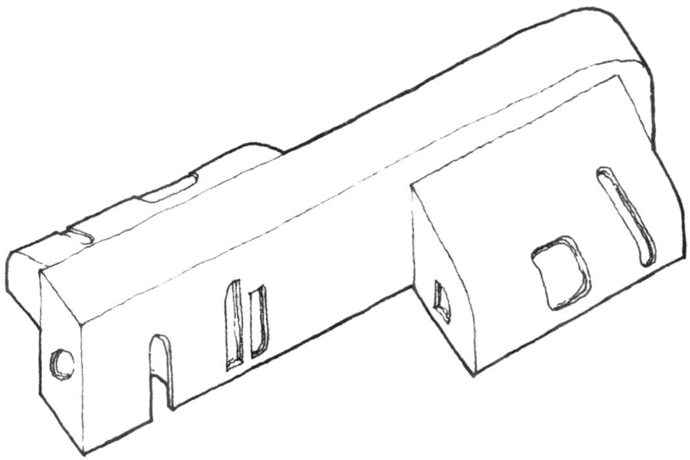

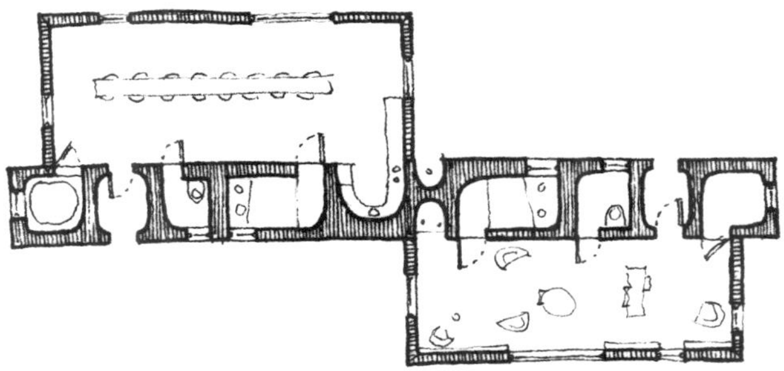

no.275

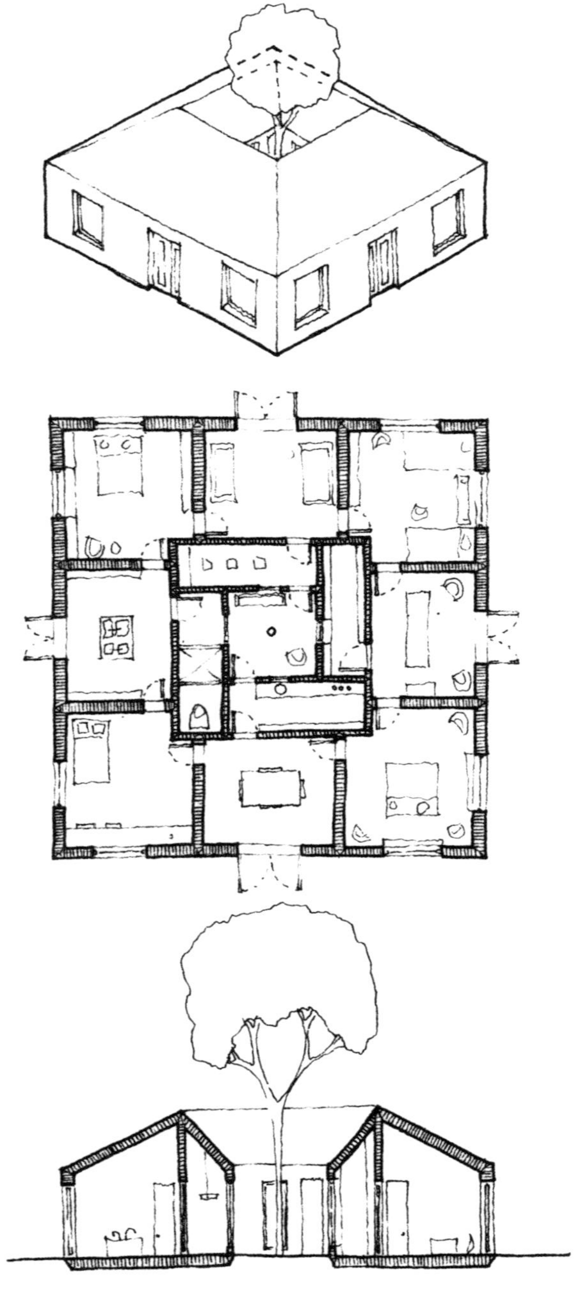

no.276

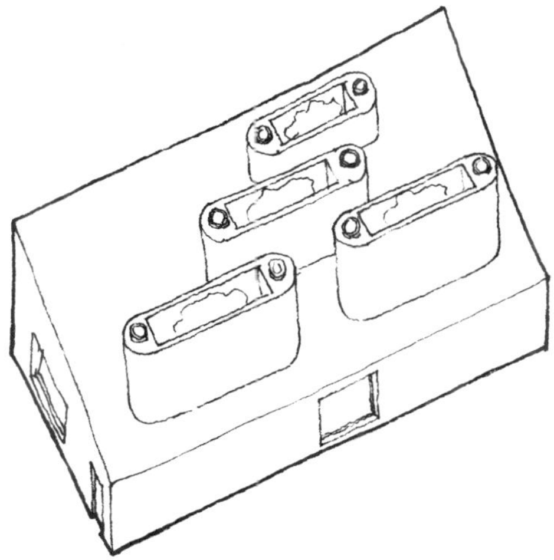

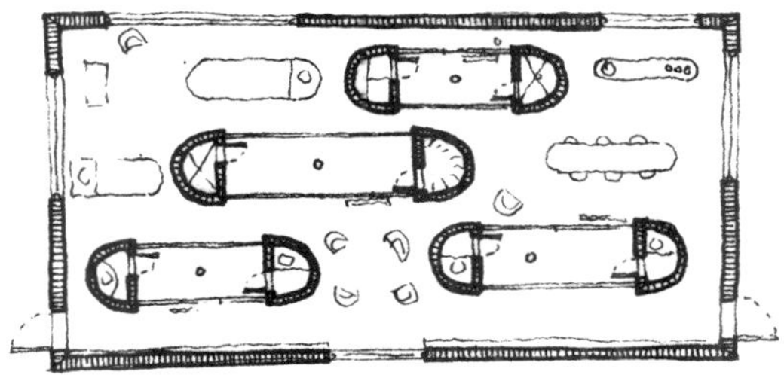

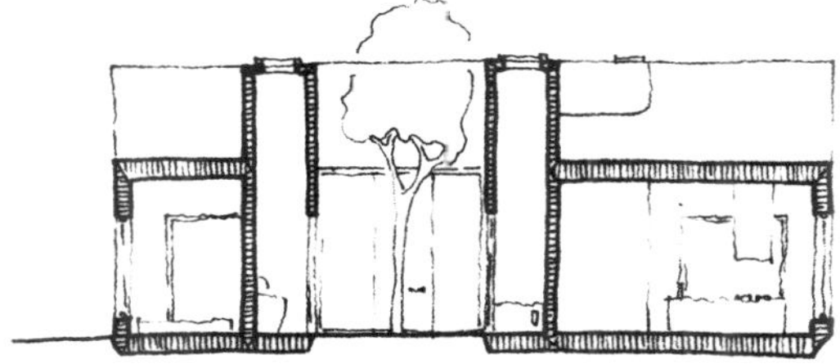

no.277

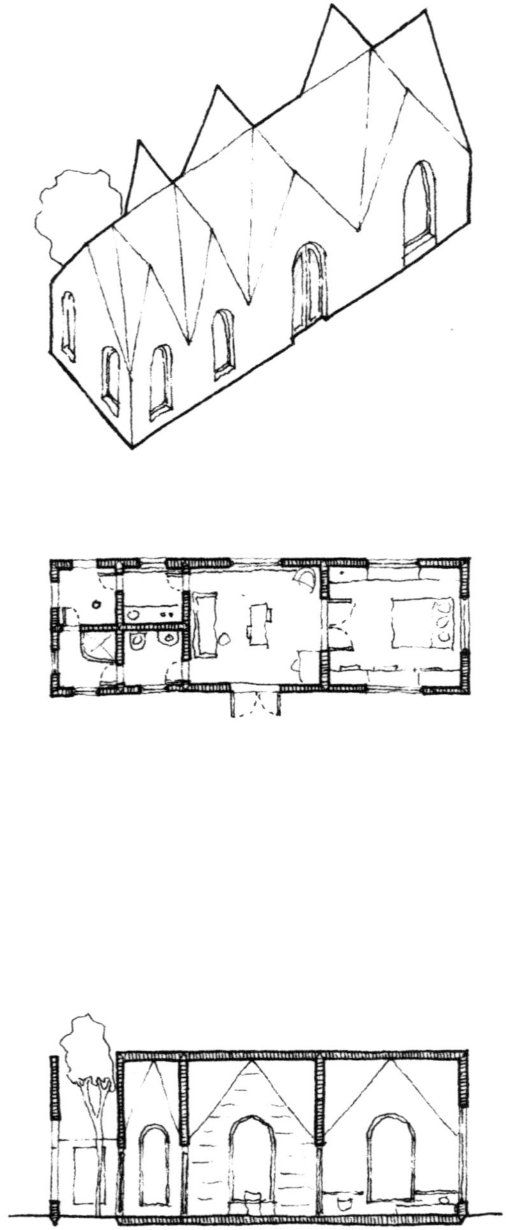

no.278

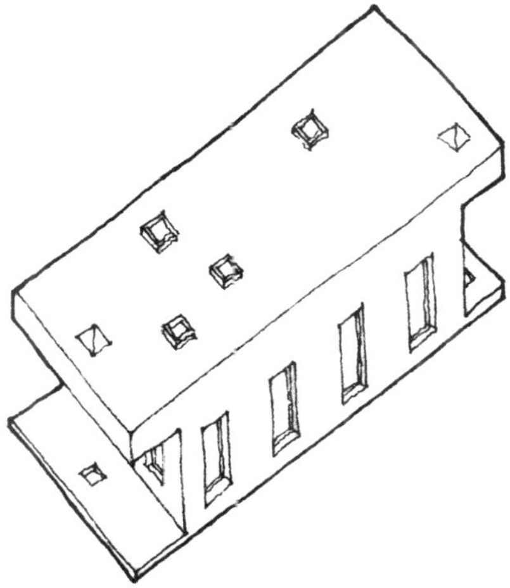

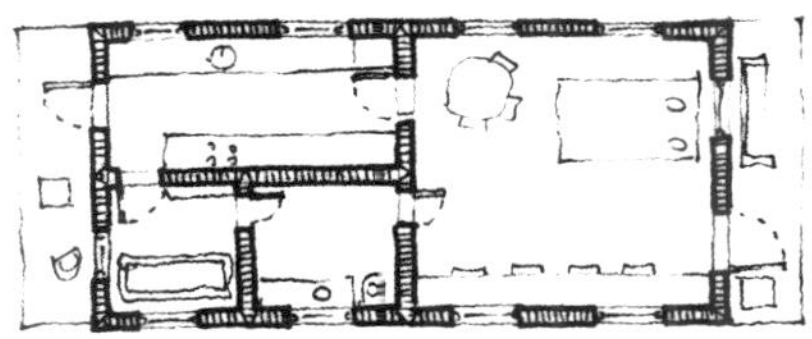

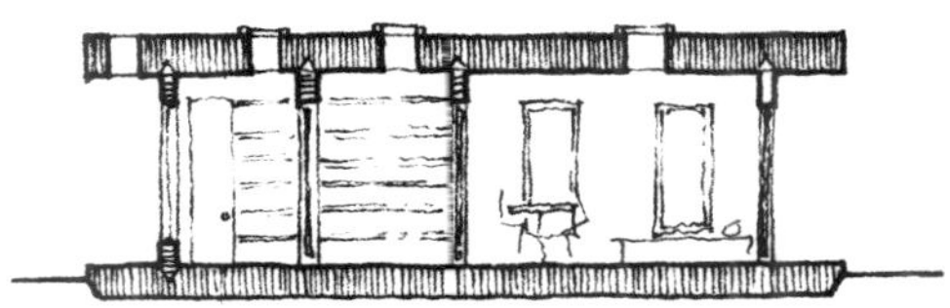

no.279

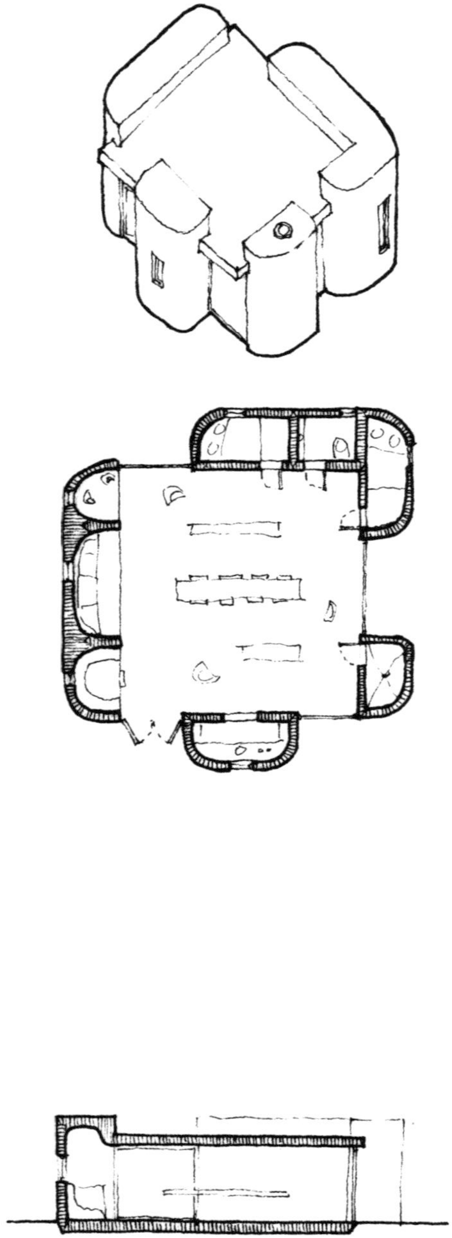

no.280

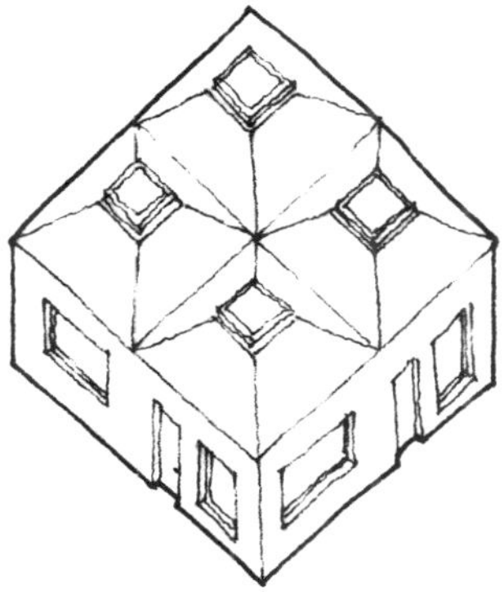

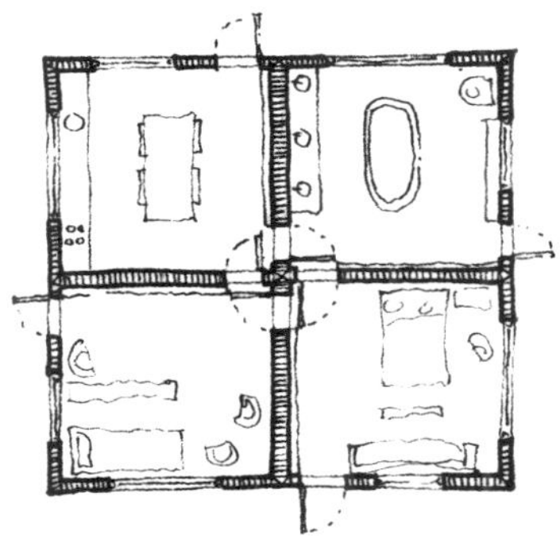

no.281

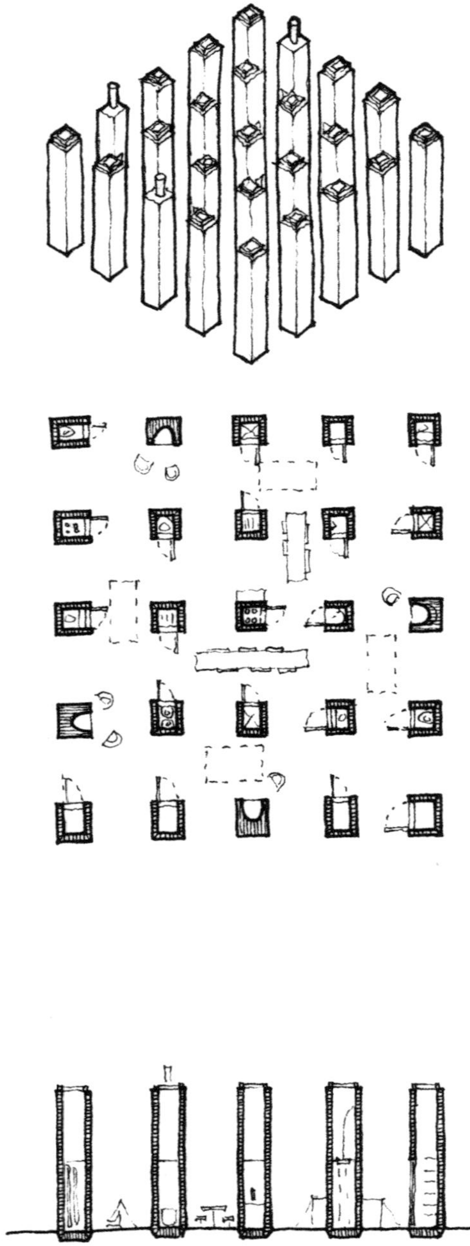

no.282

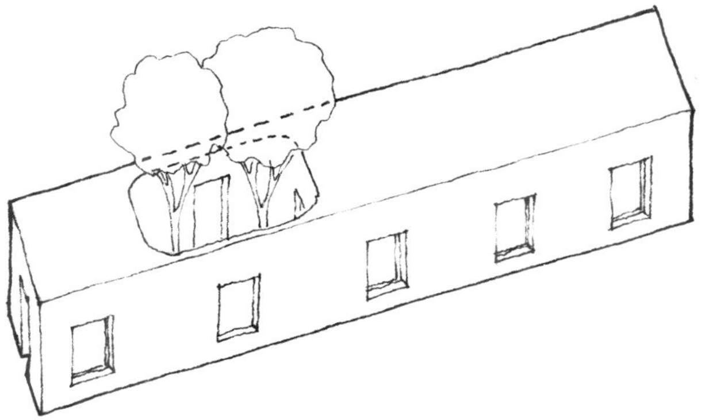

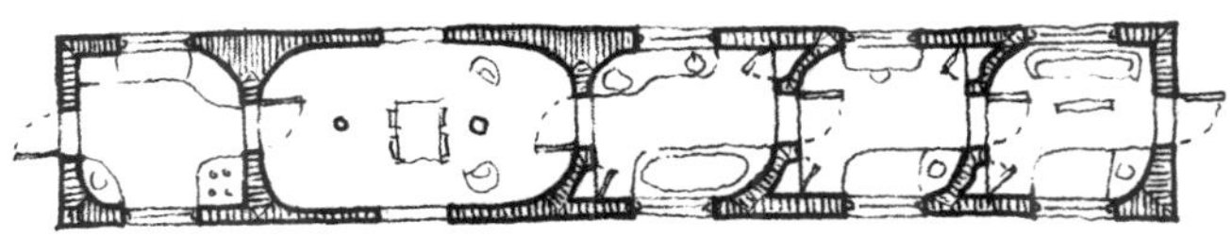

no.283

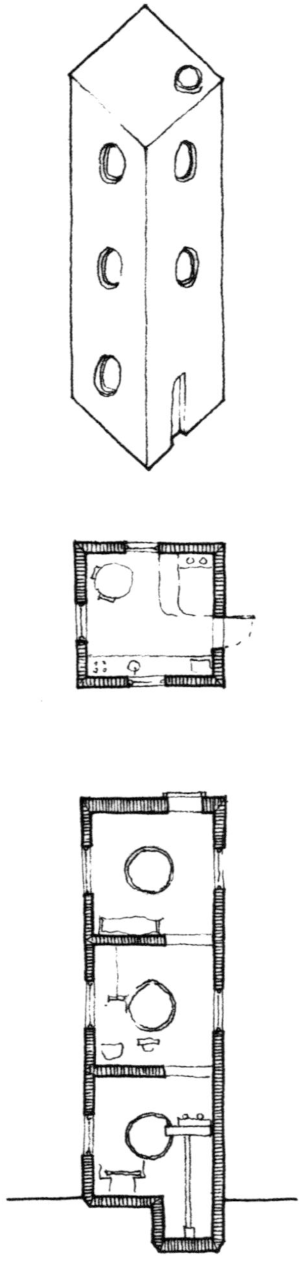

no.284

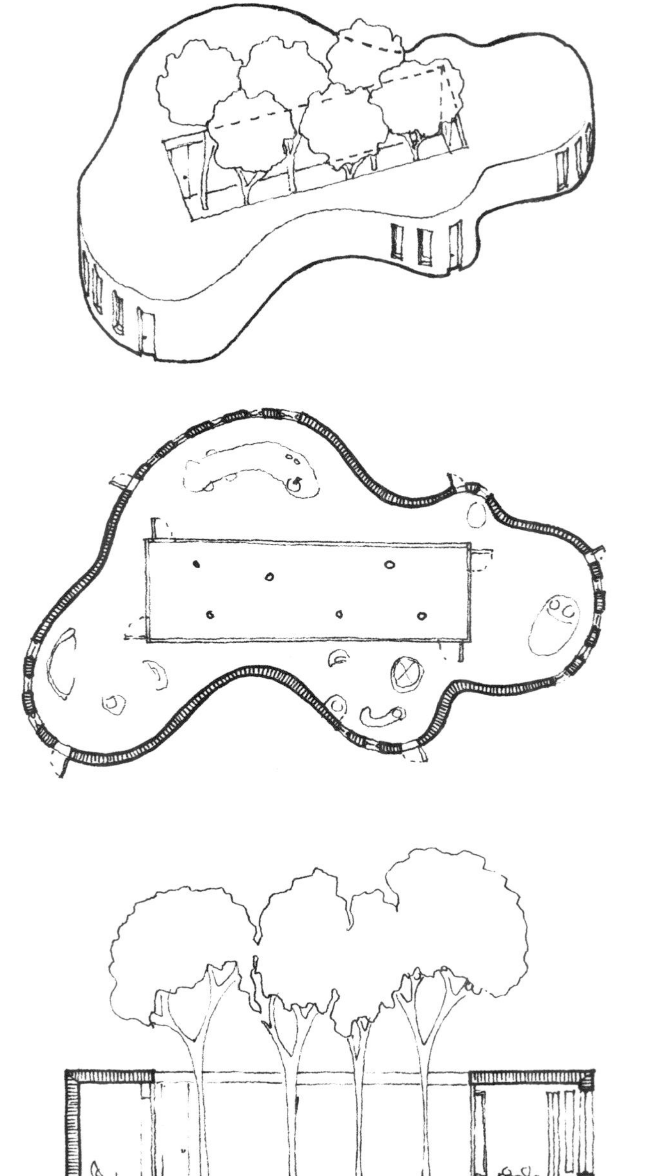

no.285

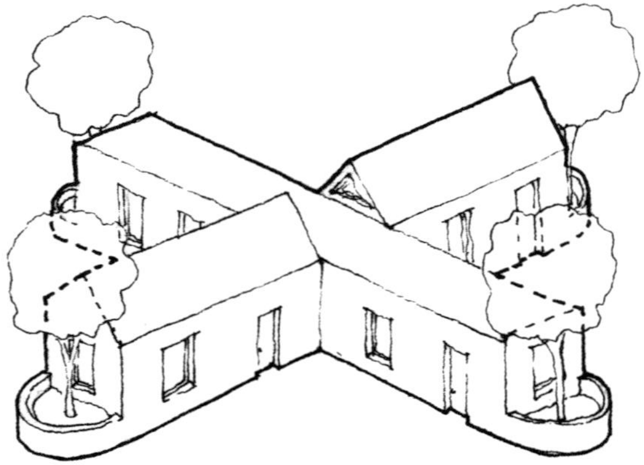

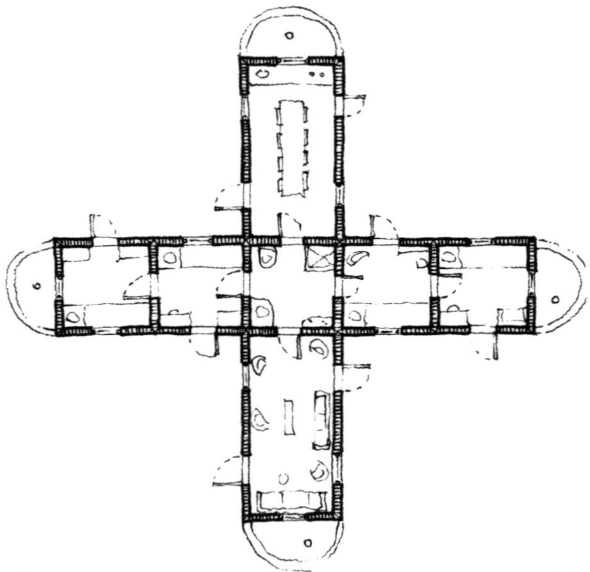

no.286

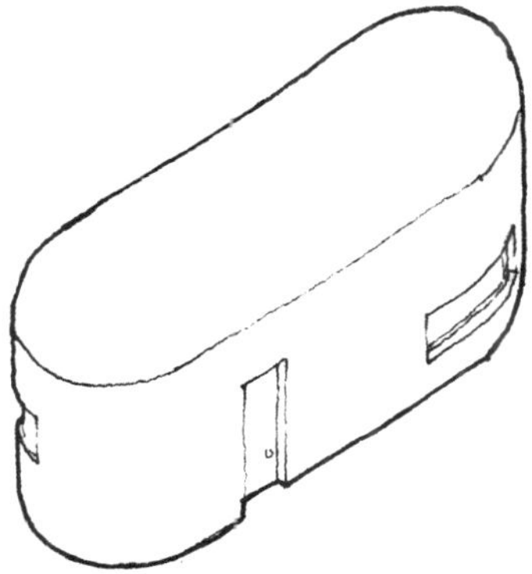

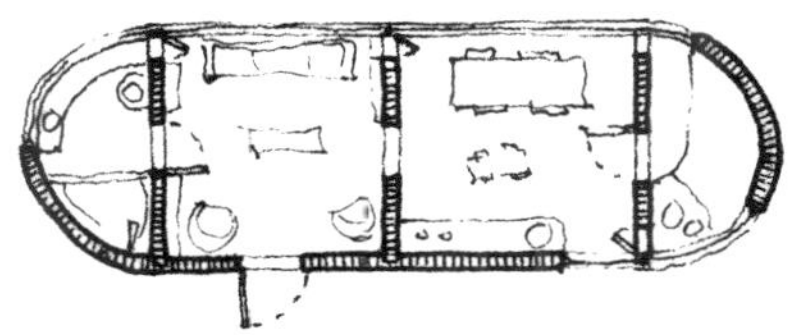

no.287

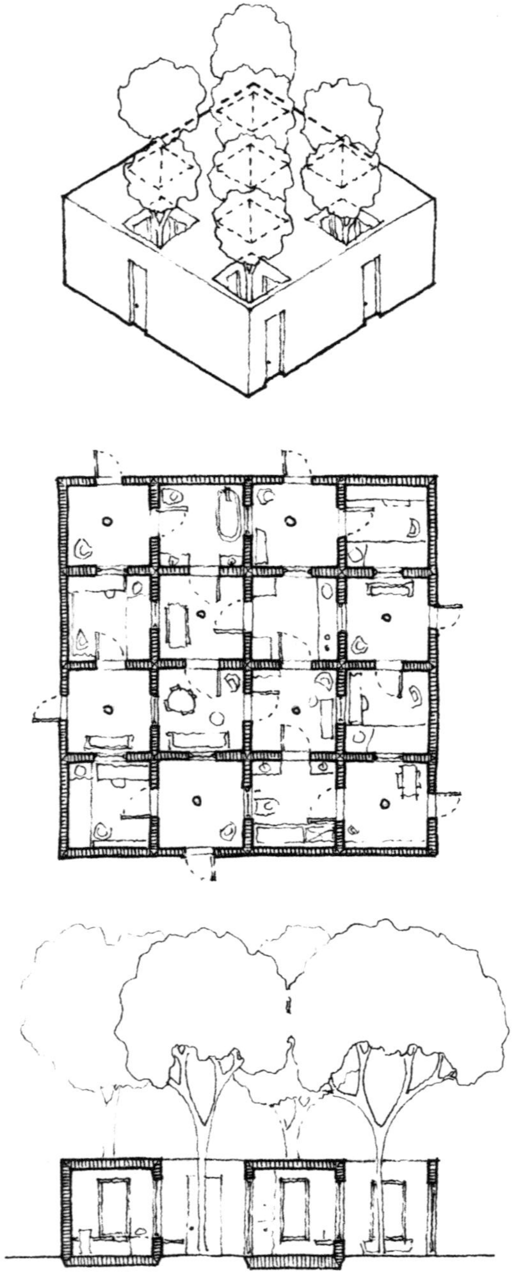

no.288

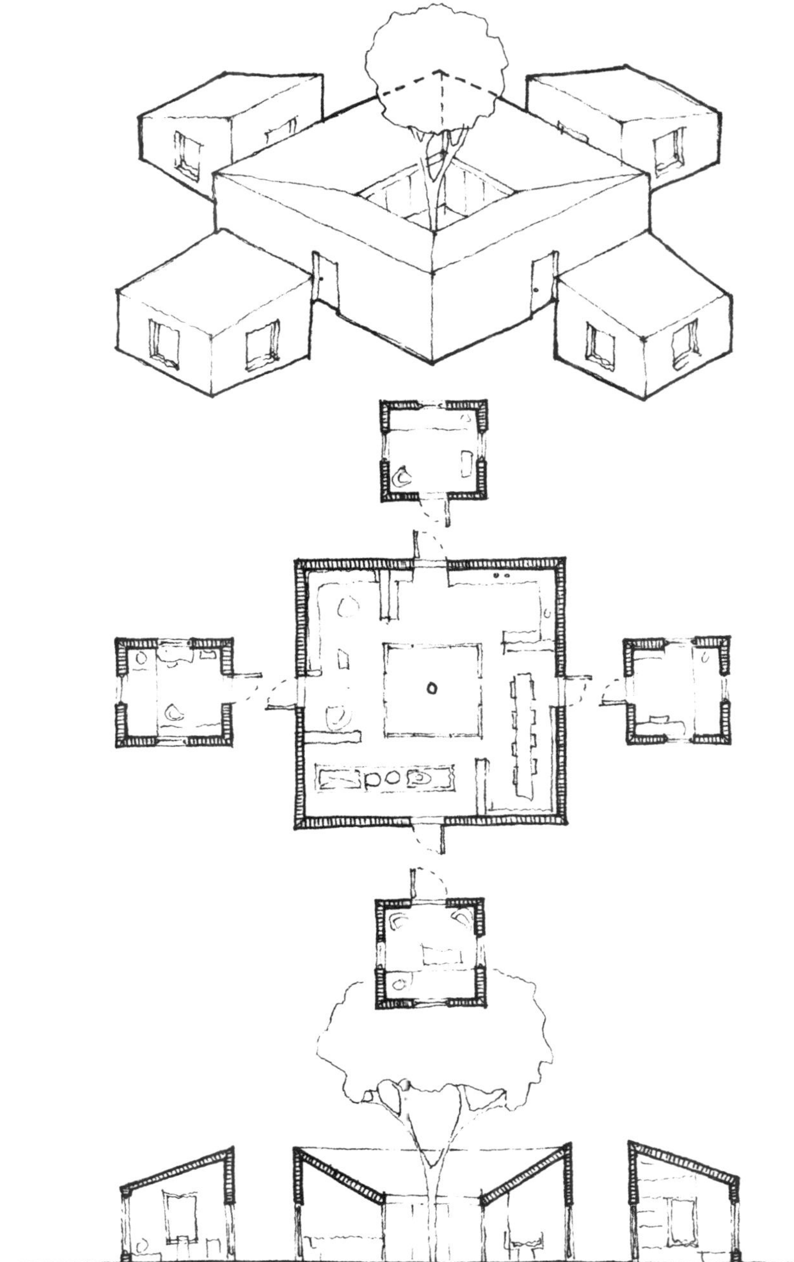

no.289

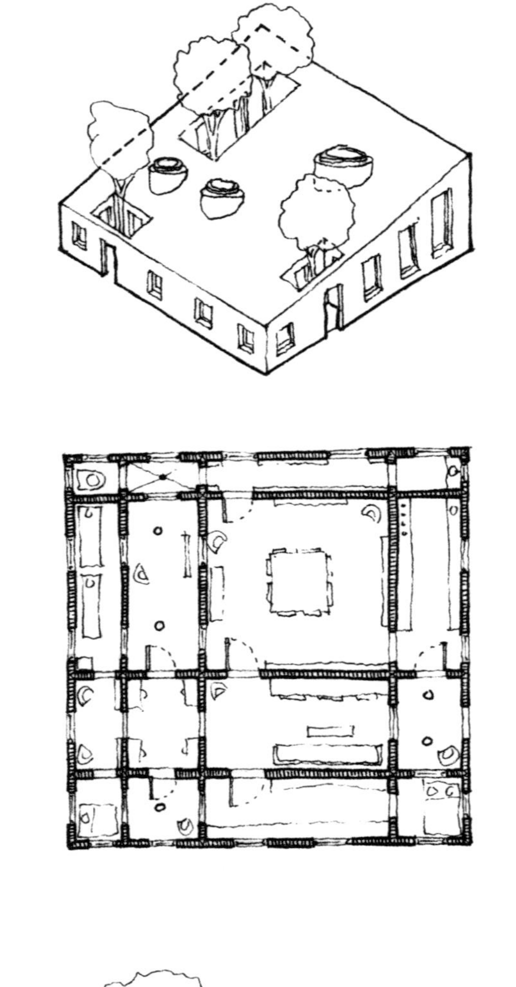

no.290

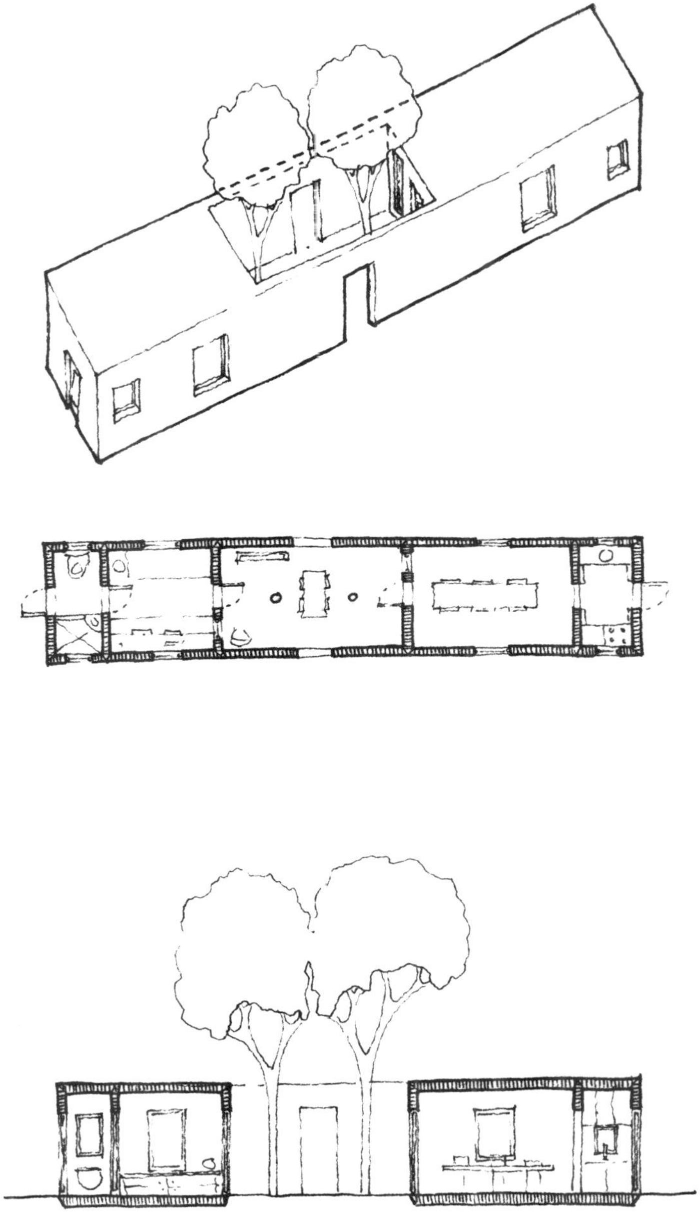

no.291

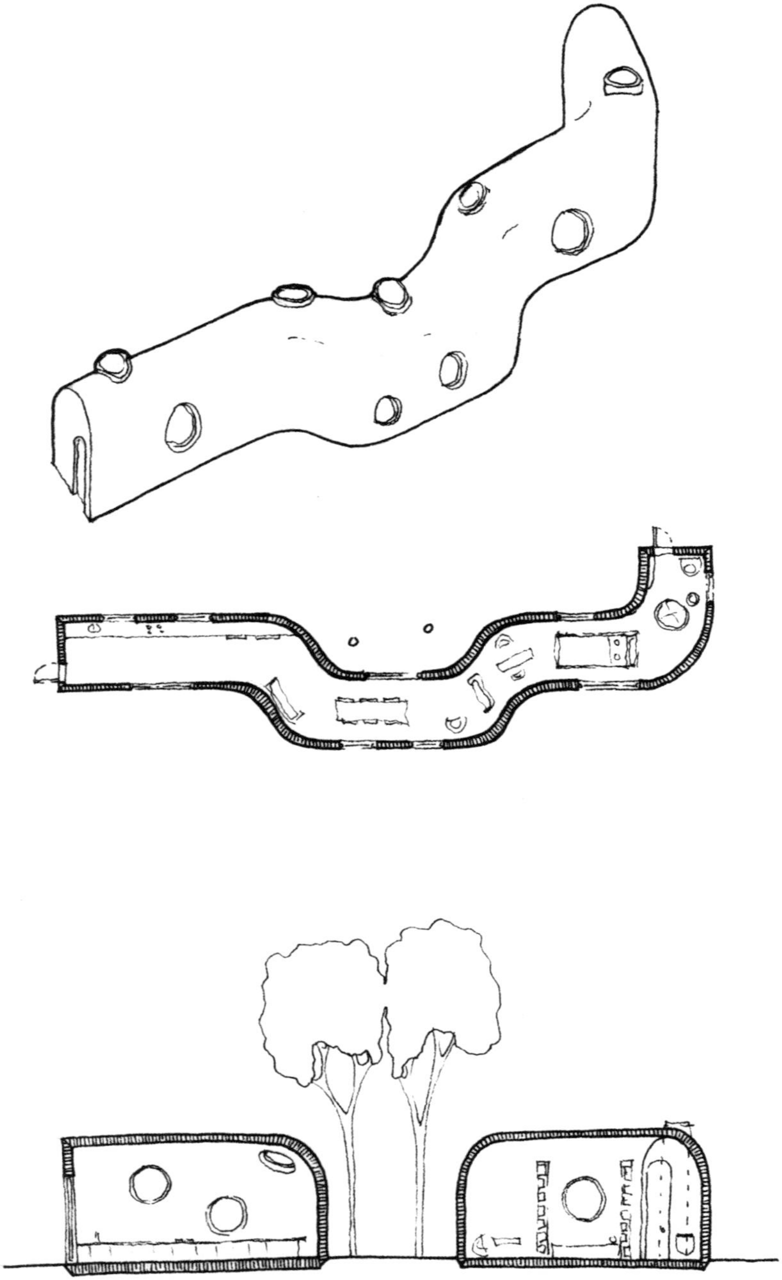

no.292

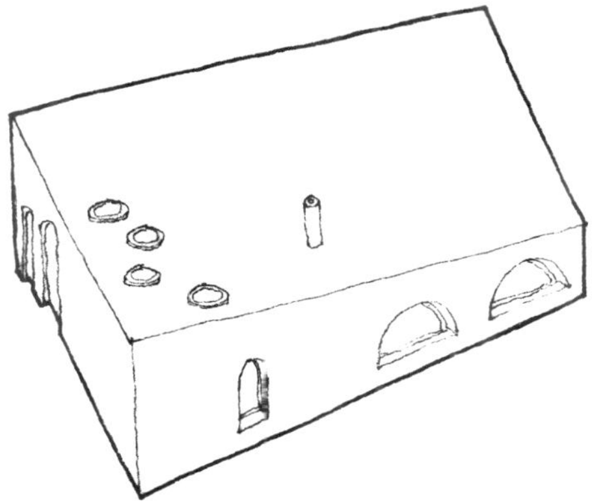

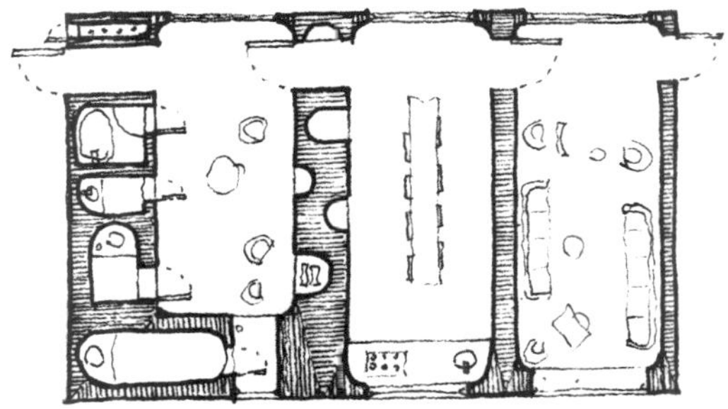

no.293

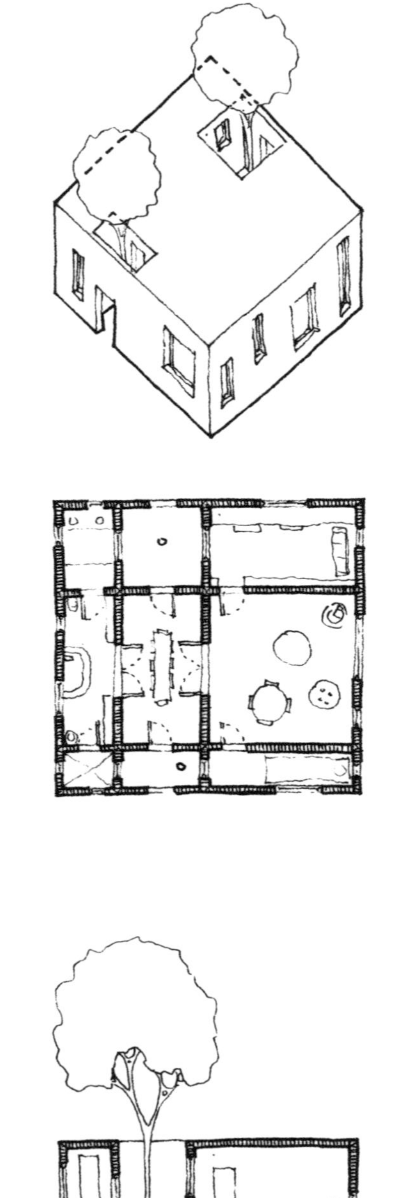

no.294

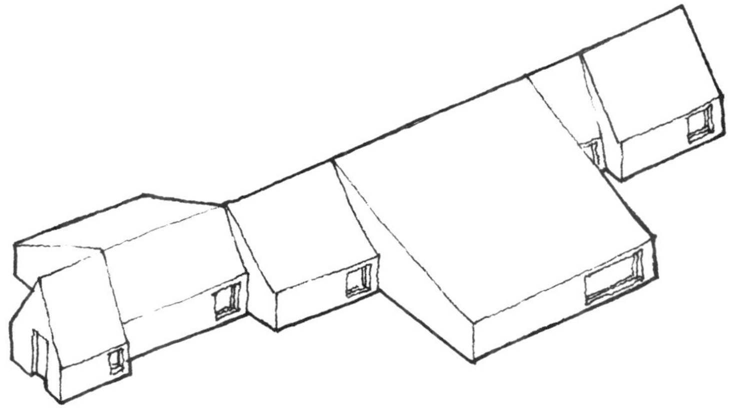

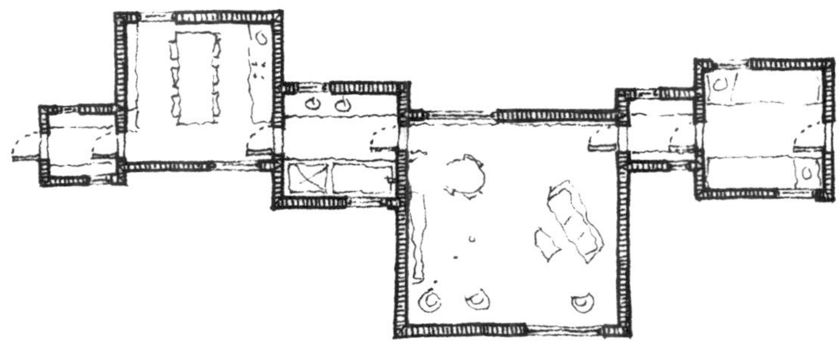

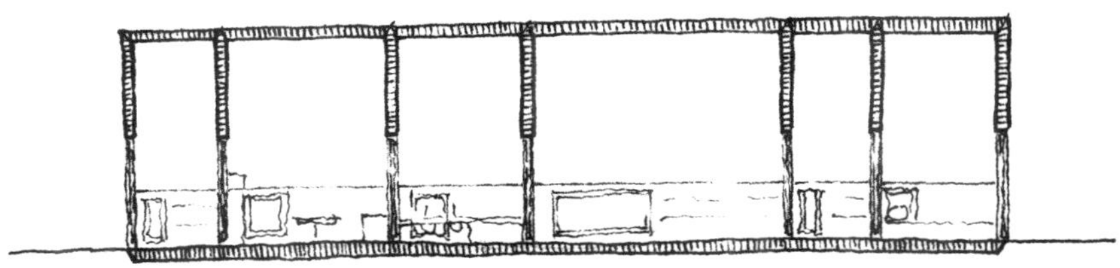

no.295

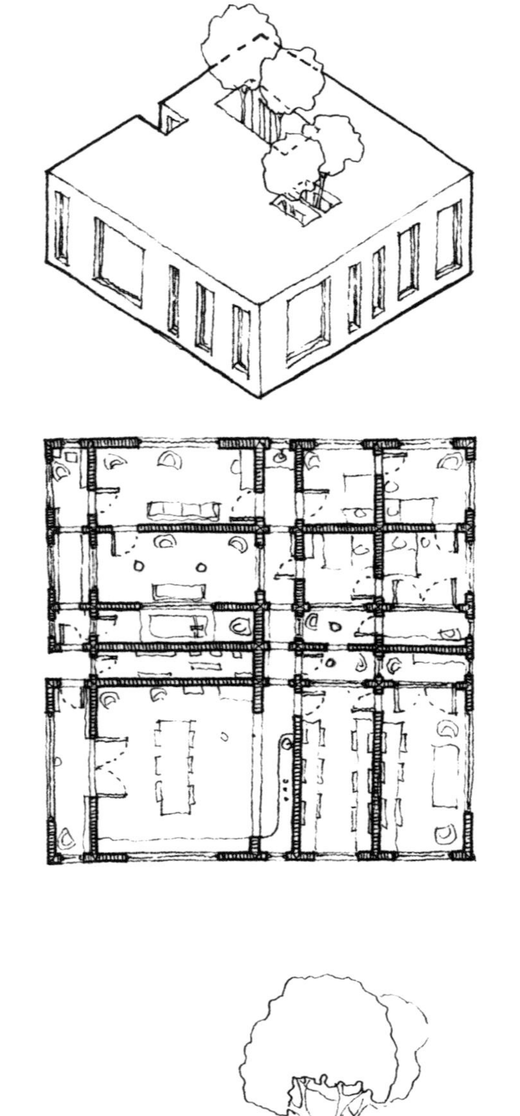

no.296

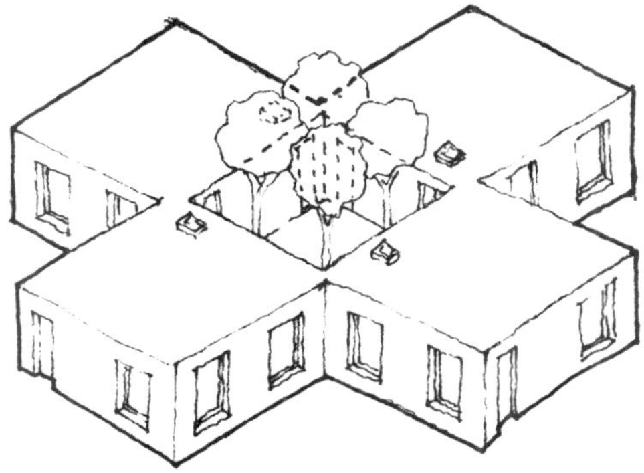

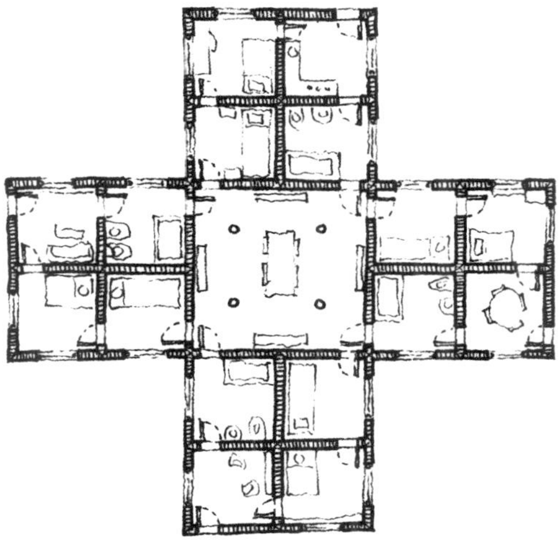

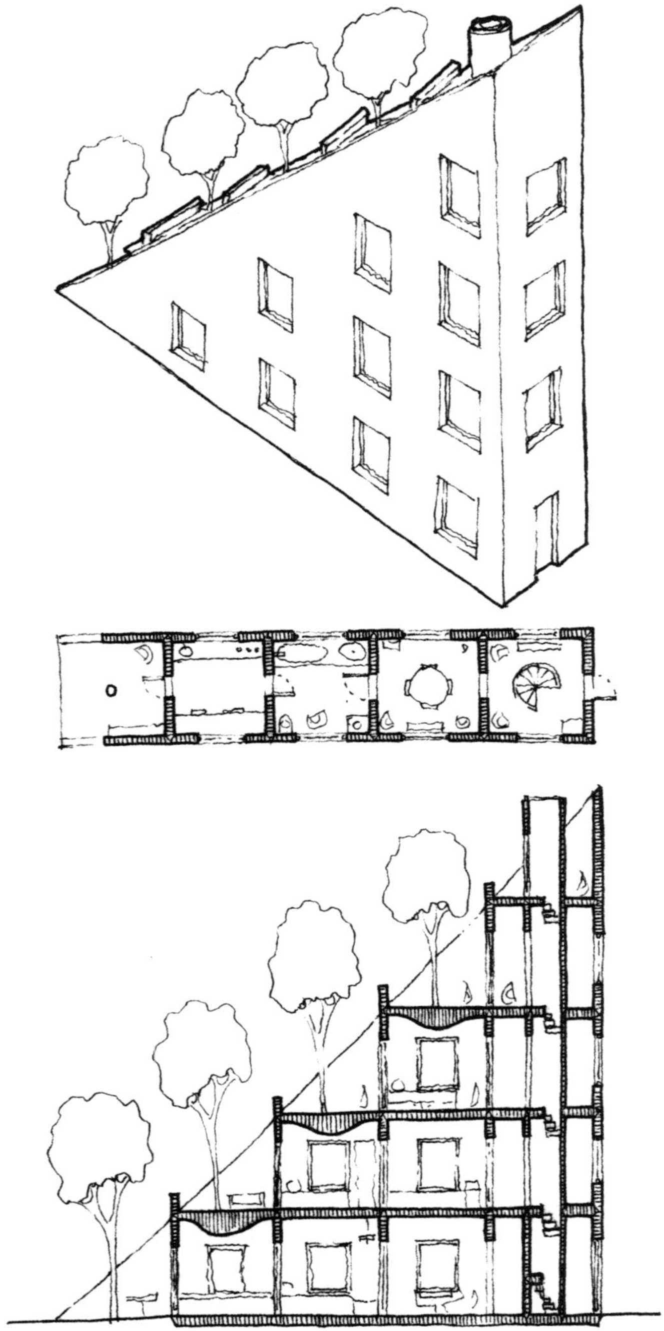

no.298

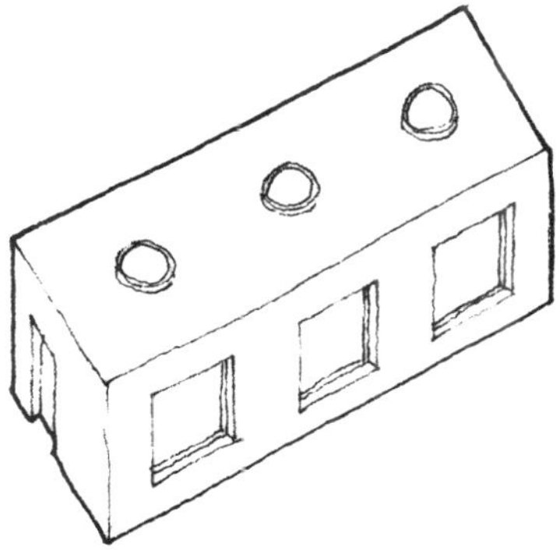

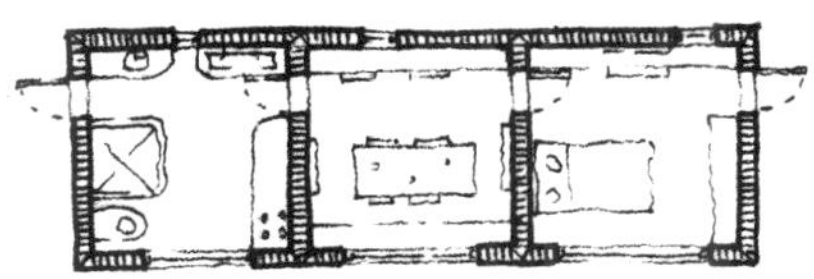

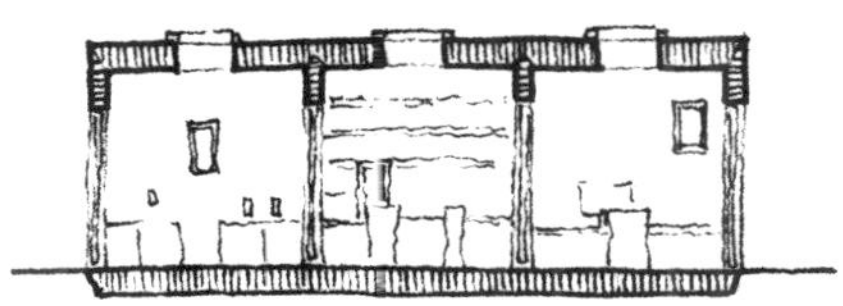

no.299

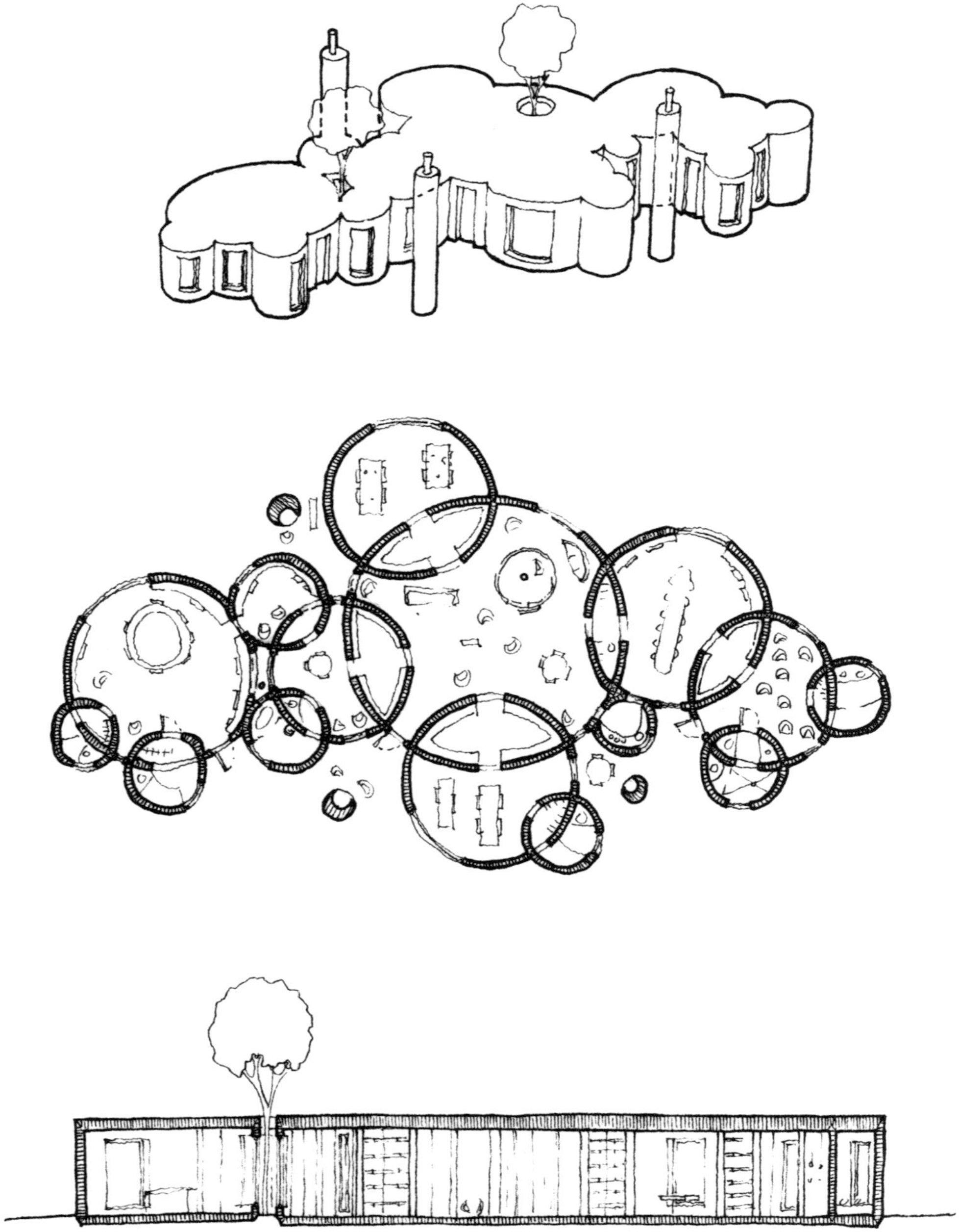

no.300

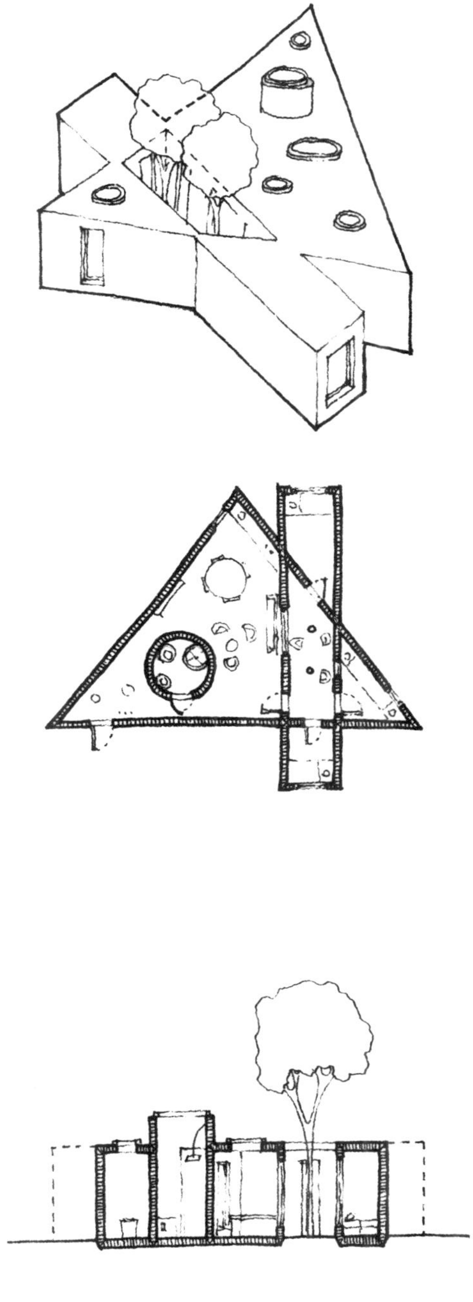

no.301

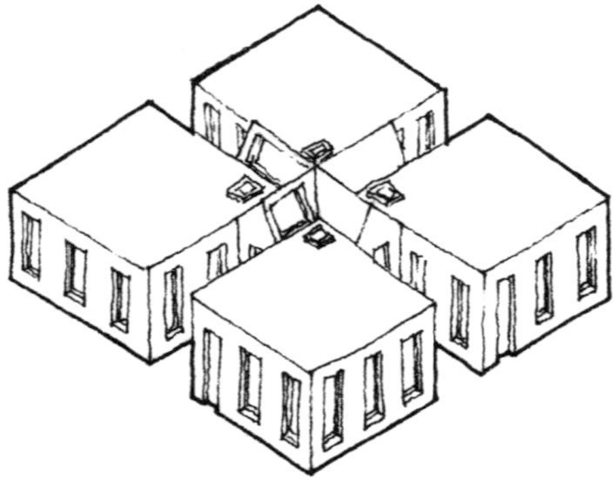

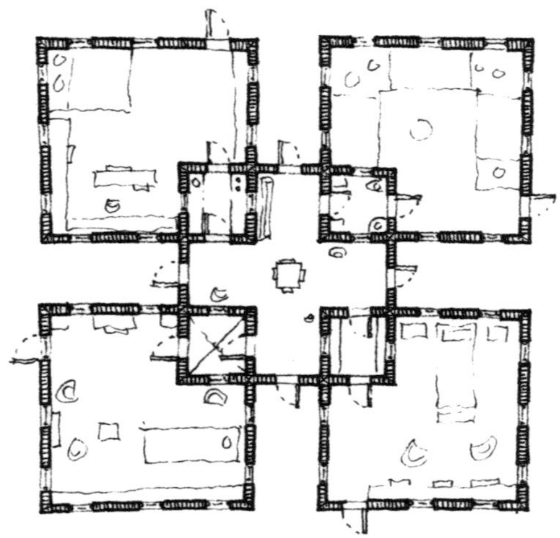

no.302

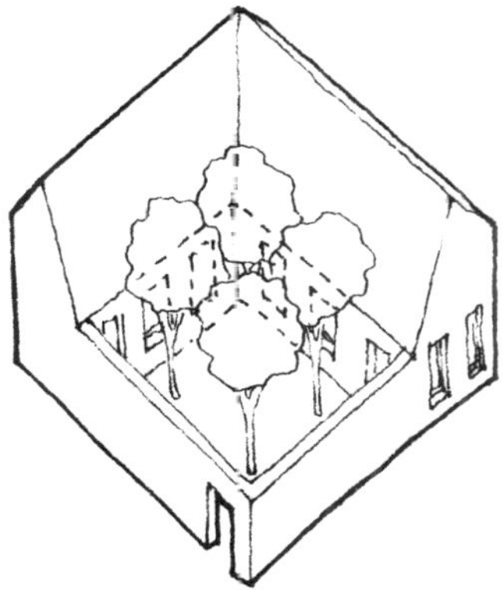

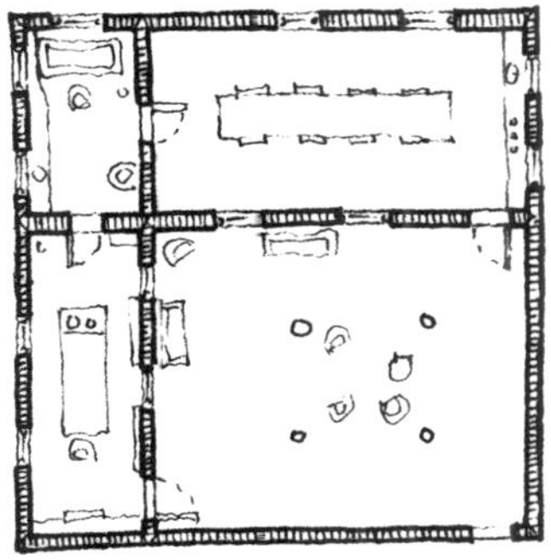

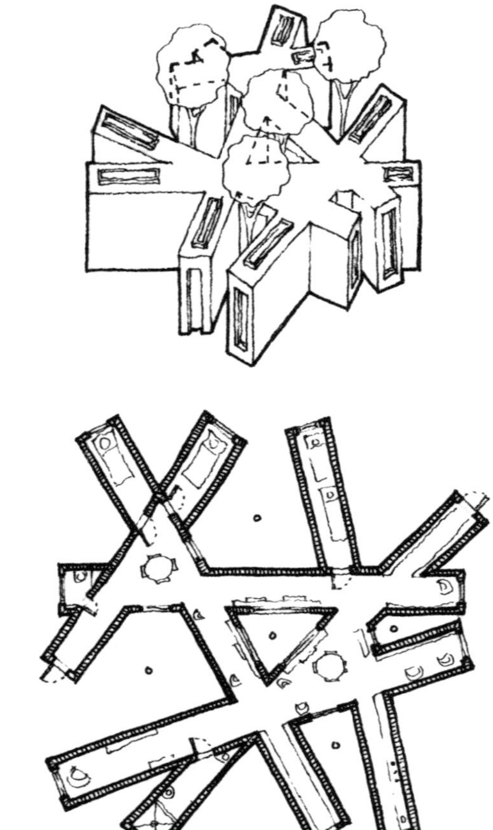

no.304

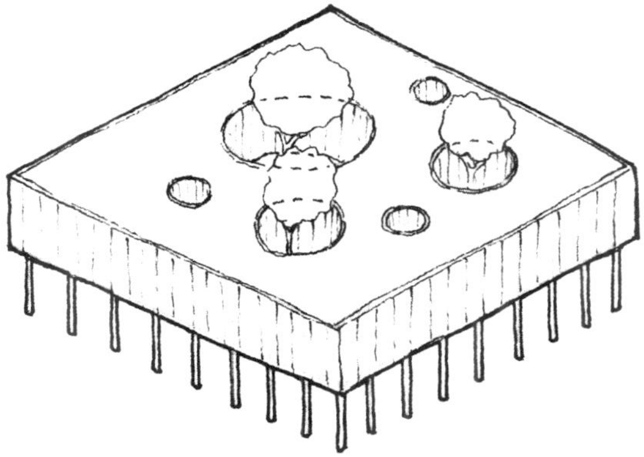

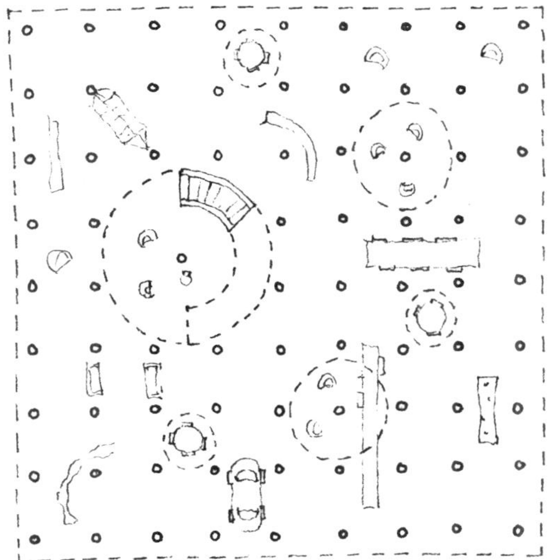

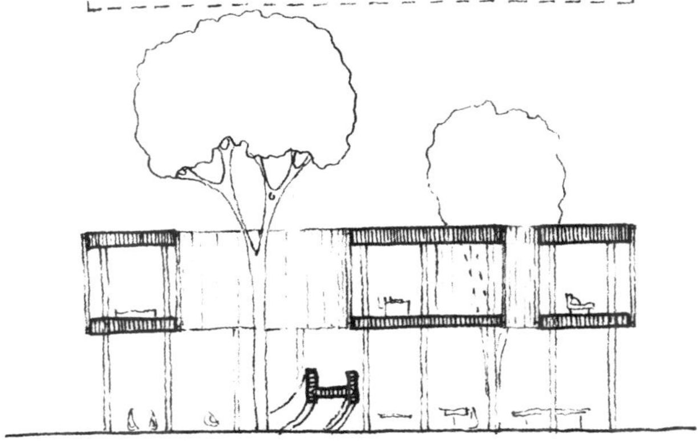

no.305

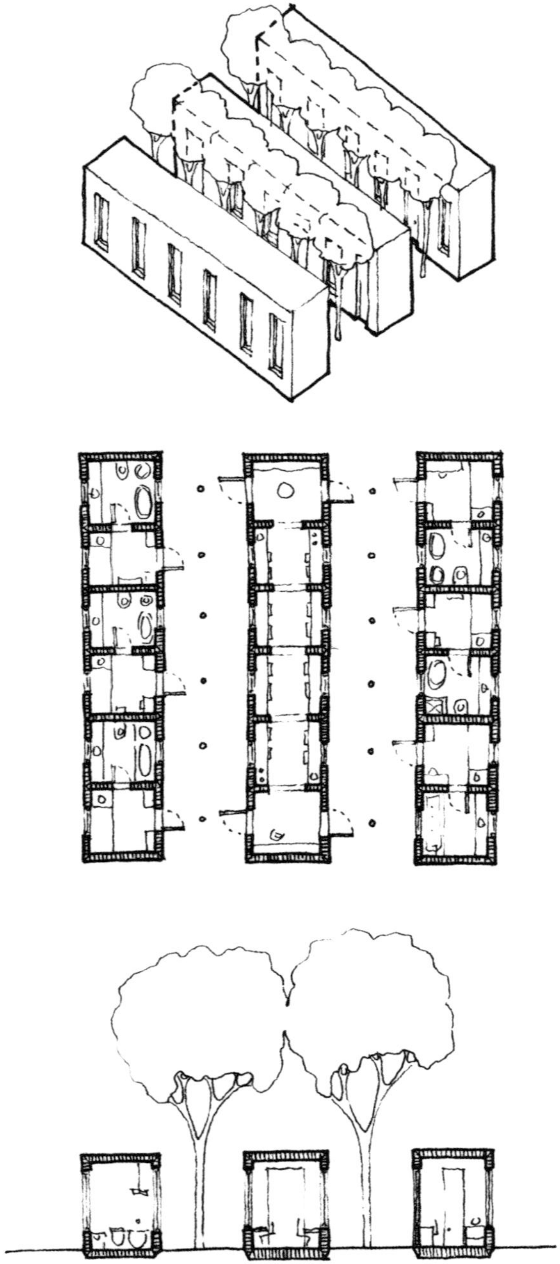

no.306

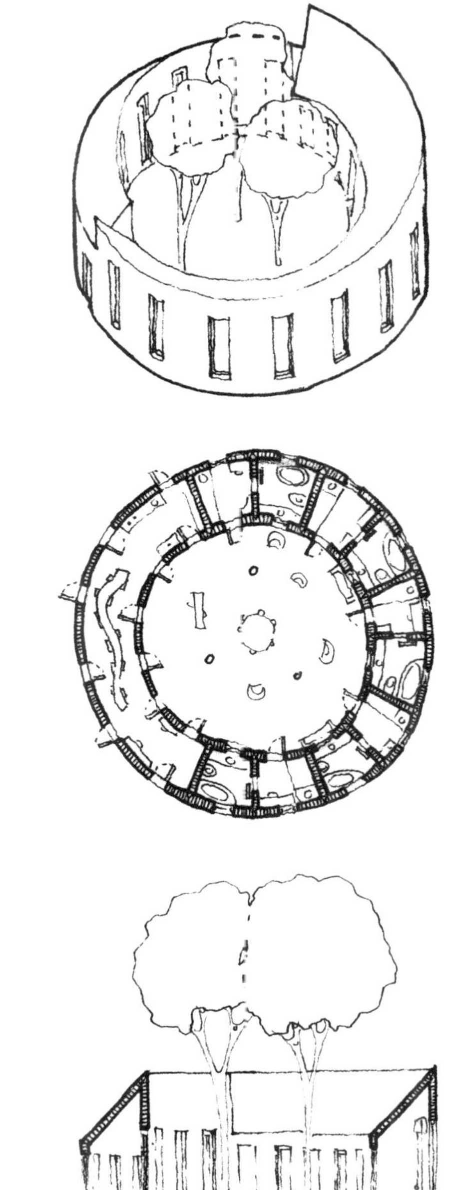

no.307

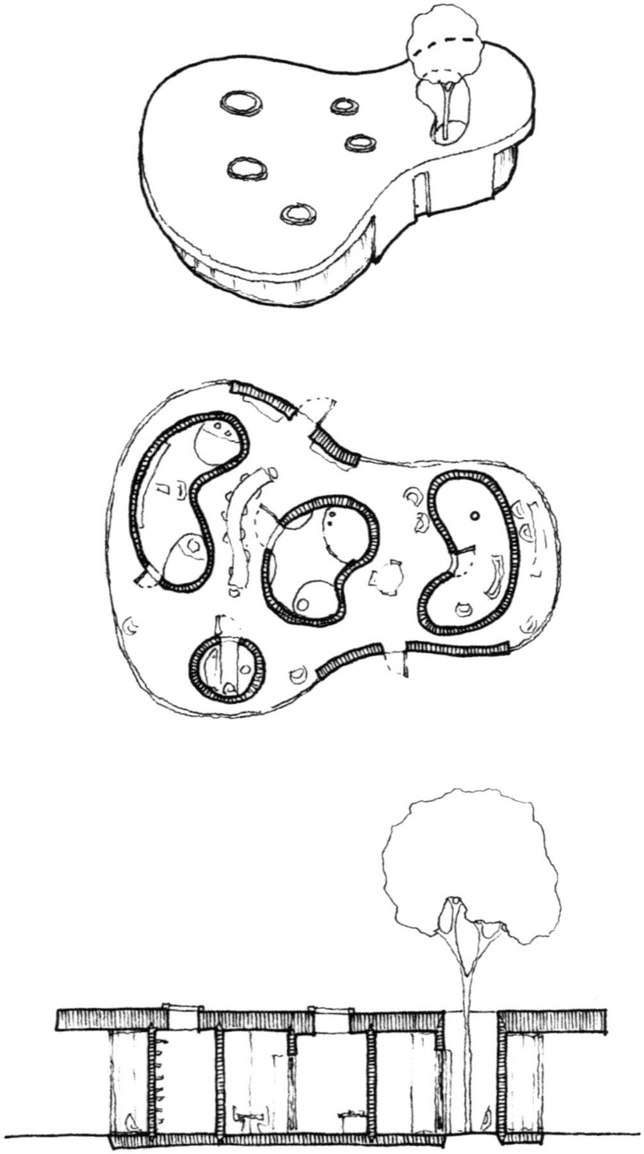

no.308

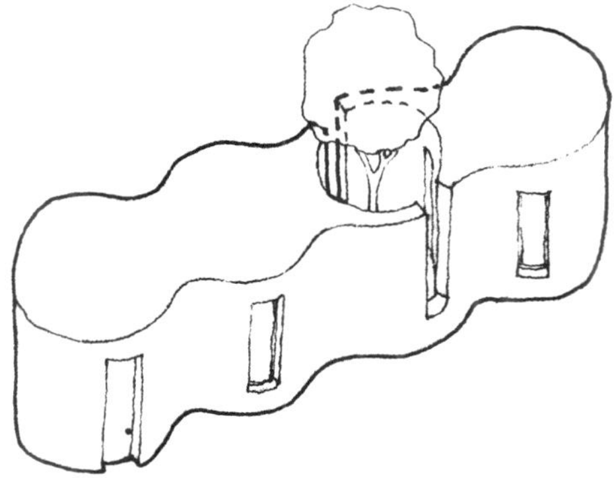

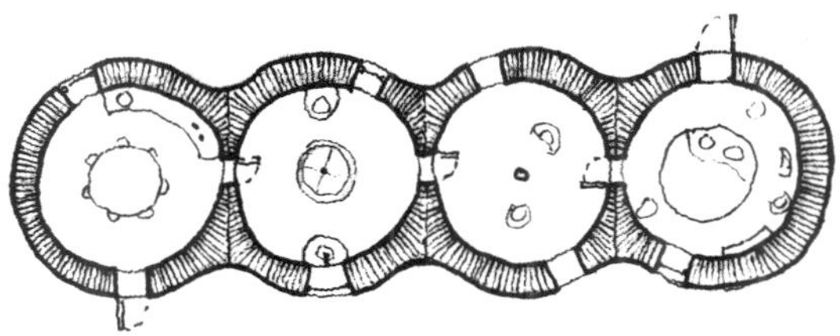

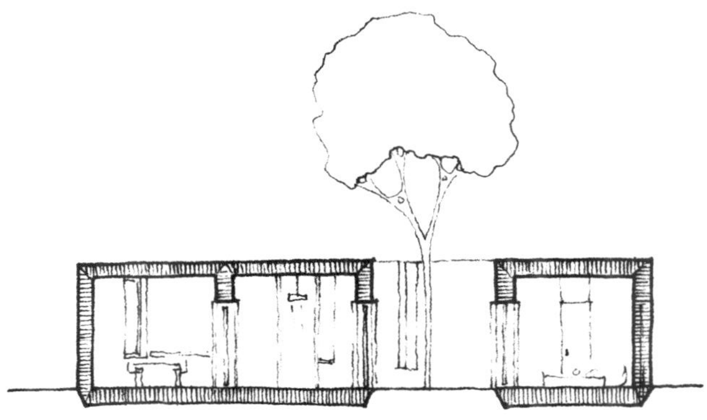

no.309

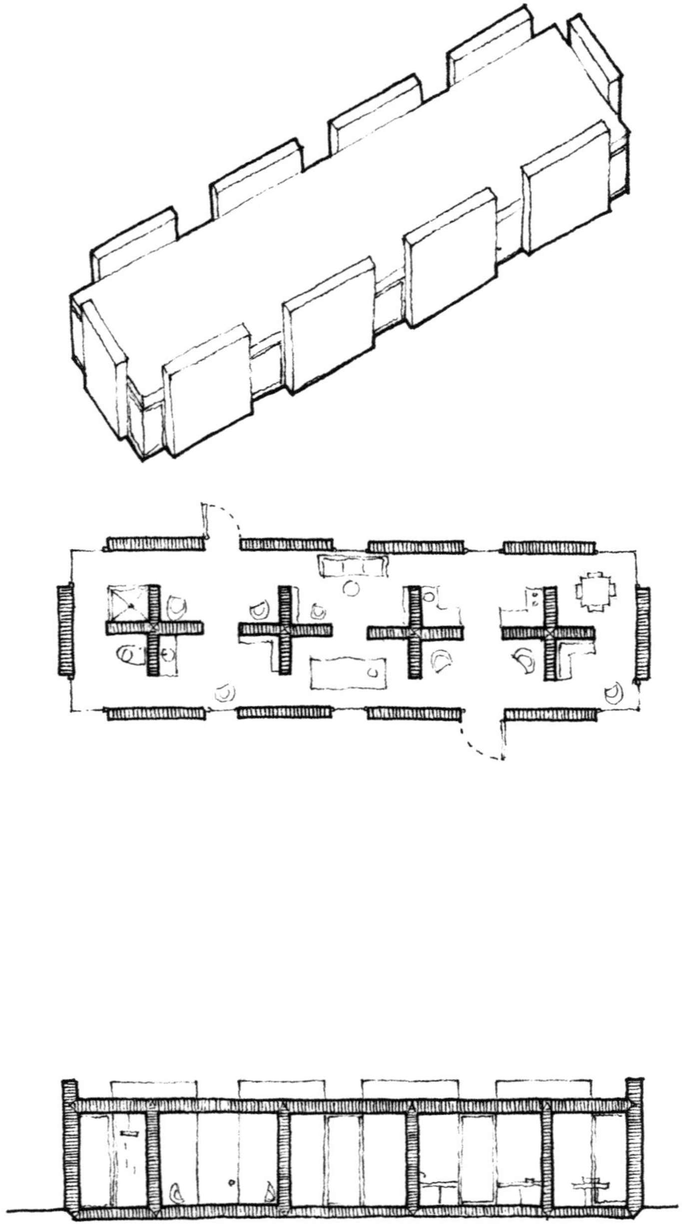

no.310

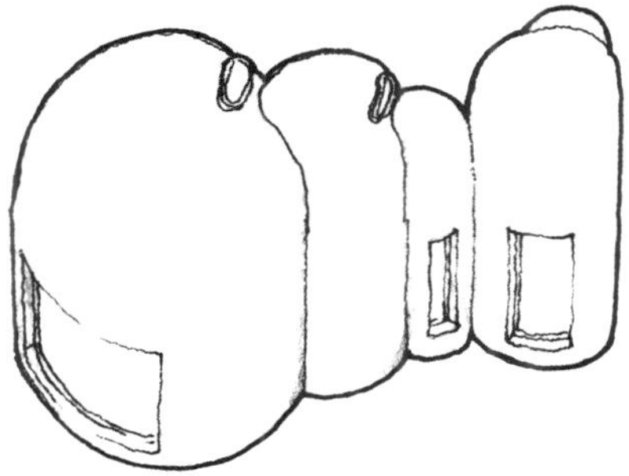

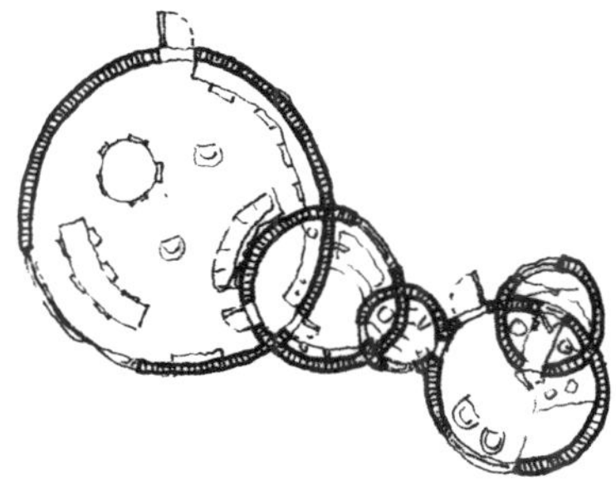

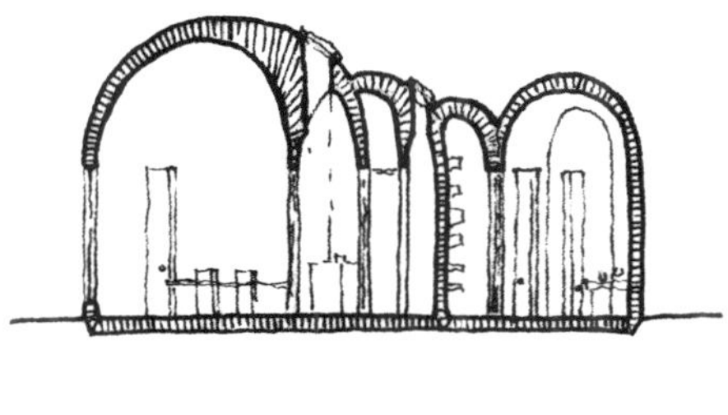

no.311

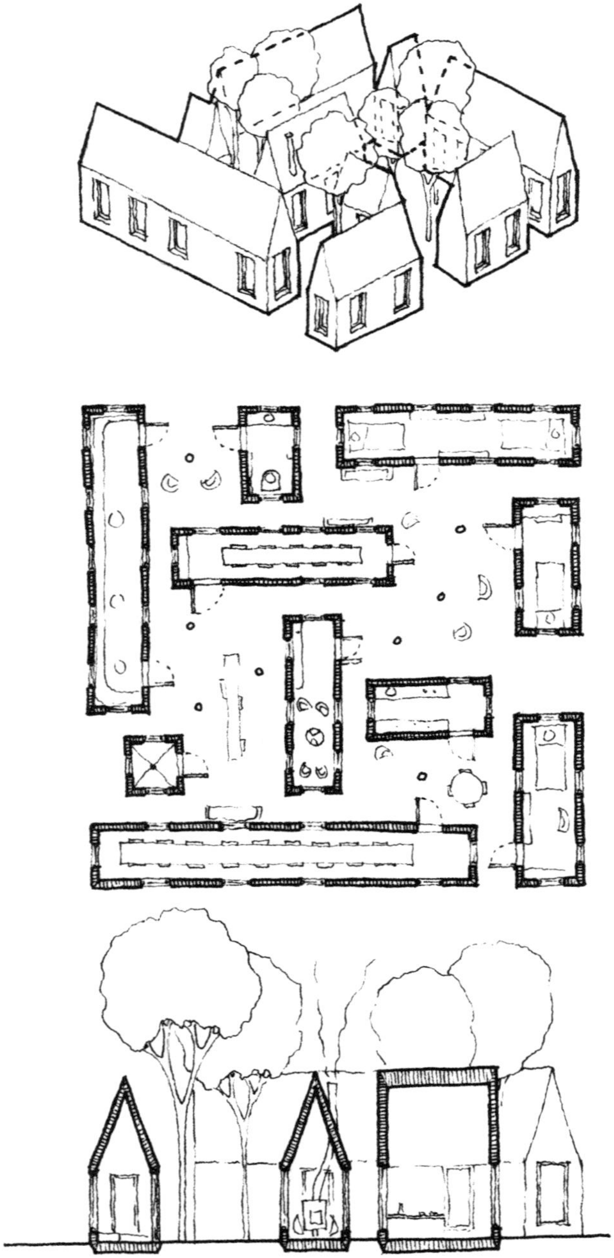

no.312

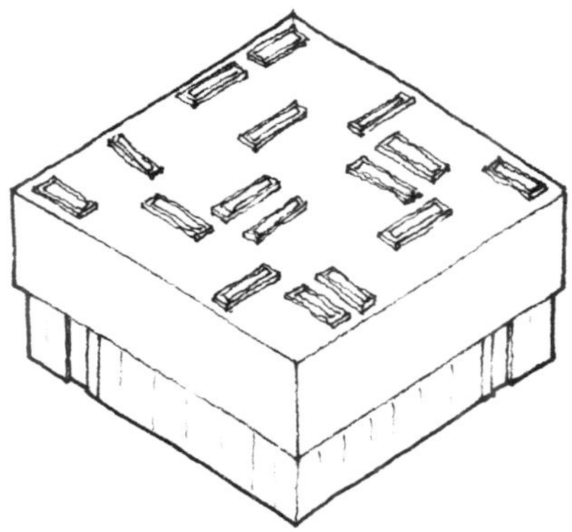

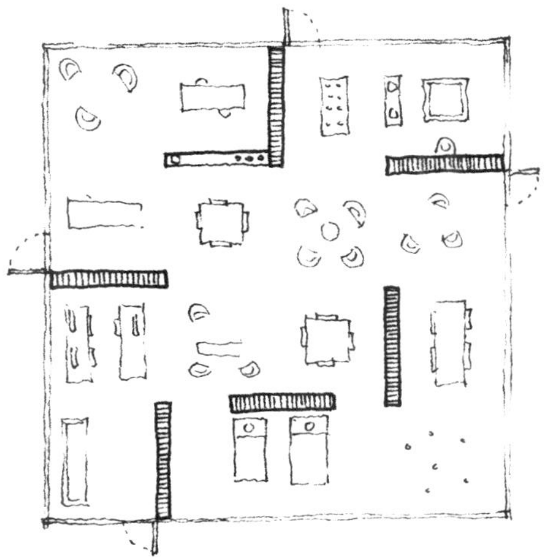

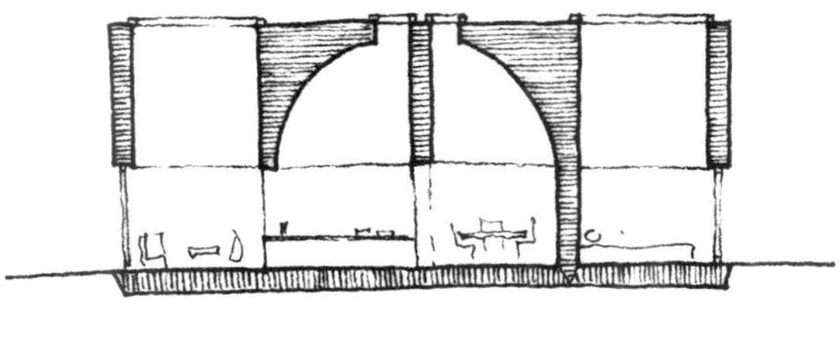

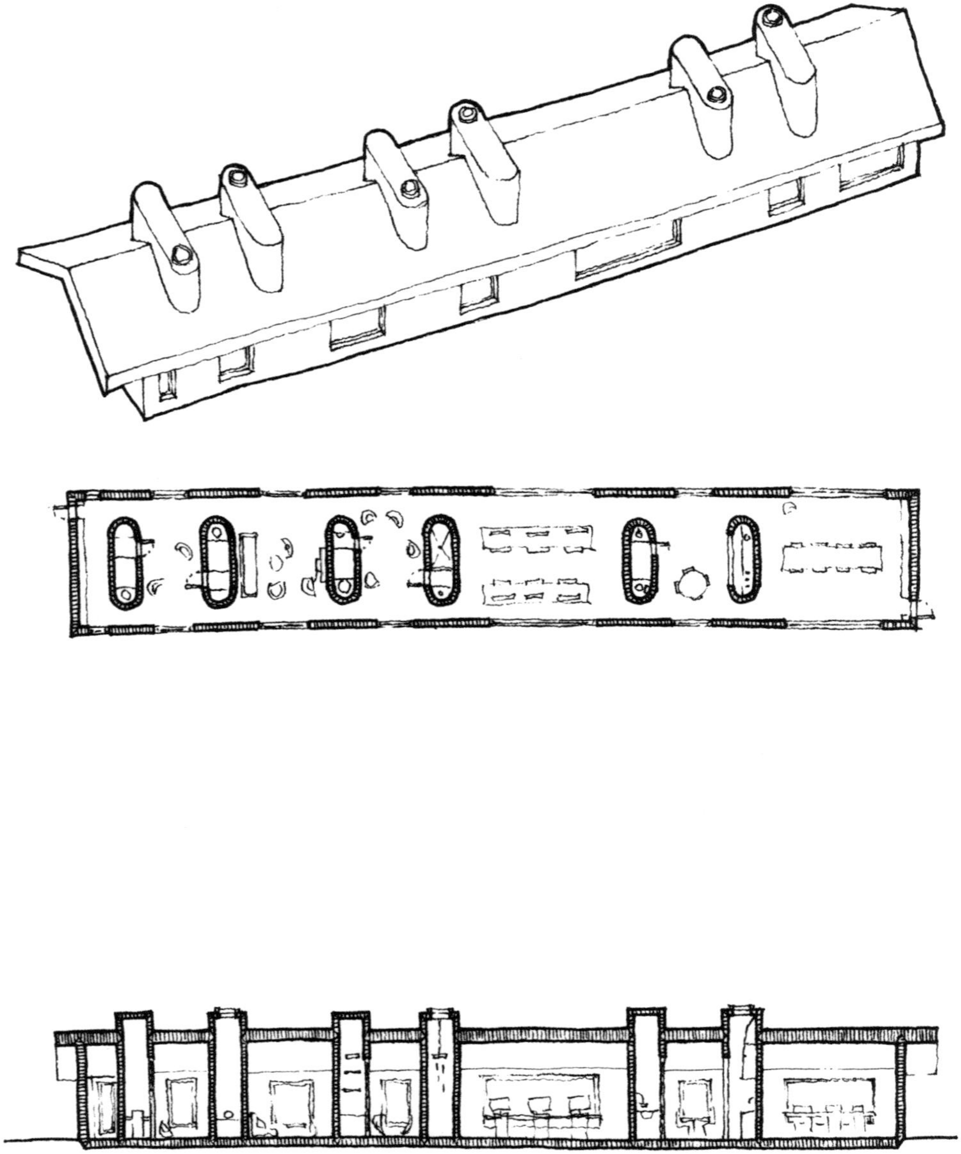

no.314

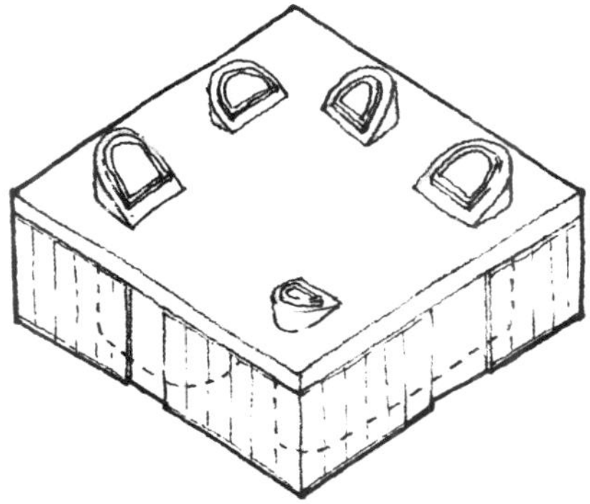

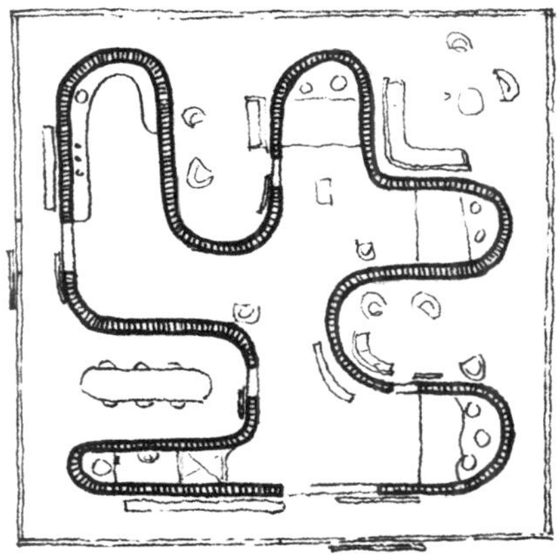

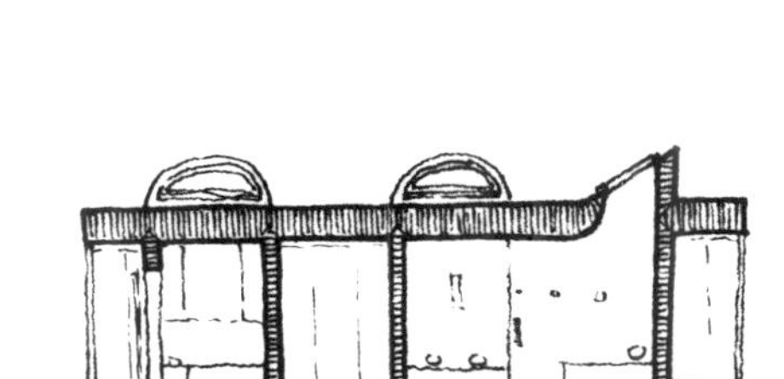

no.315

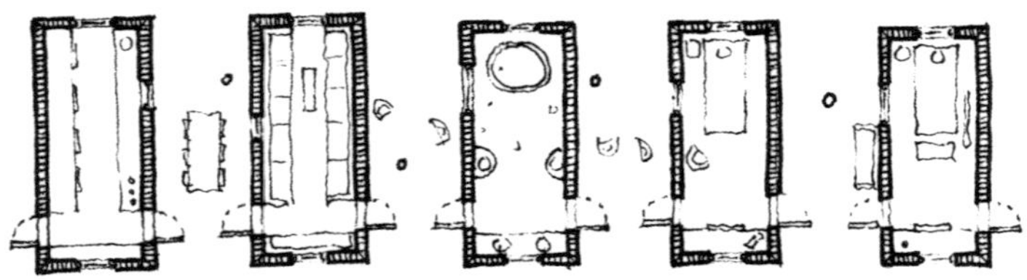

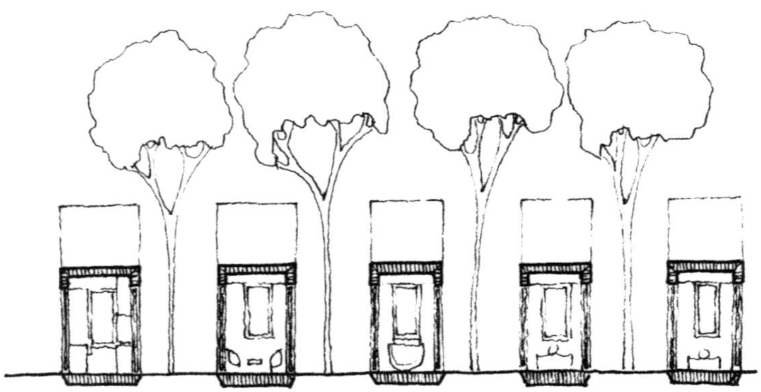

no.316

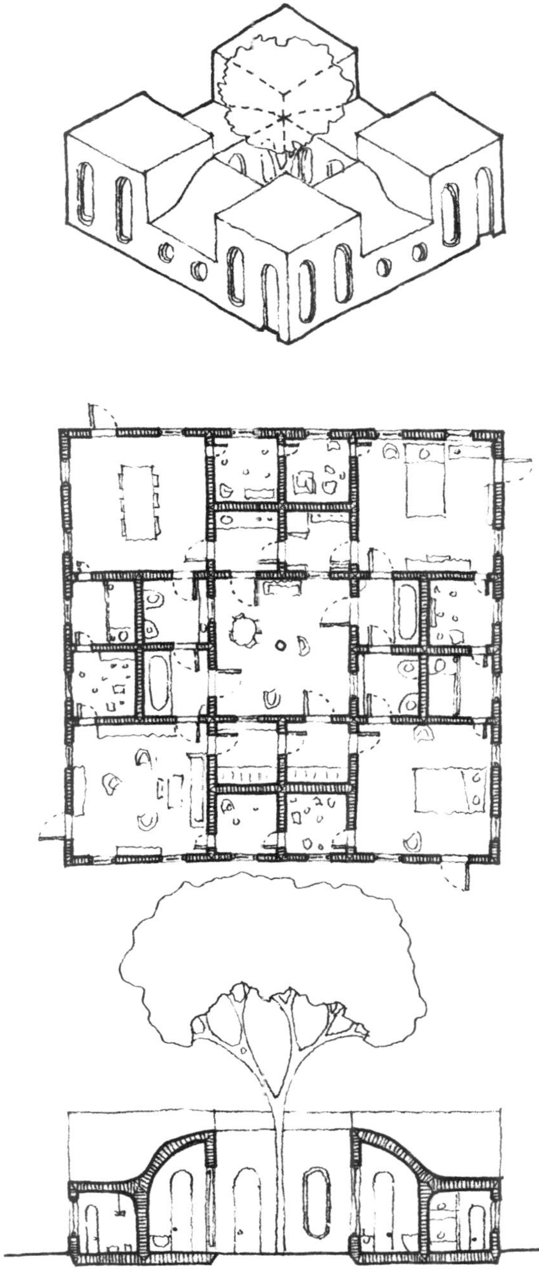

no.317

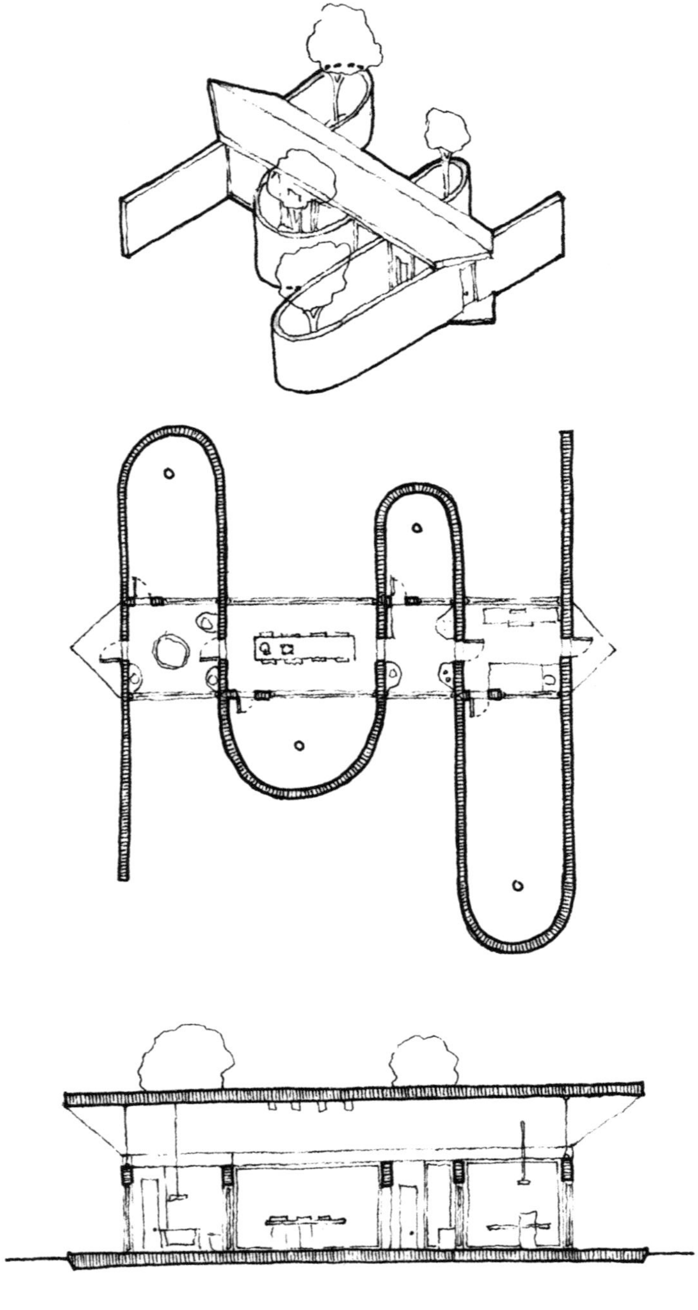

no.318

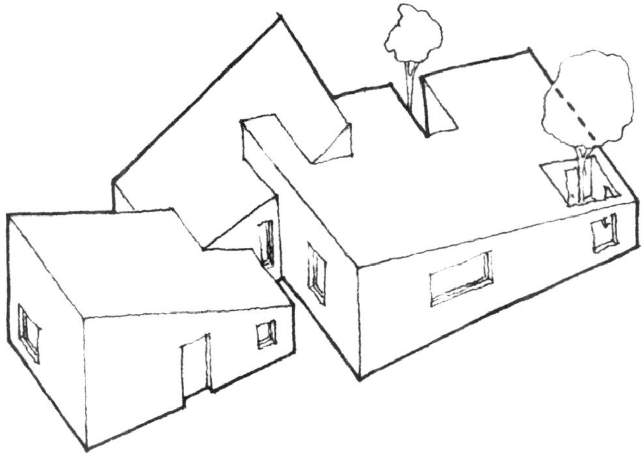

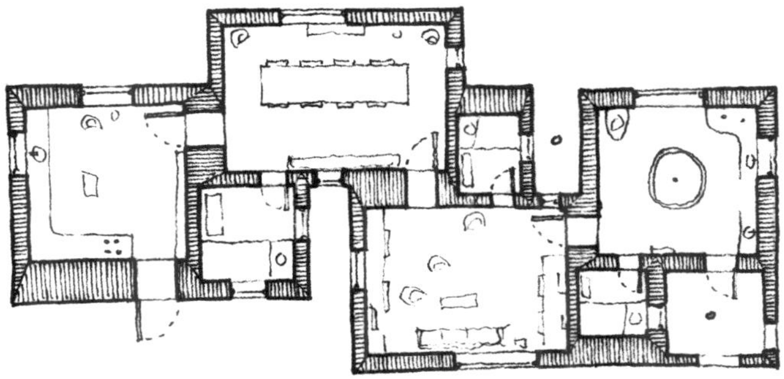

no.319

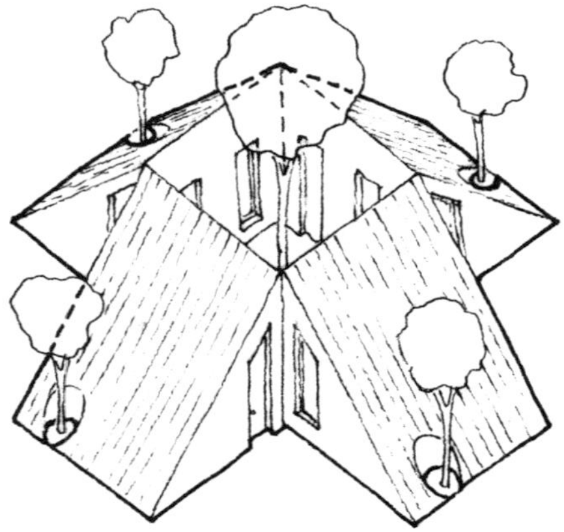

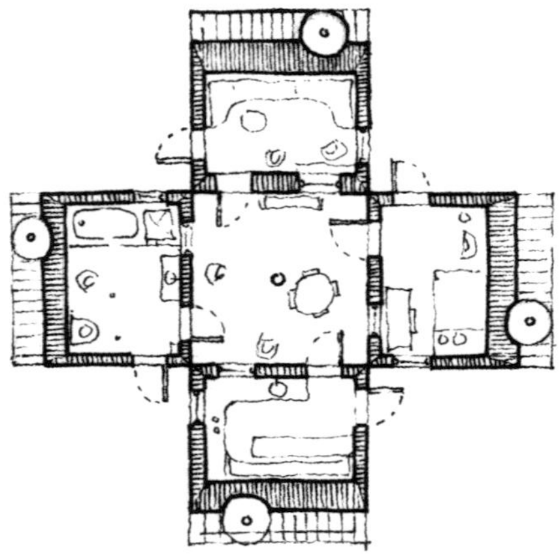

no.320

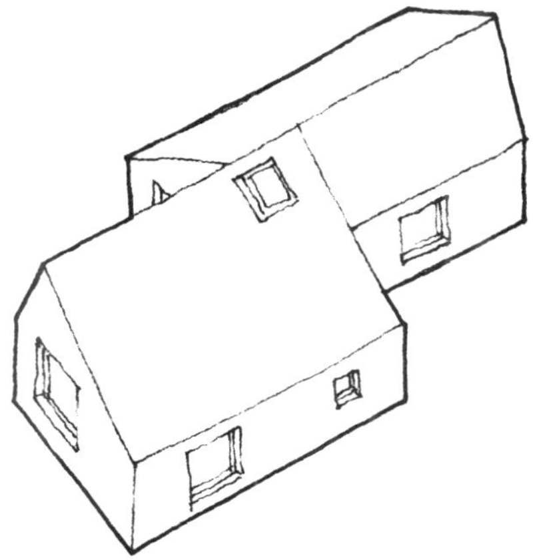

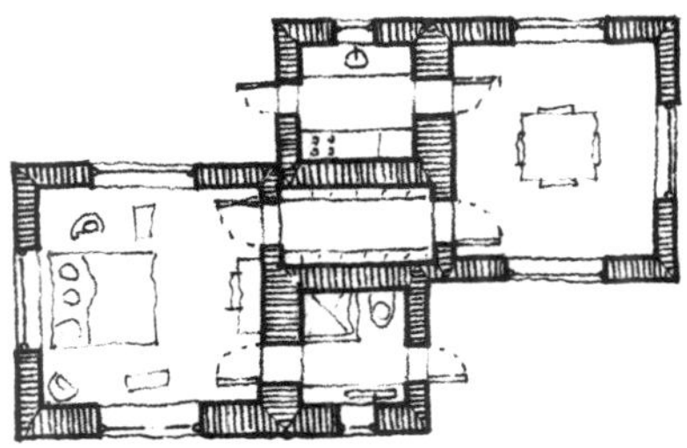

no.321

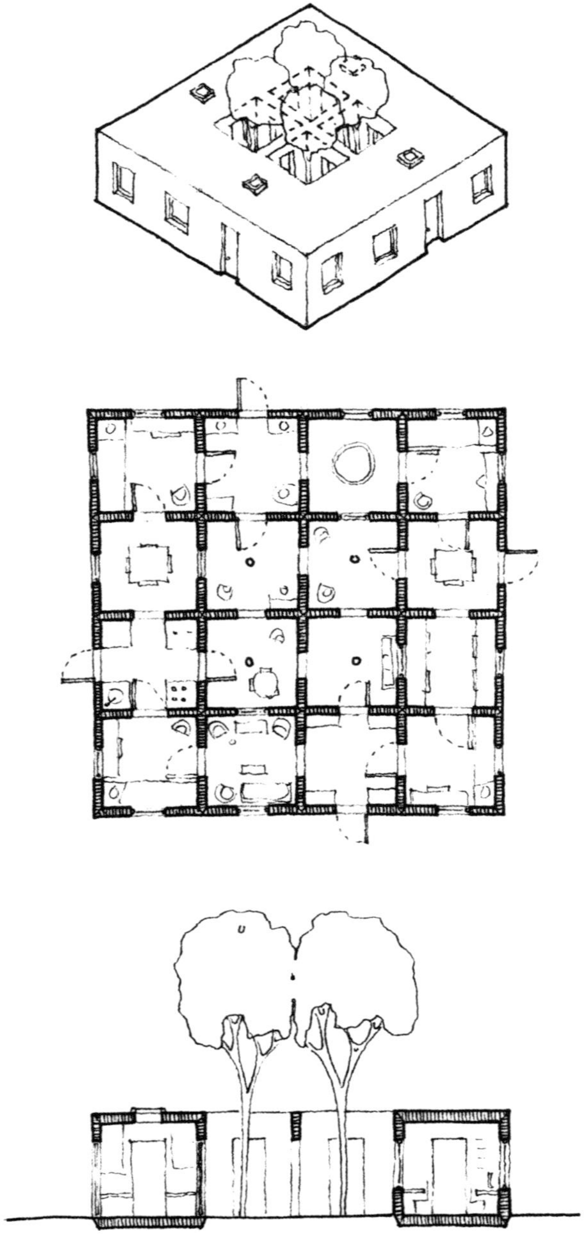

no.322

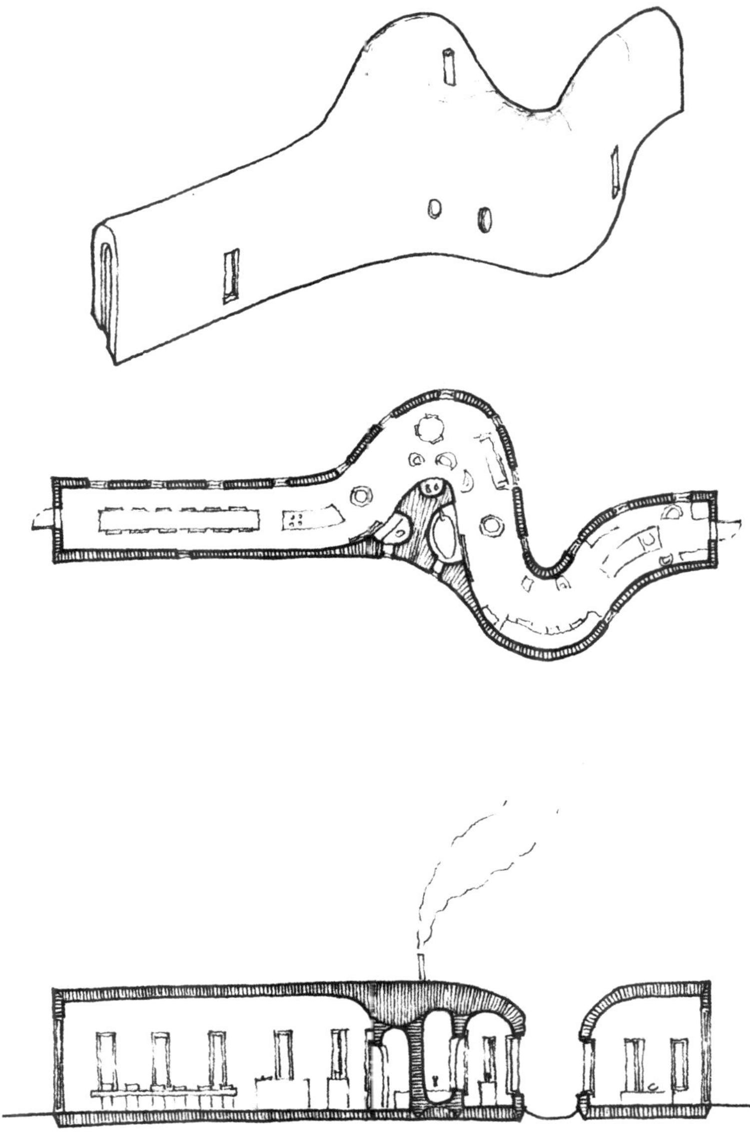

no.323

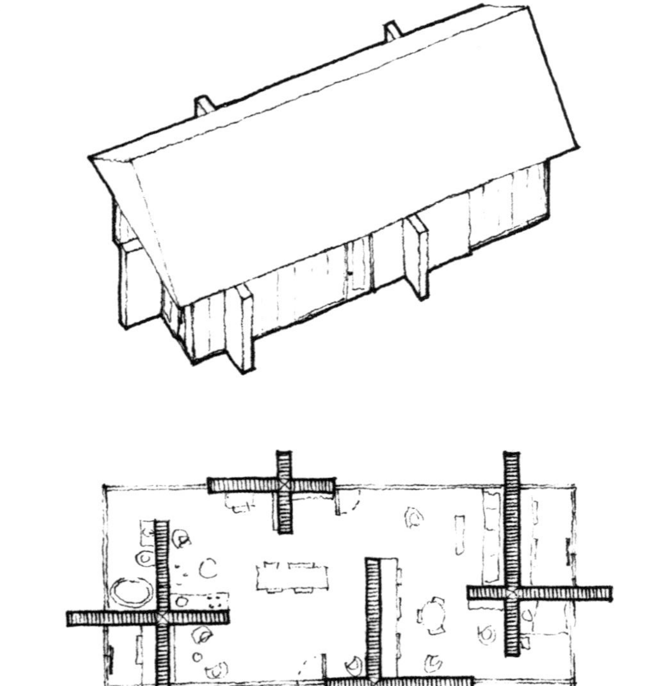

no.324

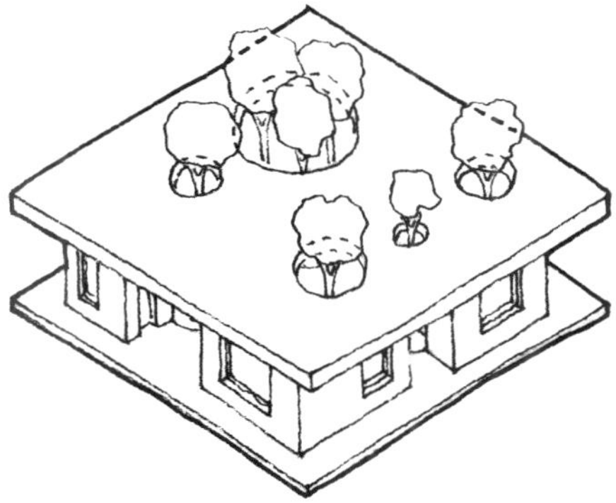

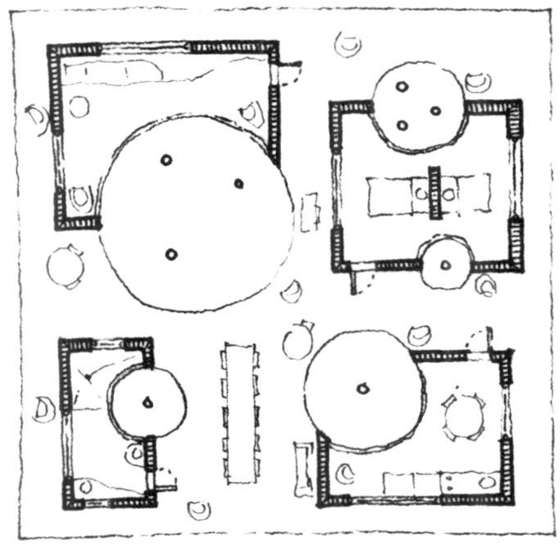

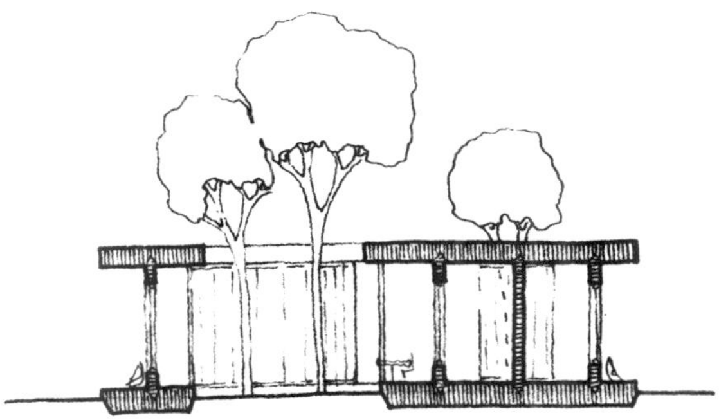

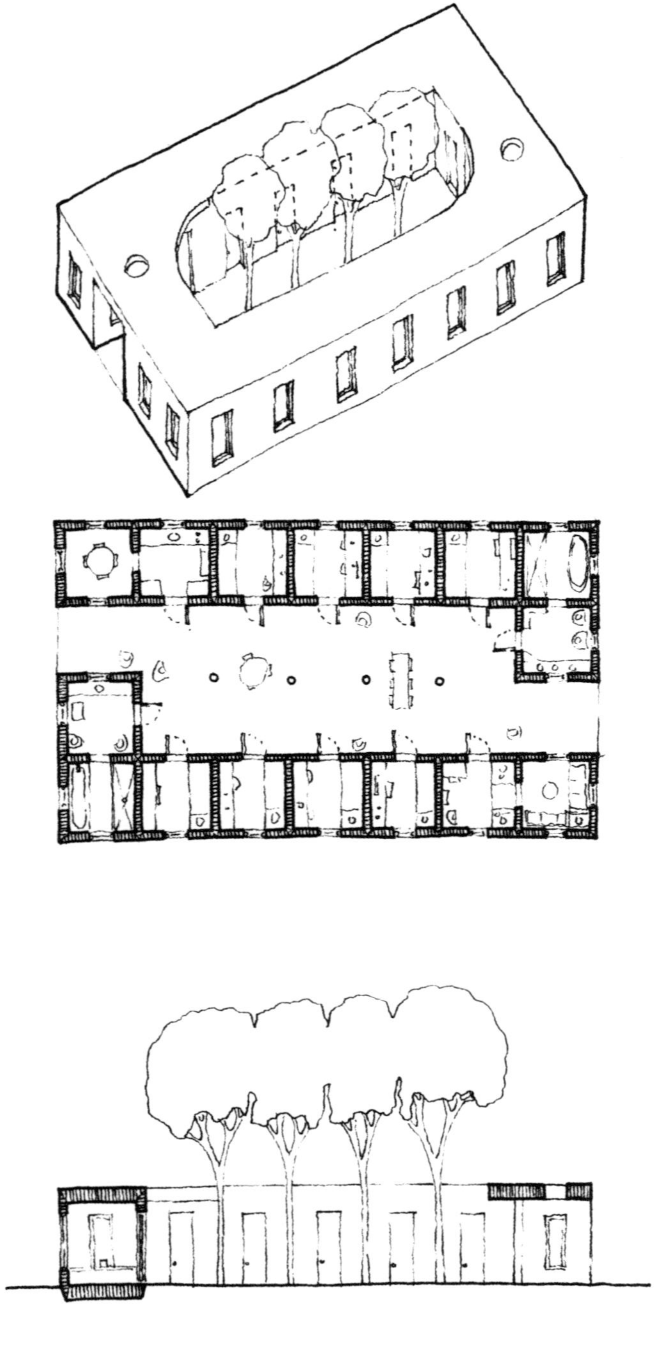

no.326

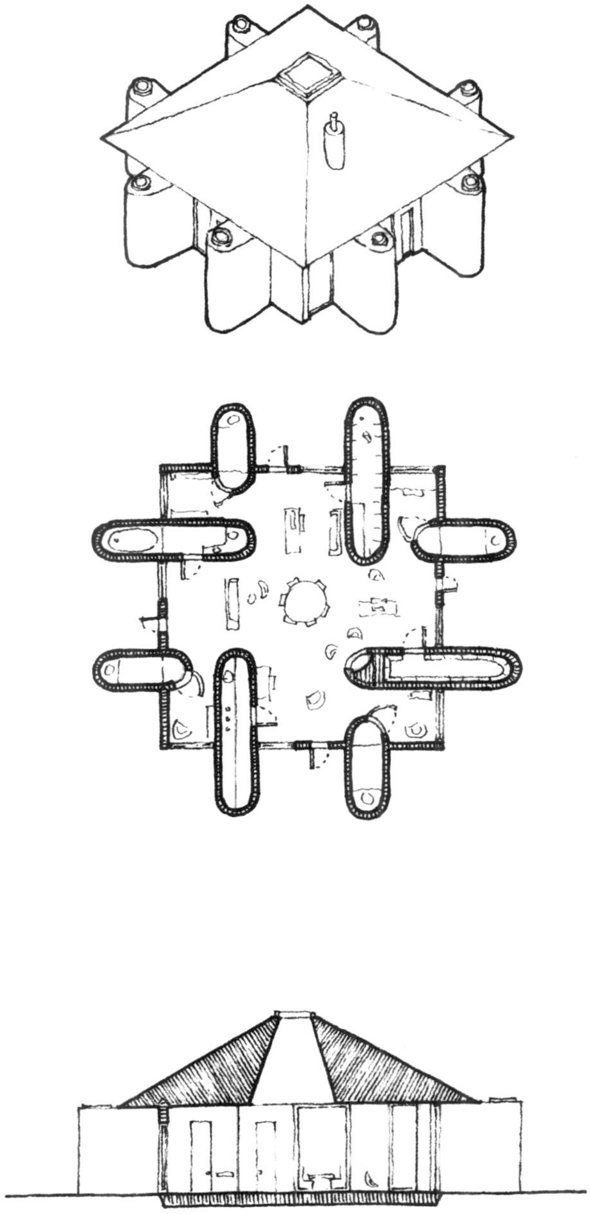

no.327

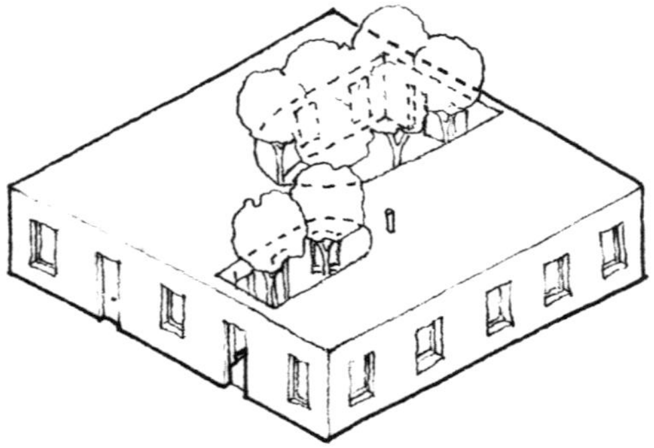

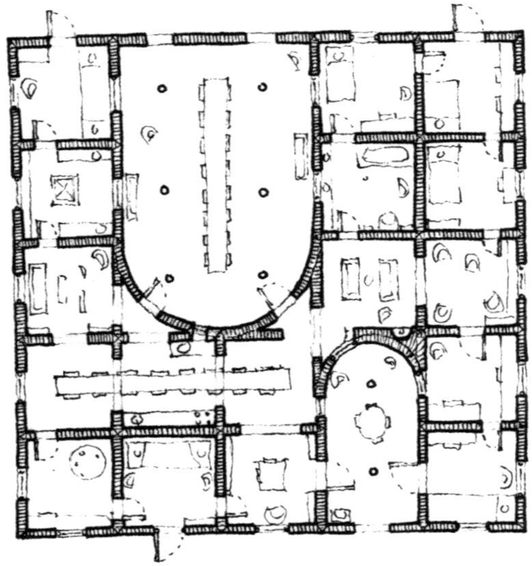

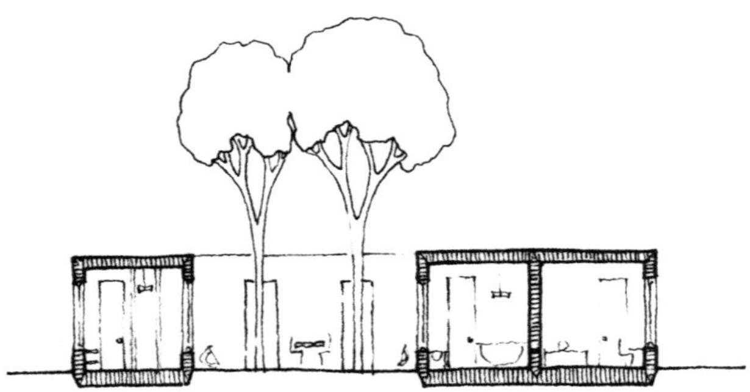

no.328

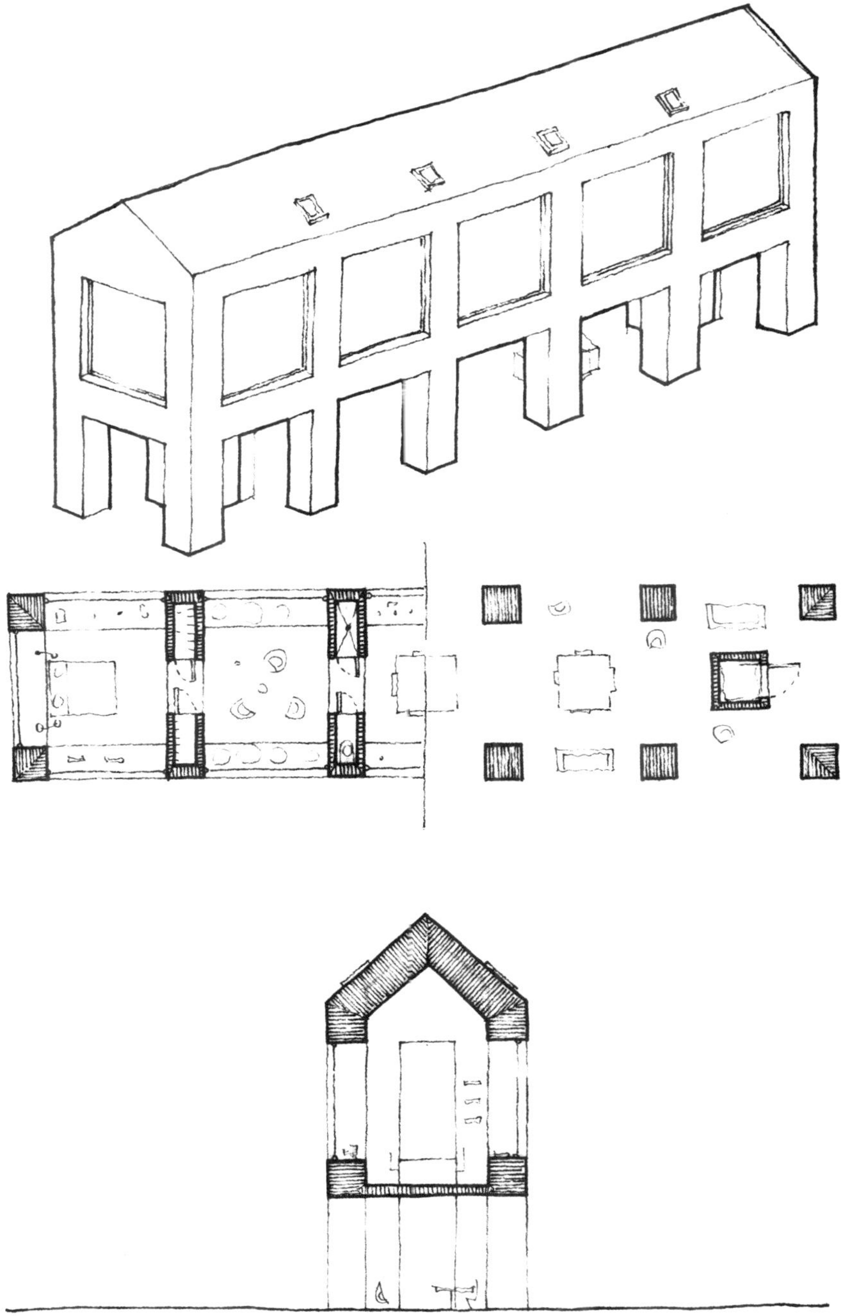

no.329

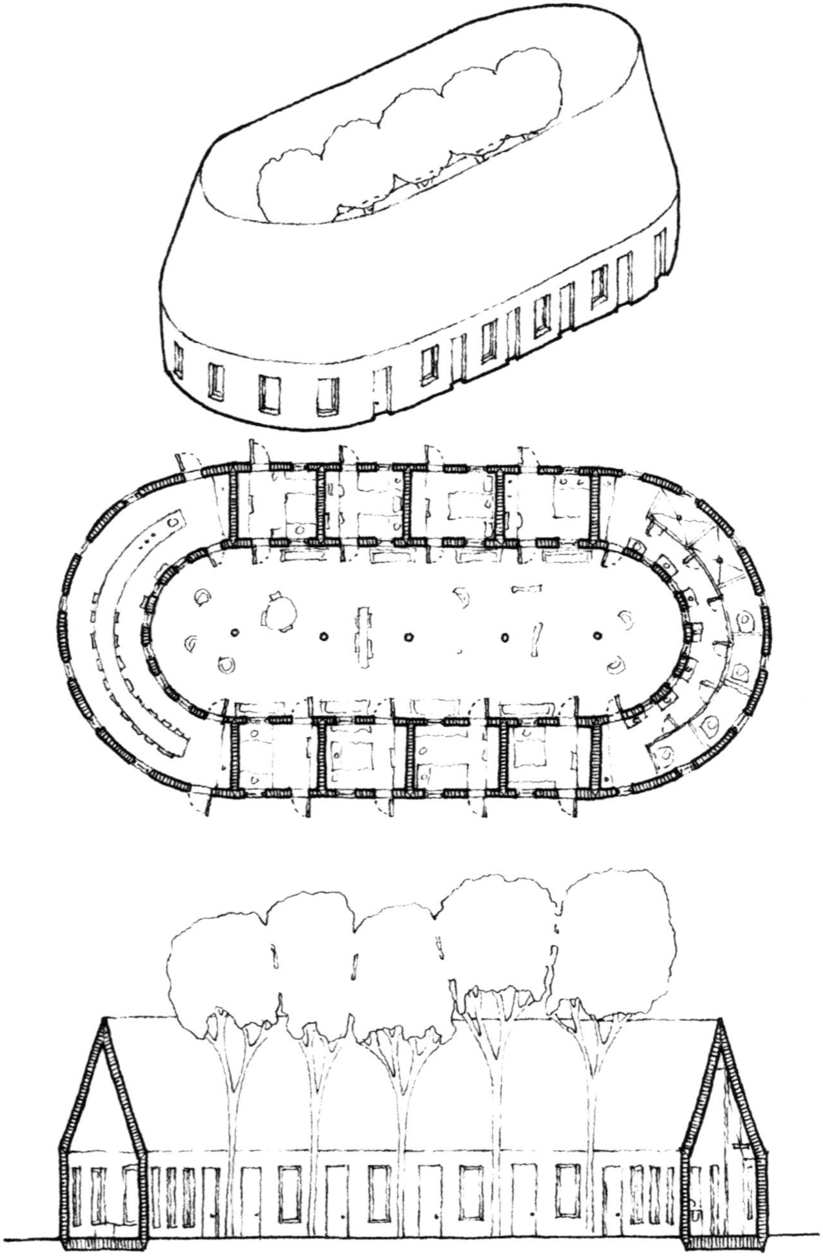

no.330

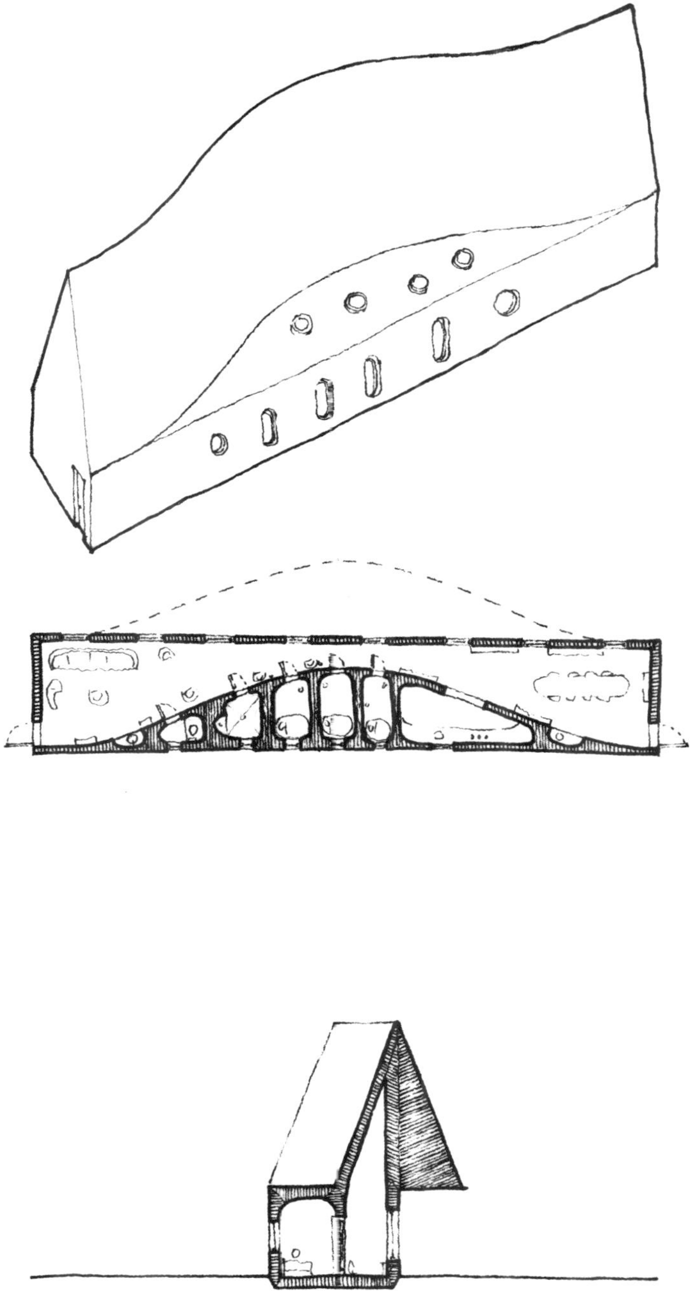

no.331

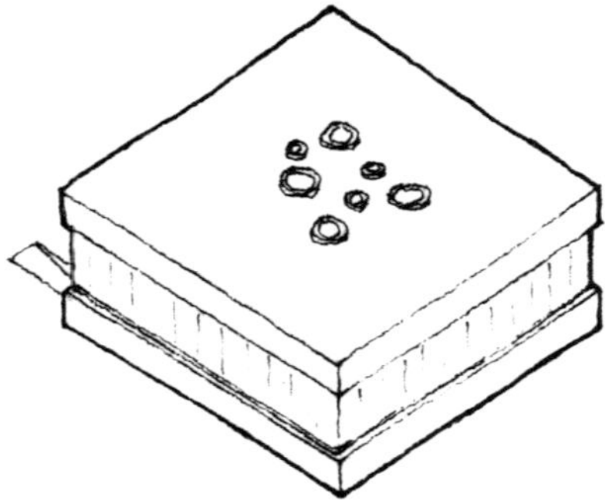

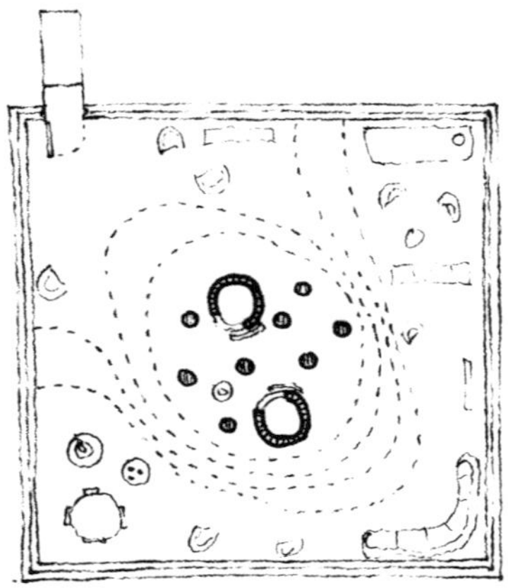

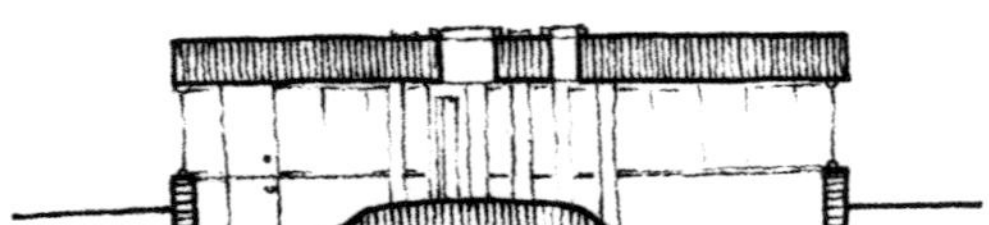

no.332

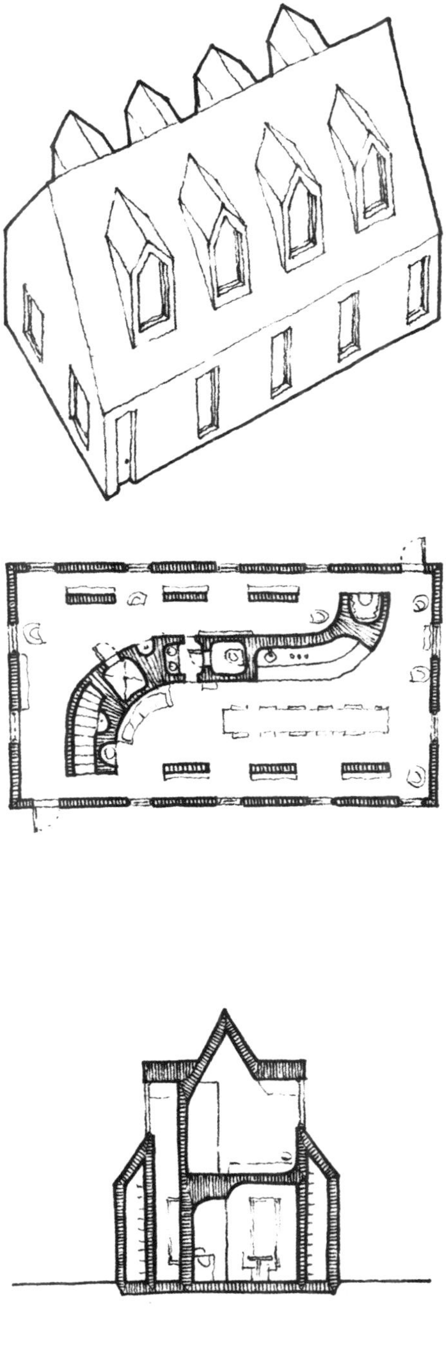

no.333

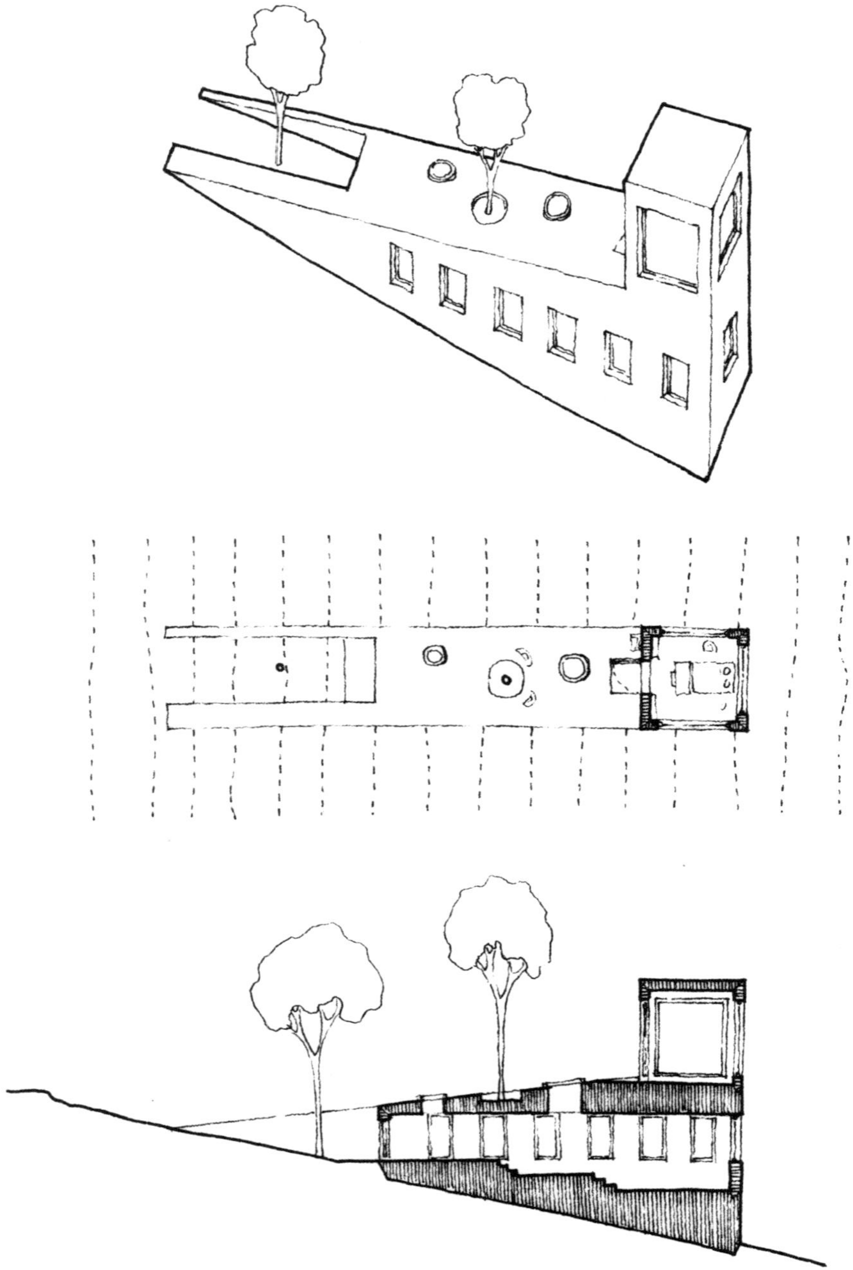

no.334

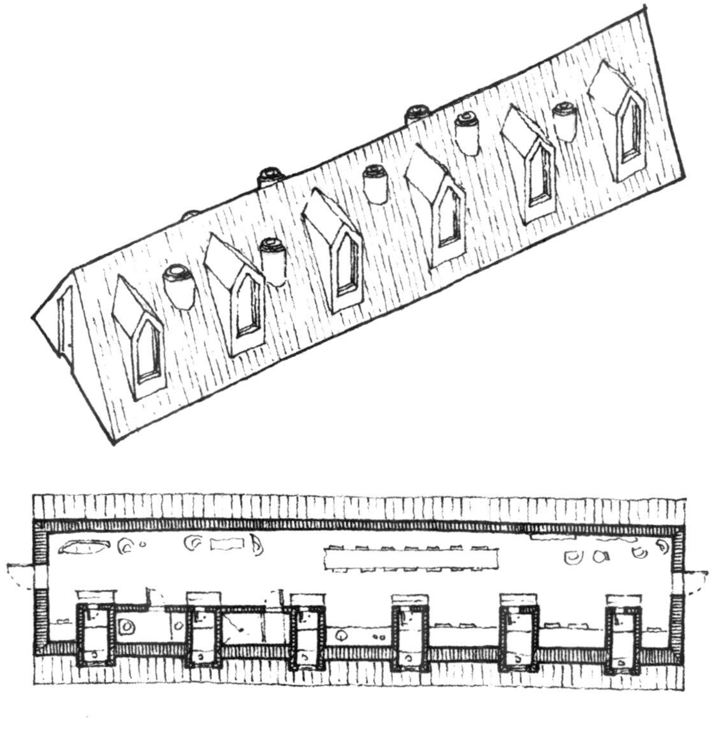

no.335

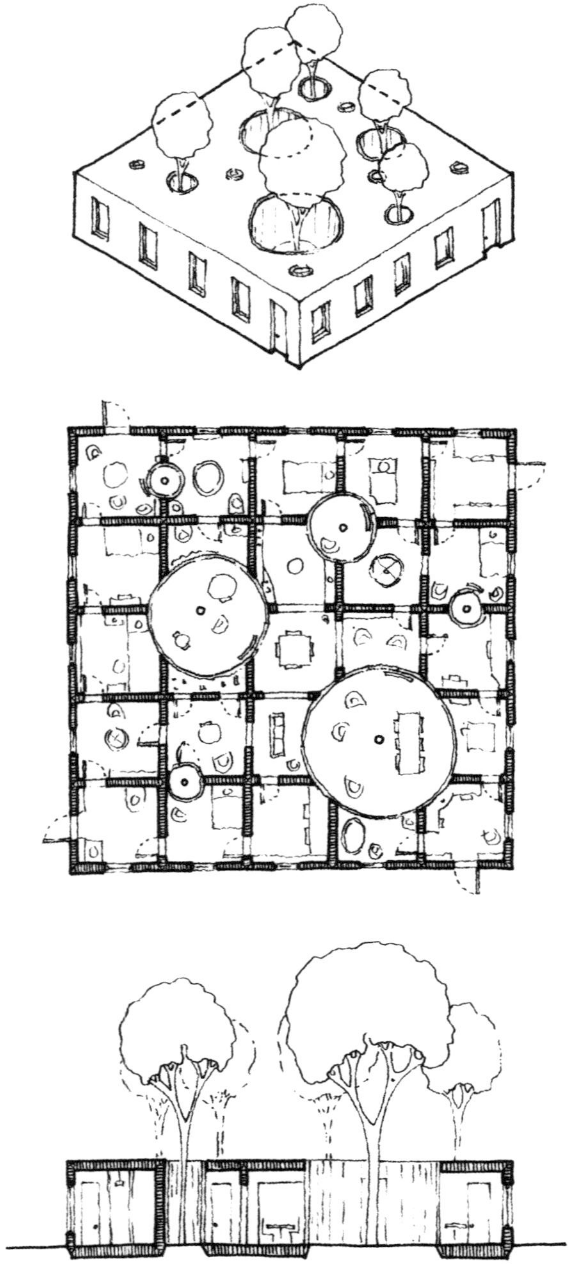

no.336

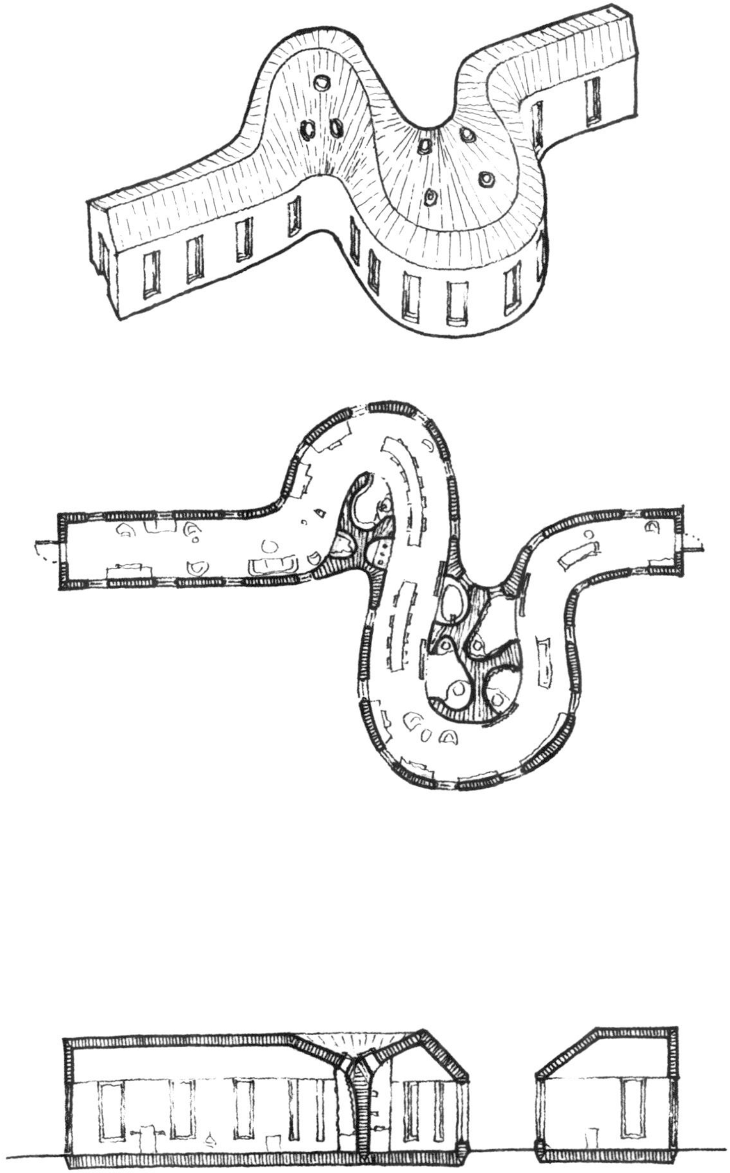

no.337

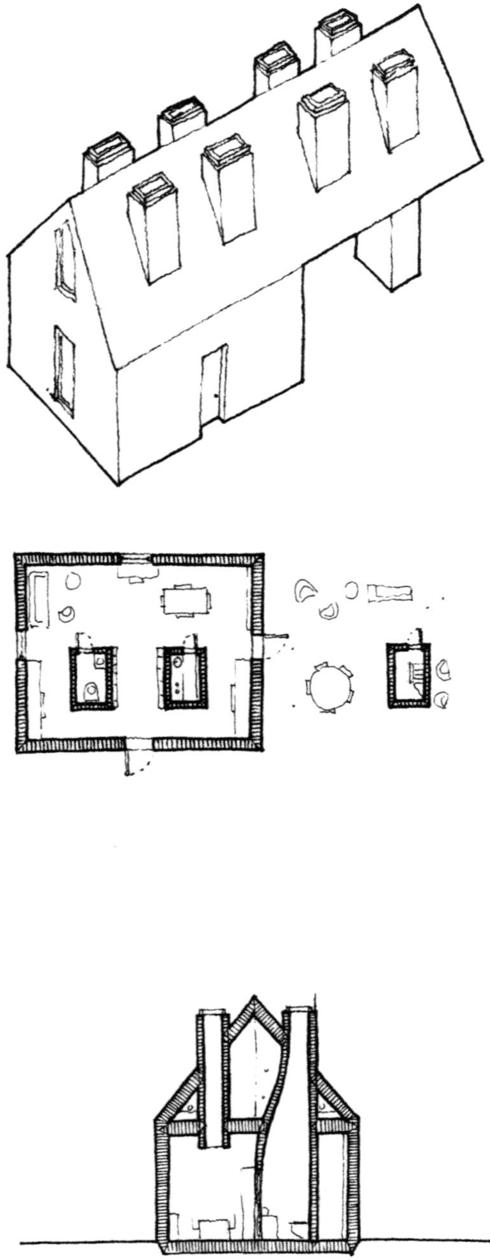

no.338

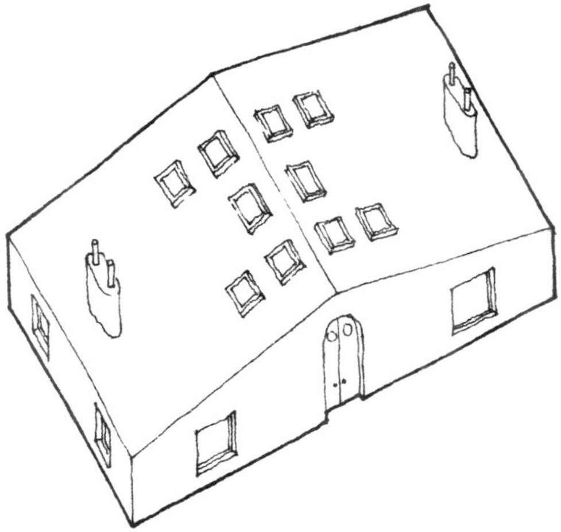

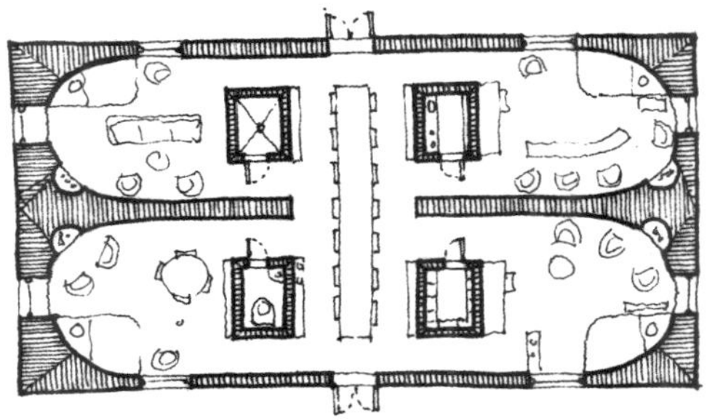

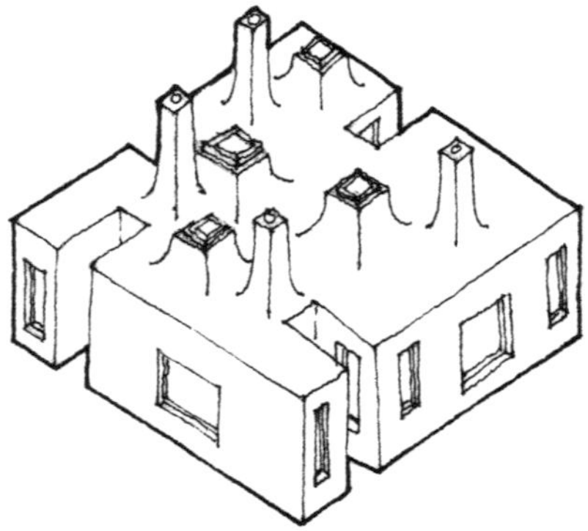

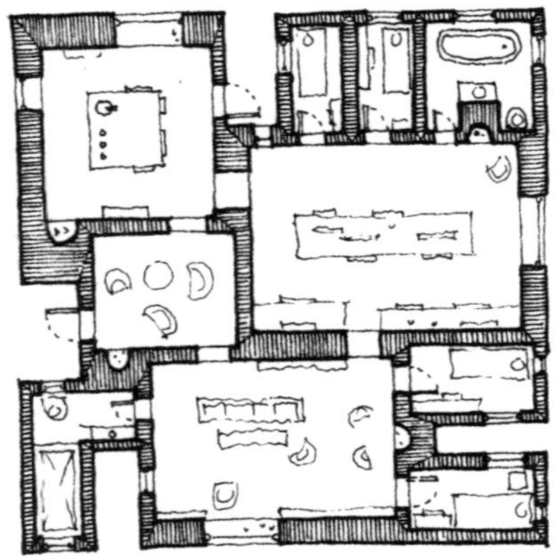

no.340

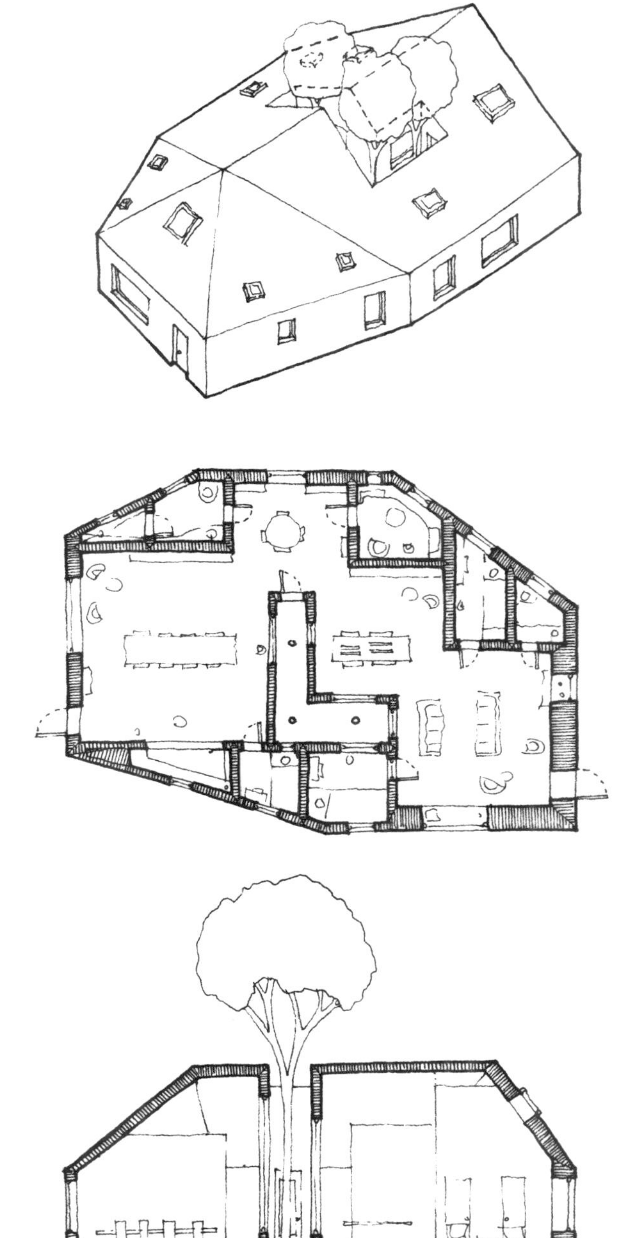

no.341

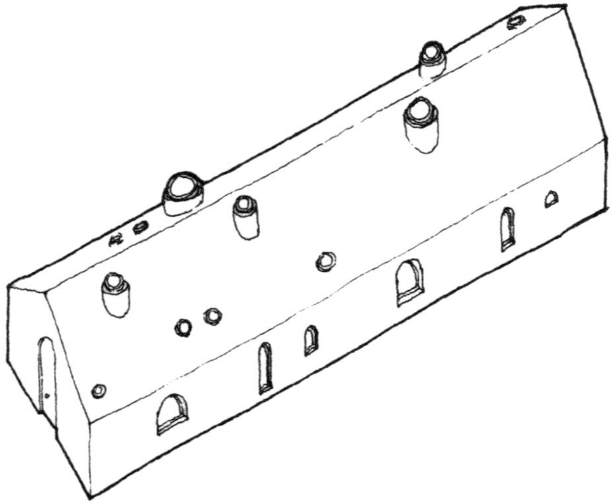

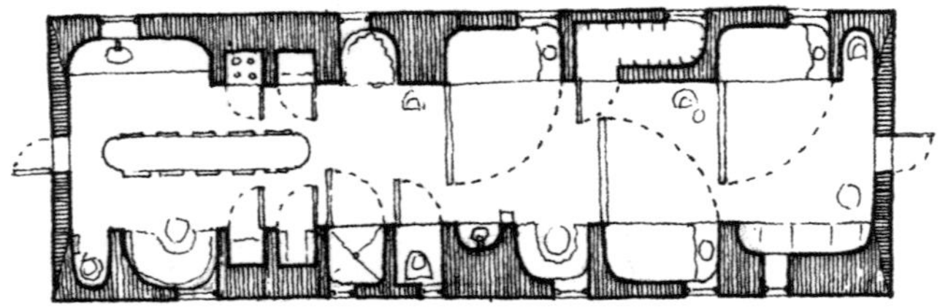

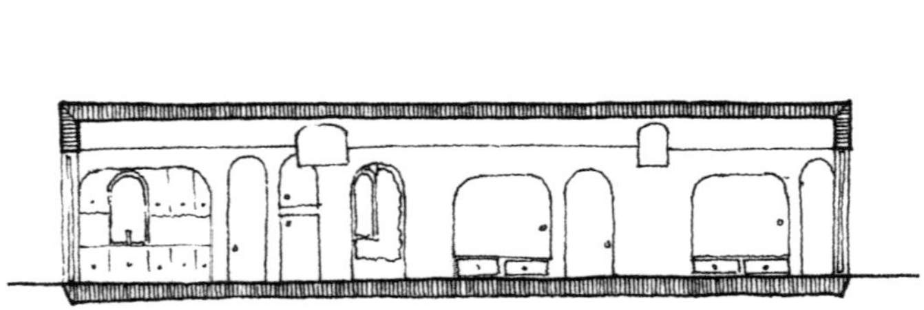

no.342

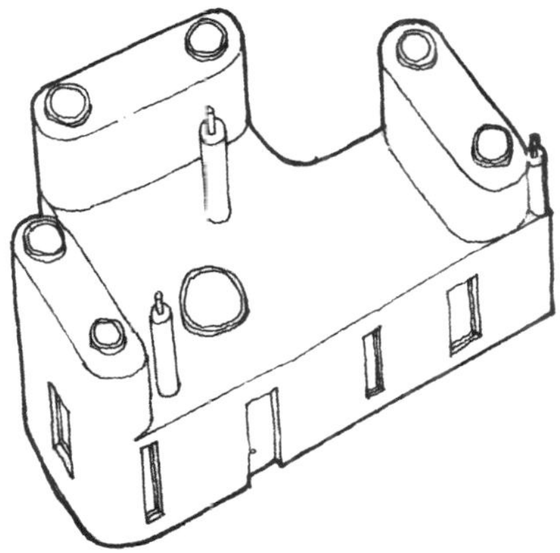

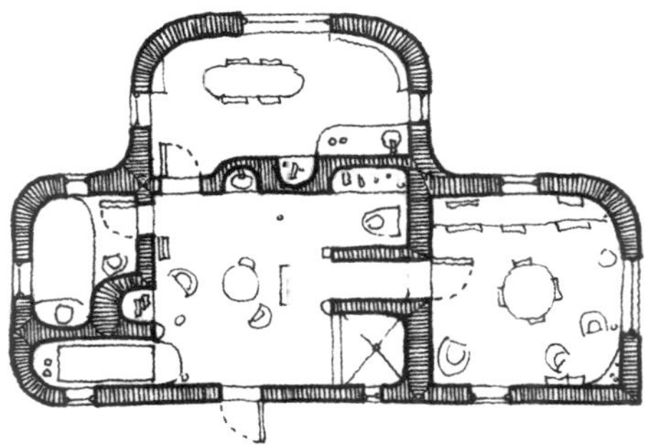

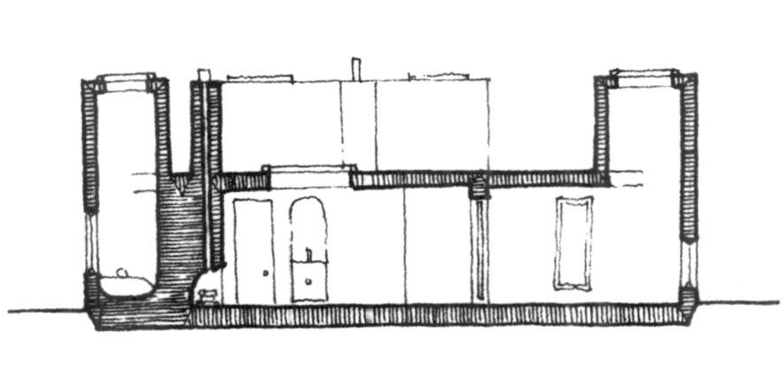

no.343

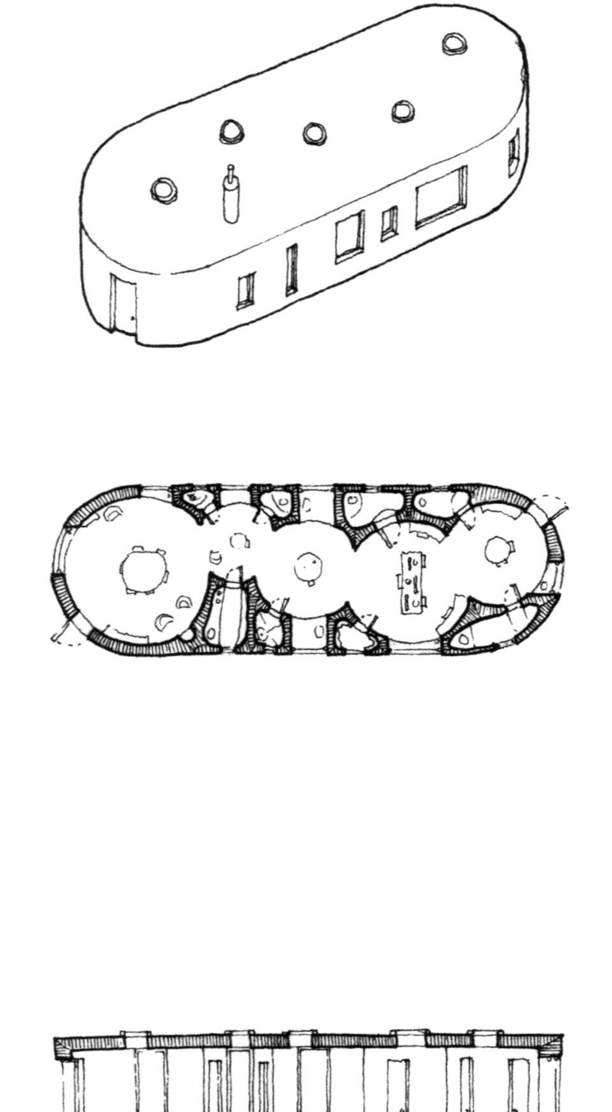

no.344

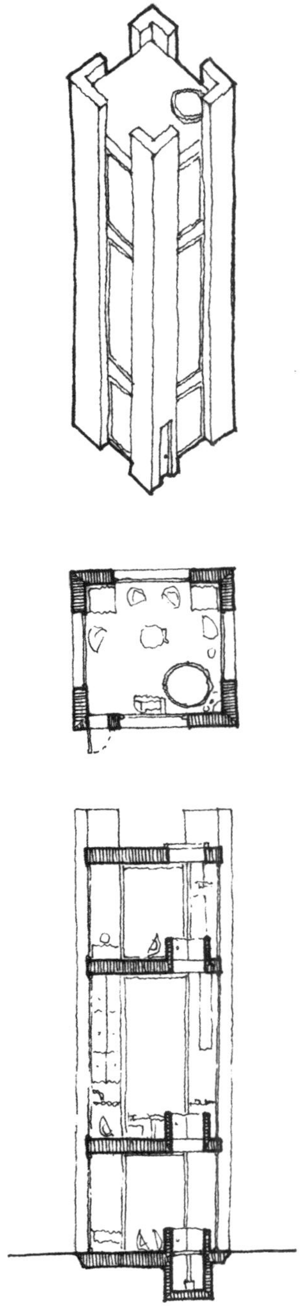

no.345

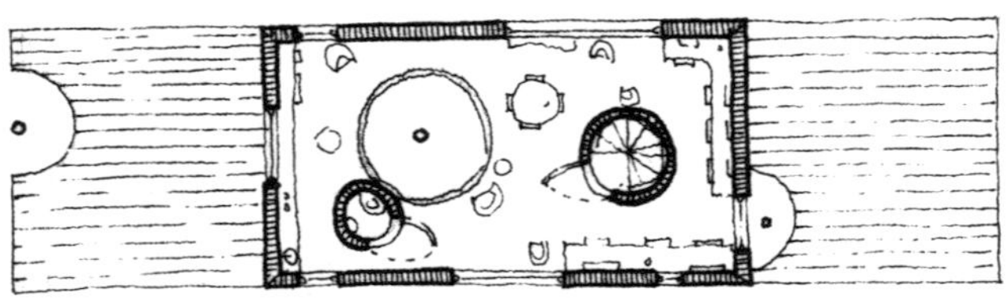

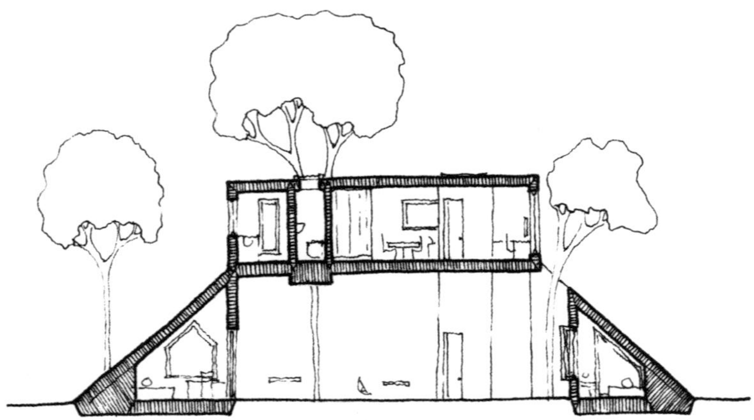

no.346

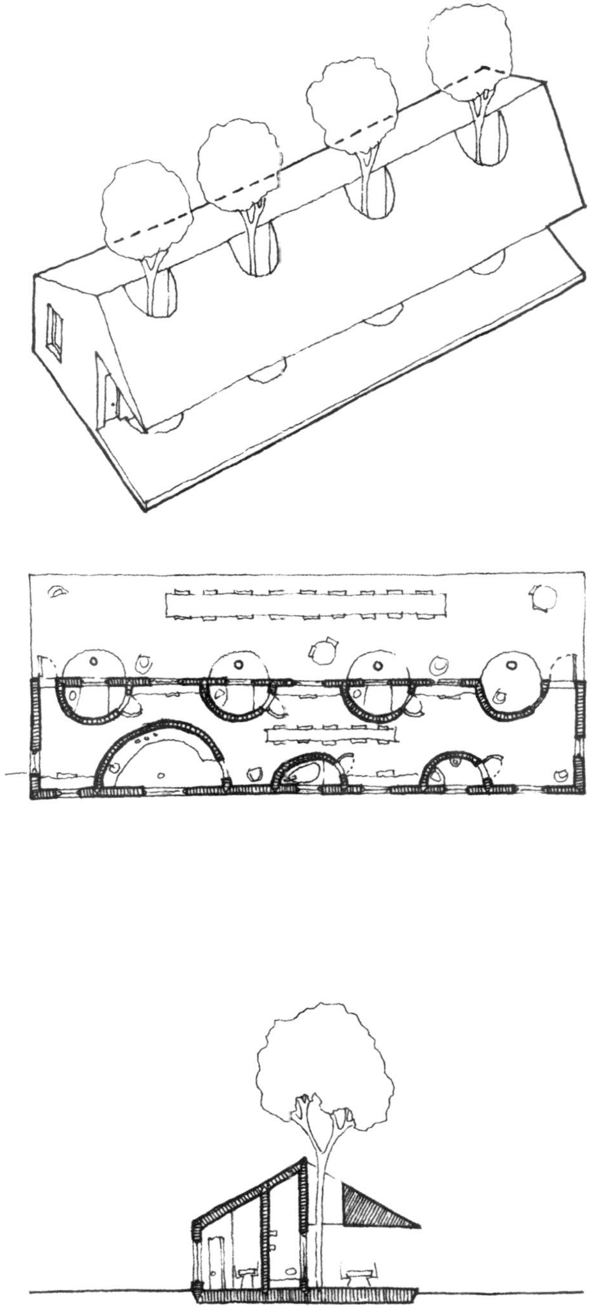

no.347

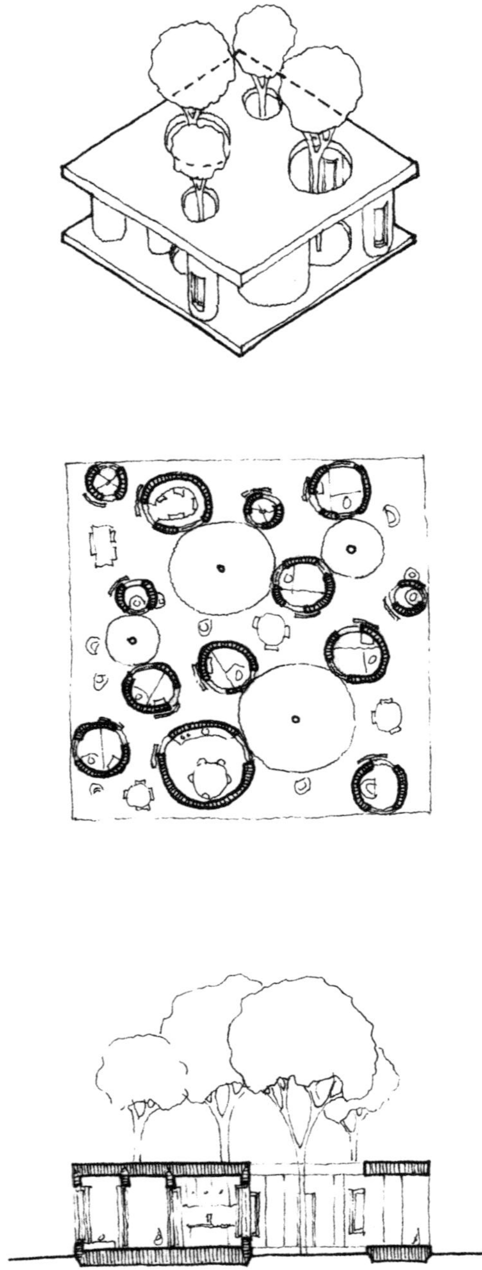

no.348

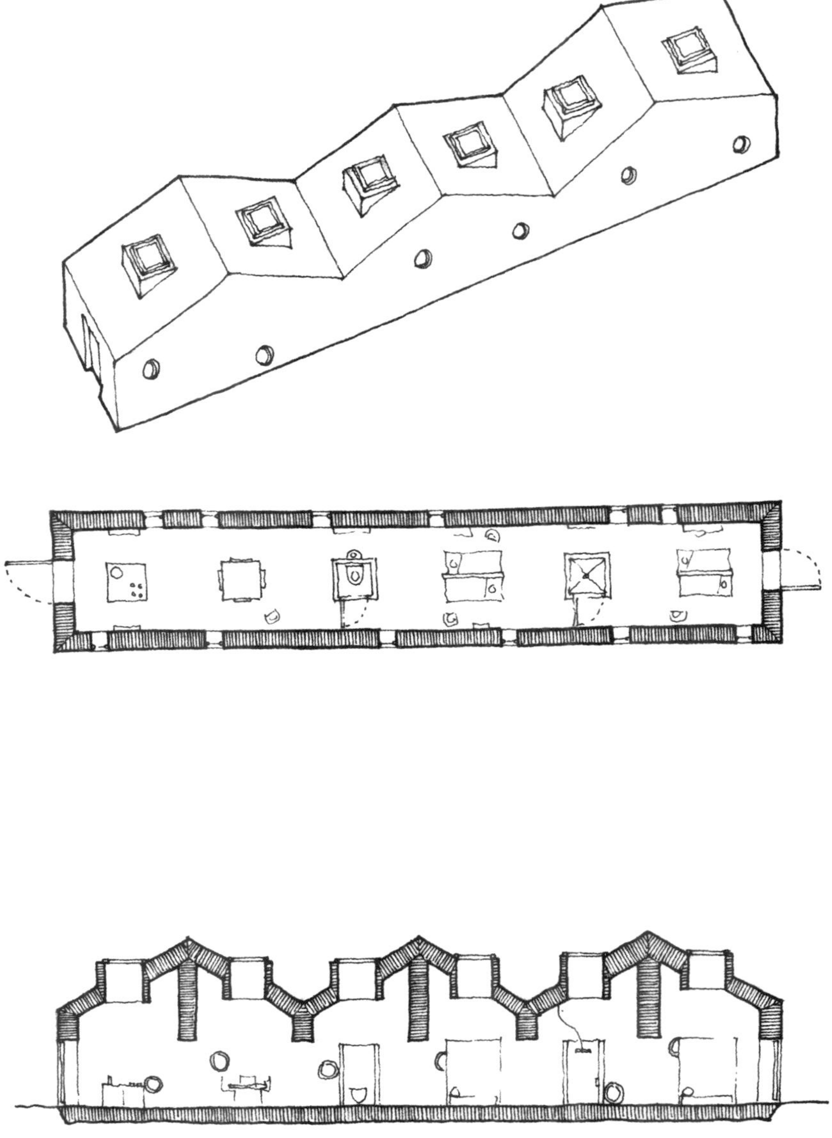

no.349

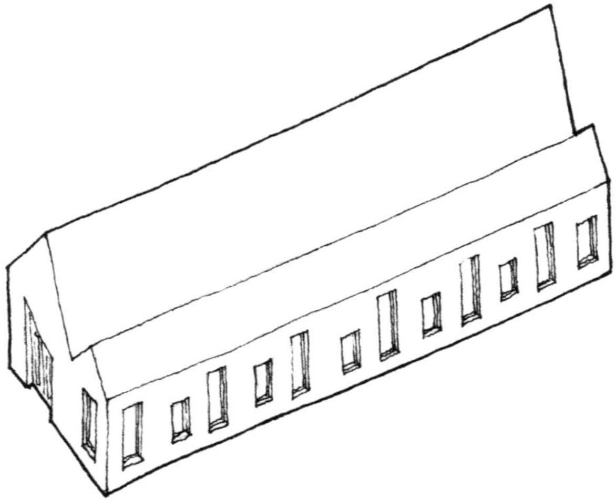

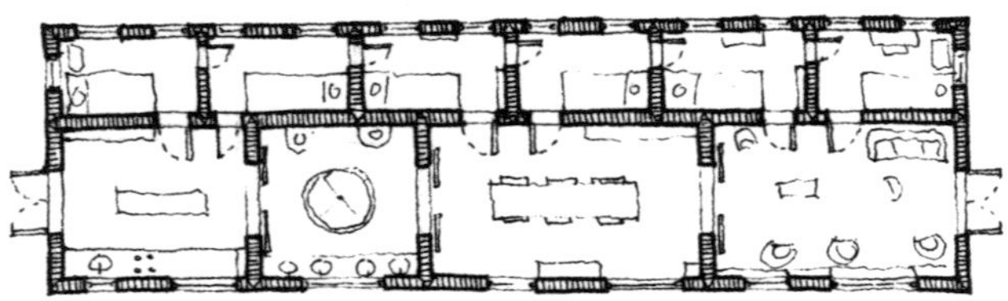

no.350

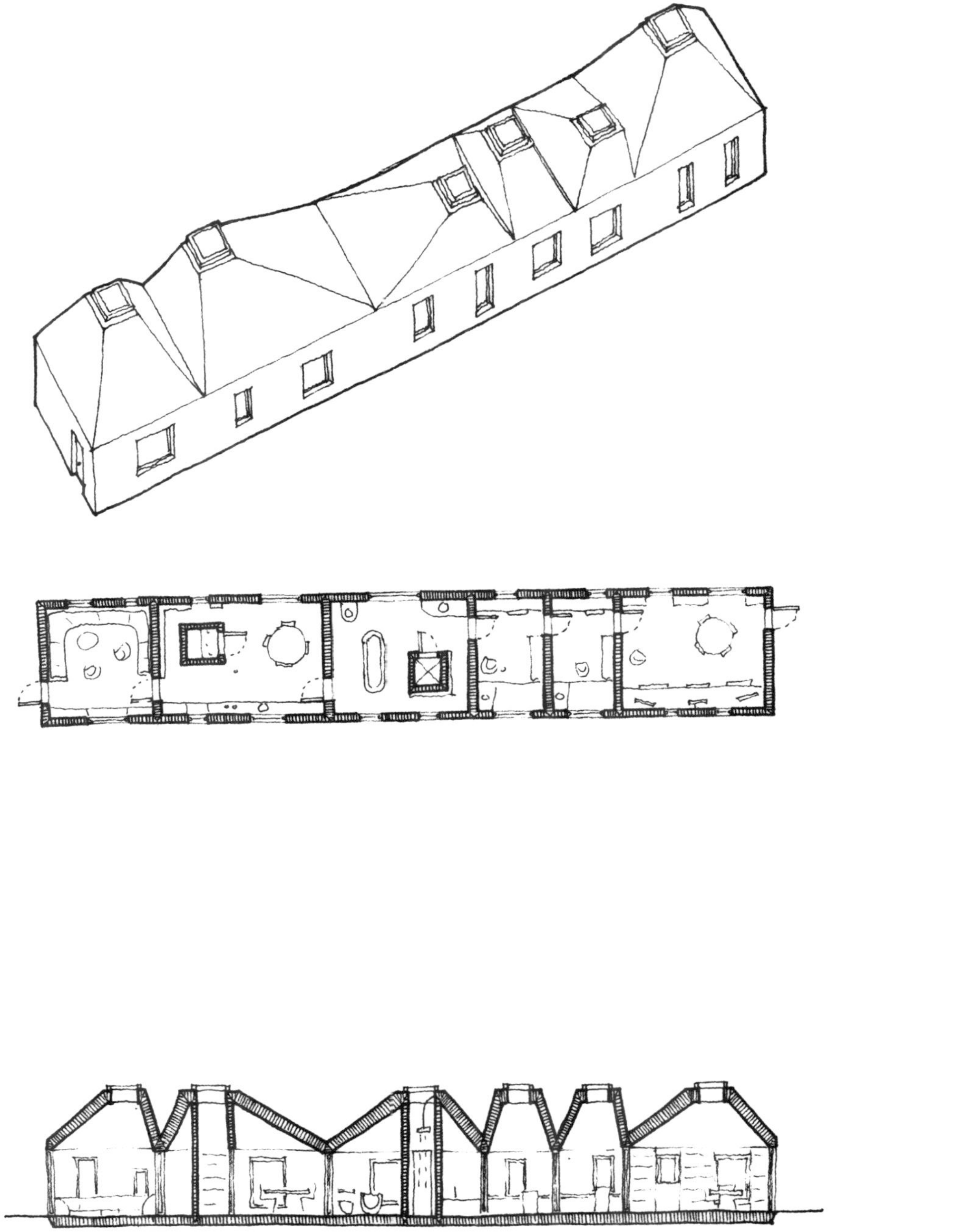

no.351

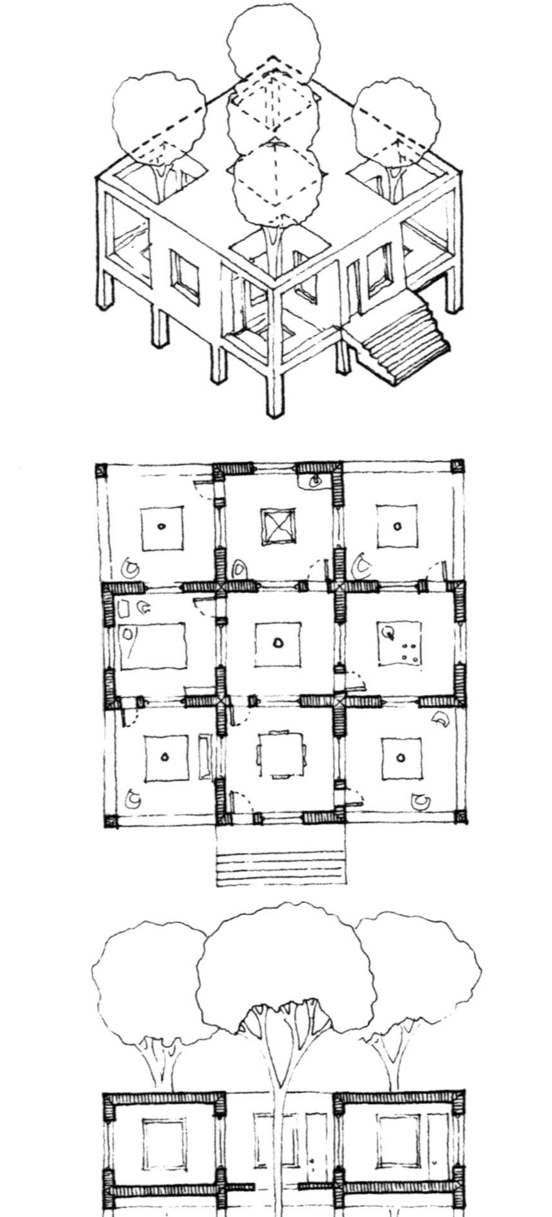

no.352

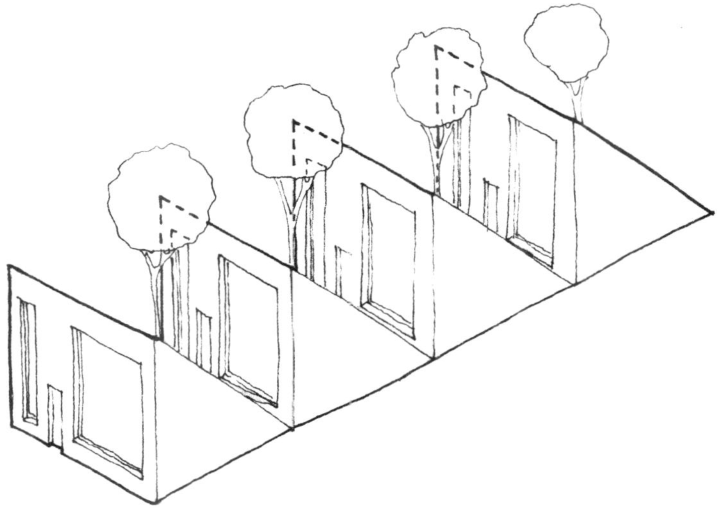

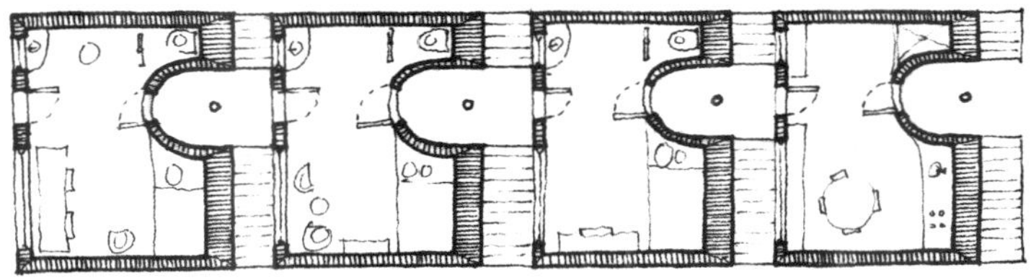

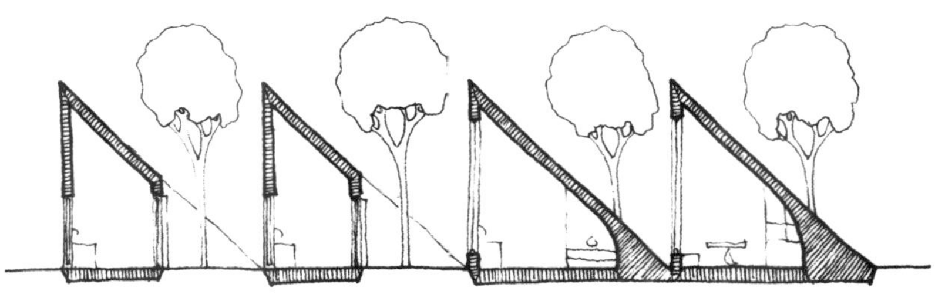

no.353

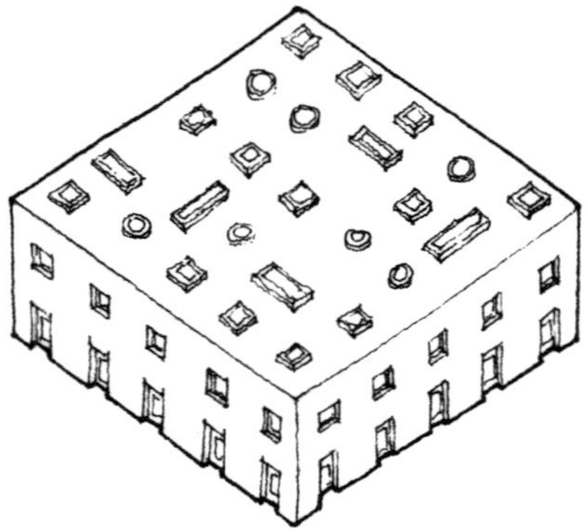

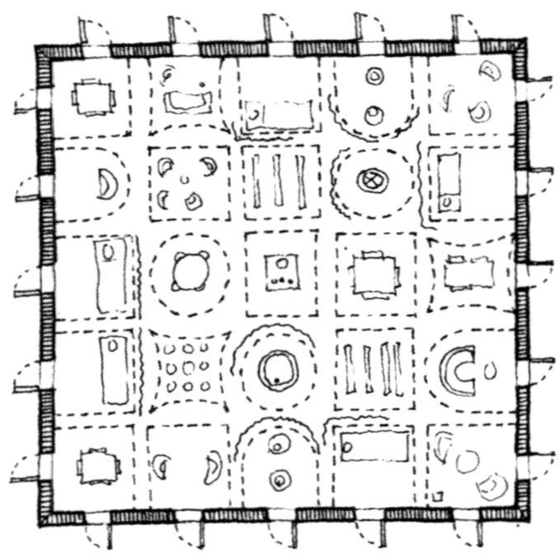

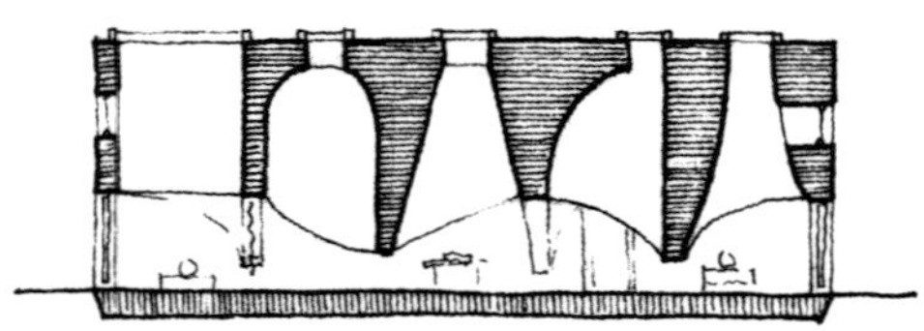

no.354

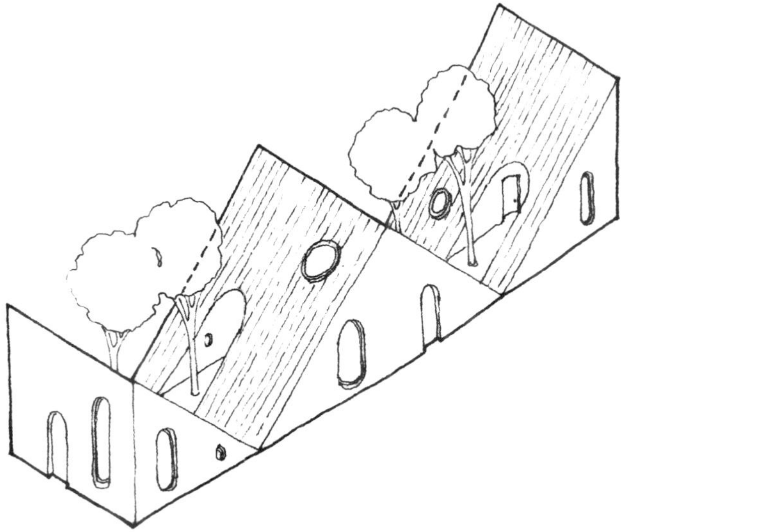

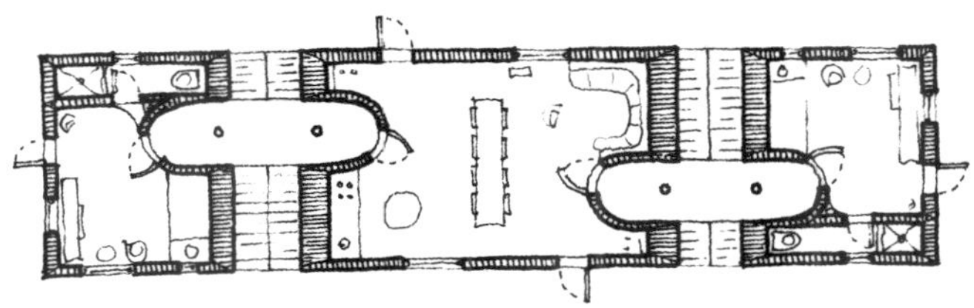

no.355

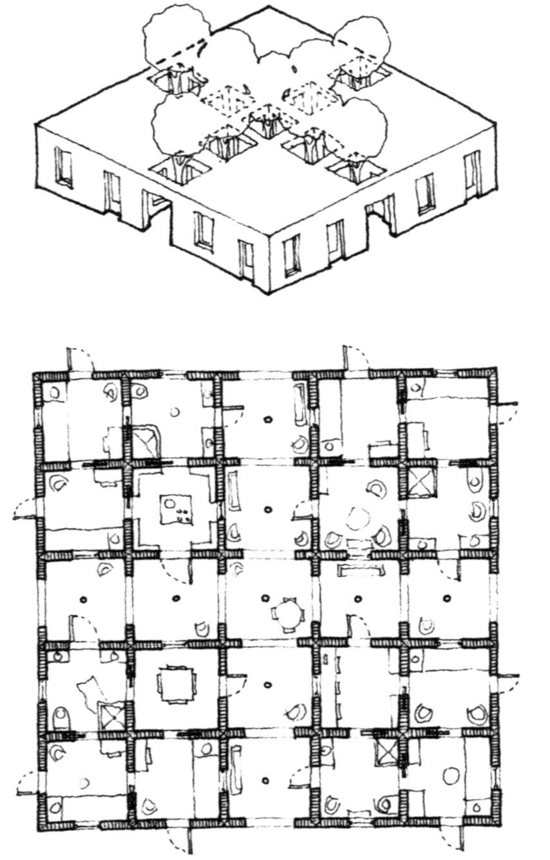

no.356

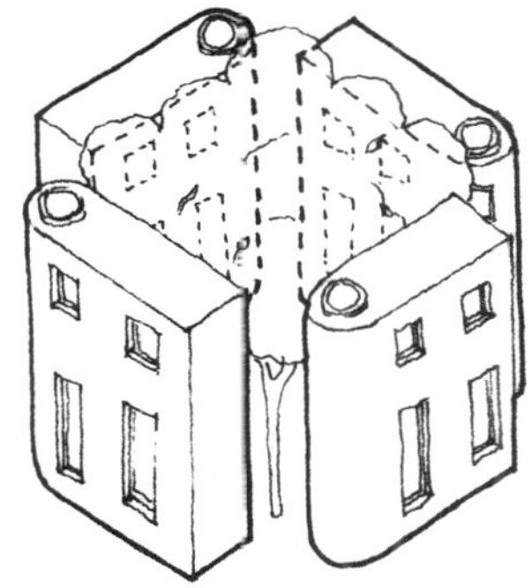

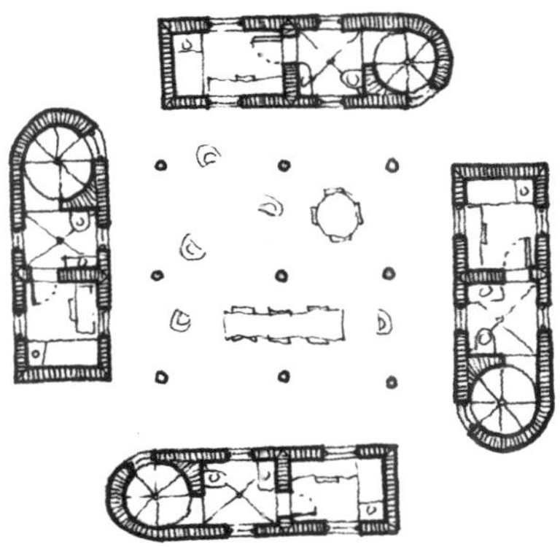

no.357

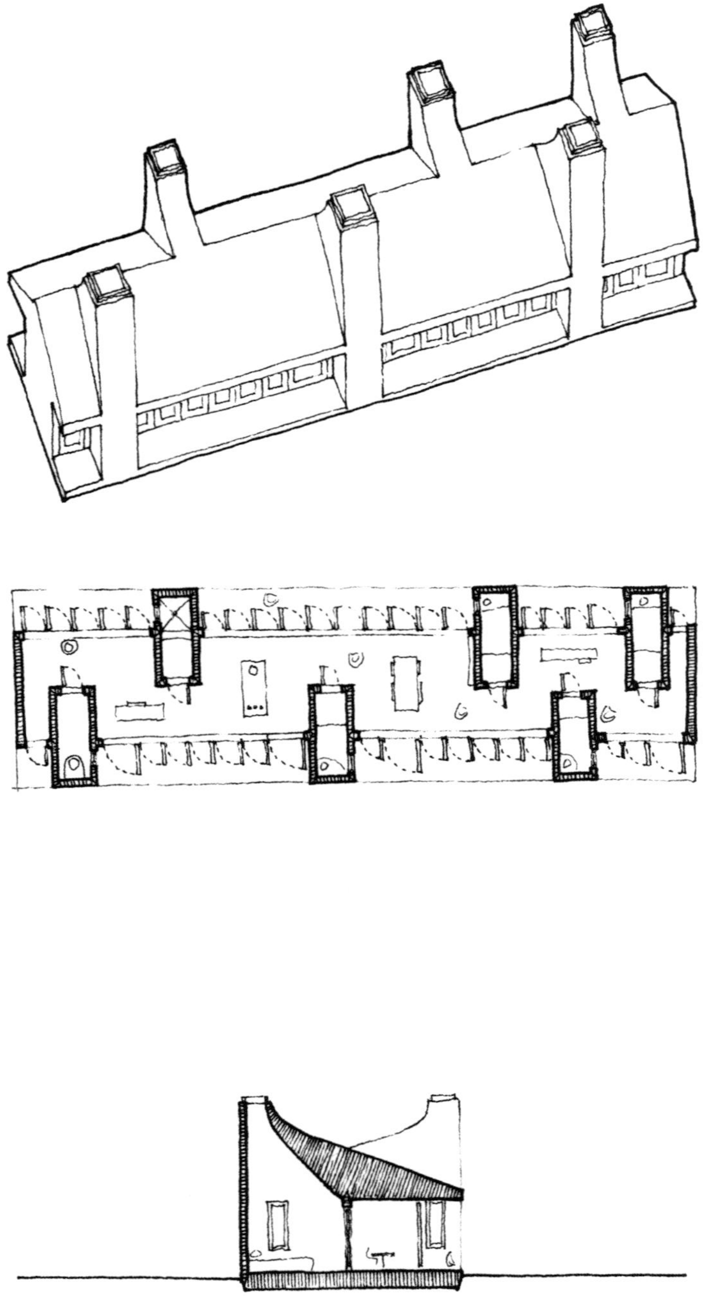

no.358

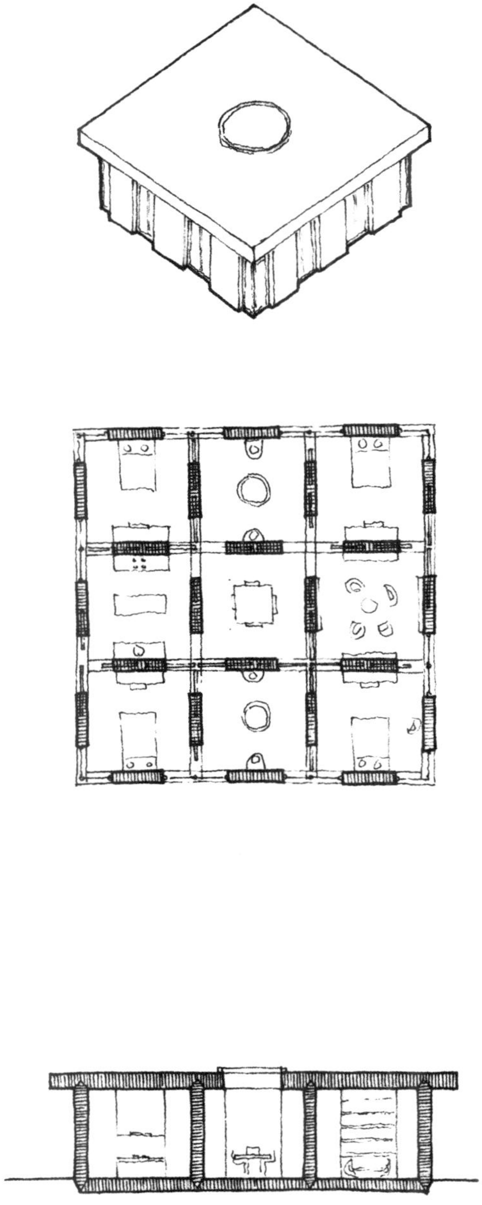

no.359

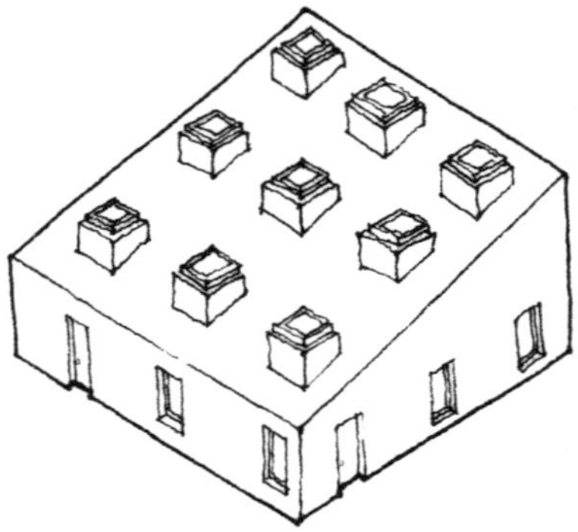

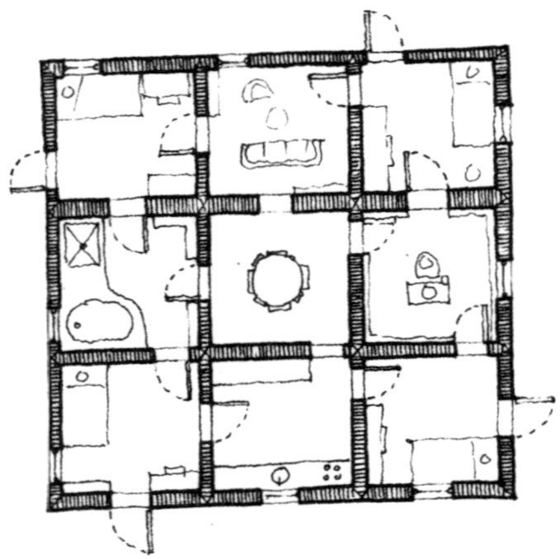

no.360

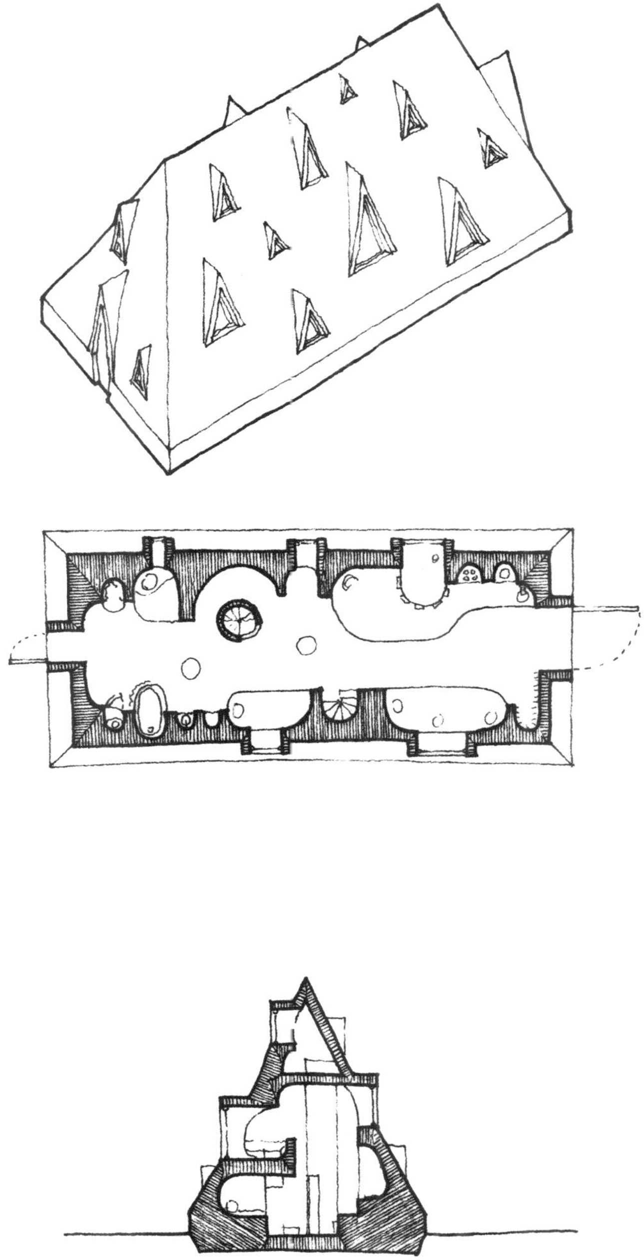

no.361

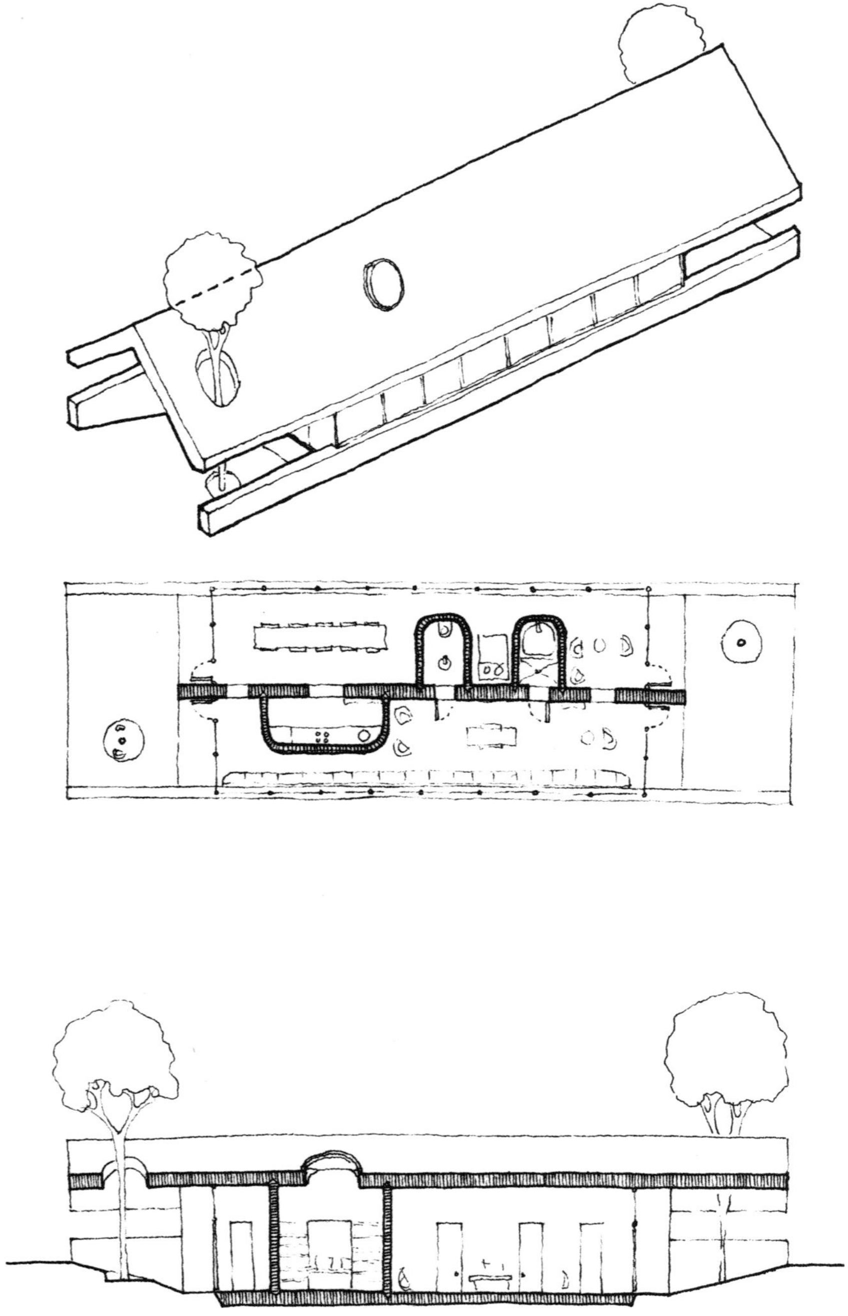

no.362

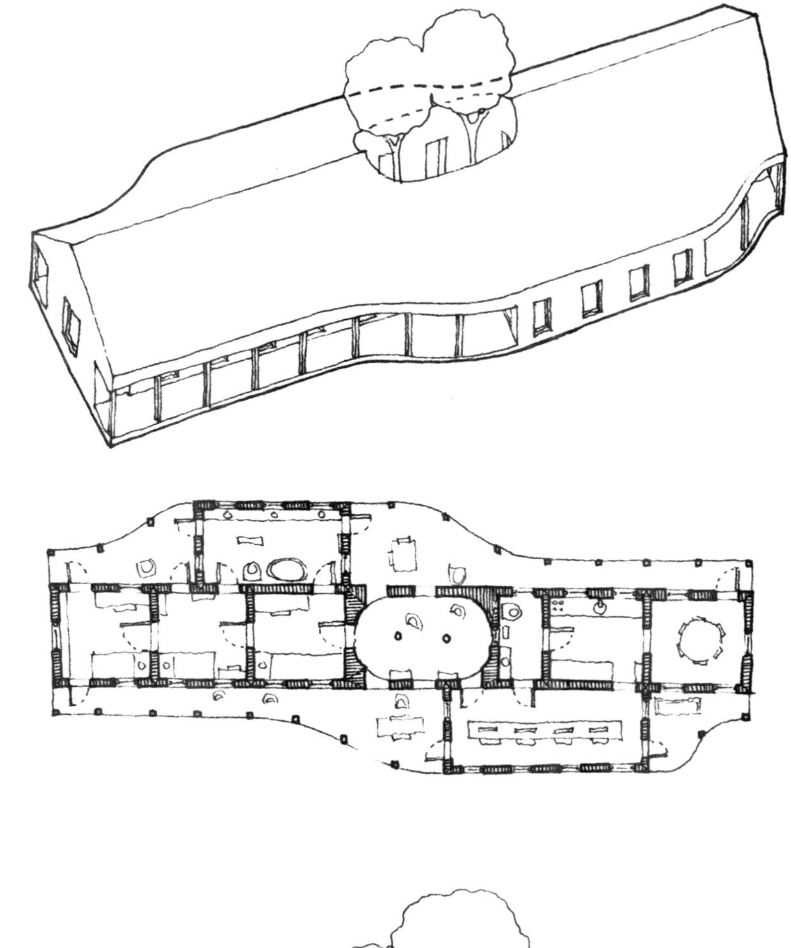

no.363

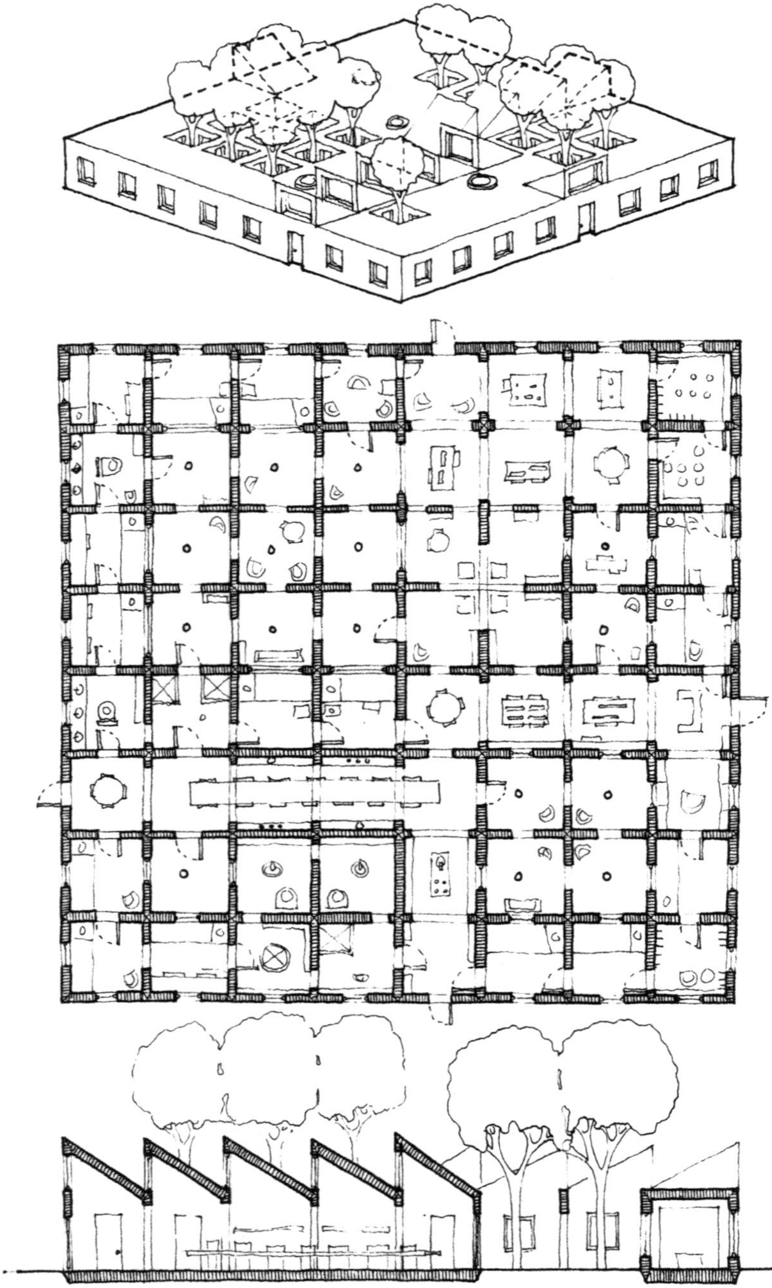

no.364

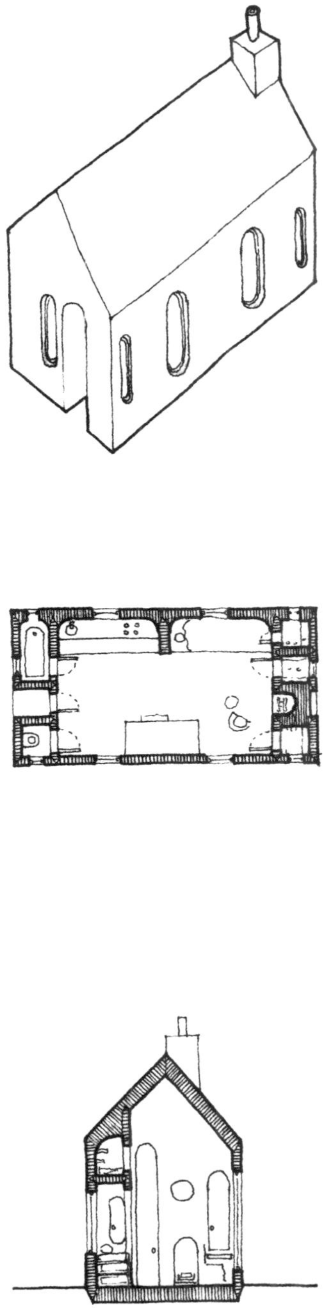

no.365

One Sentence Per Day
Clark Thenhaus

11/23/2021

As I scroll back through Andy Bruno's captivating drawings, it occurs to me that underlying the *One House Per Day* project is the ritualization of a daily practice exploring—but never exhausting—possibilities for expressions of residential architecture and that any such attempt to write about this project might benefit from following the same methodology.

11/24/2021

Therefore, I am writing one sentence per day, in earnest, to correlate this text to Andy's OHPD practice and to differentiate short-and-fast forms of thinking (both drawing and writing) from long-and-belabored.

11/25/2021

It also occurs to me, in now day 3 of writing, that Andy's project is not an appeal to short attention spans satisfied by constantly refreshed Instagram feeds, but rather the inverse: an expedient production model in which the fits and stops of fast-format daily works acquire meaning by being both incrementally accrued and sequential, yet disconnected as independent ideas and iterations.

11/26/2021

This routinization is a methodology of episodic exploration with the conscious conceit that it is the routine itself—the cyclical recurrence of isolated intuitions and momentary impulses rather than scrupulous editing, careful reflection, or durational thinking—that will foster deeper understanding or reveal new possibilities; one might see this as starting down a slippery slope into a project of autonomy.

11/27/2021

The one-per-day methodology in OHPD divorces formal and spatial value systems from social, cultural, and political circumstances to focus on expression, seriality, and familiar partis (such as the recurring use of 4- or 9-square grids), and in doing so reveals a plethora of new possibilities for organizational systems that we are—or thought we were—already familiar with.[1]

11/28/2021

So on one hand, we see abstraction and iteration underpinned by disciplinary traditions of formal organizational systems, yet on the other hand we can see this organizational abstraction as a projective technique to re-orient familiar tools and methods toward other ways of conceiving architecture for residing in, creating spaces and forms that accommodate alternative contemporary domestic lifestyles.

11/29/2021

These 365 houses divorced from external realities—yet which speculate on expressive forms of domesticity—demonstrate how abstraction can both cleave architecture from extra-disciplinary realities and tether it to future possibilities.

11/30/2021

Perhaps OHPD is a study in habituation and abstraction as techniques for distancing reality from architectural representations, and thus the one-per-day routinization fosters imagination by re-hashing, re-shaping, and re-imagining inherited sources.

12/01/2021

Today, frustration has crept in due to this incremental, broken train-of-thought methodology, and I wonder if Andy "re-read" his drawings from the day before and sought consciously to create or break linkages or connections—hidden or explicit—as I'm doing now, or if perhaps there is some other value to be found in the disconnected, fragmented thoughts that only in retrospect might be made sense of—or not?

12/02/2021

This methodology has become frustrating for me as a technique for writing, whereas it was liberating for Andy in the medium of drawing, and I start to wonder about disjunction and seriality in the context of OHPD—a disjunctive collection whose daily parts do not construct a larger whole at the end of the year, but where we find meaning in the process of serial disconnections and the ongoing plethora of expression itself.

12/03/2021

OHPD could be assessed through its day-to-day disjunctions—the atomized, singular, disconnected, and inexhaustible expressions for houses that need not be encountered or experienced in sequence suggest that a resistance to curated transitions can foster a wider spectrum of expression while also allowing compelling individual iterations to arrest one's attention.

12/04/2021

OHPD could also be assessed through its seriality—which is strange in relation to the disjunctive characterization I previously made—however, similar to Sol Lewitt's *Incomplete Open Cubes*, the collection's seriality allows us to see qualitative abundance, iteration, and potential within something many people likely feel is already deeply familiar, like the cube or the house.

12/05/2021

Whether by understanding OHPD as a daily practice of drawing houses tuned by abstraction (distancing effects), disjunction (individual expressions), or seriality (collective variations), what the project offers perhaps more than anything else is an open invitation to architects and non-architects alike to converse, re-imagine, and expand familiar forms and spaces of habitation.

12/06/2021

Unlike other daily practices, such as meme pages that are increasingly rooted in anonymous pessimism, OHPD is a project rooted in an optimism that celebrates the architectural mediums of drawing, images, and unbuilt buildings for their capacity to cultivate new audiences and interests within and beyond the discipline, and I can't wait to see how OHPD will evolve in built form as it encounters messy contextual, social, cultural, political, and environmental realities!

Notes

1 By my count, not including cruciform or courtyard plan types, 4-square organizations account for 60 versions (16.4%) and 9-square organizations account for 37 versions (10.1%), or 97 versions combined (27%) of the 365 iterations.

A Brief Reflection on *One House Per Day*
Andrew Bruno

One House Per Day emerged from the basic proposition that the detached house is a valid object for architects' critical attention and earnest engagement. In the twenty-first century, many architects seem to see the suburbs and the detached house as obsolete typologies. But this perception is starkly different from the reality on the ground. In the United States, even our largest cities are astonishingly suburban in character.[1] Ridgewood, a leafy suburban town near where I grew up in New Jersey, has a higher population density than Houston, Phoenix, and San Diego.[2] The suburbanization of the United States began long ago, and we're kidding ourselves if we think that trend is reversing. Indeed, the United States is growing more sprawling and exurban: Census Bureau data consistently shows that the number of single-family houses being constructed far exceeds the number of units in multi-family buildings.[3]

Cultivating the desire for a suburban lifestyle is a long-standing project in the United States, in which architects played a role in the creation of the nascent suburban ideal. Andrew Jackson Downing's popular pattern books of suburban cottage houses helped to establish a baseline for a desirable life in America in the first half of the nineteenth century. The suburbanization of the United States has accelerated since then. Aided by a host of policies, from FHA appraisal guidelines to restrictive zoning regulations, the house has become the dominant unit of housing.[4] The desire for a detached house in a suburban landscape is deeply ingrained in American culture, and architects risk consigning themselves to irrelevance if they ignore it.

As the house has proliferated, the scope for its design has narrowed.[5] Today, the detached house has become synonymous with the single nuclear family, and even the most architecturally radical houses are typically designed to serve the needs of a single-family patron. The words we use are important: the tendency to describe any detached house as being a "single-family house" forecloses on the possibility for the house as an architectural type to accommodate any uses or users other than the single family. *One House Per Day* responds to this arbitrary constraint by imagining over and over how the architectural form of the house might be detached from its association with the monocultural single family. Though no occupants are ever specified or depicted, the houses intentionally eschew the standardized organizational principles of the contemporary house. You certainly won't find a *One House Per Day* house with a master bedroom.

In truth, I never expected *One House Per Day* to become popular. It started as a way to contemplate these issues while engaging in the therapeutic practice of a daily drawing and helped to compensate for the lack of intellectual stimulation in my professional work. I started posting the drawings to Instagram to crowdsource my accountability to the project, but didn't imagine that they'd be seen beyond a small group of people. So it probably won't go unnoticed that some of the early drawings are not always of the highest quality, and that the specifics of the graphic language were in flux for the first twenty houses or so. There are design flaws and drawing errors throughout. In a way this is fitting of the project as a whole: the quantity of drawings, coupled with the fact that for most of the year it felt like there would *always* be another drawing, meant that there was never much pressure on any one house to be too developed. Most of the organizational ideas in the project are revisited often throughout the series, and a common through-line is the integration of spaces for work and leisure into the domain of the house, and the rejection of the traditional architectural expressions of hierarchy that are endemic to the single-family house.

I won't say any more. I hope you're reading this essay after leafing through the drawings and you've seen what you want to see in them. I also hope that *One House Per Day* can be a template for anyone to question their assumptions about how we design the places where we live. Architects love to believe we can manufacture a desire for the kind of world we want to build. What we might consider instead is to tap into the desires that already exist and imagine how those desires could be accommodated differently. The house is a fertile ground for this kind of reimagination.

Notes

1 For an incredibly compelling account of the merging of city and suburbs in the United States, see Albert Pope's *Ladders*.

2 Information on population density is drawn from the 2020 US Census.

3 Information on new housing construction is drawn from the Census Bureau Monthly New Residential Construction reports.

4 A number of works have informed my understanding of the place of the house in American culture and the suburbanization of the United States more generally. Chief among them are Kenneth T. Jackson's *Crabgrass Frontier*, Dolores Hayden's *Building Suburbia*, and John Archer's *Architecture and Suburbia*.

5 For an overview of how the design of domestic space is simultaneously contingent on culture and constitutive of the horizons of social experience, see Robin Evans's essay "Figures, Doors and Passages." No other text has been as influential on my thinking about the architecture of domesticity.

Index

no.001 has no interior walls: spaces are implied by immensely deep beams overhead, plus curtains.

no.002 is a single room in which programmatic zones are nestled by a serpentine wall.

no.003 is a classic nine-square with a serpentine wall added for extra fun.

no.004 is a funky enfilade with some dragon-scale cladding action.

no.005 is composed of overlapping rectangular rooms. Fun stuff happens in the overlaps.

no.006 is four long rooms side by side with trees in between.

no.007 is a courtyard blob.

no.008 is a single curved room with operable end walls, wrapped around a large tree.

no.009 uses an intersection of curving and orthogonal geometries to create subdivisions within one large room.

no.010 is an enfilade of three large rooms with smaller rooms appended to them. One of the large rooms is sort of outdoors.

no.011 is a large semicircular room subdivided by narrow rectangular rooms.

no.012 is four rooms staggered and shifted to allow movement and provide light.

no.013 takes its bilateral symmetry seriously, but not too seriously.

no.014 is a one-room shack with a central fireplace. Curtains hung from above allow subdivision into a four-square.

no.015 is a large semicircular room with small rectangular, top-lit rooms inside it.

no.016 is a 16-square matrix of interconnected rooms with occasional obstacles and unexpected absences of roof. It has very thick walls.

no.017 is a cruciform courtyard house with a central water source and a fireplace in each of four individual rooms. Each room is accessible only from the exterior or the courtyard.

no.018 is a single long room that develops zones of privacy through its curvature.

no.019 has sneaky dormers.

no.020 is more roof than wall and is inspired by an amazing true story.

no.021 is a classic four-square.

no.022 is composed of overlapping circular rooms. Fun stuff happens in the overlaps.

no.023 is a 16-cell grid in which all rooms are connected to neighboring rooms and the fixtures, appliances, and furniture are dispersed in unexpected ways.

no.024 is a single square room with alcoves for four trees.

no.025 is a collection of small rooms, each the size of a single bed, arranged within a large open room. The bed-rooms are lit from above, while the large room has glass walls.

no.026 has wells for light over wells for water.

no.027 is four separate rooms, each of which contains a distinct programmatic function. Each room appears as an identical volume from the outside but has a unique ceiling.

no.028 is a collection of rooms descending around a sunken courtyard.

no.029 is a gabled volume subdivided by double-sided fireplaces.

no.030 has partial-height partitions and high ribbon windows.

no.031 is a large, amoeba-shaped room peppered with tiny courtyards.

no.032 is an enfilade of five square rooms with roof scoops for light and double doors between rooms.

no.033 is a massive barrel-vaulted common room onto which smaller barrel vaulted rooms open.

no.034 is a five-room, 3x3 checkerboard of solids and voids.

no.035 is an eroded circular room with variable roof curvature.

no.036 is a triangular room with a gently curved roof and rectilinear cut-outs that divide a large room into smaller zones.

no.037 is a tree house.

no.038 is four triangular rooms created by the rotation of a cruciform partition within a large square room. A fireplace brackets each room.

no.039 has private towers that emerge from a massive common room.

no.040 is a collection of rooms with varying shapes embedded in a block of poché.

no.041 is a 25-square matrix of interconnected rooms perforated by two circular courtyards.

no.042 is a double A-frame. A large common room intersects a smaller enfilade of bedrooms.

no.043 is a composition of square rooms carved out of a solid cylinder.

no.044 is an enfilade of offset square rooms under an eroded pitched roof.

no.045 is a tapered tower.

no.046 is a bundle of four slender towers.

no.047 has hollow columns containing toilets, sinks, closets, kitchen appliances, and other accoutrements of domesticity.

no.048 contrasts heaviness and lightness.

no.049 is a pinwheeling central space with integral beehive-shaped rooms.

no.050 is a broken enfilade.

no.051 is a nine-square grid of individual rooms separated by outdoor corridors, all under one roof.

no.052 has a central top-lit library-bedroom-living room enveloped by a continuous space for cooking, bathing, and storing things.

no.053 is an irregular enclosure intersected by a series of regular walls.

no.054 is a mountainous interior bed-scape.

no.055 is a four-story, one-room-wide squiggle for 13 people.

no.056 is a rotated glass volume intersected by an orthogonal series of walls. A gabled volume rests on the walls, giving the rotated volume spatial consistency and enclosure.

no.057 is a hypostyle hall of square columns, some of which house fireplaces and chimneys. The locations of the warm columns inform the distribution of programmatic elements.

no.058 is a composition of four volumes connected at their corners and unified by a continuous circular ridge line that informs the division of rooms within the volumes.

no.059 is one room subdivided by a massive central hearth.

no.060 is a house for a dog and a cat. Fuzzy friends deserve architecture too.

no.061 is four separate rooms of different sizes whose inside corners define a central square of outdoor space.

no.062 is a single tall room subdivided by a cruciform partition that hangs from a double-gabled roof which rests on four massive columns.

no.063 is a single room with sub-rooms implied by overhead partitions. A continuous central armature contains provisions for cooking, sleeping, and bathing.

no.064 is a ribbon roof whose undulations create alternating rooms and open spaces of descending size.

no.065 is a long, low room with a continuous armature for cooking, socializing, working, and bathing. Thirteen small, tall rooms open directly onto the long room and to the exterior.

no.066 is a long common room divided by smaller private internal rooms, which are legible as dormers on the exterior.

no.067 is a collection of rooms divided by arcades with arched openings of varying heights. Openings are scaled to adults, children, and pets, so that an individual's path through the house varies depending on their size.

no.068 is a square room with an off-center circular courtyard that establishes zones of differing program and privacy.

no.069 is a long, gabled room with erosions for trees. A central armature contains spaces for storage, cooking/eating, and bathing.

no.070 is a house for humans and art. A continuous ring of rooms containing common spaces and private spaces encloses a triple-height space for work and display.

no.071 is a single cruciform room. Most furniture is arranged near the center, providing some privacy to beds at the periphery.

no.072 is a cylindrical volume sliced to create four rooms with sloped ceilings, punctuated by tree-filled voids.

no.073 is a long common room with a triangular profile, intersected by four private rectangular rooms.

no. 074 has an impluvium—for the history buffs.

no.075 is a large room with four internal sub-rooms for cooking, bathing, and storage.

no.076 is a single square room subdivided by curtains into a nine-square. Eat your heart out David Lynch.

no.077 is a single room that develops distinct zones through its curvature.

no.078 is an enfilade of square rooms of varying heights. Openings in the thick walls accommodate beds, plumbing fixtures, and kitchen appliances, among other things.

no.079 is a Boolean split. A common room and a collective bedroom are separated by a central void.

no.080 is a square block of solid poché with circular rooms carved out and top-lit by transparent domes.

no.081 is a 16-square matrix of rooms in which each room opens to every adjacent room and, for those along the perimeter, to the exterior. Four rooms are combined into a larger common room, creating a spatial hierarchy.

no.082 is a tall top-lit cruciform room containing spaces for storage, cooking, and bathing, with short square rooms in the corners for everything else.

no.083 is five gabled, interconnected square rooms in a flattened Z configuration. Three bedrooms along the central axis are flanked by a kitchen and a bathroom at the ends.

no.084 is a long gabled room with cylindrical sub-rooms, some enclosed and some open to the air.

no.085 is four L-shaped rooms arranged to form a square courtyard.

no.086 is a glassy amoeba common room with rectangular sub-rooms containing beds, sinks, toilets, showers, cooking appliances, and storage.

no.087 has a continuous underground common room with private sleeping quarters in above-ground cubes.

no.088 is a nine-square matrix of square rooms, each containing a hearth and connections to adjacent rooms or the exterior.

no.089 is a long gabled volume divided into four rooms by a cruciform courtyard, all within a continuous exterior wall.

no.090 is a cruciform arrangement of four square rooms connected at their corners with a square courtyard at the center. Each room is accessible only through the courtyard or the exterior.

no.091 is a square room with a multi-gable roof. Long walls aligned with the ridge lines create spatial and programmatic subdivisions within.

no.092 is a rectangular donut submerged below the ground and accessible by a grassy slope. Side lighting transitions to top lighting as the slope ascends.

no.093 is a long central hall illuminated by a clerestory window. Private rooms open onto the hall, which contains a continuous armature for cooking, eating, and bathing.

no.094 is five rooms alternating with exterior spaces under one long roof. The roof over the exterior spaces is translucent.

no.095 is two long and narrow gabled volumes separated by a wide tree-filled yard. Private rooms occupy one volume, while communal spaces occupy the other.

no.096 is a curving vault intersected by vertical cylinders along its central axis. The spaces typically considered private exist in the large, continuous space and those typically considered public exist in the more confined cylindrical spaces.

no.097 is four private rooms connected by corridors containing spaces for cooking, bathing, and storage—all under a large pyramidal roof, eroded by a central cruciform courtyard.

no.098 has A-frames within an A-frame. More sneaky dormers!

no.099 is a 16-square matrix of rooms on a gentle slope. The floor slopes to match the topography, while the roof stays flat. Self-leveling furniture is required.

no.100 is a square donut around a huge courtyard. Open corners provide access to common rooms, including two kitchens and two bathrooms, with an additional four common rooms for storage and relaxation. Private rooms open directly onto the courtyard.

no.101 is a crossed A-frame.

no.102 is an amoeba in a forest.

no.103 is a 16-square matrix of rooms, half of which are interior and half of which are exterior.

no.104 is a large square room with open corners, divided by eave-height partitions into a four-square.

no.105 is an amoeba of space carved from a prism of poché.

no.106 is four separate rooms connected by intersecting occupiable roofs above.

no.107 is a long house with an internal matrix of rooms and (non-sneaky) eyebrow dormers.

no.108 is a long, gabled volume subdivided into rooms of different sizes, centered around a large room for work and relaxation, with a massive central hearth.

no.109 is a circular room with a grid of square inhabitable columns containing plumbing fixtures, appliances, and storage spaces.

no.110 is two separate triangular volumes. The larger volume is subdivided into strips for sleeping, bathing, and relaxation or work.

no.111 is a 16-square matrix of interconnected rooms, in which the doors between rooms are always misaligned.

no.112 is a large public room with massive inhabitable columns holding up a private room/roof above.

no.113 is a collection of square rooms of different sizes within a square footprint. Each room has at least one connection to each adjacent room and, for those along the perimeter, to the exterior.

no.114 is a massive bed which occupies a 16-square matrix of rooms. A reversal of the normal dominance of hard surfaces, here hard surfaces become the exception in a continuous bed-scape.

no.115 is a cruciform communal workspace with private rooms in the corners.

no.116 is a continuous, long room in which the room's curvature produces different functional zones. Space for work is just around the bend from space for life.

no.117 is a large square room with a pyramidal roof, under which a cruciform private space floats over a ground-level open workspace.

no.118 is a grid of tiny top-lit rooms under a gabled roof. The largest rooms contain spaces for work. The interstitial space becomes an open sleeping room.

no.119 is composed of a series of voids carved from a vaulted solid.

no.120 is a 2x6 matrix of square rooms, two of which are open to the sky.

no.121 is a faceted volume with a central top-lit rectangular workspace surrounded by smaller spaces for sleeping, bathing, and preparing food.

no.122 is a basic four-square in which one of the squares is a workspace with a separate entrance.

no.123 is a square donut with fat columns.

no.124 is a series of vaulted rooms of different widths contained in an austere rectangular prism.

no.125 is a collection of separate circular rooms of different sizes and opacities under one large canted circular roof.

no.126 is three separate volumes, one for sleeping, one for cooking and bathing, and one for work. They are visually united by a continuous curving ridge and roof geometry.

no.127 is a nine-square grid of rooms connected by off-center openings. The single-slope roof creates different ceiling heights from room to room.

no.128 is a long central room off of which room-nooks of varying depths are arrayed. The central room has walls full of doors.

no.129 is a triangular room with a circular horn triangle void as a courtyard. I had to brush up on my geometry terms to describe this one.

no.130 is a single room structured by hollow glass columns containing trees. Shoutout to Terragni's Danteum.

no.131 is a 25-square checkerboard of open and closed spaces.

no.132 is four aligned rooms with misaligned passages between them. It's more roof than walls.

no.133 is four rows of two separate rooms with breaks between them. Trees fill the interstitial spaces.

no.134 is a house without a kitchen.

no.135 is a house with only a kitchen and dining room.

no.136 is a house with only rooms for bathing.

no.137 is a large square room with a pyramidal roof and four cylindrical sub-rooms within.

no.138 has an organization informed by Iñaki Harosteguy's "Forest of Columns."

no.139 is informed by Iñaki Harosteguy's "Technified Walls."

no.140 is informed by Iñaki Harosteguy's "Geometric Support."

no.141 is informed by Iñaki Harosteguy's "Non-Specific Frames."

no.142 is informed by Iñaki Harosteguy's "Matrix of Units."

no.143 is two right triangular prisms facing off across a square courtyard.

no.144 has a four-square organization with square sub-rooms.

no.145 is informed by Iñaki Harosteguy's "Spatial Columns."

no.146 is informed by Iñaki Harosteguy's "Perimeter Rhythm."

no.147 is informed by Iñaki Harosteguy's "Elementary Square."

no.148 is informed by Iñaki Harosteguy's "Compositional Support."

no.149 is a house inspired by my first NYC apartment. A tiny studio, it bears some resemblance to the Unabomber's shack. Only one of these windows existed in the apartment.

no.150 is a visualization of the dwelling Reyner Banham describes in his 1965 essay "A Home is not a House": a "standard-of-living package" of HVAC equipment hovering over a floor totally open to the elements. Conditioned enclosure is provided by a curtain of air around the perimeter.

no.151 is a house inspired by my second NYC apartment, a two-bedroom that my wife and I shared with a succession of amazing people. Again, I've been generous with windows and omitting some messiness.

no.152 is a separated four-square. Each room's single-pitched roof contributes to the overall reading of a gabled form.

no.153 is a house inspired by my third NYC apartment. This one was an illegal two-bedroom, as the lower right bedroom had no windows.

no.154 is a sunken square room with clerestory windows and four access points.

no.155 is a house inspired by my fourth NYC apartment, a one-bedroom, turned into a squat A-frame.

no.156 is a two-story, 2x6 matrix of cubic rooms with square windows composed to obscure the spatial divisions within.

no.157 is a long room with two small sub-rooms and a lopsided, reversible pitched roof.

no.158 is a grid of nine separate gabled rooms with trees and outdoor furniture occupying the interstitial spaces.

no.159 is a truncated pyramidal volume with rounded edges. Inside, four rooms are linked by a central void.

no.160 is a long arcing room with small top-lit rectangular sub-rooms within.

no.161 is a single square room with a curved courtyard that creates spatial differentiation within.

no.162 is three separate gabled volumes, each intersected with an additional cubic or cylindrical volume to produce a Boolean split effect.

no.163 is a triangular half of a 16-square matrix of rooms. The half-rooms become exterior entrance courts to the inhabited full rooms.

no.164 is a cylindrical room perceptually subdivided by extremely deep beams overhead. The grid of beams informs the location of carve-outs for entries and a courtyard.

no.165 is three intersecting gabled volumes with different widths but the same ridge height.

no.166 is an enfilade of four rooms with an enormous table that runs the length of the enfilade.

no.167 is a nine-square matrix of rooms with staggered doors in one direction and aligned openings in the other. This arrangement of doors creates three three-room zones.

no.168 is a stereotypically urban house, in that it has lot-line neighbors on both sides.

no.169 is four courtyards surrounded by narrow living spaces.

no.170 is a long room with two sub-rooms, a fireplace, and an overhanging pitched roof.

no.171 is a hipped-roofed volume with a narrow courtyard between small private rooms and a large public room.

no.172 is a 2x3 matrix of rooms under an upwardly curving roof.

no.173 is a double-gabled volume with a long central space for cooking and work, flanked by bathrooms and bedrooms with individual exterior entrances.

no.174 is three individual pill-shaped volumes for eating/work, bathing, and sleeping.

no.175 is a 3x3 matrix of cylindrical domed rooms, two of which form outdoor entry courts.

no.176 is two overlapping triangular prisms. Wet stuff happens in the overlap.

no.177 is a four-square with corner chimneys.

no.178 is a saltbox with two levels and cylindrical courtyards.

no.179 is an enfilade of four square rooms with varying sizes under the same roof ridge. One room is outdoors.

no.180 is a four-square with intersecting gables and corner entry courts.

no.181 is a single long room split into two curving branches, establishing gradients of privacy.

no.182 is five linear strips of space, three of which contain small courtyards.

no.183 is one long vaulted room and four small domed rooms carved from a vaulted volume.

no.184 is a 36-square matrix of rooms, six of which are open to the sky.

no.185 is a grid of columns and a roof. Textile curtains provide enclosure and interior partitioning. This house was inspired by mid-century weaving master Anni Albers, about whom I first learned on the day I drew this.

no.186 is a cruciform organization of five rooms. Only the central bedroom is enclosed; the other four rooms are open to the sky.

no.187 is a 16-square matrix of rooms, of which the outer ring are all open to the sky.

no.188 is a 2x6 matrix of rooms. Four rooms on each side are open to the sky.

no.189 is a zig-zagging arrangement of L-shaped volumes linked by corner entry courts.

no.190 is three intersecting bars of varying height. The overlaps are subtracted to form courtyards.

no.191 is a four-square with a four-square. One of the small squares is open to the sky.

no.192 is a single long room that snakes through a grove of trees.

no.193 is a balancing act. Unlike most OHPD drawings, this drawing depicts two levels using a break line.

no.194 is a hashtag in which the protruding rooms are outdoor entry courts and the intersections are double-height rooms.

no.195 is a long A-frame with a suspended loft that runs its length.

no.196 has dormers on its dormers. As it is built into the side of a hill, the house too is something of a dormer.

no.197 is an intersection of two volumes: one is enclosed and one is open to the sky.

no.198 is a staggered enfilade of four rooms, one of which is a triple-height tower.

no.199 is a linear array of five rooms, one of which has a cylindrical tower. The central room is a courtyard with a circular roof opening the same diameter as the tower.

no.200 is a 49-square matrix of rooms, of which a central swath are outdoor. Entry to the indoor rooms occurs in the courts. Interior rooms are connected in segments with interior doors placed only in east-west walls.

no.201 is a single room divided by an inset entryway. An outdoor cooking pit is aligned with the entry door.

no.202 is a 3x4 matrix of rooms, the central four of which are exterior. The outer two bands of rooms are interior, covered by overhanging roofs.

no.203 is three gabled volumes linked by a linear walled garden.

no.204 is a single glass-walled room containing rectangular enclosed sub-rooms and circular sub-rooms that are open to the sky.

no.205 is a gabled volume containing a four-square living zone and a matching greenhouse.

no.206 is a matrix of rooms clipped by a half-circle. The resulting edge rooms are left open as entry courts.

no.207 is an elongated checkerboard of rooms with alternating open and closed cells. The open cells are circular courtyards with storage space inside the poché.

no.208 is three rooms cascading down a hill, connected by enclosed ramps. The roof slopes more steeply than the hill, so that the rooms are taller uphill.

no.209 is an enfilade of rooms under a gabled roof with semicircular overhangs that shade adjacent patios.

no.210 is the reverse of no.209. Here, the central rectilinear space is exterior and the semicircular appendages are interior spaces.

no.211 is one long room with arms bent around a three-sided courtyard. The room's curvature establishes different programmatic zones.

no.212 is 16 vaulted volumes around a square courtyard. A patio and roof intersect with the enclosed volumes to create covered outdoor space.

no.213 is a long rectangular room subdivided by circular courtyards.

no.214 is two sloped volumes angled away from a central courtyard. Rectangular volumes housing entryways and bathrooms open onto the courtyard, while large windows face away from it.

no.215 has miniature EUR vibes with upside-down arched windows.

no.216 is a series of four staggered gabled volumes whose end walls extend to form courtyards.

no.217 is a matrix of square rooms clipped by a triangle. The clipped rooms are entry courts.

no.218 is a split donut. Two semicircular vaulted volumes encircle a central courtyard.

no.219 is a 25-square matrix of rooms in which two clumps—a total of six rooms—are outdoor.

no.220 is a cylindrical tower.

no.221 is a long common room with three offset wings on each side and an obvious drawing error.

no.222 is four short wings around a square courtyard. Three wings contain four private rooms each, while the fourth wing contains cooking and common space.

no.223 is an enfilade of four rooms with alternating roof orientations.

no.224 is an enfilade of four staggered square rooms with truncated pyramidal roofs.

no.225 has interconnected rooms with a chimney and a towering skylight.

no.226 is a bulging volume with concave scalloped edges. Trees are planted at the center points of the scallops.

no.227 has movable furniture on tracks. Rolling the bed into the kitchen is an option, but the exterior doors don't close when the pieces are outside on the covered porches. I swear I'm not a bad architect.

no.228 is a solid cylinder from which circular domed rooms are carved. Connections between rooms occur at tangent points, and cylindrical skylights provide natural light.

no.229 has materialized door swings.

no.230 is two two-room wings connected by an inhabitable roof.

no.231 is a truncated 3x4 matrix of rooms. The sliced rooms become entry courts.

no.232 is an elevated nine-square supported and subdivided by massive crossed-walls.

no.233 has inhabitable columns supporting an amoeba-shaped roof.

no.234 is a long winding vaulted room. Successive bends create courtyards in between strips of building.

no.235 is a circular courtyard encircled by a narrow glass room under an overhanging roof. A thick grove of trees in the courtyard obscures views from one side of the house to the other.

no.236 is a two-story gabled volume with a central courtyard. A covered passage connects the two separated enclosures, and there's a slide.

no.237 is skinny. A linear stair connects three levels of a one-room-wide house. Compartmentalized rooms exist below the stairs, so to speak.

no.238 is two bars of enclosed space flanking a square courtyard. Bathing rooms and seating nooks are carved into thick courtyard walls.

no.239 has a wraparound porch under an offset truncated pyramidal roof. A grouping of enclosed rooms contains the kitchen, bathroom, and bed and sits below the high point of the roof.

no.240 is a 16-square matrix of rooms in which each room connects to one or two others in a clearly defined path. I usually hate circulation diagrams, but this house begs for one.

no.241 is a cruciform arrangement of four overlapping rectangular volumes whose overlaps house utility spaces.

no.242 is a pinwheeling arrangement of four separate volumes. Each volume has a single room with a single top-lit sub-room beneath the high point of an offset truncated pyramidal roof.

no.243 has small nooks and rooms carved from a thick wall which surrounds a large square room. Kind of like that castle that Louis Kahn liked.

no.244 is a composition of square rooms with heights inversely proportional to their widths.

no.245 is a ring of square rooms around a rectangular courtyard.

no.246 is a steep inhabitable hipped roof with a bulge over a short, transparent ground level.

no.247 is a square glass-walled room elevated on four inhabitable cylindrical columns.

no.248 is four private suites pinwheeling around a large square common room with a courtyard.

no.249 is two interior volumes subsumed by a hypostyle porch. The volumes extend above the porch, creating clerestories.

no.250 is two two-room volumes placed at an acute angle to one another. They support a secondary roof which covers three outdoor spaces.

no.251 has an occupiable, overhanging gable roof embraced by two L-shaped stair towers.

no.252 is six private rooms that share a pitched roof with a central outdoor space. The roof peels up to create clerestory windows for a seventh room housing a kitchen.

no.253 collects interior and exterior spaces below a precariously balanced, cantilevered gabled roof.

no.254 is two single-sloped volumes with the same high and low points. The smaller volume contains private living spaces, while the larger volume contains common spaces with inhabitable columns for bathing, cooking, and storage.

no.255 is four narrow bars with consistent roof heights descending a hill.

no.256 is an enfilade of six square rooms inserted into a hillside. The resulting gradient of burial informs each room's program.

no.257 is a rectangular bar that intersects a narrow grove of trees. The resulting erosions create complex spaces for all the stuff that is typically hidden.

no.258 is four concentric squares containing different layers of program. The outer ring is entirely open to the sky.

no.259 is four rooms arranged around an off-center courtyard, all under a shallow pitched roof.

no.260 is a large square common room plus four private rooms. Each room is enveloped with cabinets, including ones for toilets and showers. A corner courtyard completes the square.

no.261 is a long barrel-vaulted room with partitions and alternating window orientations.

no.262 is a house for one person. Without a kitchen, it pairs well with communal facilities.

no.263 is a house for communal cooking, work, and relaxation. It pairs well with multiple houses for one person.

no.264 is a cross-shaped arrangement with one bedroom and one common room per wing, and a central courtyard.

no.265 has a trapezoidal footprint and gets taller as its footprint gets narrower.

no.266 is an alternating line of two-story interior and exterior spaces. Common rooms are at grade, with private rooms above accessible by garden staircases.

no.267 has alternating courtyards with private rooms at grade on one side of each courtyard.

no.268 is a tall, narrow slab from which rooms of varying sizes are carved.

no.269 is two private rooms linked by courtyards to a central common room.

no.270 is a narrow house for one person, in which each room is accessible independently from the exterior.

no.271 is a bridge over a sunken courtyard.

no.272 has a floor that slopes with the gentle hill on which the house sits. Flat surfaces are carved as required.

no.273 is two intersecting volumes containing different programmatic elements.

no.274 has bands of programmed spaces with multiple connections.

no.275 is an inhabitable wall that contains small rooms, with larger rooms appended to it. Entry to the larger rooms always occurs through the wall.

no.276 is a nine-square with an inner donut of service spaces surrounding a central square which is open to the elements.

no.277 is a single large room punctuated by courtyards. Small half-circular rooms flank each courtyard.

no.278 is a three-square composition in which one square has been subdivided into four smaller rooms. The internal divisions are registered on the exterior by differently squished gables.

no.279 is four rooms of different sizes with two porches.

no.280 is a large square room with smaller rooms glommed onto it in various configurations.

no.281 is a four-square with low pyramids and difficult doors.

no.282 reduces the house to the bare provision of services. Shelter not included. What is a house, anyway?

no.283 is an enfilade of rounded rooms with poché closets and a courtyard.

no.284 is a tower of three rooms with a platform lift bed. Cf. Maison Bordeaux.

no.285 is an amoebic footprint with a rectangular courtyard.

no.286 crosses common and private programmatic bars.

no.287 is four rooms in a pill-shaped configuration with ribbon windows that cross room divisions. Tiny pass-throughs are provided at the intersections of wall and window.

no.288 is an insular 4x4 checkerboard of open courtyards and enclosed rooms. Common rooms are housed in the central squares.

no.289 is a donut of common rooms around a courtyard, with satellite private rooms.

no.290 is a 4x4 grid with varying cell widths. Three cells are left open to the sky to provide light to windowless inner rooms.

no.291 is an enfilade of rooms with two indoor rooms on either side of one outdoor room.

no.292 is a long room that worms around to create different programmatic zones.

no.293 has walls of varying degrees of inhabitability.

no.294 is an uneven 3x3 grid with two cells left open to the sky as entry courts.

no.295 is an enfilade of offset square rooms of varying sizes, with aligned doors and a continuous roof ridge.

no.296 is an uneven grid of 5x5 cells. Four cells are left open to the sky.

no.297 is a cruciform arrangement of 2x2 room clusters around a central courtyard.

no.298 is a one-room-wide stack of rooms and terraces with a triangular section.

no.299 is a simple three-room enfilade with a wet room, a work room, and a sleeping room.

no.300 is a collection of overlapping circular rooms.

no.301 is two prisms and a cylinder.

no.302 is five overlapping volumes. Things happen in the overlaps.

no.303 is an uneven grid of four cells. The largest cell is a courtyard.

no.304 is several narrow rooms that intersect to form larger interior spaces.

no.305 is a perforated slab on pilotis. Anything can happen on the ground.

no.306 is three bars with tree-filled spaces between them. The central bar contains common spaces.

no.307 has a donut-shaped footprint with a shed roof; the direction of the roof pitch reverses depending on whether the space below is common or private.

no.308 is an amoeba with amoebic inner rooms.

no.309 is an enfilade of circular rooms, one of which is open to the sky.

no.310 divides space with cross-shaped walls.

no.311 is a series of intersecting and tangent domed cylinders. A sleeping room is separate from rooms for cooking and work.

no.312 is a composition of separate gabled rooms.

no.313 has an open plan in which the experience of different rooms is defined by deep coffers in the ceiling.

no.314 is a long room with pill-shaped sub-rooms.

no.315 is a glass-walled square with an inner serpentine wall that defines an amoeba of top-lit spaces.

no.316 is like a regular house, but sliced.

no.317 is a nine-square with a courtyard. The cardinal-point squares are subdivided into four-squares whose outer squares are scaled down for children.

no.318 is a pitched roof atop a serpentine wall.

no.319 is a sequence of four primary rooms with ancillary sleeping rooms attached. All are encased in three intersecting volumes.

no.320 is four triangular prisms that form a square courtyard.

no.321 is two interlocked units, each containing a large room and a small room.

no.322 is a 4x4 matrix of rooms in which the central four rooms are open to the sky.

no.323 is a long, snaking, vaulted room whose exterior wall thickens to provide spaces for bathing and a fireplace.

no.324 is a big roof resting on cross-shaped walls.

no.325 has rectangular interiors intersected with circular courtyards, all sandwiched between a square floor and roof.

no.326 is a ring of square rooms around a rectangular courtyard. Common rooms occur at the corners and private rooms along the long sides.

no.327 is a big pyramidal roof with a skylight resting on eight pill-shaped walls.

no.328 is a 5x5 matrix of rooms with two large rounded courtyards and networks of common and private spaces.

no.329 is an elevated gabled volume with inhabitable columns.

no.330 is a ring of rooms with a tall roof around a pill-shaped courtyard.

no.331 has a wandering roof, under which there is a tall space.

no.332 is a big roof supported by a central forest of columns. It has a smoothly undulating floor.

no.333 is a gabled volume with dormers, some of which function normally and some of which sneakily feed light into a central armature.

no.334 is built into a hillside with a sloping roof leading up to a towering private room. Common rooms live below.

no.335 is a long roof with inhabitable dormers. I had dormers on the brain that week.

no.336 is a 5x5 matrix of rooms perforated by circular courtyards. Networks of common and private spaces run through it.

no.337 is a snaking room with a ridged roof and small rooms inside both bends.

no.338 has some symmetries and some asymmetries, with an attic room above an open and closed ground.

no.339 is a symmetrical arrangement of a large common room with four large private rooms that each also have some common stuff.

no.340 is a loop of four common rooms with private rooms attached. It has chimneys and skylights.

no.341 is a large common space composed of four overlapping rectangular volumes, with private rooms filling in the poché between the common space and an irregular outer form.

no.342 is one long room with thick walls into which are carved spaces for sleeping, bathing, cooking, and other activities.

no.343 is four rooms in which the primary circulation space is also the bathroom.

no.344 is a network of common spaces composed of overlapping cylindrical voids within a pill-shaped volume. Private spaces exist within the poché.

no.345 is a three-story, three-room tower.

no.346 is a common room with a hole resting on two triangular prismatic private rooms.

no.347 is an eroded gabled roof, one half of which has enclosed rooms underneath.

no.348 is a slab and roof, perforated by circular courtyards, with circular rooms in between. The room always have a tangency with either the exterior perimeter or at least one courtyard. Windows are placed at the moments of tangency.

no.349 is a single room with six implied sub-rooms defined by low beams and discrete pitched volumes overhead.

no.350 is an enfilade of common rooms next to an enfilade of private rooms.

no.351 is an offset enfilade of six rooms with offset truncated pyramidal roofs. Two of the rooms have sub-rooms within them.

no.352 is a 3x3 checkerboard of interior and exterior rooms elevated on stilts.

no.353 is an inhabitable sawtooth roof comprising four triangular prisms punctuated by cut-out courtyards.

no.354 is one room divided into 25 implied sub-rooms by deep coffers of varying shapes.

no.355 is four right-triangular prisms in alternating orientations, creating a larger central common room. Courtyards connect the rooms.

no.356 is a 5x5 matrix of rooms where the central cross of rooms is open to the sky, creating a cruciform network of outdoor rooms with four-room pavilions at the corners. Pocket doors make a rare appearance.

no.357 is four two-story slabs pinwheeling around an open-cornered courtyard.

no.358 is a long overhanging roof with top-lit private rooms emerging like chimneys. Operable walls with doors of varying sizes line the eaves.

no.359 is a nine-square with pocket doors at all wall intersections. Privacy is a group effort.

no.360 is a 3x3 matrix of rooms with staggered door alignments and a shed roof with skylights and articulated ceilings.

no.361 is a steep hipped roof with dormers that open onto platformed programmed spaces within.

no.362 is a partially sunken volume under a big roof. It is divided by a large central wall through which various spaces are accessed.

no.363 is a linear string of rooms, or a broken enfilade, occasionally with side rooms, under a morphing roof that covers colonnaded porches.

no.364 is an extravagant matrix of 64 rooms, many of which are open to the sky. Networks of common and private rooms permeate the matrix, with plenty of room for living and working. Loops of rooms abound.

no.365 is a single room with everything one person might need, and maybe a little extra. So much of *One House Per Day* has been a meditation on the idea of the house as a collection of rooms, or the house as a single room, so it felt fitting to end this chapter of the project with one last one-room house.

ORO Editions
Publishers of Architecture, Art, and Design
Gordon Goff: Publisher

www.oroeditions.com
info@oroeditions.com

Published by ORO Editions

Author: Andrew Bruno
Book Design: Platform
Project Manager: Jake Anderson

10 9 8 7 6 5 4 3 2 1 First Edition

ISBN: 978-1-954081-86-4

Color Separations and Printing:
ORO Group Ltd.
Printed in China.

ORO Editions makes a continuous effort to minimize the overall carbon footprint of its publications. As part of this goal, ORO Editions, in association with Global ReLeaf, arranges to plant trees to replace those used in the manufacturing of the paper produced for its books. Global ReLeaf is an international campaign run by American Forests, one of the world's oldest nonprofit conservation organizations. Global ReLeaf is American Forests' education and action program that helps individuals, organizations, agencies, and corporations improve the local and global environment by planting and caring for trees.

For Krystal and Ruby, my little nuclear family.